D1565753

Edward Winterhalder

OUT IN BAD STANDINGS

Inside The Bandidos Motorcycle Club
The Making Of A Worldwide Dynasty

BLOCKHEAD CITY PRESS
Owasso, Oklahoma

Published by BLOCKHEAD CITY PRESS, PO Box 1654, Owasso, OK 74055.

Grateful acknowledgements to the multiple newspapers that granted permission to reprint their newspaper articles contained herein can be found in Appendix E.

Book design by Edward Winterhalder
Dust Jacket Cover concept by Edward Winterhalder and Team 67, Tulsa, OK

Manufactured in the United States of America

LIBRARY OF CONGRESS CATALOGING-IN-PUBLICATION DATA

Winterhalder, Edward, 1955-
    Out in bad standings : Inside the Bandidos motorcycle
    club : The making of a worldwide dynasty / Edward Winterhalder

  p.   cm.

    1: Bandidos motorcycle club   2. Motorcycle gang   3. Motorcycle
    club   4. Methamphetamine   5. Bandidos motorcycle gang   6. Hells
    Angels   7. Bandidos   8. Rock machine motorcycle club   9. Rock
    machine motorcycle gang   10. Biker gang   11. Rock machine
    12. Bikers   13. Winterhalder, Edward   I. Title

LCCN: 2005907605

ISBN: 0-9771-7470-0

All photographs contained herein are the courtesy of the author.

First Edition: October 2005

Acknowledgements

First and foremost I want to thank Caroline Haynor for putting up with me and my ways all these years; without you I could never have accomplished what I have done in the years that you have walked beside me down the road of life. I also want to thank Taylor Winterhalder for being the best daughter a guy like me could ever wish for; thank God that you came into my life. Without a doubt, I will love the both of you, forever and always, until the end of time.

To my friends Lee McArdle, Harry "Skip" Hansen, Robert Crain and Jonathan Sutton: This world of mine could not have turned without you in my life. I can't imagine words special enough to describe you guys. It has been an honor and privilege to have your support through all of these years, and to be able to call you my friends. I am sure that without your faithful friendship and guidance, this book would never have been written. My gratitude is extended to Cathy Barber, Greg Johns, Skip Hansen, Batman Batson and Jim Sutton for their countless hours of editing, encouragement, support and numerous positive comments during this time consuming project.

Additional thanks go out to all of the members of the Bandidos Motorcycle Club that still consider me to be one of their brothers, in spite of what they were told to think. Some of those like Victor, Mark M, Chuy, Junior, Jack-E, Tucker, Buddha, Doyle, Rude Richard, Earthquake, Pervert, Bones, Ramon, Big John, Jimmie, Pinhead, Hun, Grizz, Bill Wolf, Lee, Snake, Mario, Walt, Devin, Jim (Europe), Mike (Europe), Armin (Europe), Dizzie (Europe), Mick (Europe), Buller & Big Jacob (Denmark), Kemo (Europe) and Jason (Australia), are truly men of integrity and shining examples of what Bandido brotherhood is all about.

I would also like to note the following for the profound influence that they have had on me at some time during my life: Alain Brunette, April Crump, Arthur Pearson, Batman Batson, Benny Durrett, Bill Beaty, Bill Patterson, Billy Morgan, Buffalo Connaughton, Buzz Dalesandro, Candy McGee, Cecil Pullen, Charlie West, Chris Robison, Chris Westerman, Chucky Vanacore, Clay Scwab, Dave Gruber, David Norse, Deedee Guillory, Dieter Tenter, Donnie Johns, Edd Lackey, Eric Anderson, Forrest Draper, Fred Rossomando, Fuzz Terreson, Joanne Eckmyre, Joe Hannah, Joe John Edwards, John Millman, Johnny Cerrone, Keith Vandervoort, Kevin McManus, Kitty Menosky, Kurt Newman, Larry Pearson, Laurie Pottorf, Leadhead Blackman, Lee Walkup, Linda Beaty, Linda Walker, Mac Carr, Mario Figueroa, Mike Crowe, Mike Lewis, Paula McElheney, Pete Hansen, Rich Ashby, Rick Weathered, Richie Doolittle, Sam Ceruli, Scott Hall, Scott Morris, Stanley Lynde, Stephanie Hill, Suzie Delgrosso, Thomas Chandler, Tim Thomas, Tomcat Russell, Tattoo Tommy Williams, Toni Waldrop, Vicky Salter and Wizard McConnell. All of you truly know what the words friendship and family mean.

Prologue

You are about to embark on a strange trip to a world that you could not possibly imagine, for the majority of the world's outlaw motorcycle club members are legitimate, regular working guys, that rarely cause anyone problems. Contrary to the methamphetamine addicted, violence prone image regularly portrayed by the media, most of today's outlaw motorcycle club members are productive, contributing members of society that just love motorcycles and the biker lifestyle.

By writing this book, be it known that it is my express intention to provide you with an accurate portrayal of the traditionally skewed, media-sensationalized motorcycle club member than what you are accustomed to, and I truly hope that these memoirs of mine bring a much clearer perception to you as to what the 1%er outlaw biker lifestyle really consists of in this day and age.

While you are exploring my world, you will take an extraordinary journey into the biker world. There I lived my biker life for almost thirty years, and throughout most of it I was gainfully employed. Simultaneously, I lived most days of my life as if every day were a holiday, for living that way is mandatory in the traditional biker lifestyle I maintained. And during most all of this time, I was either a member of, or closely associated with, many outlaw motorcycle clubs.

My name is Edward Winterhalder, but throughout my life in the outlaw biker world, I was known as Connecticut Ed. As a full patched member and National officer first with the Rogues Motorcycle Club and then with the Bandidos Motorcycle Club, I regularly traveled all over the world. Along the way I spent time in prison; managed the Judge Parker rock n' roll band; bought, sold and built hundreds of Harleys; produced, recorded and published three record albums and a CD of my own music; owned and managed a multi-million dollar construction management company that built a multi-million dollar county courthouse in McKinney, Texas, a million dollar child care facility in Muskogee, Oklahoma, and a million dollar Gentlemen's Club in Tulsa, Oklahoma; bought and sold millions in residential real estate; wrote this book; and as a Dad with custody, raised the apple of my eye, my daughter Taylor.

Edward Winterhalder

"You Are The Master Of Your Destiny"

"A Man Has To Stand For Something, Or He Will Fall For Anything."

"Knowledge Is Power"

This book is dedicated to the memory of my sister Julie Norse Barber, and to the memory of Earl Hastings, Marla Garber, Marvin Brix, Michael James, Robert "Rocky" Harris and Robert "Tout" Leger.

Hangaround & Prospect Information

The following document has been used over the years by various 1%er outlaw motorcycle clubs as an "orientation" document, to inform the Hangaround or Prospect, of what is in store for them if they choose to join a "traditional" 1%er motorcycle club that wears a "three-piece" patch (a "three-piece" patch consists of a top rocker, bottom rocker and center piece) on their back.

INTRODUCTION

This information has been put together to give you a better understanding of the new world that you are entering and a better understanding of what is expected of you in your new role. Once you understand the scope of the task you are under-taking, you should examine your feelings and question your motives for wanting to become a member of a motorcycle brotherhood. There are many riding clubs that require only casual participation from its members. Others require a total com-mitment to the MC lifestyle. Your degree of interest will direct you towards an organization that you will fit into.

Be certain that you are both willing and able to commit yourself to the level that will be required. Be certain that your family understands the demands that the club will make of your time, and that those demands will continue to an even greater extent once you become a Patchholder. If after reading this packet you should have any reservations about being able to meet any of the requirements, it would be better not to consider moving forward at this time. Instead, either continue your present level of association with the club until you feel that you are ready and are confident of your success or find a different organization that better suits your needs. Such a decision would be respected and would be to your credit.

CLUB

The intent of this section is to give you an overview of the structure and philoso-phy of the traditional motorcycle club (MC). This does not necessarily express the feelings or priorities of any particular club, as all motorcycle clubs differ on some points. Regardless of the basic philosophy of your club, it is important that you understand the perspectives of other clubs that you may be associating with from time to time. If your lifestyle is influenced by motorcycles, then you are part of the motorcycle community. Of all the types of organizations found within that com-munity, the traditional motorcycle club stands apart and ranks highest in stature.

RESPECT

A serious club commands respect for one or both of two reasons. Those who are correctly informed recognize the deep level of personal commitment and self discipline that a man has to demonstrate and sustain in order to wear a patch. They understand that it is akin to a religion or vocation to that man. They realize that a club's "Colors" are closely guarded and the membership process is long and difficult. Other factors notwithstanding, they respect Patch holders for what they have accomplished by being able to earn and keep the patch they wear. This is respect born out of recognition of dedication and accomplishment.

Those who are less informed see only the surface. They see the vigilance of mutual support. They see the potential danger of invoking a response from a well organized unit that travels in numbers and is always prepared for confrontation. They know that no one can provoke one club member without being answerable to the whole club, and that such an answer is a point of honor that must come, to the last man. The type of respect that this generates is one born out of fear. We strive for respect for reason #1, not reason #2! This is especially true as it pertains to those persons outside of the motorcycle community. This segment of society is by far the larger, and therefore represents a larger market for any fundraising activities that the club might undertake.

It stands to reason that cultivating a relationship with these people is important, and to be perceived by them as "Biker Scum" would not be advantageous to the club. We therefore will conduct ourselves as upstanding citizens in every way... "good neighbors" so to speak. The goal is to be admired and respected by the general public rather than feared. The serious club, and all of its members and prospects, will always conduct themselves publicly in a highly professional manner. They will not go out of their way to cause trouble or to present themselves as an intimidating force without purpose or provocation.

CLUB COLORS
The general public does not draw a distinction between different club colors. In many cases, they simply can't tell the difference: we're all "Biker Scum" to them. If one club causes a problem that touches the public sector, the offending club's identity is either confused or ignored and the heat comes down on all clubs. The clubs tend to police themselves to avoid such incidents.

OFFICERS
Within a club, officers are usually elected to the positions of President, Vice President, Secretary, Treasurer, and Sergeant at Arms. Other less traditional posts are Road Captain and Enforcer.

PROCESS
In most cases, the Patchholder was a Hangaround with the club for about a year. Before that he was a long standing acquaintance and his attitude and overall conduct were well known. He then prospected for the club for one to two years before he got his patch. Of all things in this man's life, his loyalty and commitment to the well being of the club comes first above all else. There is never any doubt, which comes first. Though most things in life can let him down, he knows that his club and his brothers will always be there because he is always committed to being there himself. To be sure that this ideal and attitude continues on with any new members, he participates in teaching, conditioning, and even testing the club's prospects.

The term "prospect" comes from the words "prospective member". Before he allows another man to wear his colors, he is sure that the prospect is as dedicated as he is! A Patchholder has the attitude that there are only two types of people, those who are brothers and those who are not. For this reason he will not discuss any club business whether it's about membership numbers, club goings on, or any member's personal information with anyone outside of the club. He will keep his voice down when discussing club business and he will be aware of anyone coming within listening distance. He understands that he is a Patchholder 24 hours a day whether or not he is wearing his colors. Everything he says or does in public can affect the club or the brothers. He also understands that if he gets out of line, he is subject to be counseled by his brothers for his own good and for that of the club.

Wearing a patch is more than getting together for good times. It also means getting together for the other times, too. It constitutes a lot of work. It's committing yourself to a lifestyle in which you do not look for how your brothers can help you, but for ways that you can be of help to your brothers. You always look to give rather than to receive. All of this may seem very idealistic, and in some cases it's just that. But it is an ideal that all clubs profess and are always striving for in principal and practice. You should be aware of the "Golden Rule" of conduct while traveling in club circles: If you give respect, you'll get respect. If you act like an asshole, you'll be treated like one.

PARTICIPATION

It is important that you understand that it is the Patchholders that run the club, not the officers. This may seem a moot point to some, but it can't be overstressed. This is not to say that the officers don't deserve respect from the other Patch holders. These members have shown leadership qualities and have probably been in the club for quite some time. They are in office to carry out the wishes of the membership in a timely and efficient manner, as it is not always possible to get the members together to make decisions or take action.

Officers are elected to act as spokesmen for the club and perform various responsible tasks, but they don't run the club. When they speak or act on club matters, it is in a manner that they believe that the members of the club would agree upon, if a quick vote were taken. If an officer doesn't understand the membership's feelings about various matters, then he is out of touch with his brothers and should step down. This is a critical point because the strongest and most representative form of rule is one in which the power comes from the bottom up. If things were the other way around and the leaders or officers continually dictated down the chain of command, a sense of apathy and noninvolvement would eventually set in.

If this were to happen, the individual Patchholder would have no intuitive sense of his club's direction and would hesitate when he feels that he should act in the best interest of the club. Having little or no say in what is going on destroys a man's motivation to get involved or voice his own opinion. It would also drain his feelings of unity with his club brothers. Without such unity, a brotherhood cannot exist. Remember that the strength of a brotherhood rests with the membership at the bottom of the chain of command and is passed up. This is why aggressive participation is such a prized quality that is expected from the Patchholder and is looked for in the Prospect.

LEVELS OF COMMITMENT

When a man earns his patch, it does not mean that he has reached the ultimate goal and from that point he can kick back and coast. Moving from Hangaround to Prospect to Patchholder is not climbing from the bottom to the top, but rather more like climbing a constantly ascending slope, and in time becoming a stronger and more committed brother. A man's prospecting rocker and later his patch are merely presented in recognition of what he has demonstrated along the way. In this fashion, the more senior the Patchholder is in the club and the more he experiences, the more of a brother he should be to all.

PURPOSE OF PROSPECTING

Prospecting is not an initiation as you would find in a fraternity. It is instead a period of training that is sustained until the prospect, in every sense, conducts himself as a Patchholder. It's a time in which: The man's attitude is conditioned so that he displays a sense of responsibility and respect toward the patch holders of the club, without which he will not develop a sense of brotherhood. He is educated in basic MC protocol and etiquette.

He is given time to develop the habits that are basic to good security and good communications: to get the man into the habit of participating, to give his family time to adjust to the demands of the club, to experience and learn an essential degree of humility, and to become accustomed to trusting the judgment, at times blindly, of those patch holders who will someday be his brothers. To break the man of habits that are self centered and self serving. The list could go on but the point here is to demonstrate that prospecting has definite objectives and that a prospect will go nowhere in the club if he is not aware of this and does not apply himself to those ends. It's not possible to make a check list of what is expected from a prospect in all cases. There isn't any formula for success, but the key is ATTITUDE. Everything else can be learned in time, but a man's attitude comes from the heart.

The testing of a prospect may come in many ways. It may be planned or sponta- neous. In any event, when a prospect is given a task, the Patchholder is going to be looking for the man's attitude and the spirit in which he carries out the task. The prospect should be alert and always attentive in looking for more to do. If he is ever in doubt of his priorities or he can't find something to do, he should ask.

The Patchholders know which of the prospects hustle, and those are the prospects that are spoken of with the greatest pride and respect. It is also the way by which confidence and trust are developed. These are the seeds of brotherhood. Remem- ber that you will be prospecting for the whole club and not just one individual or individual chapter. The Patchholders of one chapter are always held accountable for the actions of a Patchholder of another chapter. It is therefore only right that the Patchholders of all chapters have a hand in developing the prospects on their way to becoming a full Patchholder.

SOME DO'S AND DON'TS

As a prospect, strive to conduct yourself as a responsible Patchholder at all times. Always display a positive attitude. Participate as much as you think is acceptable; then participate more. If you see a Patchholder of your club that you have not met, take the initiative to introduce yourself. Always introduce yourself as "Prospect (your name)". At all gatherings, make it a point to circulate when you have the time to do so and greet every Patchholder who is there. Anticipate the brothers' needs and offer to supply them. Don't wait to be told what to do and don't get overly friendly with someone that is not a regular acquaintance of the club.

If someone outside the club has questions, refer him to a Patchholder. Never give out a Patchholder's name, phone number, address, or any personal information to anyone outside the club. Never give out any information about the club itself to outsiders. This includes, but is not limited to, where the club is based, how many members are in the club, etc. Always be security minded, look around and see what's going on around you in public places and report anything that seems suspicious. While in public places, always conduct yourself with your association with the club in mind. Remember that what you do people will remember; good or bad.

Never let a Patchholder walk off alone in an unsecured area. If he is going out to his car, his bike, or even just out to get some fresh air, go with him. Watch his back at all times. If you are at an open function and pick up on some negative attitudes, especially if from another club, quietly alert a Patchholder immediately. Keep your ears and eyes open and feed any information that you may pick up on to a Patchholder, especially information regarding another club. Remember that you are a prospect 24 hours a day. Your association doesn't go on and off with your colors.

Remember that you are every Patchholder's prospect, not just your sponsor's or just your chapter's. Never wear your colors out of your area without your sponsor's approval and never out of state unless you are with a Patchholder. If two or more Patchholders are having a private conversation, don't approach them within earshot, especially if they are talking with a Patchholder of another club. If you need to interrupt, put yourself in a place of visibility and wait to be acknowledged. If it is important that you interrupt, ask another Patchholder to break in for you.

Never use the term "Outlaw Club" when speaking to a member of another club. Never lie to a member of another club. If you are in a situation where you are asked about the club or its membership, it is acceptable to say "That seems like club business and I really can't talk about it". If this doesn't put the subject to rest, offer to put him in touch with a Patchholder for him to speak with. Always show respect to a Patchholder of another club. Even though he's with another club, he's earned his patch; you haven't.

Always carry a pen and a paper, a watch, and a calendar. Frequently ask the Patchholders how you are doing and if there's anything you should be doing differently. Never ask when you may be getting your patch. Never call a Patchholder "brother". He's not your brother. Never call a Patchholder of another club "brother". He's not your brother, either. Remember, your patch is earned; it is not given to you.

Never bring a personal friend or a stranger into the presence of Patchholders without asking permission to do so first. At an open function, never turn your back to a Patchholder of another club. This is not so much for safety reasons, but as a show of respect. Always show respect and courtesy to Patchholders of other clubs. Don't come across like you want to be best friends. Be professional in such encounters; keep it short, then move on. Keep away from women associating with other clubs.

Never be quick to walk up to a Patchholder of another club in a public setting, even if you know him well and the clubs are on friendly terms. If you want to greet him, walk up slowly and wait for him to indicate that he wants such a public display to take place. He may be on some club business and may not want to give the general public the impression that the clubs are on such friendly terms. If he looks like he's going to ignore you, accept it and keep your distance. The best approach is always to wait for them to come to you, and to let everyone else see that.

Learn what different parts of our patch represent and what the different color combination of yours and other clubs represent. As you can see there's a lot to think about. This decision is probably one of the biggest you'll ever make. Be absolutely sure this is for you, and GO FOR IT!

Table Of Contents

OUT IN BAD STANDINGS

Bandidos Motorcycle Club Active Chapters

June 2005

BELGIUM

Antverp
Tongeren

DENMARK

Aalborg
Copenhagen
Faxe
FrederiksvÆrk
HelsingØr
HillerØd
Holbeck
Horsens
KØge
NÆstved
Roskilde
StenlØse
Vordingborg

FINLAND

Helsinki
Tampere
Nomad
Harjavalta

FRANCE

Annemasse
Annecy
Avingon
Cannes
Grasse

UNITED STATES

Albuquerque, NM
Albuquerque N, NM
Albuquerque S, NM
Albuquerque W, NM
Alamogordo, NM
Amarillo, TX
Austin, TX
Baton Rouge, LA
Baytown, TX
Beaumont, TX
Bellingham, WA
Birmingham, AL
Billings, MO
Biloxi, MI
Black Hills, SD
Bremerton, WA
Carlsbad, NM
Centro, NM
Chelan County, WA
Cloverleaf, TX
Corpus Christi, TX
Dallas, TX
Denver, CO
East River, SD
Eastside El Paso, TX
Elko, NV
El Centro, Denver, CO
El Paso, TX
Everett, WA
Fort Worth, TX
Gallup, NM
Galveston, TX
Gillette, WY
Grand Junction, CO
Hill Country, TX
Houston, TX

CANADA

Toronto Ontario

AUSTRALIA

Adelaide
Ballarat
Brisbane City
Cairns
Downtown
Geelong
Gold Coast
Hunter Valley
Mid North Coast
Mid State
Nomad
North East Victoria
Racing Team
Sunshine Coast
Sydney
Sidney Northside

SWEDEN

Falun
Gothenborg
Helsingborg
Halmstad
Nomad
Saffle
Stockholm

Marseilles
Nice

GERMANY

Aachen
Allersberg
Berlin
Berlin Centro
Berlin Eastgate
Bochum
Bremen
Cologne
Dinslaken
Dortmund
Duisburg
Essen
Frankental
Gelsenkirchen
Hamm
Ingolstadt
Kaiserslautern
Kassel
Mannheim
Munich Northside
Munich
Münster
Nomad
Neubrandenburg
Osnabrück
Passau
Rheinböllen
Stralsund
Ulm
Wetzlar
Wanne Eickel

ITALY

Florence

Houston N, TX
Houston NW, TX
Houston SW, TX
Houston W, TX
Huntsville, AL
Jackson, MI
Jefferson County, TX
Kerrville, TX
Lafayette, LA
Lake Charles, LA
Laredo, TX
Las Cruces, NM
Las Vegas, NV
Little Rock, AR
Longview, TX
Lubbock, TX
McAllen, TX
Missoula, MO
Mobile, AL
Montgomery, AL
Mount Hull, WA
National Chapter
New Orleans, LA
Nomad Everywhere
Oahu, HI
Oklahoma City, OK
Panhandle, TX
Panhandle North, TX
Plainview, TX
Pueblo, CO
Rapid City, SD
Roswell, NM
Ruidoso, NM
San Antonio, TX
San Antonio Centro, TX
San Antonio W, TX
San Antonio NW, TX
San Antonio SW, TX
San Leon, TX
Santa Fe, NM
Salt Lake City, UT
Seattle, WA

THAILAND

Bankok
Bankok East End
Pattaya

UK

Guernsey
Jersey

LUXEMBOURG

Luxembourg

Messina	Seattle S, WA
Meran	Seattle N, WA
Bologna	Shreveport, LA
Pisa	Skagit County, WA
	Tacoma, WA
	Tres Rios, WA
NORWAY	Tri-Cities, WA
	Truth/Consequence, NM
Drammen	Tulsa, OK
Frederikstad	Tulsa N, OK
Kristiansand	Waco, TX
Oslo	Watertown, SD
Stavanger	Whatcom County, WA
	Yakima, WA

Bandidos Motorcycle Club Inactive Chapters

June 2005

Atchison	Kansas	USA
Champaign	Illinois	USA
Cheyenne	Wyoming	USA
Devil's Mountain	Washington	USA
Elkhart	Indiana	USA
Edmonton	Alberta	Canada
Findley	Ohio	USA
Ft Smith	Arkansas	USA
Ft Wayne	Indiana	USA
Goshen	Indiana	USA
Haywarden	Iowa	USA
Juneau	Alaska	USA
Kingston	Ontario	Canada
Los Alamos	New Mexico	USA
Monroe	Michigan	USA
Montreal	Quebec	Canada
Opelika	Alabama	USA
Pascagoula	Mississippi	USA
Phoenix	Arizona	USA
Quebec City	Quebec	Canada
Silver City	New Mexico	USA

OUT IN BAD STANDINGS

Springfield	Missouri	USA
Texas City	Texas	USA

1

The Beginning Of Bandidos Motorcycle Club Canada
April 1999 To December 2000

It was springtime in Washington State; I thought that it always rained there, but this was one of those rare and beautiful days of unexpected sunshine. It was April of 1999, and it was the day I first met Alain. We were both in the Seattle area to attend the funeral for a fallen Bandido who had actually died while having sex with his girlfriend.

Alain could have been anyone in the Red & Gold world, but the first thing I noticed was that his patch was very unusual; for it had red stitching on all the edges. The center patch was an eagle, and the top/bottom rockers and center patch were light silver on black. I maneuvered myself closer in order to read the rockers and then realized that I was looking at a full-patched member of the "Rock Machine" from Canada; actually the first Rock Machine I had ever seen. Later that day, I learned that his full name was Alain Brunette, but when he introduced himself to me in his heavy French accent, he merely called himself "Alain".

Alain and I talked for a little while and then parted ways. I tried unsuccessfully to find him again before I left, because I wanted to spend more time with him. I had no idea why, but found myself intrigued. There was no way I could have known at that time what an important part of my life he would become.

The next Rock Machine member I saw was in New Mexico, at the Red River Biker Rally in late May of 1999. I was quite surprised to see that their patch had now changed: it was red and gold, no longer silver and black. I had just heard a rumor that Bandidos MC Europe had recently designated them a "Hangaround" club, and the Rock Machine had changed their patch colors to red and gold. As the shock wore off, I found myself pleasantly surprised to see that the rumor was indeed true.

A Hangaround club is an existing club that wants to join a larger motorcycle club. Being accepted as a Hangaround club puts everyone in the biker world on notice, both in the clubs as well as the rest of the biker world, that the small club wants to affiliate with the larger club and that the larger club is considering the change. In the Bandido world, after at least a year, the Bandidos vote as to whether all members of the smaller club are worthy to wear the Bandidos patch. If the vote is affirmative, then the smaller club will become Bandidos Probationary members.

In mid-November, 2000, I traveled to Europe for two reasons. First, to attend a world meeting that was to be held in Denmark, and second, to attend the one year anniversary party of the "patching over" ceremony for the new Bandido chapters of Germany, which was to occur later that month. A patch over is a ceremony where the members of the smaller club change their patches, and start wearing the patches of the larger club. In this case, the Ghostriders MC had "patched over" to become Bandidos in December of 1999, and now they were going to receive their "Germany" bottom rockers.

Most of the time that I traveled to Denmark, I flew into Frankfurt, Germany. The Frankfurt airport officials paid much less attention to motorcycle club members than the officials at the Copenhagen airport. A close friend of mine, Dieter Tenter, who lived not far from Frankfurt, usually picked me up at the airport, or I would catch a train to the town where Dieter lived. On this occasion, Dieter picked me up and I spent one night with him and his family, and then met up with a few USA and German Bandidos. To get from Germany to Denmark, we traveled by minivan.

On the way there, before we got out of Germany, a car pulled along side of us. The passenger started making all sorts of motions at us, then pulled ahead and got right in front of us. A lighted screen popped up at the bottom of the rear window, which told us to follow the car to the next exit. At this time I was informed that the car was an unmarked police car, and that we were being pulled over. No one had any idea why we were being pulled over; we all thought it was because we were all Bandidos. In the end, it was only because we had been speeding, about twenty minutes before, in a construction zone on the autobahn interstate highway. Our driver, a German Bandido, got off with a speeding ticket, which included a large fine.

We eventually arrived at our destination in rural Denmark around 7PM, shortly after dark. Although I was still suffering from jet lag and didn't feel well, I was glad to see Bandidos there from all over the world. Many of them had become close friends of mine. There were European Sargento de Armas Helga from Norway; European Sargento de Armas Johnny and European Nomad Clark from Sweden; European Presidente Jim, European Vice Presidente Mike, European El Secretario Gessner and European El Secretario Munk from Denmark; European Vice Presidente Les and European Sargento de Armas Diesel from Germany; Australian Presidente Jason and Australian El Secretario Larry; and El Presidente George Wegers, El Vice Presidente Jeffrey "Jeff" Pike, and me from the USA. Because this was a Bandidos world meeting at which only national officers could attend, I had been appointed an El Secretario (national secretary) just for the meeting.

The meeting was held out in the middle of nowhere, in the country, in a house that was surrounded by trees and armed Bandidos. Once we arrived, we were not allowed to leave or go outside by ourselves, which was for our own safety. Shortly after we arrived, we were informed that there were three Rock Machine members in the area who would soon be joining us; they were Martin "Blue" Blouin, Alain Brunette and one other who I only knew as "Will". I was quite surprised to hear that Alain was in the area, and I soon found myself anticipating his arrival.

Because I was not feeling well, I knew that I needed to get a good night's sleep. I looked around and found a tiny sauna room where I could try to sleep, but I ended up playing "Ace of Spades" with Johnny all night. "Ace of Spades" was a game that Johnny liked to play, where Johnny would try to sneak up on you while you were sleeping and put an Ace of Spades on you without waking you up. I had told Bandido Johnny that I was a very light sleeper, and that he would be unable to tag me; he tried a few times that night but was ultimately unsuccessful.

The next day we had meetings off and on all morning and afternoon. We would meet for awhile, and then watch TV, then meet again for awhile, then eat, then meet some more. All of the cooking was done by the European Bandidos members and supervised by Europe Vice Presidente Mike, who is also known as "Kok" ("Kok" is cook in Danish). Bandido Mike had gone to chef school when he was young, and actually was a very good cook. Over the next few days, we discussed a myriad of items that were of importance worldwide, none of which were illegal. Most of what was discussed that day is reflected in the minutes I took during that time, as follows:

WORLD MEETING NOTES IN DENMARK - NOVEMBER 15, 2000

Old Business:

1. USA to provide Europe & Australia with disc of correct patch design.
2. Call Tudy regarding German MC club about patch—advise German Bandidos

New Business:

1. Canada—someday soon is OK—currently there is peace—RM removed SYLB Patch and HA changed colors on support club - as part of the peace -peace is very important to keep.
2. Relationship with Outlaws in Canada, USA, Australia & England—stabbing of Bandido by Outlaw Probate in Guernsey. George will talk to Frank and set up meetings worldwide between us and the Outlaws.
3. Consider updating Fat Mexican - drawings to be submitted.
4. Check and see if Probationary members in USA are wearing 5 yr. charter patch—if so, remove immediately.
5. Actual color of gold on patches to be determined by patch reps (USA, Europe & Australia) and standardized.
6. The shield is the official 5 yr. patch worldwide.

7. Patch reps (USA, Europe and Australia) to make decisions on officers' patches: President, Vice Pres, Sgt. At Arms, Sec-Treas, Secretary, Treasurer, Road Captain with no periods.
8. Europe—return history books to George via CT Ed.
9. Patch reps (USA, Europe, and Australia) to make decision on Life Member patch.
10. No more mandatory visits to other countries for Europe and Australia members.
11. Whispering Jim and Uncle Mad—giving away ENM patches in Europe.
12. Switzerland HA incident—Munich chapter—Sep'00—rest area.
13. Relationship with HA in USA, Europe, Germany, Scandinavia,& Australia.
14. Outlaws friendship with Black Ghostriders in Germany; Pagans friendship with Bats in Germany
15. Thailand—support club—Diablo MC
16. USA runs are: Birthday Run (1ˢᵗ week of March) & Memorial Day Run (last weekend in May) & Sturgis (1ˢᵗ full week of August) & Labor Day Run (1ˢᵗ weekend in September) & Thanksgiving (last Thursday in November).
17. Australia's triangle international patch is OK to be given to USA and Europe Brothers that have visited Australia—all gift patches given to Australia & Europe Brothers are not to be worn on vest without approval from their National officer.
18. If your death is the result of a suicide, you are not deserving of a Bandido funeral.
19. If you borrow a bike, ol' lady, or any other Bandido-owned property while visiting another area, chapter, or country, leave the property in the same or better condition than what you received it in when you leave.

During the afternoon discussions, the subject of the Rock Machine becoming Bandidos was discussed many different times. At that time, the Rock Machine had been a "Hangaround" club for about eighteen months. The European and Australian Bandidos were adamant that the Rock Machine should become Bandidos immediately, while the USA Bandidos there (El Presidente George and El Vice Presidente Jeff) thought that the Rock Machine should never become Bandidos. I had already heard a rumor that El Presidente George had made a deal with the United States and Canadian Hells Angels that the Rock Machine would never become Bandidos. El Presidente George supposedly had agreed with their argument that the Bandidos should never patch (take in) an enemy of the Hells Angels. Whether that rumor was true or not, I did not know, but the subject made for a long and sometimes heated discussion.

A compromise was reached in late afternoon, in which the USA, European and Australian Bandidos settled their differences and finally agreed: that when a peace was firmly established between the Rock Machine and the Hells Angels in Canada, *then the Rock Machine could become Bandidos.* Early in the evening, Alain, Blue and Will from the Rock Machine arrived. All of us got caught up on our personal situations, ate dinner and then sat down at a big table to discuss the Rock Machine becoming Bandidos. At that time, the Rock Machine were told that they would continue to be a hangaround club, but if they could make peace last with the Hells Angels in Canada, then, and only then, would the Rock Machine be allowed to become Bandidos. Everyone sitting at the table agreed to that, but I think El Presidente George agreed to this only because he thought that the peace would never last.

Shortly after the sit-down meeting at the table, Alain and I had time to visit awhile. He was in fairly good health, in spite of all the stress that came from being a member of the Rock Machine. At that time there were more than one hundred dead in Canada, as a result of the ongoing war between the Hells Angels and Rock Machine. Alain did have an awful cold, and I must have caught it from him, because a few days later I became very sick, and it took me more than two weeks to get rid of it. To this day, I still tell him I owe him for that cold...or whatever it was I caught from him.

I finally escaped from the house in the woods that evening. I caught a ride into Copenhagen to locate a good friend of mine, a Bandido named Kemo. Bandido Kemo and I had met on an earlier trip to Europe, and had stayed in touch regularly since. I spent the night at his home and tooled around Copenhagen with him the next day. While driving around town, he pointed out a brand new store run by the Denmark Hells Angels, in which they sold clothes and other items with the Hells Angel's support logos. It looked very upscale and since I had never seen anything like that, I convinced Kemo that I wanted to go inside. We agreed that he would go downstairs and visit a friend who had a tattoo shop there, in order to give me a few minutes to browse around the shop.

When I walked in, I was quite surprised, although I don't think I showed it. The shop was beautiful, clean and light, and reminded me of an Eddie Bauer clothing store. All the merchandise therein was related to the Hells Angels. I noticed about a half dozen Hells Angels in there, so I immediately announced myself as an American Bandido. The Hells Angels looked at me first in utter shock, then called upstairs to another Hells Angel who was apparently in charge, whose name was Bent "Blondie" Nielsen.

I had heard his name many times, for Blondie was a well-known leader of the Hells Angels in Denmark. Hells Angel Blondie came downstairs, we introduced ourselves, and then we chatted for a moment about basic world motorcycle club politics and the concept of the store. I told him that I had never seen anything like this store before, and complimented him on the quality of the merchandise. Bandido Kemo returned from the tattoo shop downstairs and we left, leaving them, I hope, with a better understanding of what the American Bandidos were all about.

Not known to us USA Bandidos at the world meeting, on September 26, 2000 the Rock Machine and Hells Angels in Quebec, Canada, had shocked everyone in the biker world when the two mortal enemies sat down in person for the first time ever to discuss peace. The Quebec City Rock Machine President Frederick "Fred" Faucher and the Hells Angel's Nomad President Maurice (Mom) Boucher, met in a room at the Quebec City courthouse to discuss a preliminary plan for peace between the two clubs in Canada.

Two weeks later, in front of the entire world, with TV and newspaper reporters present, Fred and Mom had been seen shaking hands as they announced to the world that the war in Quebec between the Rock Machine and the Hells Angels was now over. But at the time I did not know that, so I was surprised to learn that, in the days since the world meeting had been held, the European and Australian Bandidos had somehow convinced El Presidente George that now was the time to change the Rock Machine into Bandidos.

A week after the world meeting, on November 22, 2000, Bandido George met with the Hells Angels at Peach Arch Park just outside of Vancouver and Bellingham. At this meeting, Bandido George confirmed the rumor that the Hells Angels had heard; he told them then that the Rock Machine would soon be members of the Bandidos. On December 1, 2000, the Rock Machine Motorcycle Club became history and Bandidos Motorcycle Club Canada was born. A party was planned for January 8, 2001 in the clubhouse at Kingston, Ontario, Canada, at which time it would be announced to the world that the Rock Machine were now officially Bandidos.

In December, I was finally notified of the exact date of the patch party, and made my plans to go to Canada. At that time, I contemplated many different access scenarios. I had been allowed into Canada in recent years, but I had also been denied access at times, due to my past criminal record and affiliation with the Bandidos. I truly had no idea if I would be allowed into Canada this time or not. It was very important for me to be there, for I had been assigned the task of organizing the new National chapter of Bandidos MC Canada; in essence I was to teach them how to be organized and function as a club. I was to open lines of communication, compile/verify phone lists/email addresses, and establish all the membership rosters for Bandidos Canada. This was going to be a momentous occasion, and I definitely wanted to participate.

Most of the United States Bandidos members who had decided to go to the patch party had opted to fly into Toronto's Pearson International Airport. I thought that under those circumstances, with lots of Bandidos coming in and all the publicity, it would be much harder to gain entry through the airport. I had heard too many stories of Immigration Canada being well known for turning members of any motorcycle club around at the airport, even if they were not convicted felons. Even El Presidente George had been deported a few years ago from Canada for being a convicted felon. I *was* a convicted felon, and in spite of the fact that it had been almost 20 years since I had last been convicted, I had little doubt I would be caught and turned around if I tried to enter at Pearson Airport.

Eventually, I decided to attempt entry to Canada through the Windsor checkpoint, just outside Detroit, Michigan. (Later, someone from Immigration Canada suggested that I came in through Niagara Falls, and I never bothered to correct them; if you check my Immigration case records, you will see a multitude of notes regarding entry at Ft. Erie, near Niagara Falls.) I figured that if I were not welcome in Canada, the officials would simply turn me around when I presented them with my passport. I also figured that no one from the club would be expected to come in through Windsor, and therefore my chances of getting in would be much better.

On January 4, 2001, late on a dreary, winter afternoon, I successfully accessed Canada disguised as a construction worker, riding in the back seat of a car with my sister and one of her friends, who both lived in Michigan. (I did tell the Canadian Immigration officials that I rode into Canada in a van full of construction workers in an effort to protect my sister who had no idea that I might not be allowed into Canada. This statement was the only lie I ever told them.)

The Canadian Immigration Officer at the gate did not ask any of us for our ID's. I had my passport in hand ready to go, but all he did was talk to the driver for about two seconds and wave us on through. I noticed at the time that most all of the vehicles near us were going through the entry point as fast as we were, but I was told that this was normal procedure. (This was before the events of 9/11…and things were much different then than today.) I traveled with my sister and her friend to downtown Windsor, where I was dropped off at a casino. There, I called the Outlaws MC clubhouse in London, Ontario, and a member of the local Outlaws chapter was eventually sent to pick me up.

The Outlaw's name was Finn; he was a full-patched member of the Windsor chapter of the Outlaws. Finn drove me to London, Ontario the evening of January 4th, and on the trip he told me that he had joint citizenship in both the USA and Canada. As we drove through a light snow storm, Finn offered to get any member of the Bandidos across the border at any time for free, which I found strange. (Several years later, I would find out that he was a law enforcement officer. I have since heard that he was an RCMP officer in Canada and that he was an ATF agent in the USA, but either way, it didn't matter to me. It did matter to most all members of the Outlaws in Canada though, for he would be responsible for the arrest of more than fifty Outlaws in the fall of 2002.)

Outlaw Finn and I arrived at the Outlaws MC clubhouse in London about 8 o'clock in the evening. I wanted to visit with a friend and member of the Outlaws MC London chapter, Thomas "Holmes" Hughes. At the Outlaws clubhouse, I called the Bandidos MC clubhouse in Toronto and two Bandidos (Bandido Gee from Montreal and Bandido Generator from the new Toronto chapter) were sent to pick me up. It was a cold, snowy night, and because of that,

Bandido Gee, Bandido Generator and I were forced to spend the night at a local London hotel. We got up early on Friday morning, January 5th, and found our way into Toronto by late morning, in spite of the many inches of snow that had fallen the night before.

Just before noon, Bandido Gee, Bandido Generator and I arrived at the Bandidos MC Toronto clubhouse. After visiting for awhile, I had them drop me off at the train station, and I took a train to Kingston by myself, where I had arranged for some Bandidos to meet me at the train station. From the train station, I was taken to the local Travelodge Inn motel, where I was assigned to share a room with my good friend from Sweden, Bandido Clark. Clark has a personal interest in Bandidos Canada, since he had dual citizenship, in both Sweden and Canada. After visiting with Clark and some of the other Bandidos in the hotel, I turned in early to get a good night's sleep. I knew that Saturday would be a major milestone in biker history and I did not want to miss a minute of it.

Bandido Tout Canada

Bandido Clark Sweden

The next morning, I started off the day by catching up on all of the newspaper articles from around the world. I always tried to have my laptop with me to monitor the newspapers, and to keep in touch with friends and family and the club. One of the first newspaper articles I came across from Canada contained a bomb. It was a story about how the police had caught a few Bandidos at Pearson Airport in Toronto trying to get into the country for the patch party. It also mentioned that a few Bandidos had actually gotten in, *including an American Bandido from Oklahoma.* I was obviously quite concerned, for it meant that there was a giant "leak" somewhere I had been in the last two days. (Several years later, I would learn that the "leak" had been Finn the Outlaw from Windsor, who had given me a ride to the London clubhouse. I should have realized then that this was an indication of worse things to come.)

Saturday was an uneventful day; I spent it hanging around the hotel visiting with new Canadian Bandidos that I did not know, as well as some I did know. I was meeting so many new people that I was having trouble remembering a lot of their names. After consulting with numerous Bandidos, I decided not to go to the clubhouse for the actual party, due to the police presence, constant media coverage, and publicity. We heard that there were about seventy-five police around the clubhouse, and eight American Bandidos had already been detained for possible deportation.

The only thing that saved all of those American Bandidos from incarceration and deportation proceedings, was the fact that Immigration Canada officials had legally allowed them into the country, and had stamped their passports as proof of the same. But my passport did not have a stamp. Therefore, I thought it would be safer for me to skip the party and have a quiet dinner with a new Montreal Bandido who called himself "Tout", which meant "beep" in the English language.

Robert "Tout" Leger and I had met earlier in the day and discovered we had much in common. Bandido Tout had a dynamic personality and like me, enjoyed working on Harleys. Tout had what they call in Canada "stipulations"; what we call in America "non-association"; he was not able to associate with any member of the Rock Machine due to an ongoing court case in which he was alleged to have committed the crime of "possession of a firearm". In spite of the fact that most all Rock Machine were now Bandidos, Tout felt that there was no need to push the issue, so he, too, was not going to the patch party.

After our dinner in the hotel restaurant, Tout invited me to visit his home near Montreal, hang out the next day, and then return to the United States via train through northern Vermont. We planned to leave by 8 PM, in order to drive to his home and get to bed at a reasonable hour. I left the table and went back upstairs to pack and check my email. It turned out to be a decision that I would live to regret. While I never made it to the clubhouse, the patch party was a huge success for more than sixty new Canadian Probationary Bandidos. Everyone had a great time that night except me, as you can see by the following newspaper article from the Kingston Whig-Standard:

Bikers Party In Kingston

By Sarah Crosbie

January 7, 2001

Eight American members of the motorcycle gang, the Bandidos, partied in Kingston Saturday night, after Canadian Immigration officials failed to show up more than two hours after Kingston Police initially detained the men.

One man from Oklahoma was arrested later that night by Canadian Immigration officials for illegally being in the country, Kingston police media spokesman Mike Weaver said.

Kingston Police Staff Sgt. Brian Cookman said Canadian Immigration questions bikers to determine if they are members of a criminal-affiliated group, or if they have a criminal record.

Jennifer Pritchett, The Whig-Standard
Three bikers hug in solidarity as they make their way inside a warehouse in Kingston's west end on Saturday

The first bikers started showing up at the Burnett Street location at about 2 p.m. in vans and taxis.

The men who were detained by police arrived shortly after 4 p.m. They were released at 5:40 p.m. to cheers and shouts of "woo-hoo."

Jennifer Pritchett, The Whig-Standard
Police photograph bikers and check IDs on Burnett Street

Cookman said the police can detain the men to check their identification and photograph them, but beyond that, it isn't within their jurisdiction to hold them.

"This is a federal issue, not a municipal issue," he said.

Cookman said he was surprised it took Immigration officials from Lansdowne more than two hours to get to the Kingston site.

By 10 p.m. on Saturday, 53 men had arrived at 770 Burnett St., for the party called a patchover party, where the motorcycle group the Rock Machine merged with the Bandidos.

The Rock Machine was granted probationary status in the Texas-based Bandidos last year.

"The local eastern chapter are patching over to the southwestern Bandido chapter in the U.S.," said Neil Finn, a Kingston police officer who is a member of a special provincial squad formed to combat biker gangs.

Finn said until the party, Kingston's Rock Machine had seven associates; four members and three probationary members.

He said the merging doesn't mean Kingston will see an increase in bikers.

"What's going on today doesn't mean we're going to have more members," he said.

Throughout the police check system, Bandido members showed their identification and their vests' which are decorated with a cartoon Mexican man holding a gun in one hand and a sword in the other.

Some Bandidos were also wearing bulletproof vests.

The men who were not detained drove or walked to 770 Burnett St. When they reached the property, a man inside would unlock the door, walk outside and greet them and then lock the door behind them.

Throughout the day, men would come out and take photographs of the area, including police and the media, but the members themselves didn't want their pictures taken. One man covered his face with a bandanna; another pulled his vest up over his head as they walked to the building.

Although police were braced for possible problems with a heavy presence that included officers from Kingston Emergency Services, a tactical team, the provincial special squad, a joint municipal RCMP-OPP group, as well as Quebec police. Cookman said there were no problems on Saturday at the largest biker gathering Kingston has seen.

"This is the pinnacle of importance. No one's ever seen this, in this magnitude in a long time," he said.

A detective from the Albuquerque (N.M.) Police Department in the U.S. came to Kingston because of the number of bikers coming to the area.

Gary Georgia, who has studied the Bandidos for 10 years, said that while he can't say what effect the Bandidos will have on Kingston, the new relationship shouldn't go unnoticed.

"Anytime you have a criminal organization coming into your town, it does lead me to be concerned," he said.

"The Bandidos have been known to use intimidation and violence," he said, noting that they are involved in selling narcotics, motorcycle thefts and prostitution.

Georgia said it's significant that the Bandidos decided to meet in Kingston.

"It gives the Bandidos a foothold they haven't had in the past," he said.

"I've tracked them all over the world and now we have them in Canada and in Kingston."

Georgia said on Friday night, before he came to Kingston, he was called to Pearson International Airport to confirm the identities of two Bandidos members who were en route to Kingston.

They were both sent back to the United States by Immigration on Friday, he said.

Immigration officials could not be reached for comment yesterday.

New Canadian Bandidos Alain (left) & Charley (right) January 2001

2

Immigration Canada & The Kingpin January 2001

On Saturday, January 6th, 2001, at about 7pm, Bandido Tout and I returned to my motel room from having dinner. We sent a runner to the clubhouse to let everyone know that we were leaving town, and sat down for a few minutes to give the Bandidos at the clubhouse time to respond. We did not plan to wait long, for it was only about a five-minute ride to the clubhouse from the hotel. I checked my email one last time, and packed my clothes in an overnight bag. Someone from the clubhouse called Tout and asked us to wait there for a few minutes; apparently someone needed to see him or me before we left. I cracked the door open an inch or two using the night latch as a prop, and we waited. We didn't have to wait long before the door came flying open. Only problem was that it was not the Bandidos that we had expected. It was the Kingston police, the OPP (Ontario Provincial Police) Gang Squad, and at the back, two officers from Immigration Canada.

Apparently the police had gone to the front desk, and the hotel clerk gave them the room numbers of every room the Bandidos had booked. It was standard courtesy in our red & gold world to provide a hotel room for an international guest, and I had been "given" my room to stay in without having to pay for it. One Canadian Bandido had secured an entire block of rooms using the same credit card for all the rooms. I had thought that no one would be able to locate me because I never expected the hotel to give up the room numbers without a warrant. I realized later that things were much different in Canada than in the United States. I also learned later that the police had been given a master passkey, and had opened all the rooms booked by and/or registered to Bandidos, looking for anyone who was not at the clubhouse.

It took the police a mere second to realize that we were Bandidos, and immediately they demanded that we identify ourselves or be arrested. Bandido Tout and I were not wearing any disguises and we had Bandidos logos on both our belts and our shirts. When the police asked us our names we told them who we were, for neither one of us had done anything illegal, nor was there anything illegal in the room. At first I did not know that there were immigration officers there, so Tout and I both thought the police would run our names and let us go. That was, in fact, a drastic oversight on my behalf.

When I told them my name was Edward Winterhalder, the Immigration officers stepped to the front of the pack of police. "You're Connecticut Ed, aren't you, from Oklahoma", one of them stated. As soon as they looked at my ID to verify who I was, I was arrested for violating Canadian immigration laws and handcuffed. One of the OPP Gang cops, who was not very bright, came running out of the room with Bandido Clark's belt, screaming that I was a Nomad, like he had made some sort of major find. It was too funny. Even most all of the other cops were laughing, because Bandido Clark was a large man and I am not; it was obvious that I could have almost wrapped the belt around me twice. I denied owning the belt, but the more I denied it, the more the OPP Gang cop swore it was mine. I finally figured it was not worth arguing with a moron and agreed it was mine. The cops packed the belt up in my belongings, and I eventually mailed it back to Clark (who was by then back in Sweden) months later, after I returned to the United States.

Simultaneously, as I was being arrested in the hall, the Kingston police were talking inside the room with Bandido Tout. They rapidly ascertained that Tout was who he said he was, that there was nothing illegal in the room, and that Tout was not violating his bond conditions by associating with me. One of the Kingston police asked me if I owned the laptop computer, and I told them that it belonged to another Bandido who was sharing the room with me, so they left it. Tout was not allowed to stay in the room, and the last I saw him that night was out in the parking lot as I was loaded into the police car. He was smiling, and waved to me as I was driven off.

From Kingston, I was transported to an Immigration holding cell at Lansdowne, about forty-five miles from Kingston, for my initial booking. Lansdowne, ironically, was located less than one thousand feet across the river from the United States. I could have thrown a rock and hit a United States Customs Office, it was so close. I even joked with them that I would walk across the river to the United States if they would let me go, and we all laughed at my suggestion. One of the immigration officers later told me that their bosses had requested that I be transferred up to Ottawa (the national capital of Canada) for a public deportation in front of the media. Immigration Canada was all abuzz, claiming that I was a big fish and a prize catch, but I had no idea what they were talking about at the time.

I've got to admit that the immigration officers assigned to book me were unusually respectful. At one point, when the antique digital computer equipment that was being used to download my pictures from the digital camera to the computer failed, I volunteered to assist them and they allowed me to do so. While waiting in my holding cell, another immigration officer asked me what he could get for me. I requested the Canadian Immigration Statutes and he was kind enough to give me the complete manual. He seemed surprised at my request, and I am sure had no idea of my legal knowledge. At the time I was contemplating waiving my deportation hearing, but by the time I read through the manual I decided that I wanted to fight. Sometime after midnight I got transferred to a small city jail in a town nearby called Brockville. Once again I was surprised to see how respectful the jail guards were. Being way past my normal bedtime, I fell asleep easily, in spite of my surroundings.

On Monday, January 8th, I was transferred to the Ottawa Carleton Detention Center and advised that I had had a deportation hearing scheduled for

Wednesday, but that it was being postponed for one week until January 17th. I was placed in the hole for security reasons, and on Tuesday morning, January 9th, an arraignment hearing was held via telephone. I argued the hearing myself, and over the objections of the Crown attorneys, I convinced an Immigration Adjudicator to grant me a bail bond in the amount of $20,000. I rapidly calculated the amount of cash I would need to be released at $2,000 (10% of $20,000) and thought that it would be very easy to obtain. Imagine my surprise when I found out that in Canada there was not a 10% bail bond system like there was in the United States. If I was to obtain my release, I was going to have to come up with $20,000 cash.

I was being held on an administrative charge, not a criminal charge. I had not been arrested for committing a crime, and was not going to be formally charged with any criminal violations. Even if I was found guilty of this administrative charge that I was being held on, incarceration as a punishment was not an option. The only punishment available was deportation back to the United States, which is where I wanted to go anyway. It was ludicrous, but the Immigration Canada attorneys did not act so. They were serious and acting like I had committed murder. And to make matters worse, according to the immigration laws, I could be held in jail without bail for up to two years, pending my deportation hearing. I was apparently extremely lucky to have been granted bail; I was told that I was the first biker ever granted bail on a deportation matter, and I believe that was solely because I had custody of my eight year-old daughter.

I contacted one of my new Canadian brothers, Jean "Charley" Duquaire, and convinced him to lend me the money to make my bail. Bandido Charley, at the time, had been elected as the first National President (Presidente) of the Bandidos in Canada. It was imperative that the money was from legal sources, and that we left an easily recognizable "paper trail" for the source of the money. Bandido Charley borrowed the money on his credit card by doing a cash advance at the Bank of Montreal, converted the cash advance into a bank cashier's check, and then had the $20,000 check hand delivered to the Ottawa Immigration Canada office. (I had promised that I would pay him back as soon as I was released, and I did by sending him a wire transfer from my construction company business line of credit to his account at the Bank of Montreal.) Early Wednesday afternoon, January 10th, 2001, I was finally released from custody, and the first thing I saw was a newspaper with an article that shocked me:

Big-Wheel Biker Wins $20G Bail

By John Steinbachs

January 10, 2001

A HIGH-RANKING Bandidos motorcycle gang member is expected to be released on bail today after cooling his wheels in an Ottawa jail.

Edward Winterhalder, 45, appeared before an Ottawa Immigration and Refugee Board adjudicator yesterday for a detention review hearing.

The adjudicator ordered that he be detained but allowed him to be released on a $20,000 bond.

The border-bouncing Bandidos biker was busted after a Kingston patchover Saturday where several local Rock Machine members were inducted into the international club.

The closed event -- attended by an estimated 53 people -- came just one week after the rival Hells Angels patched over dozens of members from smaller Ontario gangs.

The Tulsa biker -- reputed to be one of the most powerful men in the club -- was detained by Citizenship and Immigration Canada on charges that he entered the country illegally.

Winterhalder has been ordered to appear on Jan. 17 for a board inquiry, where an adjudicator will rule if the allegations against him are founded and decide whether or not to issue a removal order.

DIDN'T TELL GUARDS

According to a Citizenship and Immigration report, Winterhalder -- who admitted to being a member of the brazen Bandidos -- told investigators he entered Canada on Jan. 5 through Fort Erie but didn't tell border guards of his gang affiliations.

In 1995, he tried to cross at the same border point but was turned back by immigration officers.

The immigration report also said he has told officials that he has a criminal record, including criminal convictions for concealing stolen property, uttering a forged treasury cheque, possession of a stolen vehicle, carrying a prohibited weapon and carrying a concealed weapon. His last admitted conviction noted in the report was in 1983.

With bikers taking a higher profile in Canada recently, immigration officials have been keeping their eyes peeled for possible spottings at ports, including Pearson International Airport in Toronto.

Officers said the alerts led to the interception of four members of the Bandidos bike gang arriving here for the opening of the Kingston chapter.

Police said two members of the group's Denver chapter and one each from Washington and Amsterdam were turned around at the airport. A senior member of the Washington chapter did slip into the country but left on Sunday.

In the article it had noted that I was a "reputed to be one of the most powerful men in the club" and it referred to me as a "Big Wheel Biker". I was neither, and I was beginning to think that I was going to be railroaded, no matter what I did to defend myself. From Ottawa, I was driven back to Kingston, where I spent a few days at the home of another new Canadian Bandido, Marc "Garfield" Yakimishan and his family. As a condition of my bail, I had been ordered not to leave Canada, to reside in the care and custody of Bandido Garfield, and to appear at my next hearing. Garfield was, at that time, scheduled to become the new El Secretario for Canada, so staying with him for a few days was ideal.

While waiting for my next immigration hearing (which was scheduled for January 17th) I went to Toronto one evening with Bandido Alain "Alain" Brunette to meet with Peter from the Toronto Loners MC, and to visit some of the new Toronto Bandidos at their clubhouse. Bandido Alain, at the time, was the National Vice President of the Bandidos in Canada (Vice Presidente). The meeting with the Loners MC took a while, and by the time we got to the Bandidos clubhouse, their weekly meeting had just finished. To our dismay, we discovered that the entire Toronto chapter, that night, had voted out of the club, a Bandido Prospect by the name of Eric "Eric the Red" McMillan.

Bandido Prospect Eric was a young, tough kid from a Toronto suburb called Oshawa, and he harbored a deep resentment for some of the bikers that had joined the Hells Angels in the Toronto area. Bandido Alain and I saw him as one of the brightest stars of the entire Toronto chapter, while the rest of the Toronto chapter saw him as too "anti-Hells Angels". We left the Toronto clubhouse with a bad feeling about that meeting, and a worse feeling about the chapter. We did not think that it would survive, and we wondered if some of the members would quit and become Hells Angels in the near future. Alain and I went directly to Oshawa, picked up Bandido Prospect Eric, and went out to eat breakfast at a local restaurant.

After talking to Eric, and hearing his side of the story, Bandido Alain and I decided to reinstate him into the club, and transferred Eric into the Kingston chapter, which was also under the direct supervision of Alain. When we called the Toronto chapter and told them what we had done, they were pissed. Less than a month later, the entire Toronto chapter quit the Bandidos. Most went on to become Hells Angels, and the rest just retired and became independent bikers/citizens (not in any motorcycle club).

One of the nights that I stayed in the Kingston area, I went out to the old Kingston Penitentiary to visit a Bandidos member from Montreal. His name was

Brett "Lucky" Simmons, and he was incarcerated for his part in an ill-fated bombing attempt on the Hells Angels many years earlier. Bandido Lucky had been the only one to survive, when the bomb that they had intended to be used against the Hells Angels blew up a car prematurely, killing three other men. All the prison wanted from me was my ID, and the prison authorities eagerly let me in to have a face-to-face visit in the visiting room. My visit to him was reflected in an email Bandido Lucky somehow sent to the Bandidos Internet website guest book shortly thereafter:

> **Name:** Lucky
> **Hometown:** Montreal
> **Sent:** 01.52 - 15/1
>
> I would like to send out my respect to BANDIDO ED from Oklahoma for going out of his way to visit a CANADA BROTHER doing time it is always good to have a visit from a bro but it takes a special bro to be in another country and take time out of his trip and visit a bro inside I would like to send all my respect to BANDIDO ED and I will see you soon on the outside also I send my love and respect to all the brothers worldwide
>
> LLR. BANDIDO LUCKY 1%er MONTREAL PROBATE CHAPTER CANADA BFFB

A few months later, Bandido Lucky sent me a handmade Bandidos belt buckle as a thank you for coming to see him. Just before his release from prison, to my surprise, Lucky had a major change of heart; *he quit the Bandidos and joined the Hells Angels.* (In June of 2005 Hells Angel Lucky would be arrested for a myriad of drug charges while a member of the Ontario Nomads chapter.)

The highlight of my extended vacation in Canada was a trip, a few days later, to Montreal to meet with a bunch of the new Montreal Bandidos, and then go stay with my good friend Bandido Tout, whom I had not seen since my arrest. Bandido Alain and I traveled by car to Laval, a little town just outside of Montreal. Laval was the place where, in 1985, the Hells Angels had killed some of their own members, and dumped the bodies in the water of the St. Lawrence River. The Montreal Bandidos had rented a room in an upscale hotel there in Laval, for us to meet in. I remember that the room we rented was up high, for it had a tremendous and quite beautiful view of the surrounding area.

Prior to this meeting, it had been decided that Bandido Garfield would not make a good El Secretario, and that we needed to find someone else better qualified to do the job. Bandido Presidente Jean "Charley" Duquaire, Bandido Vice Presidente Alain "Alain" Brunette and I decided that Bandido Robert "Tout" Leger would make an excellent El Secretario. The only problem was that Bandido Tout did not want the job, so we devised a plan to okie-doke him. (An Oklahoma expression that means to fool, or play a joke on someone.) We lined up ten men and asked for a volunteer to step forward, who wanted to be the next El Secretario. We had previously told nine of them to step backwards three paces when we asked for a volunteer to step forward. So when the "volunteer" was asked to step forward, nine men actually stepped back, and Bandido Tout was left out in front all by himself, looking like he had stepped forward to volunteer. It took Tout a few seconds to realize what had happened, and all he could say was, "I don't even own a computer". We all laughed, and it was done. Bandido Tout was now the El Secretario for all of the new Canadian Bandidos.

After the meeting, we all went to a fancy Italian restaurant in Montreal for dinner. Other Montreal Bandidos joined us there, and we had a great meal. I parted ways with the Montreal Bandidos and Vice Presidente Alain after the dinner, and went with Bandido Tout to his home just south of Montreal. I spent two days and nights with Tout and his family, and had a blast there.

Tout took me to the local Indian reservation gift shop to make me feel like I was back in Oklahoma, and we talked about going up to his lake house for a few days if I was not able to go back to the United States soon. I felt like I had found a long, lost brother and I wished I could have stayed there longer. Tout gave me a ride back to the Ontario border the day before my next immigration hearing, and that was the last time I would ever see him.

My next immigration deportation hearing was on Wednesday, January 17th. It seemed almost funny, for I had only planned on being in Canada for a few days to visit, and by now I had been there almost two weeks. I was still not able to return home to Oklahoma, because the Canadian Government wanted me to stay just so Immigration Canada could deport me. Go figure! Sure made a lot of sense, didn't it? Talk about an exercise in futility; but I figured that it would be all over soon. Another underestimation of what I was up against.

From the beginning, as soon as I was released from jail, I had hired one of the best criminal defense attorneys in all of Canada, Josh Zambrowsky from Kingston. Josh was well known for all his Pro Bono work representing prisoners with major crimes, and he also had an excellent reputation with the Montreal and Kingston Bandidos. Josh had represented some of them a few years earlier, and they thought he was "neater than sliced bread".

Josh was willing to work with me, and hear out my opinions on my own legal situation, since I had had some experience with the criminal justice system. As part of our plan to prepare a character defense for the hearing, two attorney friends of mine from Oklahoma, Jonathan M. Sutton and William J. Patterson, each wrote tremendous reference letters on my behalf. Jonathan wrote the following:

01/15/2001

To Whom it may concern:

I am writing for and on behalf of Mr. Edward Winterhalder, an American citizen and good friend of mine. As I am intending to provide a reference for Mr. Winterhalder, it may be important for you to know something of myself. I am an attorney practicing primarily in Oklahoma, and admitted to practice before all Courts in Oklahoma, as well as the Northern, Eastern and Western Federal District Courts of Oklahoma, the Tenth Circuit Court of Appeals, and the United States Supreme Court. I have previously worked as a corporate attorney for United Parcel Service, and the Tulsa County District Attorneys Office, prior to establishing a private practice and firm.

I came to know Mr. Winterhalder roughly five years ago, and have enjoyed my interaction with him since. I have found him to be much like myself in so many respects, specifically, a highly motivated, intelligent, tenacious individual, possessed of a strength of character and moral code so rarely found in today' society. Having worked for Mr. Winterhalder on a variety of legal issues, I can further attest to the lack of criminal allegations brought against him during the time I have known him. Clearly, I am not able to prove a nullity, thus I can only state that for the entire time I have known him, I have never known of conduct that would likely give rise to such charges. He is a loving father, a respected member of the business community, and a valued friend. I know of less than five people I would say this about, but I personally trust Mr. Winterhalder.

Truly, I wish more people in today's society were like Mr. Winterhalder: we would all be far better off. Every time he has stated he would do something, he has, every time he made a commitment, he carried it out, every time he was placed in a situation where he could do the easy thing or the right thing, he did the right thing. I have great respect for Mr. Winterhalder, and trust that whatever the situation is there in Canada, that you do the right thing and release him.

Our only problem was that this was not a criminal matter; it was an administrative matter. And we were not dealing with the criminal justice system; we were dealing with Immigration Canada, which was quite accustomed to doing things however they wanted, with no interference from the Justice system. Most of what happened at the deportation hearing on January 17th, was best explained in another newspaper article published in the Ottawa Sun the following day:

Bandido's Departure Stalled
Biker Told To Stay In Country Until May

By John Steinbachs

January 18, 2001

Bandido biker Edward Winterhalder is accused of being in the country illegally and Citizenship and Immigration Canada wants him out.

That's why it seemed bizarre yesterday when a lawyer for the government asked for a four-month adjournment during Winterhalder's Immigration and Refugee Board hearing, effectively stranding him on Canadian soil until May.

If he leaves the country and tries to come back, he'll be denied entry by Immigration and forfeit his bail money.

The border-bouncing Bandido -- reputedly one of the highest-ranking men in the organization -- was busted at a Kingston Travelodge after a biker patchover Jan. 7 where several local Rock Machine members were inducted into the international club.

After five days in jail, he was ordered released on $20,000 bail.

Winterhalder, who says he owns a construction company, wants to go home to take care of his young daughter.

But the adjudicator at the hearing, who admitted his hands were tied in the matter, ruled for an adjournment and denied Winterhalder's request that he be allowed to return to Oklahoma and return for the May hearing.

He ordered Winterhalder to remain on bail and be back in Ottawa for the May hearing.

Immigration officials say they need more time to put together their case against him, which includes entering the country illegally with a criminal record and being a member of the Bandidos, an alleged criminal organization. Winterhalder bristled at the suggestion.

"It's certainly not a criminal organization," he said of the Bandidos after the hearing.

He said he didn't enter the country fraudulently and was waved through the border stop in Fort Erie before he could identify himself and describe his criminal record.

Once again, I was quite surprised to see that I was now "one of the highest ranking men in the organization". At the time, the only office I held in the club was Secretary of the Bandidos Oklahoma chapter. True, I was on another temporary assignment from the United States National chapter, but by no means was I "one of the highest ranking men in the organization". By now, everyone in Canada believed the lie that was being told by the Canadian Government. And to make matters worse, the Immigration Canada attorneys had successfully argued that I needed to stay in Canada for four more months. I was absolutely amazed at their arrogance and lack of common sense, but Josh explained to me that this was just their way of trying to get me to capitulate. Immigration Canada thought that if

I were forced into staying in Canada for four months, I would eventually give up and waive my deportation.

In spite of the fact that it was not reported, Josh actually argued that I did not need to stay, that I would be happy to return to Canada for my next hearing May 10th. I was extremely fortunate and finally caught a break, for the Adjudicator agreed and in his final written ruling, he ordered me to return for the hearing in May, but also Ordered me to live "wherever I wanted" while waiting for the next hearing. The Adjudicator also Ordered that if I decided to return to the United States while waiting for the next hearing, I should notify Immigration Canada at the time of my departure. In his own way, the Judge had opened a door and given me an opportunity to return home to the United States. I could now go back to my family, the Oklahoma chapter and my construction business.

On January 19th, I said my good-byes to all that had helped me, and traveled by car through Lansdowne into the great state of New York; through Watertown into Syracuse. From there, I caught the night train to Cleveland, and in Cleveland I caught a Southwest Airlines flight back to Tulsa, Oklahoma. Oklahoma was a sight to behold; it had never looked so good. It was great to finally be back home.

3

Bandidos Motorcycle Club Canada & Immigration Canada
January 2001 To July 2001

On the evening of January 18th, 2001, the night before I left Canada, the killing started again. As soon as I arrived home in Oklahoma, I received word that the first Canadian Bandido had been murdered while sitting in his car. His name was Real "Tin Tin" Dupont, and he was a full patch member of the Montreal chapter. Bandido Tin Tin had been on parole, and was trying to keep a low profile by staying away from other Bandidos; in fact, he had "parole stipulations" that required him to avoid contact with Bandidos members. Up until now, the dead had all been members of the Rock Machine, so for us as Bandidos world wide, this was a very serious situation. We had anticipated that our arrival in Canada would keep the peace, not provoke more violence. Before we even got over the death of Tin Tin, another bomb fell, but this one was anticipated. As Bandido Vice Presidente Alain "Alain" Brunette and I had so profoundly predicted a few weeks earlier, the Toronto Bandidos chapter fell to pieces. It was so bad that even the Toronto Sun ran an article about it:

Toronto Bikers Close Up Chapter

By Rob Lamberti and Jack Boland

February 6, 2001

The Bandidos biker gang has shut down its Toronto chapter.

It's the second Ontario chapter to close since the Hells Angels arrived in the province last year.

The rapid implosion follows the defection of more than a dozen Ontario Bandidos since the Hells swallowed four Ontario gangs Dec. 29.

The Hells moved into Ontario in response to the Rock Machine – with chapters in Montreal, Quebec City, Eastern chapters in Kingston, Toronto and Western in London -- becoming probationary Bandidos on Dec. 1.

Police said the Hells' plan was to squeeze competition from the world's second-largest biker gang out of the province.

'ONTARIO PHENOMENON'

When the Rock Machine became probationary Bandidos, five members instead joined the Hells Angels, including Paul "Sasquatch" Porter, president of the Eastern chapter.

About 10 members of the Bandidos' Toronto chapter quit with president Bill Miller and last week joined the Hells' Lanark County chapter -- west of Ottawa -- headed by Porter.

The four remaining members of Toronto's Bandidos chapter refused to join the Hells and have retired.

"It's an Ontario phenomenon," said Surete du Quebec Sgt. Guy Ouellette. "These guys are there just to enjoy the advantages of being bikers, money-wise."

Joe Halak, who briefly became the Bandidos' Toronto president, refused to comment.

The Rock Machine and Hells Angels were locked in a bloody six-year turf war in Quebec until hammering out a truce last Thanksgiving.

Although the newspaper reported that we already had a chapter in London, there never actually was a London chapter of the Bandidos. Some of the Toronto Bandidos did try to put a chapter in London, but it never really got off the ground. All we ever had in London was a few Bandidos from our Toronto chapter living there. And most of those Toronto Bandidos members were too "pro Hells Angels" to be like us. We were trying to convince all of our guys that they needed to have regular employment, and we told them that if they wanted to be big time drug dealers they needed to leave the club.

We also tried to teach them that to get respect, you had to give respect….that you could never get respect (and keep it) through fear. We believed then, and still do, that to survive long term in Canada as a member of a 1%er club, your members had to have "visual means of support", such as employment, income from disability or your wife/girlfriend working, and *to not be selling drugs for a living.* Most of the Canadian Bandidos understood what we were trying to do, but it appeared as though most of the ones in Toronto didn't. It did not take long to find out who was who; when most became Hells Angels and the rest retired.

A little more than a week later, the bullets were flying again, and this time they hit very close to home. My good friend Bandido Alain was almost assassinated on February 13th, 2001, as he drove his white Pontiac Grand Am along Highway 15 near Mirabel in the Laurentians. A stroke of luck allowed him to survive, for his attackers had used machine guns to try to kill him and William "Bill" Ferguson, a Bandido prospect. The newspapers reported it as a "flare-up" in the war between rival biker gangs, but I saw it as an attempted assassination of one of my best friends. I also wondered if I had been the target of the attempted assassination as well, for the car Alain was driving happened to be the same car that he and I were in for the entire time we were together.

In spite of having been almost killed and a bullet pass through his belly, Alain was in good spirits when I talked to him that night as he recovered in his hospital bed. While talking to him I learned that the car had multiple bullet holes through it and that most all of the windows had been shot out. He told me that he had been driving down the highway, when he and Bill noticed a car that appeared to be following them. At first they thought that it might be the police, but at the same time they realized that the occupants of the car were not the police, the car was beside him and the shooting had begun. To escape the bullets and save their lives, Alain swerved their car into the opposing lanes, heading the wrong way, driving against traffic.

A few hours later, the police found a handgun and bullets that had been used in the shooting, as well as a burned out car in Piedmont, about thirty kilometers from the scene of the shooting. The burned vehicle, a common trademark of a biker gang hit, matched the description of the shooter's car. No one had to tell us that the Hells Angels had sent the shooters; we knew that for sure. It seemed that the truce between us and the Hells Angels had been broken, and it was time for all of the Bandidos in Canada to be ready to defend themselves.

That same day, February 13th, in Quebec City, another bomb got dropped on us. The President of the Bandidos chapter in Quebec City, Frederic "Fred" Faucher, who had already been arrested in early December of 2000 and was being held in jail on multiple drug charges, was arrested again on new charges of attempting to murder some Hells Angels. Bandido Fred had been at the forefront of changing the Rock Machine into Bandidos, and had actually become a member of the Bandidos while incarcerated. He was also instrumental in getting the Hells Angels to agree to the truce just a few months ago. Fred was now accused of a total of twenty-six criminal charges, seven of which involved the manufacturing of bombs. The next day near Montreal, Michel Gauthier, a friend of some of the Montreal Bandidos, was killed as he drove off in his car around 8am. It seemed as though it would never end. The heavens were literally raining bombs on Bandidos MC Canada, and it did not look like it was ever going to stop.

A few days later, our luck changed. At a Holiday Inn near Montreal, the police arrested eight Hells Angels members while they were planning to kill Bandidos members. Seven of the arrested were either members or prospects for the Quebec Nomads Hells Angels chapter, and when arrested they were in possession of a "hit list" and pictures of their intended murder victims. One of the pictures recovered was that of my good friend Alain Brunette. Since Maurice "Mom" Boucher, the President of the Quebec Nomad Hells Angel chapter was already in jail; we hoped that this signaled an end to the fighting, as well as an indication that the police were all over the Hells Angels.

We did not have long to wait. On March 28, 2001, more than one hundred twenty-five Hells Angels and their associates were arrested. Many of them were charged under a new federal anti-gang law. At least sixty-five of the one hundred or more full-patch members of the Hells Angels in Quebec had been arrested, or were going to be arrested as soon as they were located. The entire Hells Angels Nomad chapter was in serious trouble, for all of their members had been charged with multiple murders. All of the Nomad members that were not in jail either had a warrant for their arrest, or had already been arrested. Those already in jail had been charged with a myriad of new crimes. All the members of the Rockers and Evil Ones, (well-known Hells Angels puppet clubs) were also arrested. It was as if we had gotten a breath of fresh air, and we were now certain that the killing would stop.

In mid March, in the United States, at the annual Birthday Run for all United States Bandidos, Bandido El Presidente George "George" Wegers assigned me the task of supervising Bandidos Canada until the end of their probationary period in December, 2001. Bandido George wanted me to handle all the legitimate club business with Canada, which would include communications and the hiring and/or firing of their National officers. In early April, I fired Bandido Presidente Jean "Charley" Duquaire, and appointed Bandido Alain "Alain" Brunette as the new Presidente for Bandidos Canada. Alain was already all over the country doing that job anyway because Charley had left the country and was no longer in touch with current events.

By the time April rolled around, things were running smoothly and it was time for me to get ready for my immigration deportation hearing. As I prepared my plans to return to Canada, Immigration Canada surprised me by requesting a postponement only two weeks before my hearing was scheduled. Immigration Canada wanted six more months to investigate my case, but the Adjudicator ruled against them and set the new court hearing date for October 5th, 2001.

In May, Bandido Fred Faucher from Quebec City plead guilty and got sentenced to twelve years in prison for the crimes he had been charged with in December of 2000 and February, 2001. At the same time, another prominent Quebec City Bandido, Marcel "LeMaire" Demers, also plead guilty and was sentenced to nine years in prison. Bandido LeMaire had gotten arrested with Bandido Fred in December, 2000; and had been charged with Bandido Fred for numerous drug crimes.

That entire spring, ever since Alain and I had met with them in mid-January, Bandido Presidente Alain had kept in close contact with the Loners Motorcycle Club in Toronto. The Loners were well known for having a real lion as a pet, which they kept on the grounds of their clubhouse. Ever since the fall of our chapter in Toronto in January, it had been our intention to open another chapter there; we just needed the right group of guys to do it. The Loners seemed to be the right bunch, and they had another chapter in Italy that was aligned with the European Bandidos.

On May 22, 2001, twelve members of the Loners MC became a new chapter of Bandidos headquartered in a suburb just outside of Toronto. Bandido Presidente Alain soon appointed Pietro "Peter" Barilla as Vice President over Ontario, to oversee our growth in that area. Bandido Peter had been a member of the Loners MC since the very early 1990's, and knew everyone in Toronto's motorcycle club world. He even had an uneasy rapport with some of the Hells Angels in that area; for Bandido Peter had known them well when they were in other clubs prior to becoming Hells Angels. I had met Peter at the meeting in the Toronto area in mid January while I was awaiting my Immigration hearing; I had a great deal of respect for him and thought that he was an excellent choice.

In early July everything was going fine, except we were having a multitude of problems crossing the border. On some days we would have no problems, and others we would have plenty. Many of us got turned around at the border, both by the United States and Canadian authorities. But by and by, for most of us, all was well. About half of the members of Bandidos Canada in Quebec were now gainfully employed, as were nearly all of the Ontario Bandidos (or their wives/girlfriends were working and they were "stay-at-home house husbands"). Since we believed that the fighting was now over for good, and summer had come to the area, many started riding their bikes around, and for the first time were able to proudly wear their Bandidos colors.

Simultaneously, in Montreal, things were not going as well for the Hells Angels. We all took notice when a National Post newspaper article mentioned that some of the remaining Quebec Hells Angels (who had not been arrested earlier in the year) were no longer wearing their colors, and some had even been reported to be covering their tattoos. The Bandidos in Canada could not imagine being in a motorcycle club and not being able to wear their colors; it was what they lived for.

Later that month, Gary Dimmock from the Ottawa Citizen wrote an interesting article about my immigration situation that was not very favorable to Immigration Canada:

Canada Fights To Ban Biker Kingpin
Senior U.S. Gang Member Insists On Right To Take Up With Canadian Brothers

By Gary Dimmock

July 21, 2001

Edward Winterhalder, reputed to be one of the most powerful members of the U.S.-based Bandidos, a ruthless, worldwide biker gang, is trying to position himself closer to new Canadian chapters, mostly ex-Rock Machine bikers, amid police fears of an intensified street war against the gang's rival Hells Angels.

Though Mr. Winterhalder, 46, insists the gang's presence "brought an end to the supposed (biker) war," the federal government is trying to stop him from entering the country because of his criminal record and alleged links to organized crime. They say he is a danger to the public.

The highly placed biker told the Citizen he's determined to fight the Immigration and Refugee Board to win the right to travel freely across the border.

"I'm absolutely fighting it. It's a case of personal liberty, and I want to travel," Mr. Winterhalder said.

It's also a matter of business.

"I'm not an undesirable. I'm a legitimate businessman," said Mr. Winterhalder, a single father of a young girl who describes himself as a respected member of society.

Corporate records filed in Oklahoma list Mr. Winterhalder as owner of a construction firm that won contracts worth $20 million U.S. in the past two years -- including the construction of a county courthouse.

And his business keeps him moving, according to statements recorded during an immigration hearing.

"In the process of conducting my construction company, I have traveled frequently all over the world," he said.

The Texas-based Bandidos, formed in 1966 by disillusioned Vietnam veterans, is organized much like a corporation, with approximately 5,000 members and more than 100 chapters in 10 countries, including Sweden, which recently saw the gang engage in a murderous war with Hells Angels. They turned the countryside upside down, using shoulder-fired anti-tank missiles to attack rival compounds.

The gang's expansion into Canada in January brought about 60 former members of Rock Machine into probationary membership. The probationary chapters include Eastern Ontario, Montreal and Quebec City.

Intelligence agents say the probationary members are trying to prove themselves by making money for the outlaw empire any way they can -- including money laundering, drug distribution, loan sharking and prostitution.

The Bandido prospects have waged war for Quebec's drug market since 1994. So far, the battle has claimed the lives of more than 150 people – including an 11-year-old boy killed in 1995 when he was hit by shrapnel from an exploding bomb.

Besides the death toll, the biker war has seen 124 attempted murders, nine missing persons, 84 bombings and 130 reports of arson.

Intelligence agents fear that if Mr. Winterhalder wins the right to enter Canada, it will grant him a license to take care of business.

Police say the criminal corporation will flourish with much bloodletting in what they call an intense attempt to wrest control of the drug market from the Hells Angels, who currently have a tight grip on 75 per cent of the trade.

Mr. Winterhalder told immigration authorities there is little to worry about.

"I am certainly not a danger to society. My criminal convictions in the early 1980s were for a non-violent activity. I am a member of the Bandidos motorcycle club, but our presence (in Canada) has brought an end to the supposed war. Since November, there is no more war and now that we are here, there will be no more war," Mr. Winterhalder said.

Intelligence agents dismiss his declaration of peace, saying the war is bound to escalate now that ex-Rock Machine members are linked with the Bandidos, the second-most powerful motorcycle gang in the world.

And any suggestion that the drug war has been over since November is dead wrong, police say.

So far this year, there have been several biker gang fistfights, a bombing and a handful of shootings.

In February, four armed members of the Nomads, an elite Hells Angels crew, gathered around a table in a suite at Montreal's Holiday Inn Crown Plaza while a security detail kept watch in the hotel lobby.

It was a study of the enemy, with each elite member taking turns thumbing through photographs of probationary Bandidos, police say.

They included snapshots of Denis Boucher, a rival biker who was almost killed last September, and Alain Brunette, reputed president of the Bandidos chapter in Kingston.

Earlier in the week, Mr. Brunette had been targeted in a drive-by shooting while making his way down Highway 15 outside Mirabel.

That same week, Michel Gauthier, a Bandidos associate, was found dead in his car on a lonely road in the Laurentians. Some 20 kilometres away, police discovered a burned-out car -- the trademark of a biker contract killing.

The shootings made clear that the biker war is far from over, with the Hells

Angels unable to accept a shared drug market.

But police could be wrong about an escalation, judging from how Bandidos do business south of the border.

In Oklahoma, where Mr. Winterhalder was the reputed leader of a chapter in Tulsa, county, state, and federal law agencies report no problems with the Bandidos.

Most of the gang members, according to a U.S. intelligence agent who monitors bikers in Oklahoma, make honest livings. Of the 10 motorcycle gangs operating in Oklahoma, the Bandidos have been the most quiet. And there is no biker war.

"It seems to be bloodier up there in Canada. Down here they all seem to get along pretty good," said Lieut. Alan Lansdown, an intelligence officer with the Osage County Sheriff's Office.

The last known time Mr. Winterhalder crossed the border was Jan. 5 at Fort Erie, Ont.

Seated in the passenger seat of a van, Mr. Winterhalder had his passport ready in his hand. He had been turned away in 1995 because of his criminal record, and he did not know if he would be allowed to cross the border.

The border guard spoke briefly with the driver and waved them through.

They then drove to Kingston to oversee the induction of about 60 probationary members, mostly ex-Rock Machine bikers.

But the visit didn't last long for Mr. Winterhalder. It wasn't long after checking into a Travelodge that Immigration officer P. Cooper, accompanied by a special police team, arrived at his door.

In an interview with the Immigration officer, Mr. Winterhalder appeared co-operative. He had only $217 U.S. in his pockets.

Police later arrested him, saying he had entered the country illegally. They said he posed a danger to the public because of his alleged links to organized crime.

They also said he lied to Immigration officers, saying he should have identified himself as a gang member to border guards.

But it was the driver that did all of the talking at the border, and if the border guard had inquired about his membership, Mr. Winterhalder would have likely told the truth. He says it is against club law to lie.

And they said he had a duty to tell them about his criminal history, a record that led Mr. Cooper to believe the U.S. visitor would do something against the law.

Mr. Winterhalder says he paid his debt to society years ago. His last conviction was in 1983. His crimes include carrying a prohibited firearm (a .45-calibre handgun) possession of a stolen vehicle and forging a $5,000 U.S. cheque.

Under the Immigration Act, an exception can be made for visitors with criminal records, so long as they are reformed and that at least five years has elapsed since the end of the person's last sentence.

Mr. Winterhalder finished serving his sentence some 14 years ago.

In any event, police threw him in jail for three nights until he appeared at a detention review hearing. Immigration officer Lynn Leblanc portrayed Mr. Winterhalder as a dangerous criminal who should remain locked up.

Mr. Winterhalder then made his case, saying he is not a flight risk, nor a danger to society, and that he is reformed.

The board adjudicator, Rolland Ladouceur, released Mr. Winterhalder on $20,000 bail on the condition that he would appear at an upcoming hearing -- which he did.

Immigration officers then requested that Mr. Winterhalder be detained in Canada for up to six months so they could have time to look into certain criminal allegations against the biker.

The adjudicator concluded that the government's motion was unreasonable because the visitor would be separated from his daughter and business in the U.S.

Mr. Winterhalder has enlisted a respected lawyer to help him fight for the unfettered right to set foot in Canada at an upcoming hearing.

Although a lot of the details about me in the article were accurate, and in spite of the picture of the club that Mr. Dimmock portrayed, I did laugh about the notion that I was "one of the most powerful members" of the Bandidos. But I did not have time to laugh for long, because Bandido Alain and I would be leaving for Sturgis, South Dakota in the very near future.

4

Bandidos Motorcycle Club Canada & The Trip To Sturgis
August 2001 To September 2001

Sturgis is the largest biker event in the United States, if not the world. It always takes place the first full week in August. It actually starts the Friday before the first full week, and ends on Sunday after the first full week; the event lasts for about ten days. In the last few years, there have been more than 500,000 motorcycles there, and some reports indicate more than 750,000 people. The Bandidos Motorcycle Club has a chapter and clubhouse near Sturgis, at Rapid City, South Dakota, and every year Sturgis has been a major event for the entire Bandidos Motorcycle Club. This year was going to be exceptional, for I had convinced my good friend from Canada, Alain, to come to Tulsa and ride with me all the way to Sturgis and back on a borrowed Harley.

Bandido Presidente Alain "Alain" Brunette arrived in Tulsa by bus a few days before we were planning to leave for Sturgis. Alain had taken a Greyhound bus from Toronto to Tulsa on purpose, to confuse anyone at the border crossing who was involved in immigration enforcement. The plan worked well, with the only problem being that it took a long time to make the journey from Toronto to Tulsa. We stayed at my home outside of Tulsa for a few days while Bandido Alain got over the bus ride. There he finally got to meet, and spend some time with, my girlfriend Caroline and my daughter, Taylor. I borrowed a 1999 Harley FXDX Superglide from my attorney friend, Jonathan Sutton, for Bandido Alain to ride, and we left Tulsa August 4, 2001 around 9am to avoid the stifling, Oklahoma afternoon sun.

Bandido Alain and I proudly rode side by side together for the first time, traveling northeast up Interstate 44 through Joplin to Springfield, Missouri. I was proud of the fact that I had done my part to get Bandidos Canada to where they were, and prouder of the fact that I was riding next to Alain. Alain later told me that this had been the first time in many years he had been able to ride without having to worry about who was going to shoot him off his bike while he rode. In Springfield, we stopped and had lunch with a childhood friend of mine, Kurt Newman, then met up with two members of the Ozark Riders Motorcycle Club from Arkansas, Andy and Nick.

Bandido Alain, Ozark Rider Andy, Ozark Rider Nick and I all rode together out of Springfield mid-afternoon, and traveled another sixty miles northeast, up near Ozark Lake, to visit a group of guys who thought they might want to join the Ozark Riders. It is beautiful country in southwest Missouri in early August, and the treed areas we rode through provided quite a bit of shade and pockets of cooler air, for which we were extremely thankful. We arrived there by early evening, and after dinner and a short meeting, we spent the night there.

Early the next day, we set out for Kansas City and a meeting with the local chapter of the Boozefighters Motorcycle Club. It was our intention to get there before it got too hot, but unfortunately, that was not the case.

By the time we got to the north side of Kansas City, it was very hot, and probably near one hundred degrees. Most of us could tolerate the heat ok, but Bandido Alain was from Canada. He was beginning to look like a tomato, so stopping for the afternoon for him was a welcome relief. We spent a few hours there in Kansas City, had a good meal, and took off around 6pm, hoping to make Omaha just after dark. We rolled into Omaha according to plan, got a motel room, and spent the night. It had been a good day with no major breakdowns, just plenty of water breaks, food and gas stops. Tomorrow would be another story, for we were now far away from all of those shade trees and rolling hills of Missouri, and headed into the hot, dry plains of South Dakota.

The next morning, we got up early and headed for Sioux Falls, South Dakota. We knew that we needed to be there before noon, if we wanted to avoid the heat. It was going to be one hundred degrees by noon, and that was just too hot for us to be out there, riding the Harleys. It was not good for the bikes or good for us, and I was very worried about Bandido Alain. The heat was literally kicking his ass. His face and neck were bright red from the sun, in spite of the sun block we all had been using. Fortunately the ride went well, and Bandido Alain, Ozark Rider Andy, Ozark Rider Nick and I got into Sioux Falls just after noon. I was supposed to meet a friend of mine, Mike, there in Sioux Falls; he rode with the Sons of Silence Motorcycle Club in Minnesota. Sons of Silence Mike and I had previously agreed to meet at a local tattoo shop, where we both had a mutual friend.

We spent most of the early afternoon hanging out and catching up at the tattoo shop. Sons of Silence Mike and I both knew the piercing girl that worked there; she was the widow of a Bandido from Louisiana. It was quite cool in the shop, watching TV and relaxing in the air conditioning. Later that day, Monday, August 6th, after the heat of the day had passed, we all headed west on Interstate 90 for Chamberlain, South Dakota. By now it was Bandido Alain, Ozark Rider Andy, Ozark Rider Nick, Sons of Silence Mike, my girlfriend Caroline, Nick's girlfriend and I. We were hoping to meet up with about fifty other members of the Sons of Silence at Chamberlain just before dark. There were a couple of small motels in that town, and earlier in the day while waiting at the tattoo shop we had all made reservations for that night there. By now, Interstate 90 was crammed full of Harleys, hundreds and hundreds of them, all going west towards Sturgis. It was a sight to see.

We had all been this way many times, and most knew that it was very easy to get stranded out here with no gas, water, food or lodging; that is, all of us except for Bandido Alain. He still looked like a kid in a candy store, albeit a kid that had a bright red head and neck. I asked Alain what the name was for a human's head in French and what the name was for a tomato in French, and he was dumb enough to tell me: Tete Tomat, which is pronounced in English as "tight toe mat". So now we all affectionately referred to him as "Tomato Head", or should I say correctly in French: Tete Tomat.

We got into Chamberlain just about dark thirty, and I found our motel rooms ok. I was surprised at how much the heat had affected us, in spite of the lay over at the tattoo shop in Sioux Falls during the heat of the day. I took a quick shower and headed up to the local bar to visit with some of the Sons of Silence, and there were plenty of them there to visit with. By this time, I was pretty weary from the ride, so I did not last long at the bar. I wanted to get a good night's sleep, for once again we were going to try to get an early start to beat the heat. We only had about two hundred miles to go, and we figured if all went well we could make it into Rapid City around noon. And we probably would have if not for the Probationary bottom rocker Bandido Alain was wearing.

In our world, when we take a patch holder that has been in another club into the Bandidos, it is our rule that they become "probationary" members for at least one year. This is based upon the fact that the probationary member already has some motorcycle club experience, and that this previous experience will give them a good foundation to build upon, while learning what it is like to be a Bandido. While you are a probationary member, you wear a bottom rocker that says "Probationary". After you make it through your probationary period, you would then get your 1%er patch and your chapter bottom rocker, your chapter bottom rocker replacing your probationary bottom rocker. When you get your chapter bottom rocker, it usually will designate the geographical area that you come from. In Bandido Alain's case his bottom rocker would eventually be Canada; in my case it was already Oklahoma.

The next morning we ate breakfast and actually got back on the road fairly early, which was a good thing, for it did not take long for the heat to return. We were minding our own business, riding along in a small pack at the speed limit, most all of us on fairly new, stock motorcycles. About mid-morning, without any warning, a South Dakota State Police car nosed right into the middle of our pack, effectively cutting us into two groups. We were very fortunate that the cop did not cause an accident, for it was obvious that he did this on purpose. At the time, we had no idea why, but we later learned that he wanted to know who the "new" Bandido was, riding the bike from Oklahoma, who was wearing the "Probationary" bottom rocker. It has always been a part of law enforcement's job in South Dakota to *figure out who we are*, that was no surprise. But this one wanted to know who we were so bad, he didn't seem to mind if some of us got killed in the process.

Ozark Rider Andy was riding next to Bandido Alain at the time, so he pulled over when the State policeman motioned for Bandido Alain to pull over. As soon as everyone came to a stop, the State Policeman ordered Ozark Rider Andy to get lost; to get back on his bike and resume riding. The front part of the group had already ridden farther down the road about four miles to the next exit. We had gotten off at the exit and parked under the bridge to stay out of the sun, so it did not take long for Ozark Rider Andy to catch up with us. By then we knew that the cop was solely after Bandido Alain, and we wondered what would happen. We were quite concerned that Bandido Alain would be arrested for some sort of immigration violation. I can only imagine the look of surprise on that cop's face, when he discovered that Alain spoke with a heavy French accent, was a Canadian Bandido riding a motorcycle he had borrowed in Oklahoma, and had a driver's license from Quebec.

It took the State policeman quite a while to check out Bandido Alain and he never did find out that Alain was the Presidente of Bandidos MC Canada. The policeman did write Alain a $100 traffic citation for having too loud an exhaust system, *even though the policeman had never gotten out of the car to test the exhaust system, and in spite of the fact that the bike was brand new and still had the stock factory exhaust installed on it.* We were all very happy to see Bandido Alain coming down the highway in the distance, and when he got close to us, we had him get off the exit and join us under the bridge. Over all, we lost more than an hour because of the cop…and once again, it was now getting hot.

The last part of our journey was uneventful, with the exception of having to stop more often for water. We finally got into Rapid City about 1pm and headed straight to the clubhouse property on the east side of town. Everyone at the clubhouse was very happy to see us, and quite surprised to see Bandido Alain. Alain was just happy to be there, for he had taken the longest ride on a bike in his entire life; he was truly happier than a pig in shit.

We spent almost four days in the Sturgis/Rapid City area. We had actually arrived the morning of Tuesday the 7th; and we eventually left around 4pm on the 11th. While we were there, I made sure that Bandido Alain got to see some of the tourist sights, including the four Presidents' faces carved in the mountain rock at Mount Rushmore. I took a great picture of Bandido Alain out in front of the rock faces there, standing with Ozark Rider Andy and Ozark Rider Nick, as you can see:

Ozark Rider Andy, Bandido Alain & Ozark Rider Nick

While there, we spent our nights at a house we rented in Rapid City for a week. The entire Oklahoma chapter stayed there, as well as all of the Canadian Bandidos that made it across the border, and Andy and Nick from the Ozark Riders. It was a decent, furnished four-bedroom house in a nice neighborhood, with a huge open room in the basement and a nice kitchen. We bought a bunch of inflatable mattresses at Walmart, used them for everyone to sleep on, and then shipped them home through the post office the day we left. The girls cooked every day, and we made sure that there was always food in the fridge. By the end of the week, the house had been a hotel for more than twenty people, and we left it just like we found it – immaculate.

Late in the week, a carload of Bandidos from Canada showed up. In the pile was Vice Presidente Peter from Toronto, the ex Loners MC member that became a Bandido a few months earlier, and another Bandido named Pork Chop. Bandido Peter and Bandido Pork Chop drove all the way to Rapid City from Toronto non-stop, spent two days there, and drove all the way back non-stop. I felt bad for them because all they ever saw while they were there was the clubhouse property and the house we rented. They never had a chance to see the tourist sights like Bandido Alain did.

I was really hoping that my friend Bandido El Secretario Robert "Tout" Leger was going to be with them, but unfortunately, he was not. I had talked to Bandido Tout nearly every day since I had left Canada, and Bandido Alain and I had been talking to him as much as we could since Alain had arrived in Oklahoma. Bandido Alain and I both tried unsuccessfully to talk him into coming and meeting us at Sturgis. One of the times we both talked to him, we actually thought that he was going to come. But Bandido Tout was very hesitant about leaving Canada, for he did not want to chance getting caught; he was on bond stipulations that prevented him from leaving the Montreal area, and in the end he decided it was too risky leaving Canada. I talked to him two or three more times while I was in Sturgis, and he felt as if he had made the right decision in not coming. Instead, he had decided to go to his other house out in the country, and spend the weekend there with his family; a decision that would ultimately cost him his life.

After four days of fun in the sun, and visiting with Bandidos from all over the world, Alain and I hit the road for the long ride back to Oklahoma. We left late Saturday afternoon the 11th of August, and rode all the way to North Platte, Nebraska before we got a room for the night. We had planned on making the trip in just two days, for Bandido Alain was scheduled to fly back to Canada on Tuesday morning, and he wanted a day to relax before the flight. We got up early the next morning at North Platte, and hit the road. It was a cloudy day, and it looked like rain as we rode east bound on Interstate 80 across Nebraska. When we ran into the rain, we turned south and east to get around it. This took us way off the beaten path, traveling down a bunch of little used county roads. We got to see a piece of Nebraska that no tourist ever sees; small country towns and miles upon miles of cornfields. There is a certain sweet smell in those cornfields baking in the sun; things like that are one of the joys of life only known to a biker.

At one desolate point I thought I would run out of gas. I was riding a 99 Harley FXDL Superglide very similar to the one Bandido Alain was riding, but I was packing my girlfriend with me, and burning more gas per mile than Alain. I discovered that day my bike would go almost twenty-five miles on reserve, and I must have coasted into that gas station on fumes. Bandido Alain and I crossed into Kansas, running south on Kansas state highway 81, heading through the wheat fields for Salina and Wichita. We finally hit the Oklahoma border in the very late afternoon and stopped at a Conoco station for gas, just north of Blackwell on Interstate 35. I checked my cell phone for messages and there were a bunch for Alain. All of the messages basically said to call home immediately, and each voice did not sound very happy. We had just checked for messages two hours ago at the last gas stop, and there had been none. We both knew that this was not going to be good news.

If it had just been bad news, I would have been thrilled. It was worse than bad news: it was the worst possible news I had heard for many years. I knew it was real bad when I saw a tear run down Alain's face before he got off the phone. I had no idea what was going on because he was talking in French; and the only word I recognized was "Tout". When he got off the phone, Bandido Alain sadly explained to me that Bandido El Secretario Robert "Tout" Leger had been murdered by the Hells Angels a few hours ago.

Apparently Bandido Tout had been assassinated right in front of his wife and kids, while at his home in the country. Bandido Tout had seen his assassins coming, and got in between them and his family. One assassin had fired a machine gun and the other a pistol, Bandido Tout was hit with many bullets. My good friend Bandido Tout died instantly just as he lived, a man of courage and action; always thinking of others before himself. Tout was a hero in my eyes for saving the lives of his family; it was a shame that his killers got away. Bandido Alain and I both sat in stone silence at the gas station, stunned, for what seemed like an eternity; for we both had lost a hell of a brother that day. It was also a sad day for Bandidos, for Bandido Tout was the first National Chapter officer to be killed by another motorcycle club in the history of the Bandidos.

As I sat there, I thought about the history that Tout had told me about in the last eight months since I had met him. Bandido Tout had been the first Rock Machine to ever come to the United States back in the mid 90's. The Rock Machine had sent him here to meet the Bandidos in Houston because he spoke excellent English, was a real Harley mechanic, and he actually rode a motorcycle. Most Rock Machine members back then did not ride motorcycles at all; the Rock Machine had originally been an organization of small time drug dealers that got together to protect themselves from the Hells Angels. Tout had gone to Texas not knowing a soul, and somehow located some Bandidos at a bar. When he told them that he was a member of the Rock Machine from Canada, and that he had been sent there to make contact because they wanted to be aligned with the Bandidos, the United States Bandidos told him to get lost. He told me, laughing, that he was fortunate that day not to have had his ass kicked all the way back to Canada.

Bandido Tout had also been in Mexico when the very first member of the Rock Machine had been killed by a Canadian Hells Angels prospect. Tout and Normand Baker had taken their girlfriends/wives on a vacation to Mexico in August of 1994. When they got on the plane in Canada, they had noticed a few members of the Hells Angels on that same plane, but did not think too much about it. A few nights later, Normand and his wife went out to eat dinner, and Tout and his wife decided to stay at the hotel. While Normand and his wife were eating dinner, Normand was shot in the back of the head; pieces of him actually landed on his wife. Normand Baker died instantly, and so began the fighting between the Hells Angels and the Rock Machine, which eventually cost Bandido Tout his life, seven years later. The prospect for the Hells Angels that killed Normand was caught, but only spent about a year in jail. The Canadian Hells Angels came to his rescue, paying off the corrupt Mexican justice system to get him released and the charges dismissed.

I immediately missed Tout a lot, but unfortunately there was not much I could do. Bandido Alain and I needed to get home, and we were only about one hundred miles west of Tulsa. We sadly got back on our bikes and rode about halfway, stopping just south of a town called Pawhuska. Every year at Pawhuska Oklahoma there is a huge biker party; it is Oklahoma's version of a little Sturgis. I had already promised Alain that we would stop and take his picture at the site of the Pawhuska biker party; for he had always wanted to be there but until now, had never been able. As I promised, I took the picture.

As you can see, Bandido Alain is red in the face just like I described earlier. When taken by my girlfriend Caroline, although we tried in vain to look like we were happy, we clearly were not. It had been a horrible end to a wonderful week. But sometimes that is life, and you have to take the good with the bad. So we got back on our bikes for the last leg of our journey, and returned to my house just after dark on Sunday, August 12th. We both took hot showers and went straight to bed. Tomorrow would bring the funeral arrangements, and we would have to tell the world what had happened. We both knew that it was not going to be a good day.

On Monday, we did what we could and of course, talked a bunch about Bandido Tout. Alain had known Tout for years, and they were very close. Alain told me then that Bandido Tout had prospected for the Rock Machine for almost seven years; not because he was a screw up, just because he did not care if he ever made it into the club. Bandido Alain flew home on Tuesday, and slowly my life returned to normal. But in Canada it would not be normal, at least not for any of the Canadian Bandidos. On Friday, August 17th, while on the way to the funeral for Bandido El Secretario Robert "Tout" Leger, William Ferguson, a Kingston Bandido, was arrested by the Quebec police for having a gun in his possession. Go figure…like he didn't need it?

It didn't stop there. It continued to get worse before it got better. Less than two weeks later, another National chapter officer in Canada was murdered. This time it was Sargento de Armas Sylvain "Sly" Gregoire and it happened in downtown Montreal. He owned a used car lot, and refused to hide that fact from the world. While selling a car to what Sly thought was a pair of potential buyers on Friday, August 24, 2001, Sly was shot in the head and died instantly. Bandido Sly was only thirty-three years old, and just like Bandido Tout, he left behind a family. Once again Bandidos Canada was caught in the middle of a war zone, and it seemed that the only option left was to go to the media. On September 2, 2001, Bandido Alain and I drafted what would become Bandidos Canada first public statement; and it said:

"The Bandidos Motorcycle Club is about riding Harley Davidson motorcycles, having fun and brotherhood. We are just a bunch of guys that like to ride motorcycles when we are not working. Just because we show up in a town or bar somewhere we have not been before, does not mean that we are there to 'take over the territory.' More than likely we are just there to visit some local friends that have invited us there, and then ride our motorcycles down the highway to another town or place. There is no reason at all for the public to be alarmed or scared of any member of the Bandidos Motorcycle Club."

Unfortunately, it did little or no good defusing the public sentiment against us; it seemed as if the only alternative was for Bandidos Canada to start fighting back again, just like they had done before when they had been Rock Machine. Bandidos Canada was now surrounded by four enemies: Hells Angels from the rear, law enforcement from the front, public sentiment from the left, and the media on the right. Many of the Bandidos members were getting tired of taking shit. And no Bandido was ever in the shit business: we did not ever give anyone shit, nor did we take any shit.

As individuals, some members of the Bandidos through their associates, hangarounds and friends, started fighting back, each in their own way and on their own terms. In September, 2001, many of the bars that did business with the Hells Angels were burned to the ground. Some of the bar owners lied about the fact that they were doing drug business with the Hells Angels, and some probably did not know that their employees were selling drugs for the Hells Angels. Other bar owners and building owners jumped on the bandwagon and burned their own places down just to collect the insurance.

The bar arsons continued into October, and sixteen people were eventually arrested for investigation concerning the bar fires. The newspapers articles explained that the arsons were part of a struggle for control of the illicit drug trade, but that was not even close to the truth. The truth was that all we wanted was peace, but to get the Hells Angels to agree, their illegal business ventures had to be impacted.

5

Bandidos Motorcycle Club Canada & Immigration Canada
October 2001 To December 2001

In mid-October of 2001, I decided that I did not want to return to Canada to attend my upcoming immigration hearing, scheduled for October 22. This decision was made as a direct result of two recent major events: the horrible destruction of the World Trade Center in New York City on 9/11, and the biological contamination of the United States Senate building with Anthrax. In early October, the planes were still not considered to be a safe means of transportation, travel was extremely difficult because of a general state of heightened security, and there was a general climate of fear everywhere.

Day and night, the media constantly exposed the American public to the premise that more attacks on the United States were imminent. My eight year old daughter Taylor, understandably so, did not want me to leave her. Taylor was afraid if I went to Canada, that Canada might not let me return. So being the Dad that I was, I made the only decision I could possibly make: I was not going to leave her, no matter what the cost.

On October 18, 2001, my Canadian attorney Josh Zambrowsky wrote a letter to the Adjudicator assigned to my immigration case, Mr. Rolland Ladouceur, and advised him that I would not be attending the next scheduled hearing. Mr. Ladouceur had always been an extremely fair and impartial Judge, and was well respected by all of the attorneys on both sides of my immigration hearings. He was the same Adjudicator that had allowed me to return to Oklahoma, at my immigration hearing in Canada back on January 17th.

Mr. Ladouceur also had been the only Judge I had ever seen laugh openly at a prosecution attorney, when the female attorney for Immigration Canada had suggested that I needed to stay in Canada for six more months so that they (Immigration Canada) could deport me, when all I wanted to do was just go back to Tulsa, Oklahoma as soon as possible. It wasn't like I wanted to stay in Canada, nor was I fighting my deportation just to be able to stay in Canada. I always thought that the whole immigration case was ludicrous, a waste of government time, and a giant waste of taxpayer money; and I had always believed that Mr. Ladouceur thought the same.

So it was no surprise to me, when, on October 19, 2001, Mr. Ladouceur rendered a bomb himself by dismissing my case. Josh, my attorney, was surprised that he had the balls to stand up to the morons at Immigration Canada, but readily admitted that the Adjudicator's logical way of thinking was profound, brilliant and an act of pure common sense. Mr. Ladouceur dismissed my case solely based upon the fact that I was already in the United States. To continue my case by bringing me back up to Canada just to send me back to the United States, in Mr. Ladouceur's opinion, was a total exercise in futility that only an idiot could comprehend.

Subject: Edward Warren Winterhalder File No : AI-00022

Following your letter of October 18th 2001, I understand that your client is still outside Canada and will not be present for the continuation of his inquiry scheduled to continue on October 22nd.

Considering that the allegations made against your client were pursuant to paragraph 27(2)(a) of the Immigration Act of Canada, and that your client is no longer "...a person that is in Canada..." I thereby consider the inquiry of Mr Edward Warren Winterhalder to be concluded.

Concerning the documentation presented by the parties, since they were not yet introduced as evidence, it has been destroyed.

Concerning the $20,000 bond, your client's passport and his Bandido Vest, I recommend that you contact Immigration Canada for restitution.

Please inform your client accordingly.

Rolland Ladouceur
Adjudicator

The Immigration Canada prosecution attorneys went ballistic. The next day, they sent a letter back to the Adjudicator, asking for a clarification of his Order. Those morons asked Mr. Ladouceur things like, "What do you mean by concluded?" and "Is the inquiry still adjourned?" I have to think it must have been a task for the Adjudicator to respond in the polite manner he did, and that Mr. Ladouceur must have had a hard time keeping his composure, when he wrote this back to the Immigration Canada counsel on October 31st:

Ms Lynn Leblanc and Mr Toby Hoffman
Citizenship and Immigration Canada

BY FAX : (613) 952-4770

Subject: Edward Warren Winterhalder File No : A1-00022

On October 19th 2001, after receiving confirmation that Mr Winterhalder would not be present for the continuation of his inquiry, I informed the parties that the inquiry was concluded. Here are the reasons.

The inquiry was opened on January 17th 2001. At the request of Citizenship and Immigration Canada, the case was adjourned until May 2001. A second adjournment was granted, as requested by the Minister, until October 22nd 2001. In the mean time Mr Winterhalder had returned to his country of citizenship (U.S.A.) and was expected to return by October 22nd 2001, to attend his inquiry.

On January 17th 2001, Citizenship and Immigration Canada presented a direction for inquiry and a report pursuant to paragraph 27(2)a) of the Immigration Act.

"An immigration officer or a peace officer shall, unless the person has been arrested pursuant to subsection 103(2), forward a written report to the Deputy Minister setting out the details of any information in the possession of the immigration officer or peace officer indicating that a person in Canada, other than a Canadian citizen or permanent resident, is a person who

a) is a member of an inadmissible class, other than an inadmissible class described in paragraph 19(1)(h) or 19(2)c)"

On October 19th 2001 Me Zambrowsky, Mr Winterhalder's counsel, informed the tribunal that his client would not come back to Canada for his inquiry.

Considering that the *Immigration Act* is silent with respect to the conclusion of an inquiry in such cases;

Considering that the objective of the inquiry was to determine if Mr Winterhalder should be removed from the Canadian territory;

Considering that the Mr Winterhalder is no longer on the Canadian territory;

The tribunal decided to conclude the inquiry because the question has become moot.

Should Mr Winterhalder return one day to Canada, Citizenship and Immigration Canada can seek his removal from Canada by causing another inquiry to be held as provided by section 34 of the *Immigration Act*.

Furthermore, at a pre-hearing conference held on October 5th 2001, Citizenship and Immigration Canada presented over 100 documents that they wished to introduce as evidence. Considering that these documents had not been disclosed to Mr Winterhalder's counsel, they were not introduced into the record. The Board reserved its decision in that respect which was to be taken at the continuation of the inquiry, scheduled for October 22nd.

Considering that these documents had not been entered into evidence, they have been destroyed upon the conclusion of the inquiry.

Rolland Ladouceur

Adjudicator

I was elated, and the folks at Immigration Canada were pissed. The only thing left was to have them return to me the twenty thousand dollars ($20,000) in bail bond money that I had posted to secure my release and property. Josh Zambrowsky wrote Immigration Canada a few letters demanding the return of my bail bond money, but the Immigration Canada officials basically told me to screw off. An Immigration Canada manager by the name of David Olsen claimed on November 29, 2001, that my cash bond was being estreated (forfeited) pursuant to section 94 (1) (e) & (f) of the Immigration Act. The peg they were trying to hang their hat on was that I failed to appear for the hearing. The only problem with that reasoning was that my case was dismissed for being moot.

I eventually waited for years for the return of my bond money. Through the years, three or four different Canadian attorneys aggressively pursued its return. More than three years after I posted it, and more than two years after my case was dismissed, their last position was that I never posted the bail money because Jean "Charley" Duquaire did. In the end, we all did the right thing and finally gave up fighting. It was going to cost a fortune to argue this in the

Canadian Appeals Courts, and I finally decided that it would be a waste of money for it was more than likely that I would never win.

As for the club, things still had not returned to normal. Maybe violence *was* the norm, in spite of our intentions that peace would prevail. On November 12, 2001 at a park just outside Montreal, some of our own guys got involved in a heated argument. One Bandidos member, Stephane Lalonde, was shot and killed. It was a sign of the times, for the stress level was unbearable. On November 27th, a friend of a few of our club members was charged with murder; it was alleged that he had shot to death a friendly Hells Angels associate during an argument on August 11th, 2001, just to impress his Bandido friends.

For a brief moment, the 1st of December was a welcome day of hope in a deep sea of despair. On that day, some members of Bandidos MC Canada officially became full patch members. All members who had completed one year of membership received their 1%er patch and their new Canada bottom rockers. This ended my official involvement with Bandidos Canada, but to this day I consider many of the Bandidos I met up there to be my friends.

A full patch party was held in Kingston again, and widely reported in the media. At the patch party, in a true testament that accurately reflected our club's worldwide sentiment, Bandidos Canada patiently explained to the world that it still desired peace in spite of all that had occurred, as reported in the Ottawa Citizen the next day:

Birth Of The 'Bandidos Nation'
Outlaw Bikers Speak Of Peace With Rivals, But Police Fear War

Gary Dimmock

December 02, 2001

The U.S.-based Bandidos, one of the world's most powerful biker gangs, secured a foothold in Canada last night after granting 45 full memberships to prospects who spoke of peace with rivals Hells Angels.

Inside a Kingston motel, some 100 guests, including new probationary recruits, talked business over steak dinner and toasts to the birth of a new "Bandidos Nation."

In conversation with the Citizen, new leading gang members spoke of a lucrative and peaceful future for expansion chapters in Eastern Ontario, Montreal, Quebec City and Toronto.

"It's a great day and we are all really proud to be part of the best motorcycle club

in the world," the Bandidos said in a statement to the Citizen. "We work hard and the public has nothing to fear. We do our best to bring something to the community."

In rare statements, even gang members who survived Hells Angels' gun attacks earlier this year, spoke of an end to the so-called war. "We don't have to party (with Hells Angels) together, but there's no reason we can't all behave together."

Now that the expansion gang has been granted full membership, it is empowered to start new chapters. "We're not just looking for anybody, we are looking for good family men with good backgrounds," the Bandidos Canada statement says.

Before last night, probationary members had to seek permission from its U.S.-based parent gang, Bandidos U.S.A. The new Canadian chapters have been granted full membership amid police reports of an intensified drug war with rival Hells Angels.

But the "war" has not materialized and the Bandidos have so far been calling for peace, not blood.

Police fear that the new members will now try to prove themselves, notably by wresting control of the drug market from the Hells Angels. Police insist the Bandidos make money any way they can -- including money laundering, drug distribution, loan sharking and prostitution.

By 10 p.m. last night, police had yet to make any arrests at the Kingston patch-in ceremony. They had vowed to arrest and deport any visiting U.S. gang members, but they couldn't find any.

Though the Bandidos are outnumbered by more than two-to-one, they still pose a threat to the longstanding Hells Angels' monopoly.

Over the past year, some probationary Bandidos defected to Hells Angels, including high-profile members with deep roots in Lanark County. Still, Hells Angels appear worried by the Bandidos presence.

In February, four armed members of an elite Hells Angels unit met at Montreal's Holiday Inn. It was a study of the "enemy," with each elite member taking turns thumbing through photographs of probationary Bandidos.

Formed in 1966 by disillusioned Vietnam veterans, the Bandidos are organized much like a corporation, with approximately 5,000 members and more than 100 chapters in 10 countries.

Early in the morning, on Wednesday, December 5, 2001, Bandido Eric "Eric the Red" McMillan, who was by now a Sargento de Armas in the Bandidos Canada National chapter, had his abdomen sliced open when he was knifed during a fight with three men in downtown Oshawa. Eric was outside leaving a nightclub around 2:15 am, when he was apparently ambushed. Three local Hells Angels members were later taken into custody as a result of the altercation.

On December 12, 2001, Bandido Presidente Alain "Alain" Brunette once again went to the media to try to explain to the world our intentions. The newspaper article was published worldwide, and unfortunately was very symbolic of the public resentment of the "biker wars", which at this point had been going on for more than six years. The headline screamed "Greed, Not Peace, Is Behind Biker's Bid For Peace With Quebec Hells". In the article, the writer stated that "a quest for money and good publicity, not peace, is behind the bid by the biker Bandidos to make nice with the Hells Angels". We obviously were extremely disappointed that the truth had not been told, and once again, what we had said, had been skewed and sensationalized just to sell newspapers.

We were serious about ending the violence, and all of us were willing to try anything to get it to stop. Alain even said during the newspaper interview with the reporter, "We're holding out our hands. We just want to live in peace and be able to work and have fun. We want the situation to stay quiet for a long time." And what Alain said clearly echoed what Bandido and Hells Angel leaders from all over the world wanted; the only people that were refusing to listen was the Quebec Hells Angles.

A few days later, Tom Mann from CBC Radio in Canada convinced me to do a live radio interview, which was broadcast all over Canada. It was a very cold day in Tulsa, during a light snow storm, when I made my way across town to the Tulsa University radio station. As I stood outside the building gathering my composure, I wondered if the war in Canada would ever be over, and if there was anything more I could do to stop it. For more than a half hour, Tom asked me all sorts of questions about my immigration case in Canada, as well as some expected questions about the Bandidos and our quest for peace in Canada. Although I was a little nervous, the interview came off without a hitch, and I was extremely proud of the end product.

6

Bandidos Motorcycle Club Canada
January 2002 To March 2002

On January 7th, 2002, the new Canadian federal anti-gang bill C-24 went into effect. C-24 made it illegal for a criminal organization to recruit new members. It really only strengthened the resolve of Bandidos Canada to get legal (if you weren't already) and stay legal (if you already were). Every member knew by now that this was the only way that the club could survive long term. Unfortunately, for all of Bandidos Canada in Quebec, their futures had already been set in stone, and the passage of C-24 just set the stage for what was coming. By now, no matter what Bandidos Canada Quebec did or tried to do, their world would soon come crashing down. The one enemy they had in front of them which they could plainly see (law enforcement), was finally ready to terminate the biker wars once and for all, in the very near future.

The beginning of the end for the Bandidos in Quebec might have been imminent, but the hammer dropped first in 2002 on the Outlaws Motorcycle Club. The sweep of motorcycle club members nationwide in Canada, which started in 2001, continued in London, Ontario, on January 8th with the arrest of Thomas "Holmes" Hughes. Holmes was the president of their London chapter, and a prominent leader in the Outlaws hierarchy. He was charged with attempting to murder four members of a Hells Angel support club in an altercation the night before; the shootout being the culmination of a tumultuous winter in which most all of the London Outlaws had switched sides and become members of the Hells Angels.

In late January, as a result of the decimation of the Outlaws MC London chapter, Bandidos Canada and the Outlaws formed an informal alliance to hang out together as much as possible, as a show of unity against the Hells Angels. At a bike show organized by the Hells Angels in London on the first weekend in February, a group of twenty Bandidos and thirty Outlaws arrived unexpectedly. The arrival and joint show of unity took almost everyone by surprise: the public, law enforcement and the Hells Angels. Surrounded by police and Hells Angels, the Bandidos and the Outlaws arrogantly walked through the swap meet, checking out the exhibits. Bandido Presidente Alain "Alain" Brunette later told me that the tension was so thick you could cut it with a knife, but it was well worth the effort. After only twenty minutes, law enforcement personnel escorted the Bandidos and Outlaws out of the bike show to defuse the situation.

London Outlaw President Holmes would be hammered some more when, a few days later, on February 7th, he was charged with a total of twenty-three more crimes that resulted from a post-arrest search of his home and the Outlaws London clubhouse next door. I was surprised when I heard on Wednesday, February 27th; a new Hells Angel named Brett "Lucky" Simmons was arrested in Oshawa for violating parole. I took notice because that is the same Bandido Lucky that I had visited in prison back in January 2001, while I was waiting in Canada for my next immigration hearing.

In the middle of March, near Toronto, in a suburb called Woodbridge, there was a big explosion in front of a social club. The club was connected with the new Toronto chapter of Bandidos Canada. Rumors that the biker war had arrived in Ontario were flying everywhere and fueled by media versions of the event. Fortunately, no one was injured in the bomb blast. Back in Quebec, it was still bad, but fixing to get worse. There seemed to be no stopping the violence; it was like a runaway train with no engineer.

In spite of the fact that most all of the Quebec Hells Angels were in jail, as well as most all of the members of their support clubs, there were still multiple teams of killers hunting for Bandidos to murder. On March 11th, the police shot and killed a man during a shootout in the middle of a busy Canadian interstate highway. The dead man turned out to be a hit man working for the Hells Angels, and he was on his way from Montreal to Kingston. In Kingston, that assassin was supposed to have killed Bandido Presidente Alain "Alain" Brunette, but Bandido Alain's life was spared simply because the police had stopped the assassin for speeding.

The killing continued. This time, Thursday, March 14, 2002, the victim was a totally innocent man by the name of Yves Albert, who was shot to death while gassing up at a gas station near his home. Mr. Albert's only "crime" was that he looked similar to a Bandido named Normand "Norm" Whissell. The specter of similarity between the two men were bizarre: Mr. Albert drove the same kind of Intrepid that Bandido Norm drove, the license plate on Mr. Albert's Dodge Intrepid was almost identical as the license plate on Bandido Norm's Intrepid, and both Intrepids were green. Mr. Albert was a family man, not even a biker, and Bandidos Canada was outraged at his senseless death. Normand Whissell was President of the Montreal chapter of Bandidos Canada at the time and it obvious to anyone that Bandido Norm had been the intended target. An article that ran in the newspaper reported the story as follows:

Biker Wars Starting To Take Big Toll In Quebec

March 15, 2002

By George Kalogerakis

Since 1994, the turf war has killed more than 150 people, both bikers and innocents.

The cost of dealing with biker activity-things like trials, prosecutors and investigators, is staggering, in Quebec alone the province has spent $100-million.

The violence pales even in comparison to the traditional Mafia in New York. And the battle is threatening to blow wide open. Here's why. The Hells Angels now control most of the U.S. and almost all of Canada.

Another rival gang based in Texas called the Banditos controls much of the U.S.. Where they overlap is Ontario and Quebec--and that means a battle for turf.

As these violent gangs are now attempting to grow by raiding each other's territory.

That battle seems to be behind a drive-by shooting in Montreal overnight. A particularly brutal murder that as Global National's Mike Armstrong shows us, killed an innocent man.

He is the wrong man.

Yves Albert was gassing up at the local corner store last evening when a mini-van pulled up. The side door slid open and nine shots were fired. The gunman continued firing even when Albert was on the ground.

A short while later, a burned out, stolen mini-van was found a 10 minute drive away. The fire was to destroy the evidence, things like hair and fingerprints. It's almost a biker sig-nature.

The problem was Yves Albert had nothing to do with bikers. Police believe he was not the man the killers were after.

Normand Whissell may have been the target. He is the president of the Bandidos Montreal chapter. Hit men have tried to get Whissell before: most recently in January, but he got away. At the time he was driving a green Intrepid, with no hubcaps, and the license plate 404 HYM.

Last evening Yves Albert was also driving a green Intrepid, with no hubcaps and a similar plate , XPM 404. The hypotheses is that the Surete de Quebec is holding is that it could be a mistaken identity that is very possible.

A breakdown in biker intelligence is how an expert explains what happened. The hit men were following orders.

They took the news hard this morning, at a local restaurant, just a few blocks from the murder. They normally share a few laughs over breakfast, but today they shared anger.

"If they want to kill each other, that fine," one man said. "But to get the wrong person, it's ridiculous."

Yves Albert leaves behind a wife, two children and many friends. He was involved in the community.

At the scene today, workers were cleaning up, while customers went about their business, many with heavy hearts. Both of these men knew Yves Albert.

"There are men who deserve this," one said. "Yves Albert was not one of them."

I felt bad about the death of Mr. Albert, but there was certainly nothing I could have done to prevent it. I spent quite a bit of time wondering if the killing in Canada would ever end. I was amazed that it had gone on for so very long. For once, I was happy to be living in Oklahoma, where all the motorcycle clubs got along. In Oklahoma there were Bandidos, Outlaws, Mongols and Rogues, and we all hung out together regularly. The gravity of the situation in Canada, where the police had killed the Hells Angels assassin a week earlier, was further sensationalized in a newspaper article published in the Ottawa Citizen a few days later:

Biker Killed In Shootout Was On Deadly Mission
Daniel Lamer, The Man Who Died In A Gun Battle With Police Last Week, Was On His Way To Assassinate A Prominent Member Of A Rival Biker Gang

By Gary Dimmock

March 17, 2002

The Hells Angels associate killed in a gunfight with police on Highway 401 last week was on his way to assassinate a prominent member of a rival biker gang in a contract-killing campaign to defend its crime monopoly, the Citizen has learned.

After reviewing a file containing an address, license plate and photographs, Daniel Lamer, 37, headed to Kingston sometime last week only to find that his target, a Bandido member, was on holiday.

Then, last Sunday morning, the parolee-turned-hit man set out again, figuring he'd execute the contract and finally earn a place within the ranks of the bikers he admired. Only this time, the police pulled him over, for all things, speeding.

At first, Mr. Lamer, a career criminal who started shooting people at 17, said he couldn't speak English to buy time while the OPP officer called a bilingual member for help. Minutes later, there were now four officers in the rear-view mirror. Armed with a revolver and wearing a bullet-proof vest, Mr. Lamer figured he'd shoot his way out, and opened fire on police.

The police returned fire, killing him on the side of the road, thus thwarting what would be the first of two assassination attempts on leading members of the U.S.-based Bandidos, a powerful gang that secured a foothold in Canada in December.

(The Citizen has learned that the assassination contracts on Kingston-based Bandidos remain open amid police fears of an intensified power struggle between Bandidos and rivals Hells Angels for control of drug, loan-sharking and prostitution networks.)

The next assassination attempt came four days later in Montreal when someone gunned down Yves Albert, a 34-year-old father of two young children. But the assassin shot the wrong man.

Though the Bandidos are outnumbered by more than two-to-one, they still pose a threat to the longstanding Hells Angels' monopoly. In the past year, several probationary Bandidos defected to Hells Angels, including high-profile members with roots in Lanark County. Still, Hells Angels appear worried by the Bandidos presence, according to intelligence reports.

It is believed that this year's assassination campaign against rival Bandidos in Canada was originally hatched in February 2001, when four elite members met at a Montreal Holiday Inn. It was a "study of the enemy," with each member taking turns thumbing through photographs of probationary Bandidos.

Bandidos U.S.A. granted new Canadian chapters full membership in December. Police fear that the new members, who no longer need to seek permission from its U.S.-based parent gang, will try to prove themselves by wresting control of the drug market from the Hells Angels.

But the "war" has not materialized and the Bandidos have so far been publicly calling for peace, not blood.

In statements to the Citizen, leading Bandidos members have said "the public has nothing to fear." Even former members of Rock Machine, since absorbed by Bandidos, who survived Hells Angels' gun attacks in the past, spoke of an end to the biker war staged in Quebec during the 1990s.

The war has claimed more than 150 lives, including six innocent bystanders -- one an 11-year-old Montreal boy killed in 1995 when he was hit by shrapnel from an exploding bomb. Besides the death toll, the biker war included 124 attempted murders, nine missing persons, 84 bombings and 130 reports of arson.

The first clear indication that Quebec's biker war has spilled into Ontario came in December, when a Hells Angels gang ambushed a rival Bandidos biker in Oshawa, first thrusting a knife into his stomach and then opening fire in the streets as he ran for his life.

Eric (The Red) McMillan, a 25-year-old Bandido, found himself alone outside a strip club. His assailants attacked him, but he managed to run down the street to a friend's waiting car.

The biker gangs reported a truce last year, but police say it was merely an attempt to appease politicians pushing to strengthen anti-gang legislation.

Gang members have told the Citizen otherwise, saying the fight ban remains in effect -- leaving some outlaw bikers wondering if the recent attacks were launched to settle old, personal scores.

Either way, both bikers and police are probing the events that led to last week's botched assassination attempts.

The hit man who was killed last Sunday by police is linked to The Rockers, a Hells Angels puppet gang used as enforcers for the Quebec Hells Angels Nomads chapter. Before the parole board set him free two years ago, Mr. Lamer worked as an assistant to a prison drug network controlled by the Hells Angels.

The Texas-based Bandidos, formed in 1966 by disillusioned Vietnam veterans, are organized much like a corporation, with approximately 5,000 members and more than 100 chapters in 10 countries.

Bandidos' expansion into the north is considered a defeat among law-enforcement agencies that had vowed to keep the gang from extending operations into Canada.

The article was quite well written and extremely accurate, except for the quote from the police that said, *"amid police fears of an intensified power struggle between Bandidos and rivals Hells Angels for control of drug, loan-sharking and prostitution networks."* What a crock of crap that was! Let's set the record straight once and for all: There has never been a power struggle over drugs, loan-sharking and prostitution, and there is never going to be. This "biker war" was simply a battle that had started over one thing: *not being told what to do*. Bandidos Canada (originally the Rock Machine when the "biker war" started) was not going to be told what to do by the Hells Angels in an area that they (Hells Angels) claimed to be theirs, *and that was all there was to it*. It was so simple an explanation, but to continue to get funding and to sell more newspapers, the police and media had to get on the drugs, loan-sharking and prostitution bandwagon.

On March 19, 2002, one of the Hells Angels Quebec Nomads associates was shot while eating lunch at a sushi bar in Montreal, in the middle of the day. The newspapers all claimed that the shooting of Steven "Bull" Bertrand was probably payback for the botched assassination of Bandido Norm, which the week before had claimed the life of Yves Albert. The truth of the matter was that a young associate of Bandidos Canada, Patrick Hénault, just by chance happened upon Mr. Bertrand sitting there having his lunch, and made a decision on his own to try to kill him. From the time that the Bandidos associate saw Mr. Bertrand sitting in the restaurant by the front window, until he shot at him, was only a matter of about fifteen minutes. Patrick Hénault was later convicted of attempted murder. Mr. Bertrand survived the attempted assassination, and I would bet he is thanking God that he is still alive.

By now, Canadian Bandido Presidente Alain and I both had a fairly decent repoire with Gary Dimmock from the Ottawa Citizen. As reporters generally go, most are unscrupulous people who never do what they say. We have found over the years that almost all of them will consistently take comments out of context, and twist those comments around to make the telling of the story turn out exactly the way the reporter wants it told. We would often wonder, after reading a story about us: whatever happened to just telling the truth? But as for Mr. Dimmock, we had learned that he was a man of his word, and that he did do what he said he would do. We found that the majority of the articles he wrote were most often extremely accurate.

That's why we were all surprised when about a week later, Gary Dimmock wrote an interesting article that shook all of the old members of the Rock Machine, specifically the ones that had come from Montreal. The article stated that the Hells Angels Nomad chapter in Ontario was behind all of the latest violence, and that the President of that chapter, who was originally a Rock Machine himself, had sent out the teams of assassins who were looking for Bandidos to kill. The President of the Hells Angels Nomad chapter in Ontario was Paul "Sasquatch" Porter. He had been an important member of the Rock Machine in Montreal for many years. The Hells Angels had even tried to kill him a few years earlier, by shooting him, and had almost succeeded. Just before the Rock Machine actually became Bandidos, Sasquatch switched sides and became a Hells Angel.

I met Sasquatch when he was a member of the Rock Machine, while on the road in Texas. We spent the better part of the day traveling together; he was driving in a truck with another Rock Machine, and I was on my motorcycle. To this day, I seriously doubt that he was behind the assassination teams that Mr. Dimmock wrote about. I am much more inclined to speculate that they were the result of left-over murder contracts issued by Maurice "Mom" Boucher and the Hells Angels Nomads chapter in Quebec. I also believe that Sasquatch did not possess the hatred in his heart that would be necessary to kill his former brothers. I have always wondered from which "source" Mr. Dimmock received his information for the article that appeared on March 27, 2002:

Hells Angels 'Hit Squads' Target Rival Biker Gang
Contracts Issued To Defend Monopoly On Illegal Drugs

By Gary Dimmock

March 27, 2002

An elite Hells Angels chapter with deep roots in Lanark County has dispatched several two-man hit squads targeting rival bikers to defend its drug monopoly, the Citizen has learned.

The Ontario Nomad Chapter issued the contracts after the Bandidos refused to be absorbed by the world's most powerful biker gang.

Paul (Sasquatch) Porter is the reputed leader of the chapter, and police consider him as powerful in Ontario as his counterpart, Maurice (Mom) Boucher is in Quebec.

In the past two weeks, the Hells Angels hit squads, mostly associates and prospects, have targeted two leading Bandidos in Kingston and Montreal.

The Hells Angels hope that killing Bandido leaders will prompt rank-and-file members to join them.

But not as full-fledged members, rather as "puppets" taking orders from Hells Angels. It is this "join or retire" policy that has sparked violence across Ontario and Quebec.

And the Nomads know their targets. Some of the chapter's leaders are former members of Rock Machine, since absorbed by U.S.-based Bandidos, a biker gang that secured a foothold in Canada last December.

At the patch-over ceremony, Bandidos denounced police fears of an intensified power struggle with rivals Hells Angels. They spoke of peace, not blood.

Months later, police fears are coming true, with tit-for-tat shootings across Ontario and Quebec.

Though the Bandidos are outnumbered by more than two-to-one, they are still considered a threat by the Hells Angels, a crime corporation known for killing competitors.

Though the contract-killing campaign has just begun, its hit squads have so far failed two reported missions.

One hit man, Daniel Lamer, was killed in a gunfight with police after being pulled over for speeding on the 401. His target, who lives in Kingston, has survived two attempts on his life. A few years ago, he recovered from several bullet wounds in a drive-by shooting on a Quebec highway in February 2001.

He escaped certain death when he swerved his car around and sped away from the gunmen, driving against traffic until he was stopped by police.

Most recently, he was on holiday when a hit man came calling.

The target is a former close associate of Mr. Porter, nicknamed "Sasquatch" for his size.

Unlike Mr. Porter, the target, also a former Rock Machine, refused to defect to the mighty Hells Angels.

Four days later, in Montreal, another two-man hit squad gunned down Yves Albert, a devoted family man whose car matched a targeted Bandido.

Days later, in what police called a retaliation attack, a two-man hit squad linked to the Bandidos, gunned down Steven (Bull) Bertrand, a close associate of reputed Quebec Nomad boss Mr. Boucher, currently on trial for charges that he ordered the deaths of two prison guards.

Police fear these hits mark a return to the biker war in Quebec that has claimed the lives of more than 150 people -- including six innocent bystanders, one an 11-year-old Montreal boy killed in 1995 when he was hit by shrapnel from an exploding bomb.

7

Bandidos Motorcycle Club Canada
April 2002 To June 2002

The first mega trial of seventeen Hells Angels who were arrested in the spring of 2001 got started in Montreal in early April 2002. One of the first pieces of evidence that was submitted at the beginning of the trial was a list of people the Hells Angels were accused of trying to assassinate. It took the court clerk almost ten minutes to read the list; it contained one hundred and thirty-two names of their "enemies", some on the list did not survive. Here is a copy of the list that I received, which includes some of the notes that I made off to the right side. Although it is not entirely accurate, it will provide a decent idea of the magnitude of the situation. On the left you will see that some of the names are highlighted in **bold**; those names in **bold** reference the fact that they were at one-time actual members, prospects or hangarounds of the Rock Machine:

Pierre Bastien		Killed Oct 98
Yan Bastien		
Claude Beauchamp		
Pierre Beauchamp		Killed Dec 96
Robert Béland		
Jean Bélec		
Marc Belhumeur		Killed Jan 97
Michel Bertrand		
Mario Bérubé		
Yves Bisson		
Serge Boisvert		
Denis Boucher		Jail
Daniel Boulet		Killed Nov 98
Martin Bourget	"Frankie"	Killed Jul 00
Alain Brunette	"Alain"	Jail
Robert Caissy		
Patrick Call		Prison
Stéphane Carriere		
Rémi Cartier		Prison
Giovanni Cazzetta		Prison
Salvatore Cazzetta		Prison
Michel Chamberland		
Leroy Clayborne		
Stéphane Corbeil	"Bull"	HA member now
Stéphane Craig		
Jean-Francois Cyr		
Serge Cyr	"Merlin"	Jail

André Désormeaux	"Andre"	Jail
Serge Desjardins		
Jean Duquaire	"Charley"	Prison
Nelson Fernandez		
Mario Filion		
Michel Fontaine		
Francois Gagnon		Killed Jun 00
Marc Godin		
Sylvain Grégoire	"Sly"	Killed Aug 01
Yan Grenier		
Marc Guérin		
Patrick Héneault	"Boul"	Police Informant
Renaud Jomphe	"Renaud"	Killed Oct 96
Sylvain Jomphe		
Steve Kelly		
Sun Chin Kwon		
Gilles Lambert	"Gille"	Parole
Simon Lambert	"Chiki"	Prison
Guy Langlois	"Guy"	HA member now
Daniel Lareau		
Michel Lareau		
Raymond Lareau	"Mon Mon"	
Jimmy Larrivée		
Gilles Laurent		
Robert Lavigne		Suicide
Roger Lavigne		Prison
Éric Leblanc		
Daniel Leclerc	"Poutine"	HA member now
Éric Leclerc	"Beluga"	HA member now
Robert Léger	"Tout"	Killed Aug 01
Richard Léonard		
Luc Lepage		
Jacques Lizotte		
Sylvio Mannino		
Marcel Marcotte		
Jimmy Mavor		
Éric Morin		
Stéphane Morgan	"Ti-Cul"	Killed Nov 98
Yves Murray		Prison
Raymond Ouellette		
Peter Paradis		Police Informant
Robert Paradis	"Bob"	Prison
Richard Parent		Killed Aug 99
Martin Camielle Pellerin		
Stéphane Perron		
Johnny Plescio	"Johnny"	Killed Sep 98
Tony Plescio	"Tony"	Killed Oct 98

Jean-Sébastien Prince	"Jerry"	Parole
Paul Porter	"Sasquatch"	HA member now
Michael Potvin		
Gilles Rondeau	**"Bazou"**	Quit the club
Jean Rosa		
Denis Rousselle		
Sylvain Rousselle		
Yvon Roy		Killed Jul 98
Rock Sauvé		
André Sauvageau	"Curly"	HA member now
Daniel Sénésac	"Dada"	Killed Sep 94
Stéphane Servant		
Brett Simmons	"Lucky"	HA member now
Rolland Therrien		
Sean Traynor		
Stéphane Trudel	"T-Bone"	HA member now
Patrick Turcotte		Killed May 00
Patrick Verret		
Andréas Vroukakis		
Marc Yakimishan	"Garfield"	HA member now

These following are/or were members of the Alliance, the Dark Circle, or associates:

Jonathan Audet	Patrick Baptiste
Luc Beaupré	Claude Bouchard
Daniel Brouillette	Serge Bruneau
André Bruneau	André Cartier
Carol Daigle	Louis-Jacques Deschenes
Michel Duclos	Éric Edsell
Leslie Faustin	Franco Fondacaro
Paolo Gervasi	Salvatore Gervasi
Jean-Francois Guérin	Reynald Huot
Jean Hyacinthe	Claude Lafrance
Gilles Lalonde	Bruno Lévesque
Mario Lilley	Maurice McIntyre
Yvan Nadeau	André Nault
Normand Paré	Nelson Pelletier
Michel Possa	Gordon Reynolds
Daniel Rivard	Gilles Rondeau Sr.
Jean-Jacques Roy	Jean-René Roy
Richer St-Gelais	Denis Thiffault
Jean Vernat	Pierre Wilhem

An associate of the Hells Angels would later tell the world in that first mega trial that there was a standard price put on the head of any one from the list that was killed:

$100,000 for a "full-patch member," meaning the highest level in the Rock Machine.

$50,000 for a "prospect," meaning a middle-level member in the Rock Machine.

$25,000 for a "hangaround," meaning the lowest level in the Rock Machine.

On Sunday May 5th, the morale for Bandidos Canada got a giant boost with the conviction of Maurice "Mom" Boucher, who was the President of the Hells Angels Nomads chapter in Quebec. Mom had been convicted of ordering the assassination of two prison guards, and was sentenced the next day to a life sentence, with no possibility for parole until the year 2027.

By early May 2002, I had convinced Bandido Presidente Alain "Alain" Brunette to come to Oklahoma again, and join the Oklahoma Bandidos first at Pawhuska, then on a trip to Red River, New Mexico. This time he also brought his girlfriend Dawn, and they arrived in Tulsa by plane a few days before the Pawhuska Biker Rally (Called the Mayfit) started, on Wednesday May 15th. The annual Mayfit was one of the biggest biker parties in the state of Oklahoma; this year it would attract more than 7,000 people. For this trip I loaned Alain my personal 1999 red Harley FXDL for the duration of his stay, and told him he could use it as he saw fit. On Friday the 17th, Alain and Dawn rode the sixty miles of winding, tree-lined roads through Skiatook and Barnsdall, up State Highway 11 to Pawhuska, while I followed in a pickup truck that was loaded with t-shirts and supplies for the party site.

After three days and nights at the rally, we all returned to Tulsa on Sunday. Alain and Dawn hung out at my house for a few days, just taking it easy. At the time, I was in the middle of a sound mitigation construction project for the Tulsa International Airport Authority. Due to my employment situation, I was too busy working and therefore could not leave town early. So on Thursday, May 23rd, my girlfriend Caroline took off early and drove out to Albuquerque, where we had planned to meet the next day. Bandido Alain left shortly after Caroline, riding out with Bandido Lee McArdle (and other Oklahoma Bandidos) headed for the Texas panhandle, where they planned to spend the night. The next day, I caught a sunrise flight to Albuquerque and met Caroline at the airport; from there we traveled up to Red River through the mountain passes.

Caroline and I were the first of the Oklahoma crew to arrive, which is the way that we planned it. Once again, I was carrying all the supplies for the condo we had rented, as well as the t-shirts that we planned to sell at the Red River Bike Rally. Almost every year we all went to Red River on Memorial Day for the Bike

Rally. It was a blast there, a beautiful place up in the mountains. The town folk always welcomed us with open arms and even the local law enforcement treated us with respect. It was a rare occasion when a Bandido got arrested there. There were only two things we ever kept an eye open for there: the first was snow (yes it sometimes snowed there in May) and the second was the thin air – it was very difficult to breath up there because of the altitude.

Up over the other side of Bobcat Pass, just east of the actual town of Red River, Bandidos USA had a huge campground right in the middle of a town called Eagle Pass. At the campsite, which covered about eighty acres, you could always get a bite to eat or something to drink. We also always had food to eat, a place to lie down and something to drink at the condos we had rented for the entire Oklahoma delegation. Once you got to Red River, between the Bandidos' camp in Eagle's Nest and the chapter condos in Red River, one did not have to spend a dime unless he chose to. It was an ideal setting for a perfect weekend. Bandido Alain and the rest of the Oklahoma chapter of Bandidos arrived a few hours later, just after dark on Friday night. By then, the town was rocking....

Between selling t-shirts, visiting with Bandidos from all over the world, and hanging out at the condo with the guys from Oklahoma, Bandido Alain and I kept very busy. In addition, we had invited Gary Dimmock from the Ottawa Citizen to join us. This would be the first time Gary had ever gone to a major biker rally in the United States, and also the first time he had ever been around the United States Bandidos. We located each other via phone on Saturday morning; both of us thankful our cell phones still worked so high up in the mountains. Bandido Alain, Gary Dimmock and I spent the most of the day hanging out on Main Street in Red River, which had been blocked off to nothing but thousands of motorcycles.

Saturday night I took everyone out to the local steakhouse called Timbers for dinner. We all had a great time there, and then spent most of the evening visiting at the Bull of the Woods bar. Sunday was meeting day for us at the Bandidos USA camp over in Eagles Nest, and by Sunday night we were all pretty tired. I got a good night's sleep and left early for the ten-hour trip back to Tulsa, driving back home in my truck with my girlfriend Caroline, Alain's girlfriend Dawn and Bandido Ian's girlfriend Shelly. Bandido Alain and the rest of the Oklahoma crew took off on their bikes shortly thereafter, and we all safely arrived back in Tulsa before 11pm.

Alain spent another day resting up at my house, before he and Dawn flew back to Canada. Once again, Alain was bright red in the face, and by now everyone was calling him Tete Tomat (Tomato Head in French). It had been the best vacation of his life he told me, right before they left. That night, I took a picture of them both, in which you can see that they are very happy:

Dawn & Alain At CT Ed's House

It had been one of those moments in time that you dream about. I had just spent almost two weeks with one hell of a man, who had made an impact on me that would last a lifetime. I was very honored that I had been able to show both of them a great time, what would become one of the greatest memories they had in their lives. It was a vacation that I had wished would never end, and one that would have to hold both of them for years to come. We spent that last day together visiting my construction jobsite out by the airport, and then they got on an airplane and flew off to Bandido Alain's date with destiny.

Just over a week after they flew home to Canada, very early on the morning of June 5, 2002, the law enforcement authorities in Canada dropped the hammer on all of the Bandidos in Quebec. One of the many arrested that day was my good friend, Bandido Alain. What happened that day was once again accurately described in a newspaper article written by my friend Gary Dimmock and published the next day:

Raids Crush Biker Gang
Bandidos' Expansion Plans Wrecked As Police Crack Down

By Gary Dimmock

June 06, 2002

Two weeks ago, in the Sangre de Cristo mountains of New Mexico, Alain Brunette met with international gang brothers who spoke of ambitious plans to expand across Canada with the hopes of one day commanding an entirely above-board club.

The 38-year-old president of Bandidos Canada said he longed for peace with his rivals, the Hells Angels, and the day he could take care of business without looking over his shoulder for hit men lying in wait. After all, in the past two years,

Mr. Brunette, who wears a bulletproof vest, has survived not one, but two attempts on his life.

The future, he said, would be different and legitimate, with every member required to hold down an honest job. Next month, the Kingston-based leader had plans to take his message for a new "peaceful" future to European leaders of the Bandidos, the world's second-most powerful biker gang.

But the gang's expansion across Canada was all but ended yesterday, with almost every single Bandidos member in Quebec -- plus Mr. Brunette – jailed on charges ranging from drug trafficking to gangsterism to conspiracy to kill rival Hells Angels members.

Operation Amigo, launched last year, culminated yesterday with some 60 arrest warrants for Bandidos gang members living in Quebec. Beyond the arrest of Mr. Brunette in Kingston, other Ontario-based members were spared.

The probe, involving some 200 police officers across Quebec and Ontario, targeted the gang for fear it would eventually fill the void left in the wake of a crackdown on Hells Angels that left some 120 members behind bars in March 2001.

Police say the early-morning raids in Quebec, Kingston and Toronto mark the "beginning of the end" of the eight-year turf war with Hells Angels that claimed more than 150 lives -- including six innocent bystanders, one an 11-year-old Montreal boy killed in 1995 when he was hit by shrapnel from an exploding bomb.

In statements to the Citizen yesterday, Bandidos members acknowledged that the police sweep marked the end of the turf war, but insisted its Canadian chapters will "survive" the crackdown.

The gang's Canadian leader was arrested at his Kingston apartment shortly after 6 a.m. and escorted to a Montreal jail cell by RCMP. Mr. Brunette, the most influential Bandido in Canada, is among 10 gang members accused of plotting to kill rival Hells Angels members in Quebec over the last four years.

The gang leader was arrested peacefully -- unlike one of his underlings. In Rouyn-Noranda, Que., about 420 kilometers northeast of Montreal, one biker refused to surrender, then waved a handgun. Police opened fire, shooting him in the head and chest. He is listed in serious condition and is expected to survive.

In all, police searched computers and seized a handful of firearms, eight kilograms of cocaine and 200 kilograms of hashish. Half of the 60 arrest warrants were for suspected bikers already in custody – including 47-year-old Salvatore Cazzetta, a founding member now serving a 12-year sentence for conspiring to import 10,000 kilograms of cocaine into the U.S.

For the first time since the bloody turf war began in 1994, police have taken an entire gang off the streets of Montreal -- leaving nearly all Bandidos, formerly known as Rock Machine, either behind bars or facing trial.

The U.S-based Bandidos secured a foothold in Canada in December 2001, granting 45 full memberships to probationary members of the former Rock Machine.

Police intelligence agents had feared that the Bandidos expansion chapters would challenge the Hells Angels' estimated 80-per-cent control of the illegal drugs market. But other than tit-for-tat beatings and shootings, police predictions of a bloody takeover of Hells Angels territory has failed to materialize.

Though the Bandidos are outnumbered by more than two-to-one, they still pose a credible threat to the longstanding Hells Angels' monopoly in Canada. The Texas-based Bandidos, formed in 1966 by disillusioned Vietnam veterans, is organized much like a corporation, with more than 100 chapters or franchises in 10 countries.

The expansion into the north is considered a defeat among law-enforcement agencies that had vowed to keep the gang from extending operations into Canada.

The recent crackdown on biker gangs has prompted police fears that the "war" will spill into Ontario, where both Hells Angels and Bandidos take care of business wearing full colors -- an act of confidence no longer seen in Quebec.

In separate statements to the Citizen, both Hells Angels and Bandidos in Ontario have called for peace -- not blood. Police say it is merely an attempt to appease politicians bent on strengthening anti-gang legislation.

It was now time for me to do what I could for what was left of Bandidos Canada. The first order of business was to appoint an acting national President (Presidente) and a new national secretary (El Secretario). The last El Secretario was a guy by the name of Eric "Ratkiller" Nadeau, and it turned out that he was an informant and a pathological liar. Ratkiller had been appointed to his position by Bandido Presidente Alain, based upon his computer skills, shortly after Bandidos Canada received their Canada bottom rockers in December 2001. Many of the charges lodged against the Quebec Bandidos members were based solely upon the word of Mr. Nadeau.

It is important to note, that during the execution of the arrest warrants on June 5th, very little illegal substances were seized from the home or on the person of any actual member of the Bandidos. Most all of illegal contraband that was seized, consisting of eight kilograms of cocaine and two hundred kilograms of hashish, was taken from the property belonging to a female associate of the club.

When the Hells Angels in Quebec were arrested fifteen months earlier, the police seized approximately ten million in cash and almost another ten million in illegal contraband; when the Bandidos were arrested, after you deduct what was seized at the home of the female associate, the police seized less than one hundred thousand in cash and illegal contraband. This fact alone is proof that the members of Bandidos Canada were *absolutely not big time drug dealers*.

Earlier in the spring of 2002, Bandido Presidente Alain had appointed Bandido John "Boxer" Muscedore to be the new Vice Presidente over Ontario, because Bandido Vice Presidente Pietra "Peter" Barilla had been arrested and was in jail, unable to make his bond. When Bandido Alain and everyone else in Quebec were arrested, the only choice for the Presidente job was Bandido Boxer. He was, in reality, the only Bandido National officer not in jail or in any trouble. In late June of 2002, Bandido Boxer took over as acting Presidente of what was left of Bandidos Canada. At this time, there were almost sixty-five Bandidos in jail, prison or out on bond awaiting trial, almost all of them in Quebec. There were another half-dozen on the run, trying to avoid being arrested, since the police already had arrest warrants for them. Left on the streets that were not in trouble, were less than fifteen Bandidos in Ontario, and none in Quebec.

The next step was to appoint a new El Secretario for Bandidos Canada. Bandido Boxer wanted to appoint a new Bandido he liked by the name of Jeff "Burrito" Murray, but I eventually persuaded him to appoint Bandido Glen "Wrongway" Atkinson. Bandido El Secretario Wrongway was a professional businessman and a devote family man, who knew computers inside and out. Glen was extremely intelligent, well respected by every one, and articulate. He had been a member of the Loners from Toronto since 1997, and had become a Bandido in May of 2001.

The very first project Bandido Wrongway and I faced was trying to take care of all of the Bandidos who were incarcerated. That turned out to be a monumental job, for the prison authorities would not allow us to make contact with them. If a letter sent to them had any remote reference to Bandidos in it or on it, it was seized as contraband and not delivered to the intended recipient. Because all the club records had been seized from the informant Ratkiller at the time everyone was arrested, we had no idea who was in the club and who was not. It took months for El Secretario Wrongway and me to configure accurate membership, phone and jail lists.

The second project was to figure out how to preserve Bandidos Canada long term, but that was really a project for Bandido Boxer and Bandido Wrongway; for there was nothing more I could possibly do for them from here in Oklahoma.

8

Bandidos Motorcycle Club Canada
July 2002 To June 2003

Throughout July of 2002, Bandido El Secretario Wrongway and I stayed in contact almost daily. We had a lot to do in the way of organizing and keeping a lid on the situation in Ontario. Everything was fairly calm until the Toronto media took a very small story and blew it into a major ordeal. As we say here in the United States, they made a mountain out of a molehill. A young member of the Kingston chapter of Bandidos Canada, who had just been released from jail, Carl "CB" Bursey, violated his parole by not living where he was supposed to be living. Instead of being there, he took off with a girlfriend and went fishing for a few days more than he should have.

Bandido CB had actually become a member of the Bandidos while he was in jail. While he was serving a three-year federal sentence, in the summer of 2000, he somehow became a member of the Rock Machine. Because the Rock Machine became Bandidos, he became a Bandido by default. When he was released from prison, everyone who knew him was either still in prison, or had just been arrested in the sweep of June 5th. When the first newspaper articles came out about him, nobody on the streets even knew if he truly was a member or not. Initially, no one in Bandidos Canada Ontario even knew who he was! It took us a few days to find out who he was and how he got in the club, but even after we figured that out, only one or two of the Kingston members were in contact with him. The more we learned about who he really was, the more we realized that he knew very little about who we were.

The newspaper articles gradually became our version of a comic strip; the details that surrounded his eluding the authorities got more and more far-fetched. At one point the newspapers claimed that he even had a grenade launcher that he intended to use against the police when cornered:

Bandido Vows To Not Be Taken Alive

September 17, 2002

By Alan Cairns

A fugitive Bandido has "numerous handguns and a grenade launcher" and threatens to "shoot it out with police," police said yesterday. The grenade launcher is believed to be a rocket-propelled grenade (RPG) system, similar to

Russian-made models that bring down U.S. helicopters in the hit movie, Black Hawk Down.

And in a strange twist to the case, Carl Thomas Bursey, 27, is apparently being hidden by rival Hells Angels. "A dangerous weapon like an RPG in the hands of a person who is as volatile and as violent as Bursey makes this an extremely scary situation," said Det. Greg Sullivan of the provincial repeat offender parole enforcement (ROPE) unit. "We have credible information that Bursey is in the Toronto area ... and he says he won't be taken alive and will get into a shootout with police."

Bursey, whose 55 prior criminal convictions include narcotics trafficking, weapons possession, threats, assaults, robberies and four jailbreaks, went on the lam in July and has since avoided an Ontario-wide dragnet. Bursey, who was once a Rock Machine member, was serving a two-year, 10-month prison term for escaping from an Ontario jail in December 1999. Bursey had only one month left to serve in his sentence when he went underground, started doing drugs and began hoarding weapons and making threats to kill his police pursuers, Sullivan said.

Prior to his latest release, Bursey twice had his early release revoked -- once in August 2001 after police seized 45 kilos of homegrown marijuana from where he was staying at his uncle's home, and again in May when police found a loaded handgun when Bursey and two other biker associates were stopped in a stolen car in Milton. National Parole Board documents also reveal that Bursey was "implicated in a weapons-related investigation in a homicide matter" in Quebec.

Sullivan said police have received information that Bursey is being aided by Hells Angels in Toronto. Bursey, who was raised in Guelph and was allowed to live with his mom upon his latest release, is 6-feet tall, about 220 pounds, with hazel eyes. He has several jailhouse tattoos, including one of a loaded gun, the motto "sworn to kill" on his right wrist and the word "anarchy" across his belly.

In addition to the incredible stories the newspapers came up with, what amazed us so much was that all he had left to do on his sentence was ten days! This media attention was for a parole violator, who, when caught, would only have to serve ten more days and he was free. Talk about making a mountain out of a molehill! My friend Gary Dimmock from the Ottawa Citizen got right into the middle of this, and helped us out by being an intermediary for Bandido CB to surrender in late September of 2002.

I admit I had to laugh a little when Gary called CB "a prominent member of the Bandidos", for the reality of the situation was that he was a very insignificant member, who had never even ridden a motorcycle. The media was the only one that ever said that he was important, and that was an outright lie. This was only done to sell more papers. Unfortunately, it perpetuated the big lie that all Bandidos were bad, which just wasn't the truth:

Fugitive Biker Back In Prison

By Gary Dimmock

September 25, 2002

Ontario's most wanted biker, Carl Thomas Bursey, surrendered on his own terms Tuesday after eluding detectives for two months.

Amid police fears that the prominent Bandidos biker would stage a "bloody last stand" rather than return to jail, Bursey kept his promise to give up peacefully.

At 4:34 p.m., the 27-year-old fugitive pulled into the parking lot of a Kingston coffee shop, where he had arranged to meet police.

Detectives Neil Finn and Brian Fleming waited in an unmarked Oldsmobile for an hour, sipping cups of Tim Hortons coffee propped up on the dash.

The fugitive, a career criminal with 55 convictions, had asked me to act as an independent observer to ensure his safe surrender.

"I just want to go back to jail and get the time over with and then get on with my life."

"I don't intend to hurt anyone and I certainly don't want to get shot when I turn myself in," he said before his surrender.

He spent the morning drinking ice-cold coolers as he watched re-runs of The Cosby Show and listened to Ozzy Osbourne. Hours later, he stuffed back a sandwich, then headed for the meet.

He pulled up alongside the unmarked police car, walked directly to Det. Finn and said "Hey Buddy," then put out his hands to be cuffed. "Are you taking me straight to jail?"

Det. Finn answered yes and assured his prisoner would not face new charges for hiding from the law.

Bursey grinned, then told his entourage -- fellow bikers and a girlfriend -- that he loved them before ducking into the back seat of the police car.

Bursey had feared police were taunting him by telling newspapers that his arsenal included shoulder-fired missiles -- a claim he flatly denied. However, the province's Repeat Offender Parole Enforcement squad says its story was based on "credible" intelligence.

"We're just glad he turned himself in and that it went down peacefully," Det. Greg Sullivan said.

Police have been hunting the outlaw biker, dubbed a "notorious escape artist," since July. He failed to check in with his parole officer with just 10 days left on a sentence for breaking out of jail in January 2000. That mistake earned him a nation-wide warrant for his arrest and put him on the top of Ontario's most wanted list.

He managed to keep one step ahead of the law for two months even though he wore his Bandidos biker vest wherever he went.

Now, though, he has had enough of running. Besides, everyone, it seemed, was urging him to surrender. His fellow bikers, parents and girlfriend all feared he'd get hurt in a standoff with police.

On Thursday afternoon, he came out of hiding to defend himself against police claims. The police said he was an "extreme" danger to the public and known for unpredictable violence.

More, they said his arsenal was vast and claimed he'd mount a shootout rather than go back to prison.

Sitting on a bench in a riverside park in Kingston last week, Bursey spoke of deep loyalty to the Bandidos Canada Motorcycle Club and understood that his membership had earned him notoriety. He insists he's not the madman of the headlines.

According to prison files obtained by the Citizen, Bursey did not break the law the last time he was at large. Police say the same is true this time.

The biker's adult criminal record dates back to 1993. His most recent federal sentence was two years and 10 months for possession of stolen property, dangerous driving, breaking probation, threatening to kill, obstruction of justice and impersonation.

He broke out of jail in early January by simply walking out the door of a storage room of a Guelph jail.

He spent a month on the run, but was captured when police searched an apartment and found him hiding under a kitchen sink.

In the biker world, Bursey is known for loyalty, notably putting the interests of

Bandidos before his own.

However, a prison psychologist's report, obtained by the Citizen, tells a different story.

The report says Bursey is an "impulsive individual with negative self-evaluation, little interest in socializing, impatient and easily irritated." The psychologist also said he drank too much, kept company with outlaws, and had "criminal values."

In a 2001 hearing, the parole board said he showed a "potential for violent behaviour."

Yesterday at least, he was anything but violent as he turned himself in.

He was later escorted to Kingston Penitentiary, the toughest 10 acres in Ontario. Police said they were glad he was off the street, even if it is for only 10 days. For Bursey, life in prison is nothing new. This time, he just hopes his brief sentence will be just that.

On September 25, 2002, the heavy hammers of justice fell on the entire Outlaws Motorcycle Club all across Canada. Almost fifty Outlaws members or ex-members were arrested on charges that were based upon the testimony of an undercover police officer who became a full patch holder in their Windsor chapter, and testimonies of other members who became paid informers. The undercover law enforcement agent, whose street name was Finn, had been spying on the Outlaws for more than two years. (Finn was the one who had given me a ride from Windsor to London in January 2001). Even the International President of the Outlaws, James "Frank" Wheeler, who lived in Indianapolis, Indiana, was arrested as a result of Finn's testimony. It was a major coup for the authorities in Canada; and almost everyone arrested was charged under the new C-24 gangsterism law.

In November of 2002, former Rock Machine member turned informant, Pierre "Peter" Paradis, published a book called "Nasty Business". It was about his life as a drug dealer and the time he spent in and around the Rock Machine. I have since read the book and found it to be quite interesting, and surmise it to be a fairly accurate portrayal of his life, the small part of the Rock Machine that he was familiar with, and the people that were close to him. I think it is important to note that he never was a biker, and except for a very small period of time, never even owned a motorcycle.

On December 17th, Hells Angels member Bill Miller was arrested on charges of possession of a gun, possession of controlled drugs, and gangsterism. Bill had started his motorcycle club life as an Outlaw, and then founded the first Ontario based chapter of the Rock Machine, which ultimately became the Toronto chapter of Bandidos Canada. In late January of 2001, Bill was one of the Bandidos who defected to the Hells Angels, causing the complete shutdown of the Toronto chapter. (Eight months later, Mr. Miller would eventually plead guilty to some of the charges in return for a one-year prison sentence.)

By the beginning of the year 2003, many members of the Hells Angels in Quebec had already pled guilty to criminal charges of gangsterism - the same gangsterism law (C-24) that had become legal just one year ago. It appears that so many Hells Angels pled guilty to gangsterism, that it will be very easy in the future for the Canadian Government to be able to prove that they are indeed, a criminal organization. I will not be surprised to see all Hells Angels charters in Canada be declared criminal organizations in the immediate future, pursuant to the gangsterism clause of Bill C-24 and all the resulting convictions pursuant to same. (The Hells Angels were eventually declared a criminal organization in June 2005.)

On January 9th, 2003, to add more fuel to the already burning bonfire, the media reported that the police and Government wanted to pass a new law classifying bikers as terrorists. This proposed legislation, if it passed, would be the death of all motorcycle clubs in Canada. In mid-January of 2003, the first member of the Outlaws to plead guilty to gangsterism was Richard Bitterhoff from the Outlaws Woodstock chapter. And as the spring progressed, more Outlaws members pled guilty to the same gangsterism charges, in spite of the fact that these guilty pleas will more than likely have drastic ramifications for the Outlaws as a club in the years that lie ahead.

In late February, ex-Bandido Carl "CB" Bursey was arrested again, this time for possession of drugs and firearms. I, for one, was not surprised at all. By now, Bandidos Canada Kingston had figured out that he was not a biker at all and that he had no business being in a motorcycle club. As a result, he was told to leave the club. Immediately he joined forces with his old friends, the Hells Angels, which once again was no surprise to us. As winter turned into spring, some of the Bandidos and their associates, who had been arrested in the summer of 2002, had already pled guilty. Everyone that had not pled guilty at that point was planning on going to trial, but the trial dates were getting postponed repeatedly. There finally appeared to be some light at the end of the tunnel, when on March 11th, a Judge ordered separate mini-trials for the remaining thirty-nine defendants.

On Friday, June 12th, Bandidos Canada was the recipient of a big defeat; Bandido Andre "Andre" Desormeaux officially pled guilty to arson, drug trafficking, and attempted murder charges. In addition, he pled guilty to a gangsterism charge, which would present a serious hurdle for the club to overcome in the future, and received a total of sixteen years in prison. Bandido Andre, at the time of his arrest, was a Sargento de Armas in the Bandidos Canada National chapter. Up until now, no Bandidos member had ever pled guilty to gangsterism, and it was a big setback for the club all across Canada. It was also the longest prison term ever given a Bandidos member in Canada at that time. Up until then the twelve-year prison sentence given to my old friend Bandido Jean "Charley" Duquaire had been the longest. The Montreal Gazette newspaper reported on the story as follows:

Key Bandido Gets 16 Years In Jail
Involved In Botched Hit At Sushi Bar. Desormeaux Offered Gang
Underlings $1,500 To Torch Clubs Used By Hells drug dealers

By George Kalogerakis

June 14, 2003

André Desormeaux brandished $15,000 in cash before underlings in the Bandidos gang. "I want it to burn in my area," he said of his Hochelaga-Maisonneuve drug territory.

Anyone who set fire to bars frequented by competing dealers for the Hells Angels would get $1,500 for each.

Thirty-five places burned down that summer of 2001, until police officers contacted high-ranking members of the Bandidos.

Police said they were not that interested in investigating the Bandidos at the moment, but that could change unless the fires stopped. The fires stopped.

Police had lied. They were actively following the gang and arrested 65 one year later.

One of the top members was Desormeaux, who yesterday was slapped with the severest sentence so far.

A judge at the Montreal courthouse gave him to 16 years in prison after he pleaded guilty to drug trafficking, pot growing, gangsterism, attempted murder and plotting arson.

Prosecutor Denis Gallant said the Bandidos were setting fires in 2001 to take advantage of the huge police sweep that jailed more than 100 people connected to the Hells drug network. "The Bandidos wanted to take over the market," he told the judge.

Desormeaux was a full-patch member of the Bandidos and had his own marijuana plantation in a Rivières des Prairies home. When police raided the 71st Ave. place, they found 400 plants as well as the shirt and badge of a Montreal police officer that had been stolen in a break-and-enter.

The 36-year-old Joliette man was also involved in trying to kill rivals in the Hells, including the failed March 2002 attempted slaying of Steven (Bull) Bertrand at a Bernard Ave. sushi bar.

Bertrand, now doing seven years in jail for cocaine importation, has close ties to Hells leader Maurice Boucher.

When Bertrand was shot, Desormeaux acted as lookout and gave the signal - taking off his baseball cap - for the shooter to fire away. "Desormeaux would say he was ready to pay to have Steven Bertrand killed and he would pay even if it failed," Gallant told the court.

Quebec Superior Court Justice Kevin Downs confiscated the home where Desormeaux had his pot plantation as well as $117,000 in Canadian cash and $11,000 in U.S. funds.

Desormeaux's wife, Nancy Paquette, also pleaded guilty yesterday, but only to helping her husband sell hashish to other inmates in prison. The inmates would deposit payment in a bank account, and she would collect the money from the outside.

The 27-year-old mother of four young children was sentenced to house arrest for one year.

So far, 49 Bandidos or associates out of the original 65 have pleaded guilty. The stiffest sentence before yesterday was 12 years for another top leader, Jean Duquaire.

A megatrial is expected as early as this fall for the remaining 16 accused. A large room is being renovated at Laval's courthouse for the case because the special biker courthouse near Bordeaux Jail is busy with two Hells trials.

9

Bandidos Motorcycle Club Canada
Quebec Ends & Alberta Begins
July 2003 To February 2004

In July of 2003, the death of Bandidos Canada in Quebec came without as much as a gunshot. No bombs, no killing, not even a whimper; only a small newspaper article in a Montreal newspaper. It told about an agreement, in which all members of the Quebec Bandidos would immediately quit the club. In return, the Hells Angels Quebec would guarantee the Bandidos' safety while they (Bandidos Canada Quebec) were in prison and/or jail. In addition, if the Bandidos Canada Quebec had a desire to continue being Bandidos after they were released from prison or jail, they could transfer to Ontario and become Bandidos again there, with no hard feelings.

Complying with this agreement meant that there would never again be Bandidos in Quebec. In a small way, this would mean that the Hells Angels had won the "biker war". More importantly, the agreement meant that the killing of Bandidos members would definitely end, and all the Bandidos members that were in Quebec jails and/or prisons would be safe and live to see freedom again. It was a difficult decision for all of the Bandidos involved. In the end, because they were all too tired of fighting, their self preservation and common sense prevailed. Initially, I was confused by their acceptance, but after a few days of thought, I understood the reasoning behind their decision. The decision to agree to the end of Bandidos in Quebec has not changed any aspect of my relationship with them; I still feel the same about them. My relationship with them was with the men, not the patch. With the patch gone, the relationship was still the same. I continued to be their friend and brother; they would still be mine as well.

So it was rather ironic, when shortly thereafter, I came across an old Christmas card I had received from them in December of 1999. I guess I had thrown it into a pile of other Christmas cards from that year, and the pile had been saved in a box to be looked at some other day. It is now, I believe, an important and significant piece of history. As you can see, it is a testament to a legacy of men who are now biker heroes held in high regard by bikers worldwide, as men of respect. A fearless group of men with principles that refused to be told what to do, refused to be controlled and who ultimately refused to sacrifice their integrity; no matter what it took. That is, except for the few that had no principles or integrity, those who were not willing to pay a price as a consequence for their actions.

By the fall of 2003, of the more than one hundred former/existing members and associates of the now ex-Rock Machine/Bandidos that had been in trouble with the law, only four had become informants. These informants were now telling their stories, and all had been either full patch members of the Rock Machine, the Bandidos, or both clubs. The informants were Pierre "Peter or Buddy" Paradis (who wrote the book called "Nasty Business"), Eric "Ratkiller" Nadeau, Sylvain "BF" Beaudry and Patrick "Boul" Heneault. It was no surprise to anyone when some of the incarcerated, now ex-Bandidos were charged with more crimes; some of which included murder. Notwithstanding the fact that some of the informants had been charged with attempted murder themselves, and/or were pathological liars, as a group they were a formidable foe, and their testimony could provide enough evidence to deliver convictions.

In September of 2003, another hammer fell on what was left of Bandidos Canada. This time, a full patch member of the now ex-Bandidos Canada Montreal (who had also been a Rock Machine member in Quebec City) chapter was charged with the murder of the highest ranking Hells Angel assassinated during the "biker war". Quebec Hells Angels Nomads member Normand "Biff" Hamel had been shot to death in April of 2000, in a carefully planned ambush outside a health clinic. His two assassins had to chase him around the parking lot before they could kill him. The next day, the media reported the arrest of now ex-Bandido Tony Duguay, who was being charged with the murder of Hells Angel Biff. In spite of the fact that there was now no more Bandidos in Quebec, the media insisted on depicting Tony as a member.

In late October the tide began to turn, as the testimony of one of the informants, Eric "Ratkiller" Nadeau, was ruled inadmissible. Apparently, the authorities finally figured out that they had a pathological liar on their hands; possibly a bigger liar could not have been found anywhere on the planet. As a result, charges were dismissed against some of the few remaining Bandidos still awaiting trial. Afterwards, there were only about a dozen Bandidos that remained of the more than sixty who had been arrested in June of 2002, waiting for justice; but the wheels of justice in Quebec turned very slowly.

Like a Phoenix rising from the ashes of the Quebec Bandidos, in the fall of 2003 arose the new Edmonton chapter of Bandidos Canada. Its conception had been planned for quite awhile. Bandidos Canada Toronto chapter members had been traveling back and forth between Edmonton and Toronto since the beginning of 2003. Some of the Bandidos Canada National chapter officers had made contact back in 2002, but the contact had been lost until early 2003, when a Bandidos Canada Toronto chapter member was visiting family in Edmonton.

The initial contact in Edmonton led to a large group that were disillusioned with the Hells Angels in Alberta, most of whom were ex-members of another motorcycle club called the Rebels. When late spring of 2003 rolled around, one of the guys in the group was allowed to become a member of the Toronto chapter. His name was Joey "Crazy Horse" Campbell, and on May 25, 2003, he became the first actual Bandido living in Edmonton. I had an opportunity to meet Bandido Crazy Horse at Rapid City during the Sturgis Bike Rally in August of 2003, but unfortunately, I missed him by just a few hours. In November of 2003, a full Probationary chapter of Bandidos Canada was formed in Edmonton. After a rough previous year, January 1st, 2004 brought in the potential for a glorious new year, and things were finally looking up for Bandidos Canada.

In mid-January of 2004, the first trial finally got under way for the now ex-Bandidos Quebec and/or Rock Machine members that had been arrested in the summer of 2002. The trial started for all the remaining defendants except my old friend, now ex-Bandido Presidente Alain "Alain" Brunette and one other, now ex-Bandido Sargento de Armas Serge "Merlin" Cyr. For various reasons, disposition of their cases would be put off until June of 2005, which would be more than three years after their arrests. (They both would eventually plead guilty and receive eight year sentences.)

It is interesting to note, that by January of 2004, the only charges that Bandido Alain and Bandido Merlin faced were very minor drug charges, possession of a gun and gangsterism. I presume that the only reason to put off their trials would be an attempt to force them to plead guilty – hoping the wait would encourage them to do so. With credit for time served while waiting for trial under Canadian law, in June of 2005 both had, in reality, served six years of prison time. More accurately stated, by the time they plead guilty, they accumulated enough jail time to discharge six years in prison.

The hope for a great new year for Bandidos Canada was smashed on January 30, 2004 when Bandido Crazy Horse was shot while leaving a nightclub in Edmonton. He later died at a local hospital with his wife and children by his side. With him, when he was shot, was Bandido Hangaround Robert "Rob" Simpson from Vancouver; he, too, was shot but died instantly. Both men were only thirty-four years old. Shortly thereafter, as a tribute to their memory, it was decided that this would be the time to tell the world that there was now a chapter of Bandidos located in Edmonton. The local Edmonton newspaper reported the shooting as follows:

Gang May Seek Revenge For Double Slaying
Gangland-style Killings Part Of A Turf War Between
Hells Angels, Bandidos, Biker Expert Suggests

By Doug Beazley

February 02, 2004

*EDMONTON - Biker gang violence could soon erupt in Edmonton in retaliation
for the deaths of Joey Morin and Robert Charles Simpson, says a retired sergeant
from Quebec's provincial police force who is an expert on the gangs.*

*The two were gunned down Friday night in the parking lot of Saint Pete's, a strip
club at 156th Street and 111th Avenue.*

*"You're going to have more shootings in the next couple of weeks," said Guy
Ouellette, who retired from the Surete du Quebec in 2001 but still testifies in biker
gang trials.*

"It will create some kind of turmoil there."

*He said Joey (Crazy Horse) Morin -- who changed his name to Joey Campbell
about three years ago -- was a probationary member of the Bandidos motorcycle
club, a Hells Angels' rival which was setting up a chapter in Edmonton.*

*City police released no further information on the double homicide on Sunday.
Police have not named the motorcycle gang thought to be affiliated with the
victims.*

*Ouellette said Morin was a former member of the Rebels bike gang and briefly a
Hells Angel. The Rebels eventually became Bandidos members, he said, adding
that Simpson was also associated with the Bandidos gang and was in Edmonton to
help set up shop. A motorcycle gang needs six to 10 people to create a chapter,
Ouellette said.*

*"The Hells Angels won't let the Bandidos organize," he said. "They don't want to
share territory with them. It's going to be interesting to see what will be the next
move, if there is going to be some retaliation."*

*Simpson died outside the club late Friday and Morin died a short time later in
hospital. Ouellette said Morin probably had a list of fellow Bandidos members in
his pocket.*

Already, messages of condolences are posted on the Bandidos website, which emits the sound of bullets when entered. Morin and Simpson were mentioned by their first name.

"Rest in peace, my brothers. You will never be forgotten," reads one entry.

"May your souls rise to heaven before the devil knows you're dead."

"This was a coward's way of doing things," read another.

One entry came from the secretary of the Bandidos chapter in Germany. Another came from the national chapter in Europe. The club has its roots in Texas.

A message from the Canadian chapter identified Joey "Crazy Horse" as a "probationary" member and Rob as a "Hangaround" who were "gunned down in Edmonton by filthy scum-sucking cowards." The chapter lauded the victims "who tried paving the road of brotherhood throughout Canada."

"You cut one we all bleed," the message concluded.

Yves Lavigne, an author and Hells Angels expert in Toronto, said there are only five Bandidos members in Canada, all in Ontario.

"Alberta is a one bike-gang province and has been for six, seven years," he said. The Hells Angels "control the province."

But he said the police have a duty to be more open about what happened.

"The police owe it to the public to say whether or not this was an isolated incident, whether it was a targeted shooting, whether these people were just victims of circumstance and whether people should stay away from that area or not."

Lavigne said just because the victims may have hung out with bikers doesn't necessarily mean this was a biker killing.

While the police haven't reported how many times the two men were shot, early reports suggested there were multiple shots to almost every part of their bodies.

"Two guys, maximum four bullets, that's a professional hit and if the whole place was sprayed, then it was either done by really frightened amateurs or by another group trying to make a very serious point," Lavigne said.

Police have yet to release what kind of weapon was used in the shooting.

David Simpson, younger brother of victim Robert Simpson, said Robert had no connections with gang activity. Robert worked in his father's motorcycle shop in Aldergrove, B.C.

"Robert had no criminal history and had never been charged with any criminal act," said David, who lives in Los Angeles. He said he talked with his brother a few days ago, but didn't know why Robert was visiting Edmonton.

"Dealing with bikes, he does know some undesirable people, but he never bought into any of that."

The 34-year-old, set to turn 35 on March 3, spent lots of time with his 12-year-old daughter, Alexis.

"He was a great father. He loved his daughter. He was funny and charismatic," David said, his voice breaking.

"The RCMP have told my dad that it just seems that Robert was in the wrong place at the wrong time."

David said his brother's funeral service will be held late this week or this coming weekend in Surrey, where Robert lived.

Ouellette said the red and gold colors of the Bandidos club will likely be on display at the funeral for Joey Morin. He said Hells Angels will likely send a spy to the funeral.

He said the police will have to be very pro-active to make sure new gangs don't get a toehold on the city.

I had to laugh when it was reported that Yves Lavigne had stated that there were only five Bandidos members living in Ontario. It only proved to me that he had no idea what he was talking about. You see, most all of the Ontario Bandidos were legal; they had highly visual means of support. Almost all had regular employment and families; they were just a bunch of guys who liked to ride motorcycles together. When there is no criminal activity going on, there is no justification for continued police surveillance; hence the police and the media (and Yves Lavigne) have no idea what is going on. At the end of the article, there was a footnote about Bandido Crazy Horse that is quite worth mentioning, for it will give you an accurate picture of the man's character:

Joey Morin (now Campbell) received a medal of bravery from the Governor General in 1991 for his role in the rescue of three people from a burning truck in October 1989 in Edmonton. Morin (now Campbell) and a friend noticed the back of a truck was on fire as they were driving by. When they stopped and approached on foot, they saw someone in the smoke-filled cab. With the help of his friend, Morin (now Campbell) grabbed the man and pulled him to safety. The man told them his son was also in the truck, so Morin (now Campbell) and his friend returned to rescue the son, who said his friend was also in the truck. The flames had reached under the cab, but Morin (now Campbell) went back a third time and was able to pull the friend from the flaming vehicle.

After the funeral, the local newspaper finally figured out that there was a new chapter of Bandidos located in Edmonton. The reason very few people had known of its existence was, once again, the same as the situation in Ontario. All of the members were legal; they had legal employment and they were not interested in illegal activities. All of the members of Bandidos Canada, both in Ontario and Edmonton, as well as the few that will return to the club from Quebec, know that for Bandidos Canada to ultimately survive, it is imperative that every member be as legal as possible. I was not surprised when the local newspaper announced the arrival of Bandidos Canada Edmonton in its standard sensational fashion, once again quoting the biker expert Yves Lavigne, as follows:

Death Predicted For Bandidos Bikers

By Doug Beazley

February 8, 2004

Edmonton has had its own probationary chapter of the Bandidos outlaw biker club since November - and their public debut at Joey Campbell's funeral Friday might mark the start of a bloody year in Alberta, says gang expert Yves Lavigne. "That funeral was the first time these guys appeared in public in Edmonton in their colours," said author Lavigne, who has made a study of the Hells Angels and their biker rivals in Canada. He said the Bandidos Canada organization in Ontario confirmed to him recently they were responsible for giving the Edmonton chapter its charter.

"We're talking six to 10 members in Edmonton, a probationary chapter that's got a year or so to prove itself. That generally means setting up a drug network of their own.

"But every one that pulled on a Bandidos vest last week is committing public suicide. Alberta is Angels territory. Setting up a Bandidos chapter there is stupid, just stupid.

"These guys are all gonna die. My big concern is civilians getting caught in the crossfire."

Word of a probationary Edmonton chapter is backed up by the fact that several Bandidos mourners at Campbell's funeral were spotted wearing Alberta patches on their vests in gang colours - red and gold. But news of a Bandidos chapter in Edmonton may have caught city police by surprise.

Lavigne's grim assessment comes from a comparison of the two gangs' relative strengths in Canada. The Angels are the dominant criminal biker gang in the nation and are, according to the last report of the Criminal Intelligence Service Alberta, the only one with chapters in Edmonton, Calgary and Red Deer.

"There's a treaty between the Bandidos and the Angels that says whoever gets into a territory first, owns it," he said. "Well, the Angels own Alberta. So what happens next in Edmonton is going to end there - it won't spread further."

Contrary to the predictions of Yves Lavigne, no more Bandidos died, but the new Edmonton chapter of the Bandidos lasted less than a year. In the fall of 2004, all of the Bandidos in Edmonton became Hells Angels, proving once again that all is not what it seems to be in the Canadian 1%er outlaw motorcycle club world. By the summer of 2005, all that remained of the Bandidos Motorcycle Club in Canada was the Toronto chapter, which had less than a dozen members.

10

The Very Beginning
1955 To Fall 1971

By now you are probably wondering where this all began, so to set the record straight, my legal name is Edward Winterhalder, and I was born in Hartford, Connecticut in the summer of 1955. On the day after my birth, my birth mother gave me up for adoption, and I was sent to a foster home pending my adoption. At the time, my biological father had no idea that I was being placed for adoption. When he found out, he tried unsuccessfully to gain my custody. Six months after my birth, I was adopted by Warren and Helen (Dolly) Winterhalder, who lived in a quiet suburb of New Haven, Connecticut, called Hamden. Warren was a business forms salesman and Dolly was a homemaker.

I spent the first five years of my life playing on Gorham Avenue in Hamden, and went to kindergarten there before moving to a brand new home in Northford, Connecticut during the summer of 1961. It was a light green three bedroom, two bath, split-level home located on Carlen Drive, smack dab in the center of a middle class neighborhood. Carlen Drive was a cul-de-sac, and at the end of the cul-de-sac was a turn-around with a basketball hoop located next to a big pond. There was also a dam for the pond there, with a bridge across it, as well as a huge field where neighborhood kids could play baseball or football.

I started first grade at the William Douglas Elementary School in the fall of 1961. I was nothing special, just another new kid on the block. But I did manage to get run over by a bunch of fifth graders playing football at recess time, causing my left leg to fracture. My earliest memory of the neighborhood was my mom, Dolly, allowing me to walk our dog, Skeeter, for the first time. I was probably about seven, and I had to work hard at convincing Mom that I could handle the dog, which weighed about as much as I did. As soon as Mom handed me the leash, Skeeter must have seen a cat, and the chase was on. I must have looked like a flag on a flagpole, as Skeeter dragged me down the street. By the time Mom got the dog to stop running, I had suffered my first case of serious road rash. My pants and shirt were all ripped open, and I was a mess, bleeding all over the place.

In the fall of 1963, when I was eight years old, I changed schools and started attending the Stanley T. Williams Elementary School in Northford. My only memory of it now was when President John F. Kennedy was assassinated on November 22, 1963. All the teachers at school were crying and we were dismissed an hour early; school was even closed for the next few days. All the kids I knew, including me, were excited to be out of school until we found out that every TV channel (all four, at the time) had nothing on except for news of the assassination.

Around that time, being the smart guy that I was, as I was exploring the woods up behind the pond at the end of our street, I discovered a yellow jacket hornet's nest in a hollow at the base of a tree. I was fascinated with the little creatures, and not knowing a thing about them, I reached my hand into the tree to see what they would do. It didn't take long for me to find out, and as a result of my stupidity, I was stung more than fifty times. It took my mom most of the afternoon to pull out the stingers and apply Arm and Hammer baking soda to my wounds.

By the time fourth grade rolled around, I had figured out that I was pretty smart. I was basically a straight A student, and spent a lot of my time reading. I soon developed a fascination with Myron Floren, who played the accordion on the Lawrence Welk show, and as a result, convinced my parents to let me start taking accordion lessons at the Betty Revegno Accordion School in Wallingford, Connecticut. Eighteen months later, I was lucky enough to win first place in a state competition for ten-year old accordion players. I soon discovered that the instrument was not very hip, and figured out that the guitar was much cooler.

However, my mom and dad would not let me have a guitar or take guitar lessons. I continued my accordion lessons just so I could learn the guitar from another teacher at the studio. I would go there early, and the guitar teacher would let me sit in the room and watch when she gave her students guitar lessons. After my accordion lesson, I was able to borrow a school guitar and practice what I had learned. It would be years before I could put all those guitar "lessons" to good work, but I eventually did.

Until my eleventh birthday and the sixth grade, my life was fairly normal, with the exception that most of the neighborhood kids ostracized me for being intelligent. I was not good at all at sports, and failed miserably when I was given the opportunity. I did join an organized Little League baseball team for one year; where I got to warm the bench, and every once in a while, play a little outfield and second base. At an early age, I figured out that sports were clearly not my forte, and I rapidly moved on to what I considered to be bigger and better things.

When I was about ten, I started shoveling snow and mowing lawns to make some money. The work didn't pay much, but it gave me a little money to buy 45 rpm Beatles records at the local discount store. I also worked at a local dairy farm whenever I could, and spent a little time watching the construction of new houses in my neighborhood. For reasons unknown to me at the time, I was fascinated with the construction process. It was like it was a part of my soul. (Thirty years later, I would learn that my biological dad, grandpa and great-grandpa were all builders and carpenters.)

Entering the sixth grade, I began junior high school in North Branford, Connecticut. Northford was a small part of North Branford, and I had to travel about five miles to get from my house to school. At the time, I thought it was a long way! The junior high school crowd was way different, and I soon fell into what some would say was the wrong crowd. It was a group of kids from the wrong side of the tracks, and I felt at home when I was with those kids, for reasons I did not then understand. I had been raised as an only child all my life, so I think that for the first time in my life I finally felt what it was like to actually have some brothers.

During my sixth grade year, I went through a massive amount of change. I had been a model student and son, but now I was starting to question all types of authority. I developed new friendships that would have a monumental impact on me. The first and foremost was Peter "Pete" Hansen. Pete was the sixth of seven sons, and he was my age. Pete had two older brothers that I knew of, Walter "Walt" Hansen and Harry "Skip" Hansen. They were all big, tough kids who had serious reputations for not taking any crap.

Pete and I did a lot of stupid things together the next few years, none of which made our parents proud of us. We found it easier to skip school and get in trouble, than to do our homework. We became the best of friends, and were almost inseparable. At the end of sixth grade, in the summer of 1967, Pete ran away from home. I hid him in the woods near my house, where there was a train and a train track. Our plan was for him to hop the train, which was supposed to take him to a land of pleasure somewhere, but he overslept and missed the train.

By the time I caught up to Pete the next day, his big brother Walter was closing in on us. As we were crossing a huge sand pit, going to who knows where, we saw his brother coming at us from about a mile away. We hid in the bushes at the side of a creek, while his brother stopped the car on the other side, only fifty feet from us. Walt started hollering for Pete, and told him that he better get home before he (Walt) found him. Walt let Pete know, without a doubt, that if Walt caught him, Pete's ass was grass. After all these years, I still wonder what would have happened to Pete if Walt had found him that day.

By now, I was totally disgusted with the accordion, and to my parents' dismay, had quit taking lessons as well as practicing. Making money had become one of the most important things in my life, for I had figured out that having money made the world go round. The summer before, when I was eleven, I had worked doing nothing else but mowing about twenty lawns, using my dad's old riding lawn mower. At the end of the season, the engine finally gave up and died from just being too old. So my dad, Warren, wanting to teach me a lesson, went out and bought himself a brand new riding lawn mower at my expense. When it was all over, he had spent every dime I had made from mowing all those lawns that summer. I had basically worked all summer mowing for free. I was upset, and I vowed to find another source of income.

So the summer that I turned twelve, being much smarter than the year before, I had pretty much quit mowing lawns and went to work at a local dairy farm, full time. I was still cutting one or two lawns on my day off and shoveling snow in the winter. I had a decent income to do what I wanted, financially. Two things happened at the dairy farm that summer that made me much smarter, two things I have never forgotten.

First, there was one cow on the milking line that I was never supposed to milk. The farm foremen called her Linda, and he had warned me to never to go anywhere near her, for she had an "attitude". One day while the farm foreman was gone, as I was milking the cows with a milking machine, I worked my way down the line until I got to Linda. After working there for a while, I thought that I had enough experience and confidence at that point to take on the world.

When I hooked the suction part of the milking machine to one of Linda's teats, she kicked me in the chest so hard that it knocked the wind out of me and cracked a rib. The kick knocked me back into the trough behind her, where all the cow shit and piss collected. I landed in a nice fresh pile of shit and a lake of piss, and because Linda had knocked the wind out of me, I was unable to move. To complicate matters, the cow then pissed all over me. I almost lost it there, lying in the trough, but fortunately the foreman came back just in time and saved my life, if not my dignity.

The second lesson I learned, while working at the dairy farm later that summer, involved feeding the newborn calves. It was my job to feed them every morning when I got to work and every evening, just before I went home. The most important aspect of my job was to never feed them too much food. Apparently, calves are capable of eating continuously and have no way of knowing when to stop.

In a natural setting, the mother cow always told them when to stop eating by refusing them any more milk. One evening, I forgot to remove the calves' source of nourishment at the allotted time, and instead, left it there all night. The next morning, one of the calves was dead, and calves cost money. I was making $0.50 per hour at the time, and I had to pay $50 for the calf that had died, for it was my responsibility. My oversight had cost me almost two weeks of pay, and I promptly quit. Once again I was upset at myself, and I vowed to never be that stupid again.

I finished that summer off working at a vegetable farm, where things were a lot easier. A friend's dad owned the farm, and there were a handful of immigrant workers there who did most of the dirty work. The one good thing that happened while I worked there was that I learned how to drive. There was an old flatbed Chevy pickup there that we used to collect the boxes of vegetables that had been harvested, and then bring them to the packing area. The Chevy was a six cylinder, with a stick shift on the column, and I soon found that driving came natural to me.

Seventh grade was the beginning of the end for me. School was a breeze and I was bored to no end. I had firmly established myself in the crowd of troublemakers that ran the school, not through brawn but with my intelligence. In the late fall of 1967, Pete and I skipped school and went walking aimlessly, looking for trouble. We ended up at a Forte's Market grocery store where we intended to purchase some cigarettes. Instead, my eyes caught the welcome sight of a car that had been left with the keys dangling in the ignition. I wasted no time in starting her up and taking off down the street, but Pete, making a most intelligent decision, refused to join me on my joyride.

It was the adventure of a lifetime for a twelve year old, and I eventually found myself back in Hamden, about twenty miles from my home and school. I was barely tall enough to see over the steering wheel, so it did not take long before an observant Hamden police officer noticed me when I stopped at a school crossing. I was arrested and transported to the Westbrook barracks of the Connecticut State Police, where my parents were called. There, I was forced to wait in a jail cell until my embarrassed adopted dad Warren came after me, and then I had to endure the long ride home. From then on, it was all downhill, and things at home got worse every day.

Somehow or other, I made it through the seventh grade, in spite of all the trouble the stolen car had gotten me into. There was a constant need inside of me to satisfy an itch, an itch that needed to be scratched. I was always in search of a challenge, something to stimulate my intelligence. Regularly stealing cars soon became the answer, and a bad habit I could not quit. I found the adrenaline rush intoxicating, almost like a fresh breath of air. The aura of invincibility was almost as powerful as the crime. And as a side benefit, I soon found the parameters of my playing field had grown twenty fold. I could now travel easily more than twenty miles from my home.

I turned thirteen in June of 1968. While Pete's older brother Skip went off to the Army to fight the war in Vietnam, Pete and I had the whole world by the balls. We had discovered girls, and I was fascinated with one in particular, who was my next-door neighbor. She and I started experimenting with sex on a regular basis, and having her next door was no less than convenient. We used to laugh our asses off when all the guys talked about sex, because Pete and I were having sex regularly while all of our friends were only dreaming about it.

It was the time of bad ass muscle cars, and by now I was an expert when it came to stealing cars. Almost every weekend, we enjoyed some type of Chevrolet hotrod car that I had stolen, but sometimes I went after mundane cars when nothing else was available. On rare occasions, we even dismantled the cars and sold the parts to a local salvage yard. Every once in a while, we would beat the car up with sledgehammers and sell the entire car for scrap. I was also regularly sneaking my dad's car out after my parents went to bed, and sneaking it back in the garage before they woke up in the morning. Eighth grade went by real fast. I even passed all of my subjects with flying colors, and before I knew it, it was the summer of 1969.

At the North Branford carnival that year, a monumental event occurred that would alter my life forever. While hanging out there watching the girls with a few of my friends, I heard this loud, unusual sound, almost a rumble. A pack of Harley choppers pulled up right next to where I was standing. The bikers were members of the local motorcycle gang from New Haven, but they had two Hells Angels with them. I was in awe of their beautiful Harleys, and vowed silently that I would someday have a motorcycle just like those I was looking at.

One night early that summer, I took my dad's 1967 Pontiac Lemans for good, and Pete and I broke into an Elk's Lodge to finance a trip to Florida. With two girls and another friend along for the ride, Pete and I headed south down Interstate 95 for Florida. We made it all the way to South Carolina, almost one thousand miles from home, before we ran out of money and gas. While siphoning some gas from a car in a rural neighborhood, we were noticed by a police officer and arrested. We were incarcerated in the Orangeburg County Jail at Orangeburg, South Carolina while we waited for Pete's dad, my dad and one of the girls' dads to come there and get us. I can assure you that the twenty-mile ride home from the Westbrook State Police barracks two years before paled in comparison to this nine hundred mile ride home; this one was a nightmare.

It was September of 1969 when I started the ninth grade at North Branford High School. I was now fourteen years old and brilliant for my age. Unfortunately, I channeled all that brilliance into the wrong things. On one of the first days of school, Pete and I were walking down the hall when some smart aleck senior made a negative comment about the Hansen family, and then asked Pete if he was related to them. Pete responded in the most normal way he could; he proudly told the senior that he was Skip and Walt's little brother, and then politely kicked the crap out of him. Somehow or other, we avoided the teachers who came running to investigate the commotion, and made it to class safely.

It was during my ninth grade year that things went from bad to worse. We had a teacher by the name of Mr. Haskell, who taught us history up on the second floor. Every day, weather permitting, when he came into the classroom, Mr. Haskell opened the windows prior to the start of class. Being bored, one day we unscrewed the latches and hinges on the windows, and gently placed them back in their locked positions. When Mr. Haskell came in and opened the windows as he always did, the window and window frame fell completely out. When the window hit the ground below with a shattering explosion, it was all we could do to keep from laughing.

In the spring of 1970, on the first really warm day, the lines at the drinking fountains were backed up forever. There was no way Pete and I could get a drink, and there was no way we were willing to wait in line. We did the next best thing; we turned off the water to the entire school. In the process of hanging out on the hillside before and after school each day, we had discovered the main water shutoff for the entire school, located in an underground concrete box. To access the box, all one had to do was break the lock, open the door and turn a giant gate valve about twelve inches across. We had previously broken the lock in the process of determining what the lock prevented us from seeing, so opening the door and turning off the water was a piece of cake. When we went back to class, we were quite amused when, before long, there was not enough water pressure to power the drinking fountains. All of the thirsty students were complaining, and Pete and I were laughing.

By the time I turned 15 in the summer of 1970, my reputation as a car thief was well known all over town. I was also turning into quite a Chevy mechanic. I loved tinkering with cars, and tried to do it as much as I could by working on my friends' cars. Unfortunately, I was not old enough to work a legal job, but I knew that I was capable, and that as soon as I was able, I would seek out some type of mechanic's job somewhere. By now, Pete Hansen's older brother, Skip, was home from Vietnam, and was driving a brand new, bad ass 1969 Chevy El Camino SS.

My tenth grade year would be my last full year in high school. I was still bored out of my mind with the drivel that was being taught to me. I had already completed geometry and algebra and was starting to learn trigonometry, but I was still bored. By now, I had fallen in love for the first time in my life with a freshman one year younger than me; her name was Cathy Newell. She was a sweetheart, cute as could be, and I had met her at a church-sponsored dance.

I spent many a night trying to be a good kid, hitchhiking across town from my house to hers, just to be with her for an hour or two. She lived right across the street from the Bondo factory, and I still think of her after all these years, every time I am near a body shop (Bondo is the trade name of a compound used by body repair men to smooth out damaged auto body panels). I dated Cathy for the better part of two years, and like every other kid that age, thought that we would be together for the rest of our lives. Unfortunately, I stretched our relationship to the breaking point by abusing her emotionally, mentally and physically, and my youthful dream to be with her until the end of time was shattered.

In late November of 1970, I got caught again in a stolen car, and this time things did not go very well. I had taken a Mercury Station Wagon, and had kept it for way too long. I had almost started to believe that the car was going to be mine forever. I liked it because it did not stick out like a sore thumb, as all the muscle cars did. Unfortunately, time was not on my side, and some observant police officer recognized the car as belonging to the local pharmacy owner. I was busted. Inside the car, to complicate my situation, was a plethora of stolen items taken in a slew of residential burglaries. My goose was cooked and I knew it. Off to jail I went, but this time I kept going. I wound up at the Orange Street Juvenile Detention Center in New Haven, Connecticut, where I stayed until just after the New Year. When I promised the Judge that I would never be back, I was finally released to the custody of my parents after spending more than a month in a very real prison environment.

I kept my promise to the Judge for only a few months. Late in my sophomore year in high school, in mid May of 1971, with my grades failing and my attention who knows where, on who knows what, I sealed my fate one day just before math class. One of the guys I hung out with had an M-80 firecracker that was supposed to be the equivalent of a small piece of dynamite, and he dared me to light it and put it in the toilet in the boy's lavatory. Not being a chicken, but obviously lacking common sense, I lit the M-80 and tossed it into the toilet, flushing the toilet right when I dropped it in. I figured that the water would snuff out the fuse, and the flush would cart away all of the evidence.

Unfortunately, this time I was not as smart as I thought I was, and before I got out of the lavatory door, a huge explosion rocked the school. Pieces of porcelain showered over me as I came through the door. I ran to my next class hoping for the best, and expecting the worst, and the worst didn't take too long. Five minutes after class started, the teacher's phone rang, and I was on my way to the office. By this time the principal was sick of me, and he was looking for any excuse to expel me from school. This was the opportunity that he had dreamed of, and he spared no time in suspending me for the rest of the school year.

In danger of going back to the custody of the State of Connecticut for more "rest & relaxation", I feverishly worked my butt off to pay for the toilet facilities that I had blown up. I still can't believe that the high school failed to press charges, and instead elected to let me study at home and work to pay the plumbing bill. But work I did, and by the time school got out, I had paid the repair bill and just barely passed to the 11th grade, in spite of the fact that I had missed more than sixty days of school. I had learned one lesson this time: I knew for sure that I had to get out of school before I wound up in prison for the rest of my life!

I turned sixteen that summer, and in June of 1971 some idiotic driving inspector at the Connecticut Department of Motor Vehicles gave me my driver's license in spite of all the trouble I had been in. I spent part of the summer working my first real, legal job at a car wash, and I hated every minute of it. At the end of the summer, I landed my first dream job, pumping gas at a local ARCO gas station in downtown Northford. Back then, we called gas Ethyl, and I told everybody that I was pumping Ethyl for a living. I saved up enough money to buy my first legal car for three hundred dollars, and promptly blew the engine in it three weeks later by over-revving it.

That summer, my friend Pete Hansen moved up the shore with his family to a small seaside town called Old Saybrook. His mom and dad had a boat not far from there in the town of Westbrook, and I started going to Old Saybrook almost every weekend. If Pete's parents were at the boat, we had the house to ourselves; if his parents were at home, then we had the boat to ourselves. Both locations provided us with abundant opportunities to play house with our girlfriends, or a place to hang out with the guys.

In the fall, I somehow got talked into going back to school for what would have been my junior year, and somehow the school allowed me back in. I always wondered who pulled that one off. By now, I was a legend at school, and knew that the first sign of trouble would be my doom. It only took a day, and some slacker called me out during lunch hour. The fight was on, and an hour later I was history – permanently expelled from high school for the rest of my life. But at that point, I didn't really care, for I felt as if a huge monkey was finally off my back. I knew that there were bigger and better things waiting for me down the road.

11

Working For A Living & The U. S. Army
Fall 1971 To Spring 1974

In spite of all the hell I had put my parents through in the last five years of my life, my adopted dad, Warren, was the one who came to my rescue when I was permanently expelled from high school. Warren had a friend and business acquaintance who owned a truck body installation facility called Connecticut Truck & Trailer in North Haven, about fifteen minutes from my parent's house. In October of 1971, I went to work there as a shop helper, where I was in charge of cleaning up the shop and every other crappy job that no one else was willing to do. No one there expected me to last more than a few weeks, but I did.

Working at Connecticut Truck & Trailer was a riot, and the shop mechanics and welders there loved to have fun. It was not unusual for the shop to come to a grinding halt for a snowball fight. The mechanics would sometimes take their creepers (a board on wheels used by a mechanic to lie on when going under a truck) and load them with snow, then roll the creepers back inside the shop, where the snowball fight was on. It was also not unusual for a welder to have his pants belt hooked up to the overhead crane from behind while he was welding, and then the crane operator would lift him just inches off the ground, where he was left to dangle for hours. Or a truck hood would be shut while a mechanic was inside the engine compartment working (without the engine running, of course), and he would be left in there for hours banging on the hood to be let out.

I loved working there. Before long, I taught myself how to weld and was allowed to do horrible mechanic's tasks that no one else wanted to do, such as repairing the hydraulic cylinders in the back of a garbage truck that was still loaded with garbage. There were days that I had to lay in the back of the garbage truck in the garbage for hours while fixing one of those cylinders. Maggots would be crawling over me most of the time and the smell was beyond belief. But I stuck with it, and by spring I was installing snowplows and dump truck bodies on brand new trucks, and quite capable of troubleshooting and/or repairing the hydraulic systems in the garbage trucks. Because I was single and not afraid to work, I sometimes worked as much as eighty hours per week, and my paychecks were showing the results of my hard work.

In the early spring of 1972, I screwed up and got in more trouble. I had bought a 1963 black, four-door Pontiac the previous fall for basic transportation back and forth to work. One cold night, after partying way too much with all of my friends and after having way too much to drink, I ran the car off a cliff on the way home. I was fortunate to escape without a scratch, but it did not take long for the neighbors to call the police, and then for the police to find the car. By the time the police figured out who owned the car, I had already been given a ride home.

And because they could not prove that I had been driving, I was lucky not to have been charged with drunk driving. But the car was a total wreck and I was back to catching a ride to work with my adopted dad again.

A few months later, in early May, at about 10 PM, I left my friend Kurt Newman's house in North Haven, two miles from my parent's home, on a small motorcycle. I thought I could make it home for work the next day without getting stopped by the police for driving an unregistered motorcycle on the street. It had been raining and I did not want to walk. I only needed to be on the main street for about five minutes, just long enough to make it to the Northford town line. Unfortunately, a North Haven police officer saw me on the unregistered motorcycle and tried to stop me, but instead of stopping, like an idiot I took off.

I was sure that I could lose him by cutting up through a school walkway because the school walkway was not wide enough for a car, or so I thought. But the police car followed me right up the walkway, with the fence scraping both sides of the car all the way. After I showed the policeman my middle finger, he was so mad that he knocked me down with the police car, and then arrested me for all sorts of things. I wound up in jail again, but this time was able to get bonded out.

When I showed up for court to face the charges, the Judge wasted no time in telling me that I only had two options: first, go off to prison at the Cheshire Reformatory for boys until I was eighteen, or second, enlist in the United States Army. At that time, the Vietnam War was ongoing, and the Army was looking anywhere it could for recruits. It did not take long for me to realize that I was screwed, and the only option I had was to enlist in the Army.

I did not want to go by myself, so I convinced my buddy Kurt Newman to alter his birth certificate to show that he was seventeen, and we both enlisted in the United States Army. Kurt wanted to get some free schooling in a trade, and figured when he was finished learning the trade, he would still be sixteen, so he could just tell the Army his true age and they would have to let him go. I did not want to go to prison, and joining the Army was my only way out, but I would have to stay the entire two years of my enlistment. Kurt signed up for electronics courses, and I told them I liked to work on trucks and knew a lot about hydraulics.

On June 15th, 1972, Kurt and I got up extra early and before dawn we reported to the downtown New Haven, Connecticut United States Army depot. From there we were taken by bus about one hundred fifty miles to Fort Dix, New Jersey for basic training. We spent about eight weeks in the same unit, bunking together, learning all of the usual Army basic training tactics. From Fort Dix I was sent to the Aberdeen Proving Grounds in Maryland to learn how to be a tank turret mechanic, while Kurt went off to Fort Belvoir in Virginia to learn electronics. While I was at Aberdeen, I studied for my GED and passed the test on the first try. I was thrilled to have my high school diploma nine months before my classmates back at North Branford High School were scheduled to graduate. At the same time

I took my GED test, I learned that my IQ was 146. I also bought myself a 1957 Chevy for transportation back and forth from Connecticut to Aberdeen; it had a 283 in it and was quite economical.

Ed At Basic Training August 1972

By late November, Kurt had experienced enough of the United States Army. He had learned all he could about electronics, and the course he was taking was scheduled to end in the near future. So Kurt marched right into his commanding officer's office and put his feet up on the commanding officer's desk. When the commanding officer ordered Kurt to remove his feet from the top of the desk, Kurt then showed the commanding officer a copy of his true birth certificate, which proved that Kurt was only sixteen years old. The commanding officer was extremely angry, but there was nothing that he could do about Kurt's behavior and attitude. Less than one hour later, Kurt was looking back at the gate to Fort Belvoir, with nowhere to go but back to Connecticut. He hitchhiked to Aberdeen where we hooked up, and I drove him home to Connecticut that weekend.

I graduated from the Army tank turret mechanic school a few weeks later, and took all the leave time I could get before I was to report back to Fort Dix for my impending departure overseas. I expected to be shipped to Vietnam when I returned from leave, but while I was home the United States Government stopped sending any more new troops to Vietnam. It was a stroke of luck for me, but at the time I had mixed feelings, for in a way I wanted to go to Vietnam. When I reported back in from being home on leave, I got new orders sending me to Germany.

After a long plane ride from the United States, I arrived in Frankfurt, Germany, on the 22nd day of December 1972. It was an overcast, cold day, and my new surroundings looked very dreary. The first thing all of us were told at orientation was to leave the German beer alone. We were told that it was nothing like the beer in the United States, but I wasn't much for being told things; I usually needed to figure that out for myself. That night I got completely snookered on only two mugs of German beer, and by the time the next morning came, I was a firm believer in what I had been told at orientation the previous day.

On December 23rd, the day before Christmas Eve, I arrived about 4pm at my new home at Ayers Kaserne, an Army base located next to the town of Kirch Goens. Kirch Goens was about thirty kilometers south of Giessen, and about one hundred kilometers north of Frankfurt. I was now a tank turret repairman and a part of the 122nd Maintenance Battalion of the 3rd Armored Division, stationed on top of a mountain, somewhere out in the middle of Germany. To complicate my predicament, it was snowing and freezing cold outside, and I hated cold weather.

My first Christmas Eve in Germany was most memorable. I first checked in with the officer on duty to get my room assignment, and then headed upstairs to locate my room. When I looked down the hall, I just about had a heart attack, for huge clouds of smoke were coming out from under the doors of about five rooms. I had heard many stories already about rampant drug abuse in Germany, some of those specifically concerning the smoking of hashish. I rapidly deduced that the clouds of smoke were hash smoke, and I prayed that I would not end up in one of those rooms. Until this time, although I abused alcohol on many occasions, I was dead set against any drug use, and had only tried marijuana once in my whole life.

As you can imagine, I ended up in front of one of those doors, and did the only thing I could think to do under the circumstances: I knocked on the door. It took a minute, but before long, to my surprise, a full-blown sergeant answered the door. When he opened the door, a wall of hashish smoke almost knocked me down. The sergeant was quite suspicious, and inquired as to what I wanted. When I told him that I was a new guy, and I was looking for the bed I had been assigned, he rapidly changed his attitude and welcomed me into the room. So there I was, in my dress greens, sitting in a room on my new bed surrounded by a half dozen men all whacked out on hash. Welcome to the Army I was told!

The very first thing one of them asked me was whether I had ever smoked any hashish before. Not wanting to appear a rookie, I told them I had, but not too many times. Before I could even get out of my dress green uniform, I smoked some hash and promptly passed out from the experience. I did not wake up until the next morning, when it was time for everyone else but me to go to work. I had no work assignment yet, but would receive one as soon as Christmas was over.

I was amazed to find my roommates getting ready for work smoking more hash! In spite of the fact that I had still not gotten out of my dress greens yet, my roommates convinced me that I needed to smoke more hash. Once again, I passed out from the experience, and did not wake again until late that afternoon. I had now been there for just about twenty-four hours, and had spent the entire time sleeping. I had not even made it to the mess hall to eat, nor had I changed out of my dress green uniform!

I finally mustered up the courage to take a shower and get changed, just as my roommates came in from work. The first thing they did was fire up the hash pipes, but this time I told them the truth – I had had enough. They did inquire if I wanted to go to Frankfurt with them that night, and I had just enough time to eat before we all caught a train to Frankfurt. On the way there, I thought about my last few days in Germany, and what I had learned so far: don't drink the beer and don't smoke the hash. I wondered if this was all I needed to know.

In Frankfurt I got my first taste of LSD. I was eager to experience everything I could, and the timing was perfect. Running around town with all my new roommates and their friends made for an exciting night. By the time the weekend was over, I was tired of partying and ready to start working. Unfortunately, the Army, in all of its wisdom, sent three tank turret mechanics to Ayers Kaserne, when the unit only needed one. One of my roommates worked on the night crew in the truck shop, and he volunteered to get me assigned there.

I quickly learned that only the best and brightest mechanics worked the evening shift, but almost all of them were hash smokers. The evening mechanics would work hard for about three or four hours until our "lunch" break. By then, we had usually done way more work than the entire day crew, and there were twice as many day mechanics as there were evening mechanics. Not wanting to make them look really bad, we would just quit when it came time to eat. The rest of our shift, we sat around and partied, with most of the guys smoking hash and listening to music.

The funniest part of this whole deal was the Military Police (MP's) that were housed on the third floor of my barracks. Some of them got high on hash regularly, and those particular MP's were assigned to guard the truck shop at night. We had it made, for none of us had to endure the daily formation inspections, and we could sleep all day. After work at night was done, we sometimes even slipped out and caught an earlier than usual train to Frankfurt.

One night, one of the ranking officers in charge somehow slipped past the MP guarding the truck shop, and caught a bunch of us getting high and goofing off. That was the end of the evening shift of truck mechanics, and the beginning of mundane duty cleaning up the barracks yard. None of us were arrested, but all of us received some form of extra duty to pay for our insolence.

By March, I was getting tired of Germany, and was hoping to get a transfer stateside to receive treatment for a persistent knee problem that had been bothering me since I had been in basic training. I also applied for a Hardship discharge based on the fact that I was an only child, and I was needed at home to help my parents out financially. When I got tired of waiting on the Army, I just packed my bags one day, went AWOL (Absent Without Leave) and took off on my own. I got a ride to the airport and paid for a one-way ticket on a plane from Frankfurt back to New York. From New York, I took a shuttle bus back to

Connecticut, where I immediately hooked up with my old friends Kurt Newman, Chucky Vanacore, Pete Hansen and Kevin McManus.

I told my parents and most everyone else I knew that I was home on leave, and pretty much came and went as I pleased for the next three weeks. I goofed off, worked part time at Connecticut Truck & Trailer, and went partying with Kurt, Chucky, Pete, Kevin and my other friends, before I got serious about my situation. I knew that I would be declared a deserter after thirty days of being AWOL, so I knew I needed to turn myself back into the Army on the twenty-ninth day.

To hopefully add credibility to my claim of medical need, as well as my hardship claim, I turned myself in at the Pentagon in Washington, DC. I was surprised at how hard it was to actually turn myself back in, in spite of all the Army personnel working there. I immediately told everyone that I was AWOL, and that I wanted to turn my self in, and I kept getting directed from one area to another. When I finally got to someone who was willing to handle the situation, he refused to accept me until I got a haircut. As soon as I got a haircut, he then listened to my story and gave me orders to go to Fort Meade in Maryland for temporary observation and medical treatment.

Fort Meade was a dream come true for me, because the base was almost devoid of people. Most of the time it was deserted, and I soon landed a job in charge of a group of barracks at night. I showed up for work at 6pm, and I got off at 6am. Most of the time at work, I watched TV or slept. The barracks buildings that I was in charge of were all empty, except on the weekends, when they were used to house groups of people usually in transit. I hit pay dirt one week when an entire troop of Girl Scouts from Pittsburgh was housed in one of the barracks under my control. I was almost eighteen at the time, and felt like a kid in a candy store, with all those teenage girls around me, and I was the only Army guy in sight.

Suzan Delgrosso & Ed At
Fort Meade April 1973

It didn't take long for me to pick out one of the oldest and prettiest; her name was Suzan Delgrosso. Although she was only fifteen at the time, she was drop dead gorgeous, intelligent and mature beyond her years. I spent as much time with her as I dared, without compromising her honor, and we promised to keep in touch after we parted ways. Less than two weeks after I had met her, I went home to take my final week's leave before I shipped off back to my unit at Ayers Kaserne in Germany.

As a gift to myself that week before I went back to Germany, I sold my 1957 Chevy and bought myself a 1968 RS SS Chevy Camaro. The Camaro was black with white stripes on the outside, and had an awesome big block 427 L-88 motor under her hood, a four-speed transmission, and 4:88 gears in the rear end. As you can imagine, she could pull a sick whore off a piss pot in nothing flat.

The last night before I turned myself back into the Army at the Pentagon, I unbolted the headers on the Camaro and ran around all over town with Pete, Kurt, and Chucky, making lots of wide-open header noise. When we got stopped by the police for the loud exhaust on the car, I told the police that I was home on leave from the Army, and that I was going back overseas the next day, and they let me go!

The next morning, on the day that I was going to fly to Germany, I got a ride to my friend Kurt's to meet up there with Kurt, Chucky and Kevin. While there at his house, just before we left around 9am, Kurt chased me all over his house with a garden hose, soaking me to the bone, as his deluded version of a goodbye gift. I had already sent my bags ahead with my dad, who was going to meet me at the airport limo, and had no other clothes to change into. I was able to change my underwear, socks and shirt before I got on the plane, and although my dress greens did dry a little on the trip, I was still damp when I landed in Germany eighteen hours later. I thought about Kurt all the way there and the many different ways I could pay him back in the future.

A week after I got back to Germany, I made PFC, but lost it the next day when I was disciplined for having gone AWOL. I quickly found one of my old buddies from the truck shop, and he got me assigned to his laundry detail. If I thought the truck shop was great, this job was going to be fantastic! We both got up at 4am, and took a loaded truck full of dirty laundry to Frankfurt, where we unloaded it at the central Army laundry facility. Then we either went to sleep for four hours, or walked around wasting time until the laundry had been processed, and then drove the truck full of clean laundry back to the base.

We soon figured out that only one of the two of us actually needed to return to Ayers Kaserne at Kirch Goens to drive the truck to Frankfurt early in the morning. The other could stay in Frankfurt all night long, as long as he got to the laundry facility by late morning before the truck had to make the return trip to Ayers Kaserne with the clean laundry. One of the side benefits of the job was that neither one of us had to get up in the morning to attend the daily formation inspections. It wasn't long before it was a major chore to keep my long hair under my Army baseball cap.

In July of 1973, my ship finally came in. The Army had decided to downsize since the Vietnam War was now over, and they were looking for ways to get rid of anybody who was willing. Fortunately for me, my application for a hardship discharge was approved, and in late July of 1973 I was honorably discharged. But before the Army let me go, my commanding officer in Germany made me get my haircut three times before he signed my final transfer papers. I went home with less hair than I started with.

I was thrilled to be back home again, and even more thrilled to have regained my freedom. I took a few weeks off to get settled in, before I started back to work full time at Connecticut Truck & Trailer. While I had been gone in the Army, my friend Pete had fallen in love with a girl from Old Saybrook whom he had met in his last year at high school, Mary Beth Garceau. Mary Beth had a girlfriend who stopped me dead in my tracks; she was the prettiest girl I had ever seen in my life.

Her name was Helen Peppas, and I immediately fell head over heels for her. She was a petite, intelligent, blonde wild child, and we were meant to be with each other. One night shortly after I met her, Pete, Mary Beth, Helen and I took off driving around in my Camaro RS SS, drinking and partying. I stopped at my parents' house for a minute to run in and get something, and while I was in the house, my adopted dad Warren figured out I was drunk.

In his infinite wisdom, Warren pulled the keys out of the ignition in my car, and made all of us come in the house. There was no way that my dad was going to allow me to drive around a carload of teenagers drunk. He called Pete's parents, and the parents of both the girls, and told them what had transpired, and then made all of us stay there that night. Helen's parents were very strict, and she was supposed to be home that night by midnight. There was no way her parents would let her be with a bad boy from the wrong side of the tracks, and after that night, her dad told her that she could never see me again. I never forgave my dad for that, for at the time I was madly in love with Helen.

On the rebound from Helen, I renewed my friendship with Suzan Delgrosso, the Girl Scout I had met a few months before while temporarily stationed at Fort Meade. I made plans to visit Pittsburgh, and not completely understanding my Camaro, and the amount of fuel it sucked, I drove it out to Pittsburgh in late August to meet Suzan's family. The Camaro ate a giant hole in my pocket and almost broke me; it only got three miles to the gallon! I spent a few days there with Suzan and her family and realized while I was there that she needed to stay in school, for she was only sixteen. We knew that there was no way our relationship could survive the long distance visits required to make it work, but decided to remain friends. With a heavy heart, I drove back to Connecticut to explore greener pastures.

Suzan & Ed's 68' Camaro August 1973

A month later, Suzan ran away from school, and called me on the phone. She wanted to come to Connecticut to be with me, but I knew that it would not work out. Besides, I didn't want her dad mad at me, and I knew that I would probably get into some sort of criminal trouble for harboring an underage girl. In spite of the feelings that I had for her, I convinced Suzie to go back home and stay in school, but it only lasted for a little while. She ran away the next year, got pregnant, and then got married. Over the years I would stop in and visit her and her family, and we remained in contact. Defying the odds, she worked hard at her marriage, becoming a great mom to three kids. More than thirty years later, we still exchange Christmas cards.

It was now the fall of 1973, and I was back at Connecticut Truck & Trailer working as a shop mechanic and welder. I was doing major jobs now that I had experience, and it was a very happy time for me. I was living at home again, and actually getting along with my parents. Once again, my dream of owning a Harley would be brought to my attention. One of the guys from the local New Haven area motorcycle gang called Hole n' The Wall went to work at Connecticut Truck & Trailer. Almost every day he rode his Harley to work, and every day I looked at it with a certain type of lust that can only be described as jealousy.

By now my friend Pete Hansen had graduated from High School, and had moved from Old Saybrook to Lamberton Street in New Haven. Pete shared an apartment there with his older brother Harry "Skip" Hansen and Skip's girlfriend Mimi. Pete actually lived in a small closet under the stairs, but he didn't care for he was finally out on his own. Skip was a serious mentor to me at the time, and I had spent many a night there sleeping on his couch while I was in the Army stateside.

My only problem in the fall of 1973 was that the workload at Connecticut Truck & Trailer was slowing down, and I needed more hours. I soon found myself a job at Cooke's Equipment Company in Wallingford. They handled all sorts of International Harvester heavy construction equipment, as well as some farm tractor equipment. It did not take me long to settle in there, and soon I was working out of the company field truck, doing on-site repairs for customers on their construction sites. I rapidly discovered that I had a knack for fixing these incredible machines, and also that I loved doing it.

Ed At His Cherry Street Apartment

Within a month, I located a nice second floor apartment nearby on Cherry Street, only a few blocks from work. It was conveniently located above a liquor store, and my downstairs neighbor was an elderly lady who could not hear very well. The apartment soon became the party headquarters for all of us. Pete, Chucky, Kurt, Kevin and I were there most every weekend, partying all night until the sun came up.

Chucky Vanacore was now working right up the street from my apartment and job, building street rods at a hotrod car manufacturing facility called Total Performance. It wasn't long before I started working there at night part time, sanding the car bodies to prepare them for paint, just to earn a few more dollars. It was there I first met Johnny Cerrone, who was about as crazy as they come. Johnny had a wicked sense of humor that kept us all laughing all day long every day.

One day, Johnny cut a hole in the bottom of a small box, which allowed his middle finger to go through the bottom of the box, protruding through to the inside of the box. He then put cotton all around his finger that was now inside the box, and then added a mixture of ketchup and water that looked like blood, to the cotton and his finger in the small box. Johnny then positioned the box just right, carrying it with his other hand, which made it look like his finger had been cut off.

He ran up to our shop foreman, screaming that his finger had just been cut off, and that he needed to get to the hospital immediately to get it sewn back on. Not knowing any better, the shop foreman immediately dropped everything, and started driving Johnny to the local hospital. About halfway to the hospital,

Johnny's middle finger came up in the box, pointing directly at the shop foreman. Johnny then told him, laughing his ass off, "you stupid asshole". The joke was on the shop foreman and as you can imagine, he was not very happy about it. But we all thought it was a riot, because we knew what was going on from the start.

I also started rebuilding muscle cars on the weekends, utilizing Cooke's Equipment Company shop, and then selling the cars to make a few extra dollars. I would buy them as is, usually with a bad engine or transmission. After fixing the engine or transmission, I would then drive them for a while, eventually selling them for a small profit.

It was apparent that I still did not know everything about diesel engines and heavy equipment, when I went out in the yard one cold morning to start a brand new piece of machinery. I used too much ether to try to start it, and when the mixture ignited, it blew the starter motor right off the engine. Fortunate for me it did not break the engine block, and I was able to repair my screw up without too many problems. But the guys in the shop sure had a good laugh at my expense!

Not long after that I had another bone chilling experience with an old bulldozer I was working on. It had a diesel engine with an oil bath air cleaner. I was servicing the piece of equipment, and in the process was changing all of its oils, including the oil in the oil bath air cleaner. Apparently I put too much oil in the oil bath air cleaner, so when I started it up, the engine rpm started increasing on its own. It throttled up more and more, and there was nothing I could do to stop it. I was scared to death that it was going to blow up right there in the shop when another mechanic jumped up and pulled the top off the air cleaner. He then put a board over the air stack terminating the supply of air into the engine, effectively shutting the engine down. The only damage done was to my pride, and once again all of the shop mechanics had a good laugh.

The next year I set my sights on getting a Harley. It was a major objective, and I was willing to do whatever was necessary to make it happen. I just couldn't figure out exactly how I was going to make it happen, for I knew no one who had a bike. Sometimes strange things happen for strange reasons, and in the spring of 1974 I answered the door to find an irate biker standing there. His home had been broken into and his stereo had been stolen, and he had been told erroneously that I had committed the burglary and was in possession of the stolen stereo.

I truthfully denied the burglary and even allowed him to search my apartment for the stereo, which of course, he did not find. Before we parted ways that evening, I told him that I was an expert Chevy mechanic and that I worked down the street at Cooke's as a heavy equipment mechanic. The last thing the biker told me was that when he found the culprit responsible for the theft, the burglar's ass was grass. A few days later there was another unexpected knock on my door, and it was the biker again, but this time he had a case of beer with him.

His name was Richard "Richie" Doolittle, and he told me that he had found the persons responsible for the burglary of his home, had recovered the stolen stereo and given the culprits an attitude adjustment in the process. He had realized then that the information given about me taking the stereo was truly a mistake, and to make amends, he wanted to drop off the case of beer. I invited him in, and it didn't take long to figure out that we both needed each other. Richie owned a Corvette that desperately needed a mechanic, and I needed a teacher, to teach me all about Harleys. It looked like my appointment with destiny had finally arrived.

12

The Birth Of A Biker
Summer 1974 To 1976

Richard "Richie" Doolittle and I started hanging around together on a regular basis the summer of 1974. We fast became good friends, and while I helped him work on his Corvette, he introduced me to the world of Harley Davidsons. In the fall of 1974, I sold my prized 1970 Chevy Nova SS to my girlfriend, and bought a 1963 Harley Panhead chopper for $2,500 from a friend of Richie's, Cecil Pullen. Cecil was a charismatic local biker who did not belong to any motorcycle club. He was also the best Harley mechanic around, so it was an honor to end up with one of his bikes. This particular Harley was very special; for the frame had been altered by "Gene the Bean". Gene the Bean was a legendary local welder, who had added about five inches to the down tubes and about three inches to the top rail of the frame, paving the way for an eighteen inch over springer style front end.

Although the bike was mechanically sound and running, I wanted to take it apart and paint it so it would be uniquely mine, and because I did not have a garage at my apartment, I decided that the best place to rebuild the bike would be my parents' house. I somehow convinced them that I would not make a mess, and used their garage to disassemble it, and the basement of their house for storage of all of the parts. I planned on using my old bedroom upstairs as a place to store and clean all of the chrome parts from the bike, but on the way upstairs with the oil tank one day, I accidentally spilled some oil on the stairway carpet. My adopted dad Warren was livid when he got home, and to make peace with him, I paid for the new carpet he had installed a few days later.

Ed On His First Harley – A 1963 Panhead

I hired a painter from Meriden to paint the bike; his name was Gary Parisi. Gary was a fantastic body man and painter, and he did a great job. The frame was pearl ice blue and the gas tank/fenders a dark midnight blue. On the gas tank, Gary painted a mural of the tattoo I had on my arm: crossed pistons and a skull with the words Harley Davidson and Budweiser on the top and bottom.

I was on top of the world, for I was just nineteen years old and owned a Harley. And not just any Harley, this one was a chopper that turned everybody's head, and I had built it myself. The first place I went was to my girlfriend's high school to pick her up after school one day, in spite of the fact that it was way too cold to be out riding. Much to my dismay, I dropped the bike in the parking lot in front of about one hundred kids. Fortunately, I did the bike no harm, and only took a large chunk out of my pride.

As 1974 turned into 1975, Cooke's Equipment Company was losing work left and right. I was barely getting in forty hours a week and it looked like I would soon be laid off. I hated the cold New England winters with a passion, and had been thinking about relocating for quite awhile. So in February of 1975, I convinced my girlfriend Toni to move to Tulsa, Oklahoma. My uncle had lived there for about ten years in the sixties, and he told me that there was lots of work there. It also was a lot warmer in Tulsa than it was in Connecticut. My buddy Pete asked to ride along with us for the adventure, and to help me drive and unload the U-haul trailer that we pulled behind my girlfriend's 1970 Chevy Nova SS.

At first we changed our minds and decided to go to Boise, Idaho, but by the time we got to Detroit, I figured out that we would never have enough money to get to Boise. So we turned south at Chicago and went to Tulsa as we had originally planned. When we arrived it was like I had died and gone to Heaven, for it was a beautiful sunny day and the temperature was in the mid 70's. We pulled into a cheap motel at the corner of 11th Street and Memorial for the night, and immediately rolled the bike out of the trailer, and took it for a ride.

Within a day, I had located an apartment complex that needed a maintenance man and was willing to trade out some maintenance work towards payment of the rent. It was called the Orchard Park Apartments, and was located just off 64th Street and Peoria in a nice area not far from Oral Roberts University. I was able to negotiate the back sliding door with the bike; thereby parking it inside my bedroom, where I knew it would be safe. To make ends meet, I also took a temporary job as a laborer on a framing crew until I located a mechanics job at one of the local heavy construction equipment dealerships.

By early April, I landed a job as a mechanic at a local John Deere dealership, and settled into a routine. I would work during the day as a heavy equipment mechanic, and evenings/weekends around the apartment complex as a maintenance man. My girlfriend Toni refused to work, and spent most of her time running around getting high however and wherever she could. I slowly realized over the summer that I had made a big mistake in bringing her to Tulsa. When we did see each other, we fought like cats and dogs. Sometimes she would not come home for days, and other times she would tell me that she was madly in love with me.

What little time I had to myself, I would ride my motorcycle a few miles down to the local Arby's Restaurant, which at the time was right in the middle of Tulsa's Restless Ribbon. The Restless Ribbon was a two-mile section of Peoria Avenue where all the kids in town hung out every summer night, all night long. Every business along the Ribbon was the temporary home to a different group of kids. All the bikers on the Restless Ribbon hung out in the parking lot of the Arby's, which is where I got my nickname, Connecticut Ed. Because I never told anyone my last name, and the fact that my bike had a Connecticut license plate, it was easy for all of the Oklahoma bikers to just call me Connecticut Ed. Within a few weeks, the name stuck, remaining my nickname to this day.

It was there that I first got arrested one night, after pulling out of the Arby's Restaurant parking lot. I originally got stopped because I did not have any goggles on, but the police officer soon discovered that I had a Connecticut license plate on the bike, so he decided to impound it. I had no idea that he could do such a thing, and adamantly voiced my disapproval. In the process, the situation soon escalated into a resisting arrest charge, my bike was impounded, and I was hauled off to jail.

There I was in jail, needing three hundred dollars for bail bond, and not knowing a soul to call to come get me. I was confused, and had no idea which way to turn. So you can imagine my surprise when I was notified that my bail bond money had been paid, and I was released from jail. When I walked outside, I found, waiting for me, some of the bikers I hung out with at Arby's. They had seen me arrested, watched as my bike was impounded, and knew I was in a switch. So they went down to the jail, and one of them, Charlie West, bailed me out. The others took me over to the impound lot and paid to get my Harley released. Three hours after I had been arrested, I was back at Arby's hanging out!

Living with my girlfriend Toni became an exercise in insanity, and I knew that I had to get away from her, but did not know how. When an opportunity presented itself in August, I left her behind (it was what she wanted) and moved to Houston to take a job at an oil refinery as a maintenance manager. That was a giant mistake, because in the process of moving, one of my toolboxes was stolen from the back of my truck. I also soon realized that I desperately missed the friends I had made in Tulsa, so after getting into an argument with my boss less than a month after I moved there, I packed up again and moved back to Tulsa.

This time, I bought a house through what is known as a Rental Purchase Contract. It was almost brand new, and was located out in the middle of nowhere between Broken Arrow and Tulsa, near the intersection of 61st Street and Garnett Road. I immediately landed a job at the Par-Ex Machine Corporation, assembling the hydraulic systems for truck mounted oil field rigs. My girlfriend Toni and I were off again, on again; one week we loved each other and the next we wanted to kill each other.

By now, my biker friend Richard "Richie" Doolittle had moved to California. He had stopped by to see me on the way out to California from Connecticut, and told me that if he did not like it, he would come back to Tulsa. It only took Richie about a month to figure out that he hated California, and I volunteered to drive out there and pick him up. I had always wanted to see California, but when I actually got there, all I could see was smog and miles of cars on the freeway. So I drove into Los Angeles, picked him up and left, all in one morning. I was only in California for less than ten hours, and could not understand why anyone would ever want to live there.

When we got back to Tulsa, Richie moved in the Garnett Road house with me, where we celebrated Christmas of 1975 together. A few weeks later, in January of 1976, another friend of his, Chris Robison from Vermont, moved to Tulsa and in with us as well. Now there were three of us sharing a three-bedroom house, so we split the rent and bills three ways. We used the kitchen as a place to work on the bikes, in spite of the fact that there was a garage attached to the house. Before long, Richie fell in love with a young Tulsa girl, and when she moved in we had a live-in housekeeper to keep the place clean and cook for us.

In February of 1976, I let the house go. I felt that it was just too far from Tulsa and was costing us too much money. Richie and I moved back into Tulsa, and split a duplex off of 67th Street & Peoria. It was a nice duplex in a good area of town, and was easier on the pocketbook. I got real down on my luck late that spring, and I sold my 1963 Harley Panhead to pay the bills. I used some of the money to buy another frame and most of an engine. This time I wanted to build my own motor, which was going to be an 80" stroker. I went out to the old Harley shop in Sand Springs, and found a set of ULH 80" flywheels and a set of decent cases for little to nothing. I sent all of the engine parts to Truett & Osborn in Wichita, Kansas, and had them build me an ass kicking stroker motor.

While I was waiting for Truett & Osborn to build my engine, my girlfriend Toni was actually trying to make our relationship work. She was working at a bar with Richie's new girlfriend, hustling guys and dancing. One day, Richie, Chris and I were in the bar having a beer, and Toni came to me and told me that a customer was giving her a hard time. I looked over to see a biker sitting in the corner by himself, so I went over to see what was going on. Before I even said a word, the biker said, "I'll fight all three of you guys, if that's the way it's going to be."

I just laughed, and told him we had no intention of fighting, that all we wanted was for him to come over and join us. The biker's name was Lee McArdle, and he had just ridden into Tulsa from Maine. He had been raised in Detroit, but lived in New Mexico for a while before spending a year in Maine. He had worked as a landscaper, an electrician, and a chef in a fancy restaurant. We all got along great, and forged a relationship that afternoon in a bar that would last a lifetime. Lee and I rapidly became inseparable, and spent all of our free time together.

By May, I had quit my job at the Par-Ex Machine Company, and was once again repairing heavy equipment, but this time it was for the local Fiat-Allis heavy equipment dealer. Richie and I grew out of the duplex, and moved in with Chris Robinson, who by now had a three-bedroom house on 4th Street over by Mingo Road. This house was less expensive than the duplex, and I was able to save more money to put into the new bike. I had a bad habit of putting all my money into the bike, and cutting myself short on food money. Lee would always come by at the end of the week to make sure I was eating.

One night Lee came by and both of us were completely broke. We went a few blocks over to the local Shakey's Pizza Parlor, and pooled all of our loose change together just to buy a pitcher of beer. While we slowly nursed the pitcher of beer, we cleaned off everyone's plate as they left the place. Almost everyone left some pizza when they were finished, and by the time we finished the beer, we were both stuffed.

In June, just in time for my birthday, the finished engine from Truett & Osborn arrived from Wichita. I spent the next few weeks putting the finishing touches on the new bike, trying to get it ready for a 4th of July ride down to Lake Tenkiller. At the last moment, I realized that I was still in need of a front axle, but did not have enough money to buy one. I substituted as best I could, and in its place I used a piece of all thread bar. It was a stupid choice, for the all thread bar was not hardened like an axle would be. By the time Lee and I got to Hulbert, about forty-five miles southwest of Tulsa, my front wheel was about as wobbly as you could get and not fall down.

Ct Ed Broke Down Hulbert, OK July 4, 1976

It was July 4th, 1976, and there I was broke down in Hulbert, Oklahoma, and it was only 1 o'clock in the afternoon. It was already almost one hundred degrees outside, and I was as stranded as one could be. Lee was forced into going back to Tulsa to get a truck, so he could then come back and rescue me. I waited in the heat all day for him, and started to worry when he had not appeared by six PM. It was only a one-hour ride to Tulsa each way, and plenty of time had elapsed since his departure. Soon it was dark, no less hot, and still no Lee.

Lee & Ct Ed Riding Together Tulsa 1976

By the time midnight rolled around, I had about given up and was starting to get mad. At 2 AM, a truck pulled up alongside of me and there was my friend Lee. He had gone to get the truck as planned, but when he got to the truck, he found himself in the middle of a big July 4th party. Lee figured he could have a beer first and then go get me, but forgot about me until a little after midnight. As soon as he remembered, he came right down to get me. To this day, I have never forgotten July 4th, 1976!

One night later that summer, while hanging around at the Arby's Restaurant on Peoria with a bunch of my biker friends, I noticed the first member of a motorcycle club that I had ever seen in Tulsa. He was a friend of ours named Johnny Cook that regularly hung out with us at Arby's. Johnny was a family man with a bunch of kids, and was a bit older than the rest of us; we affectionately referred to him as the "old man". Johnny had gone out and started prospecting for the Rogues Motorcycle Club.

Not long after that, late one night in the Arby's parking lot on the Restless Ribbon, Johnny Cook rode in again to hang out with us, wearing his new Prospect colors. This time, a stranger followed Johnny into the parking lot, and while Johnny was talking to us, the stranger walked up and pointed two sawed-off shotguns at Johnny. This stranger, I found out later, was called Shotgun, because of his habit of carrying those two sawed-off shotguns with him everywhere he went. Shotgun was standing there with a shotgun in each hand, both of them pointed at Johnny.

Within a few seconds, I figured out that Shotgun was mad at the Rogues, and he had no idea who Johnny was. So I did a very stupid thing; I got in between Shotgun and Johnny. With about twenty people watching from ten feet away, I told the stranger to go ahead and shoot me, because I was not going to let him shoot Johnny. I explained to him that Johnny was a friend of ours, and that he had a family, with a bunch of little kids. I ended my conversation by telling him that he needed to settle his problems with the Rogues he was mad at, and to leave Johnny alone. To my surprise, Shotgun accepted what I said and got back in his car, driving off into the night.

Around this time, I broke down and traded in my old, beat up Chevy pickup for a brand new, 1976 Chevy pickup. As part of the deal, I got an all expenses paid vacation for four to Six Flags Amusement Park in Dallas. I decided to take my girlfriend Toni, my buddy Lee McArdle (who had left me on the side of the road a few months before) and a cute dancer who worked at the bar with my girlfriend Toni, for Lee to play with. We were all set to take off that Friday night after work, but Lee never showed up. I could not find him anywhere, and spent the entire weekend looking for him. It never occurred for me to look downtown in the local jail.

Lee had gone down to the police station after work Friday for five minutes to pay an overdue traffic ticket. Typical Lee, he had waited just a little too long to pay the ticket, and when he got there, he found an arrest warrant was waiting for him. In spite of the fact that he had the money in his pocket to pay the ticket, and had gone to the courthouse to pay it, the officials there still arrested him and threw him in jail. It took all weekend for the jail personnel to figure out what had happened. By the time Lee got out of jail Sunday evening, we had all lost our window of opportunity to go to Six Flags for free, and Lee had missed out on what could have been the date of a lifetime.

In late September, as a direct result of the altercation at Arby's between Johnny Cook, Shotgun and me, the Rogues Motorcycle Club invited me to attend one of their meetings to get to know them. They were very appreciative of what I had done for one of their own, and they wanted to meet me as well. One of the other guys that regularly hung around at Arby's came along to the meeting with me. His name was Rickie "Smoker" Miles; he was riding a Kawazaki KZ 1000 bike at the time. At the meeting we were asked if we wanted to prospect, which meant we would have to do all sorts of things to see if we were worthy of becoming members. They told Smoker that he would also have to get a Harley if he wanted to join, and we both told them that we would think about it.

We met all of the members of the Tulsa chapter at that meeting and found out that there were other Rogue chapters in Oklahoma, as well as one or two in northern Texas and southern Kansas. At the Tulsa meeting we attended that night were the following members and prospects of the Rogues Motorcycle Club:

Edwin "EJ" Nunn	Roy "Roy" Green
Marvin "Marvin" Brix	Robert "Rob" Reynolds
Charles "T-Chuck" Schlegel	Keith "Keith" Vandervoort
Johnny "Johnny" Cook	Michael "Little Mike" Hardison
Homer "Spurge" Spurgeon	Calvin "Captain" Dorman
Louis "Bill Wolf" Rackley	Dennis "Rev" Isaacson

Johnny, Spurge, Little Mike and Captain were prospects, and the rest were original charter members of the Tulsa Chapter, except Bill Wolf, who had just transferred to Tulsa from the Oklahoma City chapter. EJ, Roy, Marvin, Rob, T Chuck, Rev and Keith had actually started the Tulsa chapter the previous year at Halloween, after getting permission from the rest of the Oklahoma Rogues.

Ct Ed's Rogues Prospect Colors 1976

It took Smoker and me a few days to make up our minds, but we decided that we would give it a try. Smoker found himself a beat up old Harley Sportster to buy, and a week later, we both started hanging around. I started prospecting a few weeks after that, and sewed my prospect patches on to an old blue jean jacket I had.

Unfortunately I soon figured out that I could no longer make ends meet living in Tulsa, and I took a job over the phone in Richmond, Virginia, working for a Richmond International heavy equipment dealer. It broke my heart, but I quit the Rogues after only prospecting for a few months, and packing all my belongings up again, I moved to Virginia just before Thanksgiving of 1976.

Once again, I took my girlfriend Toni with me, which probably wasn't the best idea at the time. We were still on again and off again; one day we hated each other and the next, we loved each other. Most of the time, we still fought like cats and dogs. It seemed as though we couldn't live without each other, or with each other. At the time, we both felt a change in surroundings would help to improve our relationship, but in hindsight, there was no way we could have ever made it work. We just weren't meant to be with each other, and that was all there was to it.

13

Virginia & Connecticut
1977 To 1978

It didn't take long for the fighting to begin once we arrived in Richmond, and my girlfriend Toni took off, back to Tulsa. I settled into an apartment on the north side of Richmond and my new job at the Rish International construction equipment dealer. I still had not forgotten the skills I had learned working at Cooke's Equipment in Connecticut a few years before, and easily fell back into the groove. Within a few weeks, I had worked my way up to a field truck, and that made life easy, for I had all of my tools with me when I came home each night.

I was still working on my bike, making it better and more reliable. Now that I was making good money, I started running back and forth to Connecticut, buying and selling Harley parts to pay for the trips. I was seeing a lot more of my friend Cecil Pullen, since Cecil had got to know me more through Richard "Richie" Doolittle and Chris Robison. I soon set my sights on having a new Harley, but knew that there was no way that I was going to be able to afford one. I did have an extra Harley rigid frame, a set of engine cases without serial numbers (I had removed them), and an Oklahoma builder's title.

So I set off to find a boatload of parts, and didn't take long to find a fairly new Superglide. The owner was a dork that had only put about one hundred miles on the bike since it was new, and he had decided that he wanted to sell it. The dork was dumb enough to let me take it for a test ride, and I never brought it back. A few hours later, back at my apartment, I had taken the bike completely apart and had thrown the stolen frame and engine cases into a local river.

Ct Ed's New Rigid Frame Superglide January 1977

Packing all the parts up in boxes, the following Friday, I set out for Cecil's house in Durham, Connecticut. He had a giant motorcycle shop in the basement of his house, and was willing to let me build the bike there over the next few months. Every other weekend or so, I traveled back and forth to Connecticut, and in the end, wound up with a reliable Harley with a stunning paint job.

The bike was, in essence, a brand new Superglide stuffed meticulously into an old Harley rigid frame, electric start and all. Once again, I emblazoned the gas tank with a mural depicting the tattoo on my arm: crossed pistons and a skull, but this time left off the words Harley Davidson and Budweiser. I was on top of the world when I brought the finished bike back from Connecticut to Virginia. I just knew it was going to be a great summer. I now had two Harleys and me squeezed into a small one-bedroom apartment, and I thought I had the world by the balls.

The first ride I took on my beautiful new bike was to the local motorcycle shop that I had been in and out of for the last few months, buying all sorts of odds and ends and Harley parts, either to sell or to use on one or both of my bikes. It was still cold outside in March of 1977, but I was so excited I hardly felt it. After showing off the bike, I took a little tour around Richmond, and before I got back to my apartment, I was stopped by a Richmond police officer.

After looking at my bike and my registration papers, the cop called in the local auto theft detectives. Fifteen minutes later, I watched my beautiful Harley get loaded onto a wrecker and hauled off to the impound yard for investigation. Seems the auto theft detective thought the motorcycle was stolen; I could not imagine why. On my very first ride on the bike, the motorcycle had been seized. What were the odds? I wondered, on the long, cold walk back to my apartment.

Over the next month, I argued with the auto theft detectives about the legality of the parts on my seized motorcycle. I had receipts for all the parts, but there was still the fact that there were no serial numbers on the engine cases, and all Harley engine cases were supposed to have serial numbers. I stuck to my story that I had bought the engine cases that way, and in the end, the tests that were performed on them to locate the hidden serial numbers came back negative.

The auto theft detective was beside himself, for the actual report he had received stated that there never had been a serial number on either of the engine case halves. He knew that it was impossible, unless the engine cases had been stolen from the Harley factory before the serial numbers had been installed on them. The detective had even contacted Harley to inquire if they had lost engine cases that were blanks. Harley Davidson had just laughed at the detective.

In the end, we made a deal. The auto theft detective would sign a release allowing me to take possession of the entire bike, *less the engine cases.* I agreed to disassemble the bike engine on the spot at the impound yard, using my field truck full of tools to do so. He told me that he wanted to use the cases for an exhibit, showing what someone could do to remove the serial numbers if they had the knowledge. I made that kind of hard for him to do, for when I took the engine apart, I smashed the engine cases into about thirty pieces, put them all in a large plastic bag, and left them at the impound yard for him to pick up. I never heard from him again, but I bet that he wasn't too happy when he got the bag full of broken engine cases!

While I pondered what to do with all the parts I now had scattered all over my apartment, my childhood buddy from Connecticut, Peter "Pete" Hansen arrived for a visit while on leave from the United States Navy. He was excited to find that I still had my other chopper, and he talked me into letting him take it for a ride. I figured that he could do no harm to the old bike, and even if he laid it down, the paint job could be easily repaired; after all, it was from a Krylon spray paint can.

So off Pete went for a little ride, and fifteen minutes later, when he had not returned, I started getting concerned. When an hour had passed, and there was still no sign of him, I became extremely concerned. While on a search for him, in my truck, on the roads that surrounded the apartment complex, I soon found the motorcycle. It was a bizarre scene; the bike was all wrecked, but there was no sign of my friend Pete. The Harley was lying on its side, off on the side of the road in some bushes. I was mystified and could not understand why no one had called me. I went back to the complex and got a neighbor to help me load the wreck, then went home and tried to find Pete.

I called the police and checked all the hospitals, to no avail. Later that night, Pete's brother Harry "Skip" Hansen called me from Connecticut, and told me that Pete was in the local Richmond Veterans Hospital, and that he had been operated on for injuries that had occurred during a motorcycle wreck. Seems I had never thought about calling the VA Hospital. When Pete had lost control of the bike, a concerned passerby had stopped, picked Pete up, and had taken him straight to the VA hospital, as Pete had requested.

The next day Skip showed up, and we both went out to see Pete. We took Pete with us and sat in the park outside the hospital, where Pete filled us in on the rest of the story. Skip and I thought it was outrageously funny, but Pete was not so sure at the time; now years later we all laugh at it. Fortunately, Pete soon recovered from his physical injuries, but it took him quite a while to recover the pride he lost that day.

One good thing came out of Pete wrecking the bike; I now knew exactly what to do with all of my parts. I took the legal engine cases and legal Harley title from the bike that Pete had wrecked, used all the parts left from the impounded Superglide, and built me a totally legal, brand new, beautiful Superglide in the privacy of the living room inside my apartment. The only real difference was in the style of engine cases; instead of having a set of stolen 1970 up alternator cases holding the engine together, this engine was surrounded by a set of 1958 generator cases. Besides that small detail, the bike looked identical to the last version that had been seized by the Richmond auto theft detectives.

This time I had learned my lesson; I made sure that it could never be impounded again. The first thing I did was to take up where I left off by returning to the scene of the "crime". I rode back down to the same motorcycle shop I had ridden down to a few months earlier, and once again I showed off my newest creation. By now most of the guys at Departure Bike Works (the bike shop) knew the story of my impounded motorcycle and the blank set of Harley cases, and everyone there was thrilled to see the bike back on the road. I spent the next few hours hoping that the auto theft detective would see me and pull me over, just so I could gloat, but I was not that lucky.

Ct Ed's Rebuilt 1958 Pan Shovel Superglide May 1977

Shortly after I got the bike rebuilt and back on the road, I was able to change jobs and go to work for the local Caterpillar construction equipment dealer across town. It had always been my dream to work for Caterpillar since I started working on heavy equipment back at Cooke's Equipment in Wallingford, Connecticut, but it seemed that I always lacked the required experience. Now that I had enough experience, I had finally found someone at a Caterpillar dealership that was willing to give me a chance.

Caterpillar was the Cadillac of the heavy construction equipment world, and it was a giant step up in prestige, as well as pay. I worked mainly in the shop, but occasionally would get to go out in the field to do simple repairs. I started getting particularly interested in their line of large bulldozers, and developed a fairly good knowledge of them in a very short time.

One afternoon that summer, I was out in the parking lot after work, screwing around on my bike, showing off for some of my fellow employees. I was doing burnouts across the dealership parking lot, and ran out of stopping room. I ended up in a line of rose bushes that hurt like hell. The bike was not hurt, fortunately, but one side of me was eaten up with thorns from the rose bushes. I learned my lesson that day, and never showed off again.

By now, my sometime girlfriend Toni had moved from Oklahoma back to Richmond and into my apartment; it seemed as though I would never get rid of her. We would still fight like cats and dogs on a regular basis, but would soon make up and go back to living together. She still had little interest in working, and seemed more concerned with spending my money and partying. At this point I was used to her little games, and knew that we had a very unhealthy relationship. It was almost as if we were addicted to each other, like a heroin addict was to heroin. She would still disappear for days at a time, but by now I took it with a grain of salt. Rarely did it bother me anymore; I figured that it just came with the territory.

Shortly after the showing off incident in the parking lot, I was welding a bulldozer blade in the shop when the chain holding the blade up broke. This caused the thousand pound blade to fall on my foot and break some bones, in spite of the steel-toed boot I was wearing. As a result, I was forced to take a few weeks off from work. I spent most of my time off hanging around Departure Bike Works on Hull Street, getting to know the employees there.

Most of them had been involved with a motorcycle club a few years before that was known as the Confederate Angels. Apparently the Confederate Angels had disbanded when some of the club decided to become Hells Angels in North Carolina, and the rest refused to make the change. To keep the peace, the club disbanded in name only, and the remaining members in the Richmond area maintained the club camaraderie and organizational structure.

It took a while, but by the end of summer they were letting me hang around socially on a regular basis. I attended my first "club" run with a bunch of them, and in spite of the fact that they did not wear any club colors, they still seemed to act just like a motorcycle club. It was then I heard of the Outlaws Motorcycle Club for the first time. One of the ex-Confederate Angels, who was living in Florida, had been killed in a bar fight by a member of the Outlaws, and I was allowed to go to his funeral which was to be held in Virginia. It was the first biker funeral I had ever been to, and I was extremely impressed at the way it was handled.

The actual burial was much different than what I had experienced up to this point. After his casket was lowered into the ground, his brothers personally shoveled in the dirt on top of it until the grave was full. They piled all of the flowers on the grave, and then had a few beers there before we all left. We traveled to the gravesite and back in a pack, and the pack had actually escorted the body from the church to the gravesite.

Because of the injury to my foot, and the amount of time that would be needed for it to heal, the Caterpillar dealership cut me loose. I received a small settlement from them for my injury, and we parted on good terms. I took the opportunity to move back to Connecticut, because my on again off again girlfriend Toni had decided that she was homesick. I had mixed feelings when we loaded up in the fall of 1977 and took all we owned back to Connecticut, but hoped that the change was for the best.

Within a few days, I located a magnificent townhouse on top of a mountain just north of New Haven, on the Hamden/New Haven town line. It was three stories tall, and had a large garage that took up the entire ground floor. It was ideal for the motorcycles, and as an added bonus, my buddy Pete Hansen was willing to rent a room from me to help pay the bills. Pete had been discharged from the Navy and had bought his first new Harley; a 1978 gray Low Rider. A few weeks later, after we got settled in, I was surprised to find myself pleased to be in Connecticut again. It was good to be back home, but once again, it didn't take long for Toni and me to start fighting. This time she moved out and took off for California.

Pete and I rang in the New Year at the apartment with a small party of old friends, and we both settled into our bachelor routines. Over the winter of 1977/1978 I bought a new Harley motor from the Clinton Harley dealer, took all my leftover Harley parts, and built another bike. Then I sold the blue 58 Pan Shovel, and kept the bike with the new 1978 shovelhead motor for my personal ride.

*Ct Ed's 1978 Rigid Shovelhead
March 1978*

*Pete Hansen On His 1978
Lowrider April 1978*

The first trip of the year in February 1978 was a trip out west, back to Oklahoma, to see all of my friends there. By now, Lee McArdle and Chris Robison had teamed up with Robert "Buffalo" Connaughton and opened up a motorcycle shop that they called the Scooter Shop. It was in a small building on North Utica in Tulsa, and I was able to sell some Harley parts to them to finance the trip. On the way back, I stopped in St. Louis to visit with some other Tulsa friends who had moved there, and wound up at a party that lasted all night.

Late that night, when I got tired, there was nowhere for me to lie down and sleep except outside in a beat-up old van. The van had no heat, and it was below freezing outside. I took a cute little drunk girl with me for heat, and we settled into my sleeping bag for the night. All was well until the girl went to the bathroom in her sleep, and soaked the sleeping bag and both of us in the process. I woke up in the van to find my leftover open can of beer frozen, most of me soaked in wet piss, and the horrible stench from the piss permeating the van.

It was my worst nightmare. All of my dry, clean clothes were in my pickup across the yard. I got out of the sleeping bag half naked, ran to my truck in below zero bone chilling cold, fetched some clean clothes and went back into the house and cleaned up. During this whole ordeal, the cute drunk girl I had slept with never woke up, so I left her and my sleeping bag there in the van, and hit the road headed back east.

From St. Louis, I headed east to the Reading, Pennsylvania area, where I first stopped into see David "Dave" Gruber, and then to visit the Harley Davidson factory/museum in York. The Harley factory was fantastic, and I felt like a kid in a candy store! It was amazing to walk beside a new bike and watch as it was built, then actually see it run at the end of the assembly line.

As soon as I got back to Connecticut, I landed a job about thirty miles away, at the Connecticut Caterpillar dealer H. O. Penn. It was a union shop, and I had never worked in a union shop before, but the pay was outstanding. I was assigned to the second shift, and found myself working 3pm to 11pm in the shop.

One weekend morning I awoke to the sound of a motorcycle running out in the townhouse parking lot. When I got to my bedroom window, I could see my roommate Pete getting ready to load his bike into the back of his Chevy van. I was about to witness one of the funniest scenes of my life. To facilitate the loading of his bike into the van, Pete had placed a wood plank from the ground to the back of the van, which he intended to use as a ramp.

As he rode the bike up the ramp, it dawned on me that Pete had not calculated the height of the van's roof, and in a second, Pete would have to stop the loading process because there was no room for him to fit into the van if he continued riding the motorcycle. I quickly calculated that there would probably only be about four inches of room to spare over the top of the handlebars. As I predicted, just as he almost got the front wheel into the back of the van, it dawned on Pete that there was no way he could fit into the van while riding the bike.

So there he stopped, dead in his tracks, forgetting that he was up in the air on the ramp and that there wasn't any way his feet could touch the ground. Pete and the brand new motorcycle teetered there just for a second, before gravity took over and both of them came crashing to the ground. Then it got funny, because the new Harley was still running in first gear, lying on its left side, with the rear wheel spinning. Pete then tried to pick the bike up, but when he did, it took off without him, all by itself. The Harley made a large circle around the parking lot with Pete chasing it, before falling over on its right side.

The 1978 Lowrider motorcycle was less than two months old, and it now was smashed up on both sides. The whole loading incident had happened in about two minutes. I felt bad for Pete at the time, but could still not keep from laughing about it. I got dressed and went downstairs to help him get the bike into the van, there was nothing I could do to repair Pete's pride: it was permanently damaged. To this day Pete's motorcycle loading is a vivid reminder to me of how to not load a bike.

In May of 1978, my girlfriend Toni came back from California, and we once again fell head over heals in love. Toni swore that she had exhausted her desire to party now that she was almost twenty years old. We had been together on and off since she was only sixteen, and like an idiot I believed her when she told me she had finally grown up. Part of me blamed her attitude and unfaithful actions on the fact that she had been badly injured in a horrible car accident when she was fifteen, and wore a wicked scar across her face as a result.

Off I dived into a sea of stupidity, when in late May, we got married. The reception should have been a huge wakeup call for me, but once again, I let it go. Toni got so completely plastered at the reception that she passed out. The combination of pain pills and alcohol kicked her butt, and I spent my wedding night with an intoxicated wife who was unable to perform her customary wedding obligations. The next day the fighting between us was back with a vengeance, and I was forced to face the prospect that she would never change.

Cecil & Angie On Their
Wedding Day June 1978

Toni & Ct Ed May 1978

Within a few days, Toni left again for California, telling me that it had all been a mistake. I took it in stride and went back to life as a bachelor. In June, my mentor Cecil Pullen and his long time girlfriend Angie got married. Richard "Richie" Doolittle and Chris Robison, came back to Connecticut from Tulsa for the wedding, and stayed with me for a few days.

My wife Toni soon had second thoughts, and after just a few weeks in sunny California, she returned to Connecticut and vowed to make a valid attempt at being a wife. I gave in and gave her another last chance, but this time swore it would be the final last chance. In July, for the fourth, we went to a bluegrass festival for my birthday, and a few weeks later we took off on the bike for a vacation ride to Bowling Green, Kentucky, where there was a major biker rally held every year. I had made plans to meet the Tulsa crew there, and was glad to see my old friend Lee McArdle. He had made the journey with some new friends of his who were members of a California motorcycle club called the Mongols. I had never heard of the Mongols before, and was surprised to hear that they were living in Tulsa, and more surprised to see them not wearing their colors.

While in Bowling Green, I ran into the Outlaws Motorcycle Club for the first time in my life. It would be a meeting that would have an impact on me for the rest of my life. I was off minding my own business, and because it was so hot, I had only a t-shirt on. The crossed pistons and skull tattoo on my arm could easily be seen. Lee had earlier kidded with me about the tattoo looking a lot like the Outlaws Motorcycle Club center patch. I guess I should not have been surprised when I was surrounded by a group of Outlaws looking for trouble. They were very pissed off about my tattoo, and their leader, who was named Wildman, demanded that it be removed immediately. I was between a rock and a hard place, with no way out, and I found myself praying for a miracle.

I explained to Outlaw Wildman the story of how I got the tattoo, and how it had been up on the wall of the tattoo shop in Rhode Island. I told him that I had no idea at the time I got it, that the Outlaws Motorcycle Club even existed. I figured that I might as well go down fighting, so I told Wildman to cut it off if he thought he needed to, and if not, let me go about my business. The look in his eyes told me that I had made a grievous mistake, and just as he whipped out his knife to cut my tattoo off, a stranger appeared from nowhere, asking the Outlaws what they thought they were doing.

The stranger just happened to be a member of the Rogues Motorcycle Club from Oklahoma City. His name was John "Little Wolf" Killip, and I knew him from when I was a prospect in the Rogues two years prior. It turned out that Rogue Little Wolf knew most all of the Outlaws that had surrounded me, and seemed to know Outlaw Wildman better than the rest. While I silently thanked God, Outlaw Wildman explained the situation to Rogue Little Wolf. Little Wolf told Wildman that he knew me well, and that I was a stand-up guy that regularly crisscrossed the country on my bike. Rogue Little Wolf requested some sort of happy medium for the situation, and Wildman complied.

Outlaw Wildman ordered me to get the tattoo covered up within thirty days, and told me to come to the Dayton, Ohio Outlaws clubhouse as soon as I could to prove to him that the tattoo had been covered up. I told Outlaw Wildman that I had no problem with that solution, and told him to expect me at the clubhouse in the near future. The pack of Outlaws dispersed, and I thanked Little Wolf for his interdiction. We talked for a while about our lives, and I learned that Rogue Little Wolf was a frequent visitor to the Outlaws clubhouse in Dayton. He told me the Outlaws were a great bunch of guys. Little Wolf also told me that these guys were the real deal, and a whole lot more serious about clubbing than the Rogues were. He told me to not be surprised if he became an Outlaw someday. Before we parted that day, Little Wolf asked me to come back to Oklahoma, and join him again as a member of the Rogues. I told him I would seriously consider it.

I went back to Connecticut, where I immediately had my tattoo covered up. As soon as I could arrange some time off from work, I took off in my truck for whirlwind trip to Oklahoma, where I planned to buy a load of Harley parts from Lee McArdle's bike shop for resale in Connecticut. I spent one night in Tulsa, and while I was there I ran into a Tulsa Rogue named T-Chuck. I told him all about the Outlaws and Rogue Little Wolf, and that I was thinking about moving back to Oklahoma again. T-Chuck told me that he would love to see me come back, and when I did move back I would be more than welcome to pick up with the Rogues where I had left off.

On the way back from Oklahoma, I stopped into see the Outlaws at their Dayton Clubhouse. This time I was not unprepared, and I carried with me a Colt 45 automatic for protection. I figured if things didn't go well, I could at least take a few of the Outlaws with me. When I arrived at the clubhouse, it was almost dark. I knocked on the door, and a mountain of a man let me in, and then closed the door behind me. As he stood between the door and me, he introduced himself as Outlaw Sampson; his real name was James Marr. I explained to him that I needed to see his brother Outlaw Wildman, but refused to tell him why. Outlaw Sampson told me that Outlaw Wildman was nowhere to be found, and I would just have to come back another time.

I told him that I was on my way from Oklahoma to Connecticut, and that I lived in Connecticut. I also explained to him that coming back at another time was not an option, and instead I demanded to speak with Outlaw Wildman's chapter President, whoever that was. Sampson laughed, and sent one of the Outlaws upstairs to wake the Outlaws chapter President up. As I stood there waiting, I noticed that there were about ten other Outlaws in the room. I knew that there was no way I could shoot them all if things went bad, and I resigned myself to the fact that I probably would die here in their clubhouse in the next ten minutes.

The President of the Dayton Outlaws at that time was Kenneth "Hambone" Hammond, and it didn't take long for him to come downstairs. It was obvious that he had just gotten out of bed, and I was thinking that this was not a good way to start off. He ordered me to come and sit down at the bar, and asked me if I wanted a drink. I then explained to him about the incident that occurred with Outlaw Wildman at Bowling Green, told him I was a man of my word, and then showed him that the tattoo had been covered up. I thanked him for his time, and got up to leave, telling him I needed to hit the road.

That is when it got tense; because he told me that there was no way he could allow me to leave. All the Outlaws in the room were on edge, waiting for the least excuse to beat my brains in, and it looked like it was the end of the line for me. Then Hambone broke the ice, and told me the reason I could not go was that he wanted to get to know me. Years later, Hambone would tell me that he was impressed that I had walked into their clubhouse by myself, and he knew right then and there that we were going to be friends for life.

While Outlaw Hambone and I sat at the bar shooting the shit, he told me that he had talked to both Little Wolf and Wildman about me, and knew that I would show up at the clubhouse before long. Before we parted, he made me promise him that every time I passed through Dayton, I would always stop there and see him. He promised me, that when and if I moved back to Oklahoma, he would visit me if he were in my neighborhood.

As I walked out the clubhouse door, I breathed a breath of fresh air, and wondered how I had made it out of there alive. I had no idea of the relationship I had just forged, or the important significance of our meeting. It would take years for me to realize that the incident at Bowling Green was a turning point in my life.

When I got back to Connecticut, after stopping for a few hours to see my old girlfriend Suzan Delgrosso and her family in Pittsburgh, my wife Toni dropped a bomb on me. It turned out that she was pregnant, and had told her dad that the child was mine. I was convinced that the child was not mine, by quickly calculating the time of conception against the time she had been pregnant. I figured that Toni had gotten pregnant on her last trip to California. I also thought I was sterile, so I went to see Toni's dad. After explaining all of this to him, her dad arranged for me to go to a local laboratory, where I submitted myself to a sperm test. The test proved beyond all doubt that I was not the father of the child, and Toni soon admitted the same to her dad and me.

Her dad was livid, and his Italian blood boiled at the thought of his daughter being unfaithful to her husband. He threw Toni in a truck, and we took her to a local psychiatric hospital for observation. While there, she had a quiet abortion, and I filed for divorce. There was no way we could ever repair our relationship after this major indiscretion, in spite of all we had been through over the years. By late September of 1978, we were divorced, and I was looking for any reason to get out of Connecticut before it got cold and started snowing.

On October 9th, my reason came when I learned that Charles "T-Chuck" Schlegel, who was the Rogue that I had talked to on my last trip to Tulsa, had been murdered by his girlfriend during a domestic squabble. There was no way I could attend the funeral on such short notice, but it did propel me to make definitive plans to move back to Tulsa. I contacted the Caterpillar dealership in Tulsa before I moved, and arranged for a job there as soon as I arrived. It was easy to do so at the time, because I worked for Caterpillar in Connecticut, and the Tulsa dealership was in need of many experienced mechanics. It just happened that the timing was right, or maybe my destiny was to live out my years in Oklahoma. Either way, I moved back to sunny, warm Tulsa at the end of October 1978.

14

Back To Tulsa & The Rogues MC
Fall 1978 To Summer 1979

As soon as I arrived back in Tulsa, I moved in with Robert "Buffalo" Connaughton, in a house he was renting off Admiral Place, just east of Highway 169. He and I got along just great; we had the same interests in Harley Davidson motorcycles and both of us loved the freedom of being bachelors. Within a week, I was working at Albert Equipment, the Tulsa area Caterpillar heavy construction equipment dealer. I had my own field truck, and was specializing in the repair of large bulldozers, specifically the D-7, D-8 and D-9 models. By the end of November, I was prospecting again for the Rogues Motorcycle Club, and everything in my life was looking good.

But in mid-December, I hit a snag in the road. As part of my work assignment one day, I was sent down to Stigler, Oklahoma, to replace the transmission on a customer's D-9 Caterpillar bulldozer. When I got to the jobsite in my field truck loaded with tools, I performed the standard performance checks on the D-9 transmission before I condemned it. I discovered that the transmission just had a bad main pressure relief valve, and called into the parts department of Albert Equipment for a new valve to be delivered that night to the local parts drop box in Sallisaw. I rented a local motel room, as was customary, and the next morning I went by the parts drop box and picked up the new transmission valve.

It took me a few hours to replace the bad D-9 transmission valve, but by noon I had the bulldozer pushing dirt just like a new machine. The customer was thrilled, because instead of a forty-four thousand dollar bill for replacing the entire transmission, we both figured that he would have to pay only about two thousand for the repair job I had just completed. He even bought me a case a beer to thank me for my service, and I headed back to the shop in Tulsa for my next assignment. When I got to the shop, I was immediately called into the office, where the field service manager proceeded to chew me out.

The field service manager was so mad I thought his eyes were going to pop out of his head. As he yelled, he explained that he had told me to replace the transmission, not test it and fix it! I told him that I was a mechanic, and if he wanted someone to replace parts for him, he should have hired a parts replacer. As he continued screaming at me, threatening to fire me, I thought that I just wasn't cut out to be working for somebody else. I had never been able to hold down a job for very long, and I thought this would be a good time to quit and go to work on my own.

So I interrupted him and as I looked over my shoulder, I asked him whom the hell he was yelling at? I then told him that it couldn't be me, because I didn't work there anymore. As I walked out the door of his office, I told him to have someone come by my house the next day and pick up my field truck, after I unloaded it. As I slammed shut his office door behind me, I optimistically walked down the hallway to the applause of a group of other field service mechanics that had approvingly watched my performance.

Since I had quit Albert Equipment, I resumed stealing motorcycles to supplement my income. I started fixing Harleys to pay my bills, and selling the parts off the stolen motorcycles for extra money. I also started marketing my special skills in changing serial identification numbers on Harley engine cases and frames, to facilitate the concealment of the stolen motorcycle parts. I had learned a lot from my experience with the auto theft detective in Virginia two years before and now was putting the experience to good use. There were only two or three bikers in town willing to change Harley serial identification numbers, but my method was by far the best and safest. Prospecting for the Rogues Motorcycle Club became another full time job, but my line of work complimented my involvement with the club.

A few days before Christmas, Rogues Rickie "Smoker" Miles and Homer "Spurge" Spurgeon and I took off to Florida to visit with my friend, Kenneth "Hambone" Hammond from the Outlaws Motorcycle Club, at the Outlaws' annual Christmas/New Years party in Fort Lauderdale, Florida. I had stopped into see Outlaw Hambone while moving from Connecticut to Oklahoma, and had told him what I was doing. Hambone had invited me to come to Florida to visit him, and told me to bring some of the Rogues if they had the balls to show up. I told him I would be there, as long as my financial situation allowed it.

The three of us drove down to Miami, Florida in a pickup truck with a camper shell on it; in the back we had a mattress to sleep on. We rotated drivers every few hours; one of us was able to sleep in the back while the other two sat in the front. This enabled us to drive all the way there, from Tulsa to Fort Lauderdale, in a little more than a day. We planned on being there for Christmas, and leaving in time to be home for New Years Eve. While we were there, we were treated like visiting royalty. In spite of the fact that I was a prospect, many Outlaws treated me as if I were a full patch holder. I took the time to establish a few relationships with some of the Florida Outlaws, which eventually proved to be well worth the initial effort. After spending a few days and nights there, we all piled into the truck for the long journey back to Tulsa. We returned home exactly as planned, just in time for the New Years Eve celebration.

I celebrated the New Year by renting a nice house on 34th Street, just west of 129th East Avenue, in January of 1979. The three-bedroom house was right in the middle of a fairly new neighborhood. Its location was perfect, nice and quiet, and the garage was twice as large as the one I had shared with Buffalo. I soon had a slew of young cuties hanging around, most of which were dancers at the local strip joint where we all hung out. I was still not emotionally over the relationship with my ex-wife Toni, so I tried not to date any one of the girls for more than a few days at a time. I moved two of them into the house with me to help pay the bills, cook and clean the house, and in return provided them needed protection and helped them save their money.

On February 24th, 1979, at a regular Rogues Motorcycle Club meeting, I was elevated from prospect to full patch holder. I had finally fulfilled my promise to T-Chuck, who had been murdered a few months earlier; I felt as though I had taken his place in the chapter. To celebrate the occasion, Rogue Rickie "Smoker" Miles and I took off on our bikes ten days later for Daytona, Florida, to attend the notorious Daytona Bike Week. We had been invited down there by some of the members of the Jacksonville chapter of the Outlaws that we had met at their Christmas/New Years Eve party in Miami, and were scheduled to actually ride into Daytona with them in their pack at the beginning of the rally.

When we got to Jacksonville, one of the Outlaws that I had met while I was in Fort Lauderdale over Christmas, Ronald "Arab" Watchmaker introduced me to their resident professional bike thief. His name was Edward "Edd" Lackey, and he was a Jacksonville Outlaw from Hogjaw, Alabama who talked with a slow, southern drawl. Outlaw Edd and I were like two peas in a pod, and hit it off immediately. Since I needed to make some extra money while I was there, it was a no-brainer to steal bikes and then sell them to the Outlaws.

Edd and I soon devised a game to challenge us a little while we were stealing bikes during the Daytona Bike Week festivities. To make the act of stealing a Harley a bit tougher, we started the game out by making a rule that you could only steal a Harley if it had less than five hundred miles on it. We rationalized this game of thievery by calculating that a Harley owner who had less than five hundred miles on his bike deserved to lose it, for all righteous Harley bikers like us rode our bikes everywhere, putting lots of miles on them. We had no problem stealing low mileage Harleys from owners that did not ride the bikes, and we affectionately called these owners RUBs (rich urban bikers). These RUBs that we targeted just owned the bike for show, like one would wear a piece of jewelry.

As a further incentive, each bike that was stolen would set a new barometer for the amount of mileage on the next one; for example, if Outlaw Edd got one with four hundred ninety miles on it, I had to get one with less than four hundred ninety miles on it. I was surprised how easy the pickings were. There seemed to be an abundance of new Harleys around that had less than five hundred miles on them. Within an hour, the new threshold to beat was to steal one that had less than two hundred fifty miles. Within a few more hours, the threshold was less than one hundred miles.

The first night, we bagged four and delivered them by van to a warehouse for disassembly sixty miles away. The next night, because we had to steal bikes that had less than one hundred miles on them, the selection pool was much smaller, and it took us a while to locate acceptable candidates. When each of us had bagged a new Harley with less than one hundred miles on it, we loaded the bikes into the back of the transportation van and headed north through Ormond Beach to catch the highway out of town that would get us to the warehouse.

Unfortunately for us, an Ormond Beach police officer recognized the driver as a member of the Outlaws, and stopped us for no reason at all except to harass us. It was March 9th, 1979, and the police officer soon figured out that something wasn't right with the new bikes in the back of the van. Within a minute, we were surrounded by lots of police officers, and ordered out of the truck and searched. I was arrested for possession of two stolen motorcycles, and three counts of carrying a concealed firearm. When we had first been pulled over, I put all three of our guns in a hidden storage area behind the dash directly in front of me. When the police discovered the hidden compartment, because it was closest to me, I was the one that got charged with the three gun charges.

All three of us were taken to the county jail at Deland, and within hours, released on bond. The Outlaws had a full-time bondsman on call right there at the county jail, to bail out Outlaws and their associates as fast as possible all week long. Every hour or so all week during Daytona Bike Week, it seemed like an Outlaw, Outlaw associate or Outlaw's ol' lady went to jail. During the next few days, the three of us pooled together all of our resources, sold all the Harleys we had already stolen, and hired the best attorney Florida had to offer, Richard D. Nichols from Jacksonville.

Fortunately, the police officer that stopped us was an honest police officer, and would eventually admit under oath at our first major court hearing that he had recognized the Outlaw driving the van, and in spite of the fact that the Outlaw or his passengers had done nothing wrong, he stopped the Outlaw anyway. It was law at the time that there had to be a reason to stop us initially, and to stop us for no reason amounted to an illegal stop; to search the van after making an illegal stop constituted an illegal search, and to impound the bikes after the illegal search constituted an illegal seizure. As a result, the presiding Judge did the right thing, and dismissed all of our charges six months later in October of 1979. Because our charges had been dismissed, the police even returned to us all three of the 45 caliber Colt firearms that had been confiscated from us that night.

On the last night of our Florida trip, both Rogue Smoker and I stayed with my new friend, Outlaw Edd, in his house on Blanding Blvd. Edd talked me into shooting off an old black powder rifle, just outside the window of the bedroom Smoker was sleeping in, to wake Rogue Smoker up. But I had been okie-doked, and Outlaw Edd had packed way too much powder into the old gun. When I shot it, it blew up. The force of the explosion threw me for a loop, knocking me back on my ass. It was so powerful that it blew the window out, and my shoulder was sore for almost two weeks. Surprisingly, Smoker slept right through the fiasco, and woke up hours later wondering where all the glass had come from.

As a result of my arrest at Daytona, I was forced to return to the Jacksonville area numerous times that spring, summer and fall for court. This turned out to be a blessing in disguise, for I soon established my self as a regular with all the Outlaws in Florida. The Outlaws Motorcycle Club had four chapters in Florida in 1979, one each in Jacksonville, Orlando, Tampa and Fort Lauderdale. Almost every time I was there for court, I stayed for at least two weeks at a time, and made sure I visited each chapter at least once. I rapidly established strong friendships with Outlaws from each chapter. Almost every Outlaw in Florida knew who I was, and many considered me to be their friend.

Outlaw Edd Firing The Black   *Edd Lackey March 1979*
Powder Rifle Before Ct Ed Shot It   *Holding The Rifle*

In April, while I was attending a Rogues Motorcycle Club party in Prague, Oklahoma, I got into a fistfight with another Rogue who was from our Oklahoma City chapter. He was a mountain of a man, who had been in the Marine Corps in Vietnam. His name was Robert Eugene Harris, but we all called him Rocky. Rogue Rocky was a little drunk and had noticed that I wore a patch identifying myself as the Tulsa chapter Enforcer. When I walked by him, he told me that there was no way a little guy like me deserved that Enforcer patch, and in fact, he thought that I was a punk with no balls. Not wanting to be thought of as a punk, and certainly not being one, I immediately stuck him in his face with my fist, using all the strength I had.

I had to jump up in the air to actually hit him, and just by luck, caught him unprepared and just right, knocking him over backwards. Then he was really mad, because I had done this in front of a whole bunch of Rogues. When he got up, he dared me to try that again, and not being too smart, of course I obliged him. As my right fist got just about to his face, he grabbed my arm and jerked me over to the ground, where we both wound up in a pile. The only problem was that he had hurt me real bad in the process, and I had to be taken to a hospital. At the hospital, I was diagnosed with having a massive AC (Arm & Collar) separation, and I was told that I needed immediate surgery to remedy the injury.

After my surgery, while I was laid up in the hospital, Rogue Rocky came by to see me. He had gotten up the next day and been told what had transpired at the party, most of which he had no memory of. So Rocky rode about a hundred miles out of his way to come visit me. By my bedside, he told me that he never intended to hurt me, and that he knew that I wasn't a punk. He ended up staying there with me until I was released a few days later, then stayed with me at my house for another week until I was able to get around pretty well by myself. Rogue Rocky apparently felt guilty for causing me so much pain, and hanging out with me was his way of making things right. As a result, we became very close, and hung out together quite a bit over the next two and one half years.

Ct Ed After Surgery May 1979   *Rogue Rocky May 1979*

While I was laid up recovering from my surgery, one of my many lucrative business ventures got busted up. I had set up an escort agency in Tulsa, out near 64th Street South and Peoria, in a nice office complex building. I had hired two fairly straight, non-bike-type guys to run it for me, and was supplying the operation with dancers from the local strip joints.

It was a mini gold mine, but the managers I hired soon got too vocal with the advertising. As a result, the Tulsa Police Department did an investigation and determined that the business was a front for an organized call girl prostitution service. The arrests of the managers produced lots of media attention, and in spite of the fact that all the charges would eventually be beaten, I did the smart thing and closed it down.

At the same time, my friend from Pennsylvania, David "Dave" Gruber, moved to Tulsa with the intention of becoming a member of the Rogues Motorcycle Club. Dave and I had met in Connecticut back in the summer of 1978, while he and a friend toured New England on their bikes. I had run into them riding down the highway, and took them to my parents' house for a free meal. We hit it off real well, and had stayed in touch. I had stopped into see him a few times, since his home in the Reading, Pennsylvania area was right on the route I traveled back and forth from Oklahoma to Connecticut on a regular basis.

On June 13th, 1979, a Wednesday night, a bunch of us went down to a local rock n' roll bar called Whiskers, where we wanted to see the show and have a good time. I was still in my arm brace from the surgery, and although I felt well enough to actually get out on the town, I was far from being fully recovered. Out in front of the nightclub, a young wannabe named Lyndon Jackson tried to start a fight with some of the Rogue patch holders that were milling around.

Jackson was a big, tough guy that regularly hung out at Whiskers, terrorizing and assaulting innocent patrons most every night. He normally loved to pick on those who were unable to defend themselves, but on this night, he was out to prove to the world that he was the toughest kid on the block. Unfortunately, no one ever explained to Mr. Jackson that it would be no less than suicide to attempt to beat up motorcycle gang members, many of whom had just returned from Vietnam or had been trained to go to Vietnam.

It all started when Jackson's little brother confronted the first Rogue he ran into, and the Rogue pissed on the little brother's leg while patiently listening to his threats that his older brother would kill all of them when he got there. After realizing that the Rogue had pissed all over him, the little brother ran off into the darkness, and the few Rogues milling around thought that the altercation was over. A few minutes later, the little brother came back with the older brother, and a few of his older brother's friends. Five minutes later, Lyndon Jackson the big tough guy, was Lyndon Jackson the walking dead guy. When Jackson confronted a Rogue with the intent to do that Rogue serious bodily harm, the Rogue did exactly what he had been trained to do; he defended himself. Lyndon Jackson had been killed in a split instant, with one stroke of a small knife. I heard later that he actually lived for about twenty minutes, but was dead by the time he got into the ambulance.

After the brawl in the Whiskers parking lot, which involved more than twenty people, all of the participants scattered to the four winds, and disappeared into the night. Every Rogue there, as well as all of their friends and associates, left that parking lot under their own power. What they left behind was no less than a scene reminiscent of a Vietnam battlefield, for there was blood and injured combatants everywhere. Only one Rogue required hospitalization for injuries that had occurred that night; he suffered a broken nose and two broken cheek bones in the melee.

Less than thirty minutes after the brawl, the Tulsa Police apprehended three people who were thought to have been involved in the fracas. Rogue Michael "Little Mike" Hardison was arrested for suspicion of murder; while Rogue Calvin "Captain" Dorman and Rogue prospect Myron Corser were arrested as material witnesses. What we all knew at the time was that Rogue Little Mike had nothing to do with the death of Lyndon Jackson, for Little Mike was inside the bar at the time the fighting broke out. His only involvement was after the fight, when he accidentally hit an innocent bystander with his motorcycle on his way out of the parking lot.

City/State

Fri., June 15, 1979

Biker Is Charged In Stabbing Death

One motorcycle gang member was charged with second-degree murder and two others were being held as material witnesses Thursday in connection with the stabbing death of Lyndon Charles Jackson Wednesday night.

The medical examiner ruled Thursday that Jackson had died as a result of a stab wound to his heart.

Michael Lee Hardison, 23, was charged with second degree murder. Myron Lloyd Corser, 28, and Calvin Proctor Dorman, 28, are being held as material witnesses. All three are members of the Rogue motorcycle gang.

Several gang members apparently were involved in a fight in the parking lot of Whiskers club, 2725 S. Memorial Drive, police said. Jackson wasn't involved in the argument but one of the gang members allegedly ran over him when they fled quickly from the scene, police said.

One witness said the brake or clutch pedal of one of the motorcycles struck Jackson in the chest. Police said they believe Jackson was simply an innocent bystander.

Police still are searching for a fourth gang member believed to be

connected with the case.

Bond for Hardison was set at $10,000. His preliminary hearing was scheduled for June 28 before Special District Judge Tony Graham.

"This thing that happened last night was an accident, a regrettable accident," said Frank Thompson, attorney for Hardison. "There was no intention for anything to happen. It's a regrettable incident that has been blown out of proportion."

Thompson said Hardison's affiliation with the motorcyle gang had prompted the second-degree murder charge.

"If he was on a 350 Honda (motorcycle) and had been by himself, he wouldn't be facing this charge," Thompson said.

Jackson graduated from the special projects class of Booker T. Washington in 1978. He lived with his parents, Mr. and Mrs. O.B. Jackson at 4349 S. Allegheny Ave. He also is survived by two married sisters, Linda Shuck of Tulsa and Laura Davis of Corpus Christi, Texas, and one brother, Lawrence Steven Jackson of the home. Jackson was unemployed.

Hardison grew up in Tulsa and attended Edison High School.

The Tulsa Newspaper Article About The Whiskers Fight

The charges against Rogue Little Mike alleged that he caused the death of Lyndon Jackson when he ran over him with his motorcycle, on the way out of the parking lot. The exact injury that caused Jackson's death was alleged to be the shifter pedal on Rogue Little Mike's bike. When the medical examiner testified at a preliminary hearing that Jackson had died from a small knife wound that had been inflicted by someone trained in military killing techniques, and not by the shifter pedal of a motorcycle, the Judge dismissed all of the charges that had been filed against him.

A few months later, when I finally recovered fully from my shoulder surgery, and regained full use of my injured arm, the Rogues transferred me to the Enid chapter, which was about one hundred miles west of Tulsa. There I set up a retail motorcycle shop to cover all of my illegal enterprises, and just after Thanksgiving, took off again for Florida. I had planned to spend a month there, and not come back until after the New Year. I loved being in Florida in the middle of winter, for it was warm there all winter and the biker world never skipped a beat.

One night during that vacation, while I was hanging around outside in the yard of the Outlaws clubhouse in Jacksonville, the full patch members of the chapter had a meeting in the house. When the meeting let out, the President of the Jacksonville chapter told me that I had been voted in as a member of the Jacksonville Outlaws. All I had to do was give up my Rogues patch, and move from Oklahoma to the Jacksonville area. As I had no intention of moving, I instantly declined his offer. His response was to hit me in the chest as hard as he could with his closed fist, knocking me down on the ground and causing the imprint of the Outlaws ring he wore to be indented in my chest.

But this wasn't a fistfight, just his way of letting me know that he was disappointed. The Outlaws President respected my decision, and as he helped me up he told me to think about it for the next few days. At the time I felt honored to have been voted into the Jacksonville Outlaws as a full patch member. I almost changed my mind about it over the next few days but there was just no way I could leave Oklahoma. I felt that Oklahoma was my home, and knew it was my destiny to remain there.

In September of 1979, some of the Rogues from Tulsa got hooked up with the owner of a trucking company, whose union employees were all on strike. These Rogues accepted his offer to drive the trucks and act as strikebreakers for a lucrative salary. When leaving the truck facility one evening after work, four Rogues in a car got into an altercation with the actual strikers at the gate, and a massive riot broke out.

Among the four were my good friends Marvin Brix, Arthur "Art" Kohring, Homer "Spurge" Spurgeon, and Rickie "Smoker" Miles. When the dust settled, nineteen people went to jail. Illegal weapons, enough to cover the trunk, were recovered from the Rogues and the car they were riding in. As a result of the fight, union representatives from Kansas City made an agreement with the Rogues, who were then allowed to continue strikebreaking without the possibility of facing any retribution for what they were doing. The strike ended peacefully after about three weeks, and all of the rioting charges were eventually dismissed.

15

Running With The Bandidos
Summer 1979 To 1985

I met my first Bandido in Mobile, Alabama in the summer of 1979. His name was Buddy Boykin and he was a Vice Presidente at the time, under Bandido El Presidente Ronnie Hodge. I was a member of the Tulsa chapter of the Rogues Motorcycle Club, and I had been visiting the Outlaws Motorcycle Club all over Florida. Arab from the Jacksonville chapter of the Outlaws knew Bandido Buddy well, and since my frequent travels from Tulsa to Florida took me directly through Mobile, Outlaw Arab thought it would be a good idea for the two of us to meet.

It turned out that Bandido Buddy and I got along well. Buddy's house was not far off my normal route, so it was a perfect stopping place, just about half way between Tulsa and Jacksonville. I would usually try to get to Mobile by early evening, spend the night, and hit the road the next morning. It did not take long before stopping to see the Bandidos in Mobile was a requirement on every trip, and I went to Florida at least a couple times each year.

Bandido Vice Presidente Buddy had a interesting effect on me; it is said that your perception of the first member of a motorcycle club that you meet will last a lifetime, and it has. Buddy introduced me to a totally different type of motorcycle club, one that truly believed in the concept of brotherhood that all motorcycle clubs projected. It wasn't long before I started thinking about the possibility of changing over the entire Rogues Motorcycle Club to being the Bandidos Motorcycle Club Oklahoma. I had no way of knowing at the time how long a process that would be.

In the spring of 1980, after I had spent the fall and winter rebuilding the Northern Oklahoma chapter of the Rogues in Enid, Oklahoma, I was appointed a National officer. Because the Rogues were a fairly large club with more than a dozen chapters spread out all over Oklahoma, southern Kansas and northern Texas, there were two National Sergeant at Arms: my friend Robert "Rocky" Harris (who had injured me so badly the year before) and me.

Rogue Rocky was a crazy son of a bitch, who was, as I previously pointed out, a mountain of a man. I was a fairly small man in relation to Rocky's size, but both of us were well known by this time for our ability to take care of business. Usually when we went into a dangerous situation, everyone there would always notice Rocky and forget about me, which is exactly how we planned it. Rogue Rocky and I were a dynamic team, and we both spent a lot of time on the road together.

At the same time that I had been cultivating my relationship with Bandido Buddy in Alabama, Rogue Rocky had been cultivating a relationship with a Lubbock, Texas Bandido by the name of Earthquake. Bandido Earthquake was also a mountain of a man, also with a well-deserved reputation for taking care of business. It was no surprise to me that they hit it off so well together. While Bandido Buddy got me thinking about leaving the Rogues and becoming a Bandido, Bandido Earthquake had Rogue Rocky seriously thinking about leaving the Rogues and becoming a Bandido.

During 1979 and the first half of 1980, I had been working on a life-long dream. I finally realized that dream in June when I completed what would later be my first record album, which I called "At Long Last". The pseudonym I chose for my project was the "Connecticut Dust Band". I hoped the name would quietly reflect the fact that there never really was a band, but my childhood friend Kurt Newman, an assortment of studio musicians, and me. In my frequent travels to Connecticut over the years, I had established a friendship with a pair of schoolteachers who owned and operated a Hamden recording studio called Grace Recording Studios, which is where the album was recorded.

I established a record and music publishing company which I called Shovster Records & Music, to promote, copyright and distribute the record, aptly named after a stroked Sportster engine. By myself, over the span of a few years, I had learned how to record, produce, manufacture and copyright the songs and music contained in the record. Although the sound quality was inferior, and the quality of the songs that I had written was not the best, I was quite proud of my accomplishment. For the first few months after it was finished, Rogue Rocky was so proud of it he carried the record album with him wherever he went.

Later that summer of 1980, Rogue Rocky and I rode into Oklahoma City from Wichita Falls, where Rocky was living at the time. When we got to the Oklahoma City clubhouse, everyone there was complaining about the fact that there were Bandidos in town, and it looked like the Bandidos were setting up a clubhouse and were planning to establish a chapter in the middle of Rogues territory. All the Rogues in the clubhouse were mad, yet none of them were willing to go do anything about it. As soon as Rocky and I heard about it, we immediately decided to ride over and confront the Bandidos about the rumors. It was no problem finding them, for their new "clubhouse" was less than a mile from the Rogue clubhouse.

Rogue Rocky and I rode our motorcycles over to the house where the Bandidos were living, ready for World War III. We both hoped for a peaceful solution, but had prepared for the worst, for it is always better to be safe than sorry. It only took us a moment to arrive there and knock on the front door. A Bandido member opened the door and asked us to come in, which we did. As my eyes got adjusted to the lack of light inside, I noticed a few men relaxing in the living room. (Years later, I would find out that there were actually four Bandidos there. Bandido Tramp, Bandido Slyder and Bandido Cannon were three of them, and that they all expected and were also ready for World War III.)

Ct Ed Enid Clubhouse 1980   *Rogue Rocky Summer 1980*

Although we knew none of them at the time, we did tell them that we both had current, excellent relationships with two of their brothers, Bandido Buddy and Bandido Earthquake. We explained to them our concerns about the rumors we had heard, and inquired about their reasons for being in Oklahoma City. The Bandidos told us that they were in Oklahoma City to help another Bandido set up and run a local strip club; that there was no reason for alarm. The Bandidos advised us that they had no intention of establishing a chapter in Oklahoma City; they were just there for business purposes. Rogue Rocky and I ended the meeting by inviting them over to our clubhouse, and they told us to drop in and see them anytime we wanted to, as well.

After we left, Rogue Rocky and I stopped and got a bite to eat, and we talked about the prospect of changing over the entire Rogues nation to Bandidos. We did not think it would be possible to change over every member, since some of the Oklahoma City chapter was heavily involved with the Outlaws, but we did agree that it would be easy to find enough people to start up chapters in Tulsa and Oklahoma City. We decided to sit back and see what the future would bring, and planned to talk to the Bandidos about it the next time either of us saw one of them. I would talk to Bandido Buddy and Rogue Rocky would talk to Bandido Earthquake.

Unfortunately, these conversations with the Bandidos never materialized, for soon after part of the Rogues Oklahoma City chapter broke away and formed the first Outlaws chapter west of the Mississippi River. This new Outlaw chapter was about five hundred miles away from the closest Outlaws chapter in Memphis, and almost seven hundred miles from the next closest chapter in Indianapolis. It posed an interesting dilemma to me, for I had good friends in the Outlaws (Florida and Ohio, as well as the brand new Oklahoma chapter), but I also had a club allegiance to my Rogue brothers to uphold. To say the least, it was a troublesome and tumultuous time for me.

To compound things, at the same time I was dealing with the Outlaws, I was also in serious trouble with the law in numerous jurisdictions. It was a navigational nightmare, for by now I had multiple, simultaneous criminal cases pending in Oklahoma, Florida and Texas; all required court appearances and it seemed as though I had to be in court somewhere every week. I had been arrested in Florida again during the summer, one night after attending court for the Daytona stolen motorcycles/gun possession case; this time in Jacksonville for possession of a fourth loaded gun.

In Dallas, on March 16th of 1981, I was arrested again for a fifth gun charge, while sleeping in my van in front of the Scorpions Motorcycle Clubhouse. This gun charge rapidly turned into an investigation of a Kansas murder, because the gun I was caught with (which was actually in the back of the van and belonged to Rogue Rocky) had been used in a Kansas murder. I lucked out when the detectives from Kansas arrived at the jail to interview me, for when they saw me; they discovered that I was about one hundred thirty-five pounds and five feet eight inches tall.

It turned out that they were searching for a really large man, and as they yelled at the Dallas detectives for wasting their time, it occurred to me that the guy the detectives were describing was very similar to my running buddy, Rogue Robert "Rocky" Harris. The hold on me of "investigation for murder" was dropped less than an hour later, and I was released from jail on my own recognizance.

The funniest part of my arrest was still to come. When I was arrested, all I had on was a pair of jeans. No shirt, no socks and no shoes, for I had been asleep up until I was awakened by the police and arrested. So at the time I was released, I had no clothes with me except a pair of old blue jeans; everything else I owned was in my van and the police had impounded the van at the time of my arrest. Out of the jail I was thrown, to find an unusually hot day. As I hopped from one foot to another to avoid the hot pavement, I decided to run across the street to avoid burning my feet, instead of going up to the corner and crossing at the light. You can imagine my dismay when I was caught jaywalking by a policeman coming out of the building. In spite of my dilemma, the Dallas policeman made me re-cross the street, go up to the corner, wait for the traffic light, and then cross the street legally.

I just barely held my anger in check, and because I kept hopping from one foot to another, I was able to avoid burning my feet. Things got worse when my good buddy Rogue Rocky came to pick me up. All he had was his motorcycle, so I was forced to ride on the back for about four city blocks, from the jail to the impound yard. I finally got to my van and my clothes, and was never so relieved to put my shoes on, as I was that day.

Between all of my court cases, trying to keep the animosity between some of the Rogues and the new Outlaws in Oklahoma City from turning violent, trying to make a living and handling our normal daily club business affairs, Rogue Rocky and I had our hands full. We spent the rest of the summer balancing our load, and in spite of a few fistfights between members of the two motorcycle clubs, there were no more major problems that summer.

In August of 1981, I moved back to Tulsa from Enid. My legal problems came to a head when I went to trial in Tulsa at the United States District Courthouse. I had been arrested earlier that year on charges of "Uttering a Forged United States Obligation" and "Possession of Stolen Mail"; both charges were the result of me attempting to cash a stolen United States treasury check at a local Tulsa bank. I had wondered about the authenticity of the check when I had received it as payment for a debt, but figured that if it were worthless, the bank would not cash it.

I figured that getting caught was no big deal, and even if I was, it would probably only result in a short stay in jail. Besides, since I was using about ten different identities at the time, I had deposited the Treasury check in one of many bank accounts that I had established under a fictitious name. Worse case scenario: I figured the fake bank account would insulate and protect me from arrest. Amazing how naïve you can be when you are young!

As a result of my trial, I missed an important Rogues Motorcycle Club run in Wyoming held over Labor Day weekend. I had actually been convicted in federal court the week before, and was out on bond waiting for my sentencing. I had already been sentenced to two and a half years in state prison, after being convicted in western Oklahoma for "Knowingly Concealing Stolen Property". I was out of jail pending appeal in that case, and now I was looking at another prison sentence. In mid-September, I was sentenced to an additional seven years in federal court for the crimes concerning the forged Treasury check.

The Rogues' National President Gerb was upset that I had not shown up in Wyoming for the Rogues national run, so he ordered my Tulsa chapter President, Marvin Brix, to make me a prospect again. Rogue Marvin was quite upset that he had been told to do so, and I was extremely mad over the deal. I had no time to prospect, for I was about to go to prison for a long time, and I needed what little time I had left on the streets to get my affairs in order. So I quit the club, which was my only option at the time, in lieu of the fact that the Rogues concept of brotherhood was nowhere the same as mine.

On October 8, 1981, in late afternoon, I answered a knock on the door of my house and found about twenty cops there. They had a warrant for my arrest regarding the Garfield County conviction from 1980; it seemed that my attorney had forgotten to file my appeal. So off I went to the Tulsa County jail for a day; then to the Garfield County jail for a few weeks, and finally to the Oklahoma state prison system in early November.

I spent about nine months in custody on the two and one-half year sentence, and paroled out of the state prison system on July 8, 1982. As I gladly walked down the steps of the Jess Dunn Correctional Center at Taft, Oklahoma, that day, I savored my release. But to my surprise, there appeared two men in suits who identified themselves as federal marshals. They told me that I was under arrest because my attorney had once again failed to file my appeal, this time in the federal case.

I spent a few days in the Tulsa County jail again, before I was transported to the El Reno federal prison in El Reno, Oklahoma. It was now the end of July, and it was very hot, probably in excess of one hundred degrees. I was put in a 3rd floor cell, way up high in the cell house. It was like an incinerator there; if you moved you would sweat a river.

I hung out there for about two weeks, and then I was sent by bus to the federal prison at Leavenworth, Kansas to serve my sentence. It was a wonderful bus ride, one that I will never forget. Handcuffed and belly chained, with leg irons to boot, I arrived there in very early August 1982, spent one night inside the walls at Leavenworth, and then was sent to the prison camp because my prison sentence was so short.

While at Leavenworth camp, I got interested in the law library. I figured that no one could help me now except myself. If I wanted to get out of prison, I would have to do it myself, so I learned how to attack my sentence through a provision of law called a 2255, and filed my own section 2255 motion in the United States District Court at Tulsa a little before Halloween in 1982. At the same time I was working in the law library, I was also starting to have severe gastrointestinal problems.

As a result of my medical condition, I was transferred to the Comprehensive Health Services Unit at the Fort Worth Federal Correctional Institution two days before Thanksgiving, 1982. I arrived there in a state of shock, for the facility was coed. To my surprise, I found males and females together all over the place. I thought I had died and gone to heaven!

I also found a huge law library there, which was enlightening. At Leavenworth camp, all I had to work in was one small cramped room. The law library at Fort Worth was fantastic, filled to the brim with everything you could ask for, and lots of room to work. Seeing that I had a pending 2255 motion, I was allowed all the time I needed to study and prepare my defense. I had alleged that I was being held in violation of the Fifth Amendment of the United States Constitution, which guaranteed that a prisoner would receive effective assistance of counsel. This was predicated on the fact that my attorney had failed to file my appeal on the federal conviction for which I was currently serving my prison sentence.

In late January, I was given an evidentiary hearing concerning the 2255 motion back in Tulsa, which I handled Pro Se (myself). I was successful in convincing the Judge that I had been rendered "ineffective assistance of counsel", and that the constitutional protection of the Fifth Amendment applied to appeals, as well as trials. As a result, my appeal bond was reinstated immediately and I was released from custody. Once again, I was thrilled to be free, and savored my walk out of the courtroom.

But once again, my glee was short lived, for there was a Tulsa Police auto theft detective, Dewayne Smith, waiting for me with another warrant for my arrest. The arrest warrant he had in his hand was for various crimes that I had committed in the spring of 1981, all involving the same stolen Chevy van, and the Detective needed to arrest me before the statute of limitations prevented him from doing so. The crimes that I was being charged with happened so long ago that it took me almost a week to remember the van in question.

I made bail on the state auto theft charges early the next day, took a few days to visit my friends all over Tulsa, and eventually settled in living with my old President from the Tulsa Rogues chapter, Marvin Brix. While I was incarcerated, Rogue Marvin had become disillusioned with the Rogues and had also quit, taking half of the chapter with him. Some of the Rogues had been caught stealing my tools, stereo and business inventory while I was locked up, and Marvin and I were not too happy with certain Rogues. (All of my tools, stereo and business inventory were returned a few days later while Lee McArdle and Robert "Candy" McGee, with Marvin's blessing, pointed machine guns at Rogue Rickie "Smoker" Miles in Smoker's house.)

By early spring of 1983, there were two completely different factions of Rogues in Tulsa: the ex-members and the current members, most of whom didn't like each other. Marvin and I had stayed in touch, and he had taken care of some of my affairs while I was locked up, so it was a no-brainer when I moved into a small apartment that was attached to his house in early February 1983. Shortly after I moved in with Marvin, the Rogues sent two armed members over to Marvin's house to order me to remove my club tattoos, one of which was Smoker, the other Jerry Nelson.

At the exact moment that Smoker rode his bike up into the driveway, one of our New England guys, Earl Hastings, was holed up in Marvin's house; he was on the run for shooting a guy in Claremore. Earl was all over the television news, for the shooting had just happened the day before and the police everywhere were looking for him. Earl thought that the guy he shot was going to die, and Earl did not want to die in prison, so he had decided to shoot it out with the police when he was caught. To facilitate his plan, Earl carried with him a fully automatic M-16 machine gun and a bunch of clips, filled with ammunition for the machine gun. Knowing that Marvin and I were having serious problems with the Rogues Motorcycle Club, and that Smoker was probably arriving with the intention to do us bodily harm, Earl volunteered to kill both the Rogues standing there in the driveway before they could harm Marvin or me.

Fortunately, I talked Earl out of shooting Smoker and Jerry that day, although I had a hard time making up my mind for a brief minute. Leaving Earl behind the door to watch over me, I met Jerry and Smoker out in the driveway. When Jerry and Smoker told me they had been sent over to tell me to cover up my Rogues club tattoo, I told them both that it would never happen, and to go back and tell their National President I said so. (Months later, Smoker would be found to be in possession of a Mac-10 machine gun and silencer that he had been instructed to use to kill Marvin and me. Smoker failed to complete the assignment, and instead, served eight years in federal prison for that gun charge.) A few days later, the guy that Earl shot recovered from his wounds and was released from the hospital. I then was able to convince Earl into returning to New England, where he avoided capture for two more years. When he eventually was extradited back to Claremore to face the charges, Earl lucked out and got sentenced to just two years in the Oklahoma prison system.

By the time I was released from prison, my roadie Rogue Rocky had sadly been killed in an auto/pedestrian accident in Alaska, and the Rogues membership had shrunk from almost one hundred fifty in the summer of 1980, to less than fifty. Most all of my Outlaw friends in Florida had all been convicted of federal Racketeering charges also, while I was incarcerated, but I was still in contact with a few of them. One of them, an Outlaw from Jacksonville, Ronald "Arab" Watchmaker, just happened to be sent to a federal prison near Memphis.

In the spring of 1983, I started traveling to Memphis from Tulsa on a regular basis to visit Outlaw Arab in prison, and to see another friend there, Thomas "Tattoo Tommy" Williams, who had opened a tattoo shop in a Memphis suburb. Tattoo Tommy had been a tattoo artist in New Orleans for many years, primarily for the Outlaws. As a result of a bomb blast that leveled his tattoo shop in New Orleans, he had relocated to the Memphis area while I was incarcerated.

While at the prison one day visiting Outlaw Arab, he asked me to try to locate Bandido El Presidente Ronald "Ronnie" Hodge for him. I had no problem with this, for I had been in contact with Bandido Ronnie years before when I was a member of the Rogues, and Bandido Ronnie knew who I was. Outlaw Arab hoped to re-establish their friendship and open a direct line of communication; they had apparently been close friends for many years.

I contacted Bandido El Presidente Ronnie by phone through some old phone numbers I had for him, and relayed to him the messages from Outlaw Arab.

While I was talking to Bandido Ronnie about Outlaw Arab, I mentioned the fact that I was frequently going to Memphis to visit him. Bandido Ronnie asked if I was stopping in Little Rock to see the Bandidos there. I told him no, for I did not know anyone there, or have phone numbers for anyone in Little Rock. Bandido Ronnie then gave me a phone number for Bandido Gary "Wiggs" Wiggs, who was the President of the Little Rock chapter and suggested that I call him the next time I went through Little Rock.

Outlaw Arab, Ct Ed & Tattoo Tommy 1984

Shortly thereafter, on my next trip to Memphis, I contacted Bandido Wiggs from the I-40 rest stop on the west side of Little Rock. After he invited me to come and visit, I rode my bike over to see him. His house, at the time, was in the city of Little Rock and not far from where I was on the route I was traveling to Memphis. I only spent about an hour there, and spent the majority of it explaining to him how I came to be in possession of his phone number and name.

Bandido Wiggs was not very friendly and seemed to be extremely suspicious at the time (in the years ahead I would learn that he was not friendly with anyone and was, at first, always suspicious of everyone he met), so I was surprised when he told me to make sure I stopped into see him on my way back through Little Rock. I was happy to be back in touch with the Bandidos, for while I was locked up I had lost all contact with Bandido Buddy from Mobile, Alabama. So I made up my mind to stop in one more time before I gave up on the Bandidos.

A few days later, on my return trip from Memphis to Tulsa, I again stopped into see Wiggs. I had planned on stopping in for just a few minutes, basically because I told him that I would, and I expected another unfriendly reception. This time I was almost shocked, for I found just the opposite. Bandido Wiggs was just like Bandido Buddy had been in Mobile the very first time I had

met him; it was like we had know each other for years. He explained to me that
when I first called, he had had no way to contact Bandido Ronnie to verify who I
was and if, in fact, Ronnie had given me Wiggs' phone number. While I had been
in Memphis, Bandido Wiggs had talked to Bandido Ronnie and Bandido Buddy
about me; both had apparently told Wiggs that they both knew me and I was ok.

From that point on, Little Rock was like a home away from home. Every
trip I made to Memphis, I would stop there both on the way to Memphis, and on
the way back. Every time I stopped there, my visits got a little longer, and it
wasn't long before I started staying there overnight. On about my third or fourth
visit, Bandido Wiggs told me that it was time for me to meet a very special Little
Rock Bandido – Bandido Robert "Cowboy" Crain. Bandido Cowboy was the
chapter Sergeant-at-Arms; he immediately reminded me of Rogue Rocky, and I
wondered if the relationship I had had with Rogue Rocky would set the stage for
my relationship with Bandido Cowboy.

Bandido Cowboy and I hit it off immediately, and soon discovered that
we made an outstanding team. Bandido Cowboy possessed an impressive
knowledge of firearms, torture and violence. I had an successful history of both
motorcycle and auto theft, knew how to alter the serial numbers on those stolen
motor vehicles in a way that the original serial number could never be
distinguished, and had an extensive knowledge of criminal law. Between us, our
knowledge allowed us to pursue numerous business ventures, both legal and
illegal.

One of the most successful endeavors that we were ever involved in was
the purchase and sale of LSD. At the time, possession of LSD, although criminal,
was nowhere as serious a charge as it is now. Simple possession back then would
get you a slap on the wrist, and selling it would usually result in a small prison
sentence at the worst. The benefits of selling it then, in 1983 and 1984, far
outweighed the cost if we were caught. In addition, we could get ourselves, as
well as all of our friends, high for free.

In the summer of 1984, Bandido Cowboy decided that he wanted a new
Lincoln Towncar, but didn't want to pay for it. We secured a 1976 model,
wrecked, from a local salvage pool and removed the serial number plate. Bandido
Cowboy and I then went to Tulsa and spent a few nights "shopping" for a similar
1976 model Towncar at local apartment complexes. We finally settled on a real
nice maroon one. It only took me a few minutes to gain entry and start the car, and
another hour to change the serial numbers and license plates. Bandido Cowboy
drove that car all over the place, and finally sold it for a tidy profit, just after he
dropped me off at the federal prison in Texas, in January of 1985.

During 1983 and 1984, my relationship with the Little Rock Bandidos
grew and solidified. By the time the fall of 1984 arrived, I had met all of, and
socialized with most of the entire Little Rock chapter. I had also met a few
Bandidos from other chapters, and had kept in touch with Bandido Buddy. I was

beginning to think that starting a chapter of the Bandidos in Oklahoma was not impossible, and in fact quite possible. I even talked to Bandido Cowboy about moving to Oklahoma to help me get it going.

While I was out of prison, awaiting the results of my court cases during 1983 and 1984, I made the time to record another record album. This time, I used the name "Warren Winters" as my stage name, and titled the work "As I Was". I recorded some of the album at Long Branch Studios in Tulsa, and some of it at Grace Recording Studio, while on one of my trips back to Connecticut. The majority of the songs on the album were written about a preacher's daughter I had fallen in love with named Keitha Millis. Keitha had been my off and on live-in girlfriend back in 1979 and 1980, but had left me for greener pastures in the early spring of 1981. My buddy Lee "Lee" McArdle took a picture of me with his German Shepard dog at my feet, which we eventually used for the album cover.

After I had been released from federal prison in the spring of 1983, the federal prosecutors appealed my release to the 10th Circuit Court of Appeals in Denver. They argued that I did not need "effective assistance of counsel" during my appeal, and that I should be put back in prison immediately. I argued the appeal myself, once again as my own attorney, and was very satisfied when, in late December 1983, the Court upheld my release. The unanimous decision was reported in the law books at 724 F2d 109 (10th Cir. 1983); and mandated that all criminal defendants in the United States were guaranteed the "effective assistance of counsel" for their appeals.

As a direct result of that legal decision, in early 1984 my original appeal of the conviction that occurred in the fall of 1981 was finally perfected and filed by a court appointed attorney. That turned out to be an exercise in futility, for ten months later, the 10th Circuit Court of Appeals in Denver affirmed my federal conviction, and I found myself back in front of the same federal Judge that originally oversaw my trial. Just before Christmas, he ordered that I should be sent back to federal prison to resume serving the sentence I had been released from in January, 1983. In a small gesture of niceness, he allowed me to spend the holidays at home; I was scheduled to report back to the federal prison at Fort Worth on January 4, 1985.

On January 3, 1985, Bandido Cowboy and I drove to Fort Worth and spent the night at the home of a Fort Worth Bandido named Cory. All three of us went out and did a giant tour of all the strip joints in Fort Worth until closing time, got up early and had breakfast, then Cowboy gave me a ride to the federal prison. I remember Cowboy driving onto the grounds of the prison, realizing exactly where he was and hoping that no one searched the car because the trunk was filled with guns. I can only imagine what would have happened to us and what the authorities would have thought, if the car had been searched that day.

On January 4th, at about 9am, I started serving what was left of a four-year sentence that I had originally started serving in July of 1982. I had calculated that I would be released in about nine months, by the middle of October 1985, and I told Bandido Cowboy I would see him then. Unfortunately, my plans to meet him would be postponed for more than six years by the events that happened in the next few months.

It took me a few weeks to get used to prison life again, and by the end of January, I had resumed working in the prison law library. Working in the law library kept my mind occupied, and also allowed me to assist other inmates with their legal problems. Some of the inmates I helped for free, some I traded my legal services for favors (like an evening sandwich or personal laundry services) that they could provide, and for others that had complicated legal situations, I would have them send money orders that would be directly deposited in my prison commissary account.

The one good thing about the Fort Worth federal prison was the fact that it was still co-ed. There actually were females and males of all ages at the same prison, wandering around all over the yard together. We were allowed to eat together, work together, socialize on the common yard area and even hold hands, but we were not allowed to sleep together or have sex with each other. As I am sure you can imagine, there was nothing the prison officials could do to keep the prison population from having sex with each other.

Most everyone there had what we called a walkie, or more accurately, a member of the opposite sex that we walked with, held hands with, or socialized with, and in some cases, had sex with. Because the prison was basically a minimum-security facility, there were a lot of rats and snitches there (informants, inmates that had testified against other inmates). Since I was a biker, and one that was very close to the Bandidos, there were only a few females that I would allow to get close to me. Two of the women that I knew just happened to be from Texas (home of the Bandidos). Both women were serving time for contempt of court, so I knew beyond any doubt that they were not informants. They both knew each other well because they had known each other while still on the streets.

One was Elizabeth "Liz" Chagra (the wife of Jimmy Chagra) and the other was Jo Ann Harrelson, the mother of the famous actor Woody Harrelson. We all spent quite a bit of time together; an independent biker friend of mine always walked with Liz and I walked a lot with Jo Ann. Jo Ann, at 44, was still a good looking woman then, even though she was almost fifteen years older than me. Although we never had sex or anything close to it, I have to admit that the thought did cross my mind a time or two. Jo Ann and I always had plenty to talk about, and she helped me pass the time. When I left the Fort Worth prison in June of 1985 we lost touch. (Jo Ann remained in prison for many years; I read that she was finally released in 1997.)

At the same time that I was in Fort Worth federal prison, across the yard from me in the STAR Unit was the brother of former President Bill Clinton, Roger Clinton, who was serving a short sentence for his involvement in a cocaine

Most of the other Arkansas guys had pled to charges that resulted in sentences which would allow them to return home in just a few years, but one received a twenty-year sentence. All in all, the prosecution of the Bandidos in Arkansas was a lot less fruitful than the federal authorities had hoped for and predicted.

In February of 1986, I got permission from my parole officer to go to Mardi Gras for a much needed, long over due "vacation". I drove to Longview, Texas, and hooked up with a Bandido who lived there. I had originally met Frances "Lenny" Bonner in Little Rock. He was a wild man, always on the edge, living in the fast lane. We traveled together by car to Galveston Island; our mission was to meet with Bandido El Presidente Ronald "Ronnie" Hodge so I could possibly get permission to set up a new Bandidos chapter in Tulsa, Oklahoma. It was Mardi Gras time on the island, as it was everywhere along the gulf coast. Every house we went to, we seemed to be just one step behind Bandido Ronnie.

At one of the houses we went to on the island, I ran into a young Bandido, John "Big John" Lammons. Bandido Big John and I did a double take when we saw each other, for we had met in Muskogee, Oklahoma in 1980 when I was a member of the Rogues Motorcycle Club. John was, back in 1980, a hangaround for a Muskogee based motorcycle club called the Drifters. The Drifters wanted to become Rogues, and I was one of the Rogues that had been sent to Muskogee to check them out. I had thought at the time that John was the best of the bunch, better than all the Drifters put together, but he was too young (16) at the time to be a patch holder. Running back into Bandido John was a fluke, and turned out to be one of the highlights of my trip.

While we tried to catch up with Bandido El Presidente Ronnie, Bandido Lenny and I wasted some time watching the Mardi Gras festivities. Lenny had to leave for a little while, so he dumped me into a van with a few other Bandidos and asked them to watch me. It was the first time I met Bandido Trash, and within a few minutes he was all over me, asking me obnoxious questions. At one point I thought I was going to have to fight my way out of there when he accused me of being a cop, but then learned that he was only kidding with me to check my reaction.

Bandido Lenny and I finally caught up to El Presidente Ronnie a few days later at Bandido Trash's house on the north side of Houston. Bandido Ronnie and I sat in the living room by ourselves, although another Bandido Sargento de Armas (a Bandidos enforcer) sat by himself over in a corner of the room. I was never introduced to him and could not see him well. Years later, I would learn that he was Sargento De Armas Dave from Rapid City, South Dakota.

It was actually the first time Ronnie and I had ever met; but we both knew each other through previous phone conversations. I thought that the fact that all of the Oklahoma Outlaws being in prison would work to my benefit, but in the end it worked against me. Ronnie decided that a new chapter in Oklahoma would have to wait until the Oklahoma Outlaws got out of prison. His decision was based on the respect that he had for the Outlaws Club as a whole, and specifically the respect he had for Outlaw John "Little Wolf" Killip, who was still the President of the Oklahoma Outlaws even though he was incarcerated.

I learned that his relationship with Outlaw Little Wolf went back many years, and Bandido Ronnie did not want to sacrifice it by starting a chapter in Oklahoma behind Little Wolf's back. At the time I was surprised, but that turned out to be very typical of Ronnie, as I would learn in later years. Ronnie suggested that I move anywhere that I wanted and told me that he would make it possible for me to become a Bandido, but I told him I wanted to stay in Oklahoma. I also told him I would wait for permission to start a Bandidos chapter there, no matter how long it took. We agreed that Oklahoma would be an ideal place for Bandidos members coming home from prison to reside while they were on parole; that I could get them a place to live and a legal job. I would also do some legal investigation work for the club, and in return I would be welcome anywhere Bandidos were, almost as if I were a Bandido.

Bandido Lenny and I left that night and traveled back to Longview; from there I headed north into an awful snowstorm. I spent the night in a motel at Hugo, Oklahoma, and made it back to Tulsa early the next afternoon. I was sad that things did not work out, but knew that someday I would get the OK to start a new chapter of Bandidos in Oklahoma. I figured that El Presidente Ronnie would change his mind; obviously I did not know Ronnie as well as I thought I did, for he never did change it.

In April of 1986, my good friend and ex-Rogue Marvin Brix died unexpectedly in the middle of the day from a brain hemorrhage. I was blasted, for Marvin was one of my closest friends and confidants; he was going to be a Bandido with me whenever I got permission to start the chapter.

Tattoo Tommy & Ct Ed April 1986   Connecticut Ed April 1986

On Wednesday, April 23rd, with heavy hearts, we buried Marvin under a nice tree in a beautiful cemetery in south Tulsa. Tattoo Tommy came over from Memphis, and out of his six pallbearers, myself and four others were ex-Rogues.

By the summer of 1986, I had temporarily put the idea of starting a new chapter of Bandidos in Oklahoma behind me, and I focused all of my energy on making a legal living by buying, fixing and selling automotive rebuilders. I traveled back and forth to Little Rock on a regular basis, and developed a small business capable of paying my bills. I was easily showing visual means of support in the eyes of my parole officer.

That summer, my best friend Lee McArdle's house burned down one night, while he was out of town. It was not a big surprise to anyone, for it was a very old house. Fortunately, it was insured, and so presented an opportunity for us to rebuild it the way Lee wanted it to be built. Lee spent the summer building the new house, and I got my feet wet helping him when I could. It would set the stage for the road of life that I would choose to travel in the near future.

In the fall of 1986 I had the good fortune of running into Howard Camron at the Little Rock Salvage Pool wrecked car auction. Howard was a small guy with a dynamic personality, and he owned an auto salvage/rebuilder company located in northeast Oklahoma, called Oak Hill Auto Salvage. We hit it off immediately, and I soon started working for him. I would travel back and forth to Jay, Oklahoma, from Glenpool. I would work twelve or sixteen hour days for Howard, for a few days per week, to help supplement my income. Oak Hill was an amazing place out in the middle of nowhere. We would take a brand new Lincoln Towncar that had been badly wrecked, completely disassemble it, cut the car in half through the windshield posts, replace the frame, weld on a new rear clip (back half of the body), and repaint the car. From the time we towed the car from the salvage pool to the shop, to the time that the car was ready for sale, usually took about a week.

In January of 1987, I had a brand new 1987 Chrysler 5th Avenue in my inventory. It had been wrecked, but had been an easy repair; I had bought all the parts to fix it legally at a local Tulsa area salvage yard. I had a contact at the downtown Ford dealer who was interested in the car, so I went down there to try to sell it. My contact called auto theft and told them he wanted to know if the car was stolen. As soon as auto theft heard my name, they immediately dispatched two rookie detectives to investigate. The rookies decided that the car was stolen, which was too funny, because it was not.

I was adamant that the car was not stolen, and by the grace of God before they arrested me, they allowed me to place a phone call to their supervisor, Detective Dewayne Smith. This was the same Detective Smith who had arrested me in January of 1983. I told him the story of the car; told him that it was not stolen, and that I had a receipt for the parts I had bought from a local salvage yard.

He asked me to go get the receipt and meet him at the auto theft impound lot with the car, as soon as I could. I told him I could be there in an hour. I was mad because my sale of the car was now ruined.

When I arrived at the auto theft impound yard, it did not take long to figure out what had happened. I had bought a part for the car that had a serial number on it; a front frame rail. The car it had come off of had been stolen, recovered, and sold to the local salvage yard where I purchased a part off of it. Only problem was no one had ever taken the parts car off of the stolen car list; so it appeared as though I had changed the serial numbers on a stolen car. Detective Smith then told the two rookies that I had been one of the best auto theft guys he had ever seen; that I was an expert at changing serial numbers. Detective Smith asked me if I would show the two rookie detectives where all the hidden serial numbers were on the car, which I did. Doing so made the two rookie detectives look like the idiots they were, and I got a small amount of payback satisfaction in return.

By the spring of 1987, I had outgrown the small shop at the Glenpool house. My girlfriend Teresa and I moved back to the north side of Tulsa, into a house I lived in for a short time in 1981. I had bought the house in the spring of 1981, about six months before I went to prison. During the last six years, I had rented it out to pay the mortgage, but now the current renters were moving out, presenting a perfect opportunity for me to move up. The house was in a little town called Turley, sat on almost ¾ of an acre, and was only a few blocks from my best friend Lee McArdle. The home was twice as big as the one in Glenpool, but most importantly, the garage was almost three times as big as what I had been working out of. I had come full circle, and it felt good to be back home.

The summer of 1987 started off with a bang. In May, my friend and employer at Oak Hill Auto Salvage, Howard Camron, got into an altercation with his wife, Karen, in the middle of the night. Karen and Howard were separated, and Karen had already moved most of her belongings out of the house. While Howard was in bed sleeping with his new girlfriend Faye, Karen snuck up on the house and fired a shotgun through the wall of the bedroom, narrowly missing Howard and Faye. When Karen came into the bedroom and attempted to shoot again, Howard took the shotgun from her and struck her in the head. Karen left the property a little beat up, but on her own power she walked to a friend's car. A few days later Karen died, apparently from the injuries that she sustained in the fight at Howard's house.

The police immediately charged Howard with murder, but were not fortunate enough to catch him when they came with an arrest warrant. I spent a day or two moving cars off the property to get them ready to sell, to prevent the police from seizing the cars. There was a little known Oklahoma law in existence that enabled the police to seize all of one's belongings that could possibly be sold to facilitate a getaway; in this case it was Howard's entire auto salvage. I wanted to get enough cars off the property to sell, in order to raise enough money to get him out of jail on bail, and to pay his defense counsel.

Unfortunately, the second evening I was stopped on my way out of the town while driving one of Howard's car haulers loaded with cars, and surrounded by law enforcement authorities who thought that I was Howard. A friend who was with me and I got out of the truck to face about twenty guns. I laughed at them and asked them what they thought they were doing, but the police were not in a joking mood, and both of us were immediately handcuffed and thrown in the dirt. They soon realized that I was indeed not Howard, and released us, but they did impound the car hauler as well as the cars on it. I asked them how we were supposed to get back to either the salvage or to Tulsa, and the police told us to walk. We were left on the side of the road to fend for ourselves.

A few days later, Howard turned himself in and spent a few days in jail before I was able to get my Tulsa bondsman, David Hamilton, to make Howard's fifty thousand dollar bond. In a few days, we hired a prominent Tulsa attorney to represent him, and life slowly returned to normal at Oak Hill Auto Salvage.

For the rest of 1987, I continued working full time as a mechanic, and between Oak Hill Auto Salvage and my shop in Turley, I had my hands full. I mainly specialized in full size Ford pickups, Lincoln Towncars and of course, Harley Davidson motorcycles. I didn't get rich, but I was comfortable. I traveled whenever I could, and tried to visit with the Little Rock Bandidos as much as I dared, while on federal parole. By the early spring of 1987, Bandidos President Gary "Wiggs" Wiggs had been released from prison, and I was able to sell him a partially burned 1984 Harley Softail FXST. I had recently purchased it at one of the salvage pools I had been dealing with.

Ct Ed's Adopted Dad Warren In One Of The Rebuilders

When I could, I tried to let my adopted dad Warren drive some the cars for a while after I fixed them. Warren was kind of like my quality control, and while he did so for free, it enabled him to drive a new car for nothing. I supplemented the income from my auto and motorcycle rebuilding business by doing paralegal work for some of the attorneys I knew in Tulsa. I would do legal research in the evenings, for complicated post conviction appeal briefs, sometimes even ghost writing the entire briefs myself. When I was finished, the attorney I was working for would just sign his name on the appeal brief, and submit it to the appeals court in Oklahoma City, as if he had done it himself. I was also making money at the time doing people searches, using an information services company in Nashville to actually do the search for me, and selling the information that I received.

That Same Car Completely Rebuilt

In late summer of 1987, I traveled to Connecticut to record my third album titled "Crossbar Hotel", with my good friend from childhood, Kurt Newman and another good friend, Mario Figueroa. Kurt, Mario, Andrew "Andy" Rutman and I recorded the entire album at Grace Recording Studios in Hamden, Connecticut again, in one long weekend, but this time the sound was a lot more professional and I was very proud of the results.

While I was there, my childhood buddy Pete Hansen and I thought up an excellent birthday gift for his older brother Harry "Skip" Hansen. It was Skip's thirty-eighth birthday that July, and we both wanted to do something really special for him, something that he would never forget. So we went by Skip's house and borrowed his extension ladder. Pete and I were pleased that it never crossed Skip's mind to ask us what we needed the ladder for.

We took the ladder to Skip's stained glass business, which was up on the second floor. We made up a banner that said, "Celebrate Skip's 38th Birthday - Free Food and Beer up on the 2nd Floor", and then used Skip's ladder to climb up to the outside of the second floor window where we securely fastened the banner. The next day must have been great, for the second floor window overlooked a major intersection with a traffic light. All day long, people stopped into wish Skip a "Happy Birthday", hoping for free food and beer in the process. The beauty of the gift was that there was no way that Skip could remove it, because he was unable to leave work to go home to get the ladder!

On the way back from Connecticut, I stopped in Dayton; I wanted to visit my old friend Hambone, President of the Outlaws in Dayton, whom I had not seen since the early 80's when I had been a Rogue. I spent a day or two with Hambone, catching up since we had last seen each other. It would be the last time I would see him before he was murdered by a rival club a year later.

I started off 1988 by socializing at a New Years Eve party hosted by an ex-Rogue in Tulsa. It was a good party, and I thought at the time that 1988 looked promising. Most all of the Little Rock Bandidos were home or almost home from prison; my good friend Robert "Cowboy" Crain would go to a halfway house in a little more than a year. I was even thinking about marrying my longtime girlfriend Teresa and settling down. We had gotten used to living in my house in Turley, and my various businesses were producing more than enough income to sustain my frugal lifestyle.

I was still working at Oak Hill Auto Salvage with Howard, rebuilding cars and motorcycles at my shop, researching/writing legal briefs, and locating people. I had by now named my three businesses Header, Connecticut Bike Specialties and Paralegal Services. I was even planning on turning the legal corner; planning on filing income tax on my business like every other normal American. My parole officer was generally staying off of my back, and allowing me to travel for almost any occasion, as long as I linked the travel to some aspect of my business. I was able to take some of my extra money and started rebuilding my house. I poured additional concrete outside the shop for me to work on, and installed a hot tub inside my den. Before long, I had an excellent place to work, as well as a nice place to live.

In the early spring of 1988, Bandido Cowboy's girlfriend Sissy had broken up with him, and to assist Cowboy in facilitating the breakup, I advanced Sissy some money to move back to Texas. Sissy had promised to pay back the money as soon as she received her income tax refund, so when she called to say she had all the money, I figured I had better get it as soon as possible. I flew to Dallas on a Southwest Airlines flight and met her at the airport, spent about an hour there and flew right back to Tulsa. All I took with me was my business briefcase, where I placed the check that Sissy gave me, for the money she owed me. I even got advance permission from my federal parole officer to travel to Dallas and back.

When I landed at the Tulsa airport I got a big surprise, for as soon as I got off the airplane, two undercover police officers accosted me. They told me that they had gotten information that I was carrying drugs or drug money in my briefcase. I asked them if they had a search warrant, and they told me that they could easily get one. Being a guy with lots of legal experience, and considering the fact that I either was, or had been, working for a half dozen prominent Tulsa criminal defense attorneys, I told them that I wanted them to go get a warrant. I figured that I would sit there for an hour, and they would give up and let me go.

Although I had no drugs or drug money, and was totally legal, I was still quite recalcitrant; I hated the police and authority in general. The two police had rapidly turned into about a dozen, all undercover. They had been stationed all over the area of the airport that I arrived in, waiting just for me. I thought at the time that they must have been expecting a huge drug bust, and I wondered who had given them so much erroneous information. I also wondered what made the cops believe all the bad information they had received.

It was like I was in the middle of a Grade B movie, surrounded by police at the airport. It turned out that they wanted to take me downtown for questioning and to see if they could get a warrant to look inside my briefcase. I am sure that you can imagine the whole pack of us making our way through a busy airport, with me in the middle of all of these cops. What a circus show! When we finally got outside of the airport terminal, I decided it would be easier to just let them look at my briefcase, than go through all the crap and time necessary to get a warrant. Besides, I thought it would be fun to see the look on their faces when they opened the briefcase and found the cashier's check.

I told the main cop in charge that I had changed my mind, and that I did not have the time to waste hanging out with them. I let them look inside the briefcase, where all they found was a check made out to me. They asked to search me, and I let them. Of course, they found nothing at all, and were forced to let me go. It ended up being a colossal waste of time and taxpayer money, but at least I felt vindicated when I saw how disappointed the police were.

In April, Howard Camron fired his Tulsa attorneys and hired an eighty-two year old attorney from his hometown of Jay, to represent him at his upcoming manslaughter trial. Howard had become addicted to methamphetamine, and was convinced that the system in Delaware County (where he was to be tried) was completely controlled by the Masons. He told me that the Judge was a Mason, the Prosecuting attorney was a Mason, and so he hired a Mason to represent him. What a mistake that turned out to be. His Tulsa attorney, who was one of the best in the state of Oklahoma, had figured the case to be fairly easy to win; we all figured Howard would get off on self-defense.

When it came time for trial, Howard was so whacked out on the meth that he ended up stealing the gun that was the state's star piece of evidence, during a noon recess. It only took about thirty minutes for him to get caught, and for Howard to admit what he did. Howard's elderly attorney immediately stood up and told the jury what Howard had done, in a self-serving attempt to explain to the jury that he, the attorney, had nothing to do with Howard's behavior. The jury should have never been told about Howard's actions, and after Howard's attorney spent the rest of the trial dozing on and off, Howard was, of course, convicted. The jury recommended a prison sentence of thirty years, and the Judge rubber-stamped it the last week of May 1988.

I got a few of my friends, as well as a few of Howard's, and all together we worked to liquidate Howard's Oak Hill Auto Salvage. We sold everything, even had an auction at the end to sell what was left. We sold the house, all of the salvage cars, and some of the tools, and paid off every bill Howard owed. We were able to keep Howard's 1964 Chevelle SS, all of his mechanic's tools, and in the end, he had about $30,000 left. We packed all of his tools and personal belongings in an old school bus, and took it all to Missouri, where I left the bus, the 64' Chevelle SS and the money in the care of Howard's brother, Dwight.

At one point, I had to liquidate a Honda Goldwing that Howard had bought wrecked and already fixed; the only problem was that the buyer I had lined up lived in Tulsa, but the bike was in Jay. There was no way to haul it, so I was forced to ride it all the way back to Turley. I did real well, staying on a bunch of back roads, for I did not want anyone seeing me ride a Honda. Unfortunately, just as I pulled into my driveway, I noticed my best friend, Lee McArdle, waiting for me there. He was laughing his ass off. I was obviously busted, and it didn't take long before everyone in town knew that I had been riding a Honda. I wonder who had the audacity to tell on me…..

In the summer of 1988, I met a youngster from Germany by the name of Dieter Tenter. He was a very intelligent German, here in the United States to buy a load of used Harley Davidson motorcycles. Dieter had run into another friend of mine who lived in Kansas, also a buyer and seller of Harleys. Dieter was brought to Tulsa to see what was for sale that he thought he could resell in Germany, hopefully at a profit. I let Dieter stay with me for a day or two, along with another German friend of his. I treated Dieter as though he were family, just like I did with all of the bikers in my world. I made sure that no one took advantage of him, and in the end, we found a bike or two that he bought. It would be the beginning of a long relationship that continues to this day.

By now, the Bandidos were stopping by on a regular basis. I would usually see them before Sturgis in August, or just afterwards. If any of the Mississippi, Alabama or Louisiana Bandidos were traveling north and or west through Oklahoma, it was a good bet that they would be stopping by for a meal and a place to rest. In late summer, I even helped move Bandido Cowboy's old girlfriend Sissy to Tulsa, in spite of the fact I believed that she had tried to get me into trouble while I was in federal prison. I moved her only because Cowboy wanted me to, and I stayed as far away from her as I could.

I decided that year to marry my girlfriend Teresa on August 8, 1988. I wanted to get married on a day that I could easily remember, so I picked 8-8-88. I knew I could never forget that. Teresa and I had a very conventional biker wedding in the backyard of my home in Turley, and invited about seventy-five close friends and family to witness the ceremony. The motorcycles were all lined up in the backyard, and we used the bikes as the aisle to walk down. We had a great wedding reception afterwards, there in the house and yard, and Teresa and I ended up eating some LSD to cap off the night. By the time we woke up the next day, because of the LSD we had no idea who gave us what wedding presents. The actual marriage announcement was kind of unusual; you would have to see it to believe it, so here it is:

The Great Harley God in the sky
commands your presence at
the marriage of

Edward "Connecticut" Winterhalder
and
Teresa K. Williams

on Monday 8-8-88 at 8 p.m.

Ceremony and Reception at
6441 N. Madison

"Believe it or not"

The Wedding Announcement   *Ct Ed After The Wedding*

In the fall of 1988 I traveled back to Connecticut for the release of my "Crossbar Hotel" album. I had finished up the cover artwork over the summer, and thought that it would be a good idea to kick the album off in Connecticut. I wanted to be with all of the people who made Crossbar possible. At the same time, we got everyone together in Kurt Newman's cabin up in the woods, and held an impromptu jam session. I even talked my friend Chris Westerman from New Hampshire into coming down and playing keyboards, and another childhood buddy, Chucky Vanacore, into playing bass; it was a great night.

By the time Christmas rolled around, I was getting antsy. Bandido Cowboy was getting ready to be released from prison, and transfer to the halfway house in Little Rock. I had also accepted a contract to establish a state of the art collision center, Tulsa's first one stop shop for wrecked cars. Up until that time, if your vehicle was wrecked and you wanted it fixed, your auto would have to go to more than one shop, depending on exactly what repairs were needed. For example, it might have to go to a frame shop, a body/paint shop, an upholstery shop or a mechanic's shop; with our shop every aspect of the repairs was located under one roof. My title was General Manager; I was in charge of setting up the business and running it day to day. We were going to call the new facility "One Stop Collision Center", and planned to open it in January.

Christmas was excellent. I gave my friend Scott Hall a motorcycle helmet in a box. It was a special helmet that no biker would ever wear; looked like something from the 60's. It was red with two huge blue stripes, and white stars all over the blue stripes .It looked like something from Easy Rider. Scott should have known better, but he actually put it on and let me take a picture of him, showing off the hideous helmet with his head bent down. Being the nice guy that I was, a few weeks later I put that picture in a local magazine called the Picture Post; in

year I splurged and sent two dancers to dance for him and help him celebrate. No tricks this time, just two knockouts for him to reflect upon for a minute or two. By mid-May, the June issue of Supercycle Magazine had hit the newsstands, and Bandido Cowboy's girlfriend Marla, using the pseudonym "Kat" (after my Akita), had done a two-page spread on Warren Winters and my Crossbar Hotel record album. It was kickass, as you can see:

Welcome to the Crossbar Hotel

By Kat

Ya' know, I got this real good buddy o' mine who's kinda sorta shy when it comes to publicity. Can't quite figure him out. He shits and showers with the door open, but he don't talk much about himself. Well, personally, I kinda like the little guy, and I even kinda like his music, so I guess it's up to me to let ya'll know about him.

His name's Warren Winters. Funny, that's what he calls his band, too, which really isn't actually a band anymore, but it was a band that put together a pretty cool tent full of tunes that must of us can relate to. You know, us guys that been in prison. Us riding guys that been in prison. Us riding guys that got burned and been in prison. There's lots of us around, both in and out. You'll like this guy.

The album/tape's called the Crossbar Hotel. First came the music back in '67. Then came the bikes in '74. A '63 Pan with an 18-over springer, a bike he wouldn't dream of riding THESE days. Instead, Warren's hogging a brand-new '89 Softail. Once he discovered blockheads he said, it's a whole new world! Anyway, then came the screw-up, the jail cell and the concept for Crossbar back in '85, while Warren was in the federal prison in Fort Worth. Crossbar didn't get recorded until '87/'88, split between Connecticut and Oklahoma (big split, huh?) and slapped on the 'Shovster' label—just an idea after seeing a Shovel top end on a Sporty bottom.

Warren spent 2½ years in prison on a couple of bullshit raps and that's where most of the songs were written.

He describes his music as a '60s flavor rock and roll, with a side order of progressive country, washed down with some adult contemporary, but basically, rock and roll.

Songs came from his experience in prison and with the system, his feelings about the system and the people he met. It was a good way to get his feelings out and a way to pass the time. The album gave Warren a chance to express his antisocial values to whoever wanted to listen. He figures every scooter tramp in jail should be able to identify with the way the government fucked with them.

"Land of Freedom"...that's a song about our fathers, all of them who fought so brave, all the battles they fought for freedom, now being laid in the grave.

"Prove My Love"...Warren met a guy in the joint who had been in for 17-18 years (from Death Row to life). He was at a carnival with a little sweetie, and someone got in her face and made her cry, so he killed the sonuvabitch. Turns out he never saw her again, yet 17 years later he was still "doing the time" for that crime.

"We Know They Lied"...This powerful song is a statement about how from the time you're a little kid, the government just forces shit down your throat—how it's supposed to be, but not how it really is—with THEIR values and THEIR lies.

SuperCycle
70

Crossbar Hotel...The title track's about living with nothing to do, something that everyone on the inside gets used to doing.

The cover of the album is a reflection of what Warren wanted to see outside of his cell every day; himself and his bike at the time, an '81 Super Glide.

As for where he's coming from and what he believes in, Winters says, "I stand for freedom and if I can't be free, then life ain't gonna matter to me. The song 'Free' (a simple song made up of two guitars and a vocal track)...says it all regarding what I'm really like,

"Police! Freeze!"

'cause freedom is an illusion brought on by you and me."

Winters is still forging ahead, writing occasionally, and planning another album in four years or so. (He's not in any big hurry.)

Winters was on parole until '88 and is currently still under the watchful eyes of his probation officer. He's still the unreconstructed S.O.B. he was when he got busted, just older and wiser.

"Freedom" was a term he took for granted back before he did time. "I didn't know what it was until I lost it," he says. "That's something that will stick with me forever".

Unfortunately, getting airplay for a little unknown, independently produced album is a bitch. Ya' need connections, money, or some big-time asskissing. Warren doesn't care, the album was something to get off his chest. And if people like it, that's fine. If not, that's okay, too.

The album is dedicated to all scooter trash still locked up, those that have been and ones that will be. Unfortunately, tapes aren't

allowed in Federal penitentiaries so none of the inmates he knows will hear it until and unless they get out.

Well, lemme tell ya' somethin' here. I liked this here album since the first time I heard it. No matter who done it, or why, I just did. It grows on ya'. The tunes are catchy and the words ring true. Whether ya' been down or not, ya'll get into his music. He makes you understand how he feels, and you can feel for him. Prison's not an easy life, nor do many people understand it. But most who've been there will swear to a one-way-out ticket only and NOT go back.

As I said, Winters doesn't give a rusty fuck if you like his shit or not, but I do and I'm bigger than he is! So write out a check with four little circles on it, two on top of each other and two to the side (that's $8 bucks ya' dummies), and send it off to Shovster Records, Route 4, Box 530, Tahlequah, OK, 74464. You'll be more than glad you did. This is a top-notch, Grade-A worthwhile musical and spiritual investment. Would I lie ta' ya'?

SuperCycle
71

On June 15th of 1991, I finally finished my federal parole term. After being either in jail, on bond, or on parole for more than ten years, I was finally a free man. I felt like I had a brand new lease on life, and I could go anywhere I wanted to without asking permission from my federal parole officer. I could not believe that I had stayed out of trouble for so long.

Meanwhile, back in Little Rock, Bandido Robert "Cowboy" Crain was very much back in the swing of things, too much so, I was starting to think. He and Marla Garber had parted ways and he was now hooked up with a girl named Cheryl. Cheryl was from the streets and it didn't take long for Bandido Cowboy to be back into his old ways. I thought that Cheryl was dragging him backwards, but could not convince Cowboy that it was so. Her daddy was a bookmaker and minor league loanshark, but Bandido Cowboy was happy, so what the hell; I closed my eyes and hoped for the best.

When we finally opened Scarlett's late that summer, it was a huge success. Mike and I had the largest and nicest strip joint in Tulsa, and had more than fifty girls working there. After all the hard work for the last eight months, I decided that it would be time to go on another vacation; but this time it would be a quick one. I packed up the scooter and took off for Eureka Springs, Arkansas, and the Labor Day Rally at Lake Leatherwood. There I met up with all of the Arkansas Bandidos, and we had a blast. Bandido Cowboy and I ate some LSD, and ran around all night laughing and howling at the moon.

In November, I got into a big fight with Axle, my Akita. He kicked my ass and gave me almost one hundred stitches. I was bitten on both arms, between the shoulders and the elbows, and he tore me up on the outside as well as the underside of my arms. When the doctor finished stitching me up, I could not use either of my arms; I couldn't even wipe my ass.

In honor of my fight with Axle, my buddy Scott Hall made me a t-shirt that said on the back in big letters: DOG TRAINER, and on the front it said "Axle's Little Eddie". It seemed as though everyone thought it was funny except me. Like the saying "what goes around comes around"; Scott Hall had finally paid me back for the helmet joke ad I put in the Bargain Post.

For Christmas 1991, I asked a friend of mine in prison, a member of the Outlaws, Edd Lackey, to make me five leather plaques for some of my close friends who were Bandidos. I had one made for Bandido Cowboy, Bandido Jack-E, Bandido Trash, Bandido Tucker and Bandido Big John from Galveston. The plaques turned out excellent, they had the Fat Mexican logo in color with the respective bottom rockers of Arkansas, Louisiana, Texas, Texas and Texas.

I also took the liberty of having one more made with an Oklahoma bottom rocker, which Bandido Cowboy said he would keep for me until the Oklahoma Bandidos chapter became a reality. Bandido Cowboy's plaque had a little extra – it said "Charter Member Eleven Years", which was a testament to the eleven years that he had been a member.

Bandido Trash, in Houston, received one more gift from me, a pup from my two Akitas, Axle and Kat, which he ended up calling "Honey Dog". Honey Dog actually rode to Houston in a nice BMW car belonging to a Louisiana

Bandido named Rooster. On the way down to Houston, Rooster stopped into see some Bandidos in Longview, Texas, and forgot to let the dog out while he was visiting. Honey Dog thanked him by chewing up the interior of the car; she even chewed the armrests on the door panels off. Bandido Rooster was not very happy about it, but could not do anything to Honey Dog because he was afraid of making Bandido Trash mad. Honey Dog made it to Houston ok, and brought Bandido Trash many years of happiness.

Bandido Cowboy & Ct Ed With Bandidos Plaque December 1991

Marla Garber & Honey Dog September 1991

18

Waiting On The Bandidos
1992 To Spring 1994

I started out 1992 by taking off in mid-February for a vacation to the Gulf Shores area, and to deliver the Bandido plaque Christmas presents to Bandidos Jack-E in Baton Rouge, Big John in Galveston and Trash in Houston. For once, my wife Teresa came with me, which was very unusual. Teresa always said she wanted to go with me on my excursions, but when it came time to go, she always came up with an excuse to stay at home in Tulsa.

While in Baton Rouge, sitting around visiting with a few Bandidos, I made a life changing decision that I would no longer ingest methamphetamine. I had never been a methamphetamine addict, but to keep me awake and alert while traveling, it was not unusual for me to do small amounts for just a day or two. It would take me years to realize and appreciate what a great decision I had made.

As soon as we got home from Texas, Teresa returned to her job as a bartender at Scarlett's, and I returned to my routines. I was now acting as the booking agent and manager for the Judge Parker band, as well as running Paralegal Services, Connecticut Bike Specialties and Header. I had my hands full, and every phone call required me to change my hat – one minute I was talking about Harleys, the next some legal work, and a few minutes later I could be booking the band. It was exciting, to say the least.

In March, the Bandidos sent a National Vice Presidente to Tulsa to visit with me for a few days. His name was Lawrence "Larry" Borrego, and he was a member of the Nomads chapter, in addition to his duties of being a National officer. Bandido Larry and I spent a few days together, and a few nights watching the dancers at Scarlett's. I was hoping that Larry's presence would signify that the Bandidos were ready to do something in Tulsa, but my hopes were premature. I heard many years later that Larry had reported back to the Bandidos, that there was nothing or nobody in Oklahoma worth having.

Later that month, I let my dog Axle inside to hang out with me while Teresa was at work. I had by now gotten over my injuries from last fall, and had developed a healthy respect for Axle since our fight. Unfortunately, Axle had developed a more arrogant attitude since our last fight. He was amazing, for he would now even piss over my pee, if I took a leak in the yard. I should have known that we couldn't live on the same property together for long. Just before bedtime, I told Axle to go outside. He raised the middle finger of his paw to tell me that he now owned the house, as well as the yard and his doghouse. I went over to grab him by the collar and throw him outside, and the fight was on. It did not take long for me to figure out that I was in deep shit for the second time, especially after I tried to stick my hand in his mouth in hopes of breaking his jaw.

Whoever told me the "stick your hand in a dog's mouth to break its' jaw" story was full of crap, or he forgot to mention how to get your hand past all those teeth. I grabbed the stun gun off the table and tried to shock Axle; boy, that was an instant I won't forget. Up until that point he hadn't really got too excited, but when I shocked him with the stun gun, he kicked it into overdrive. I vividly recalled that he had really kicked my ass last fall, and if I didn't figure out something new, I would soon be getting lots of stitches again. So I asked Axle if he had ever met Mr. Gun, and then Axle said "no, bring it on". So I complied, but missed him on the first shot and blew a hole in my living room wall, which really pissed me off. The next two shots put an end to Axle's life, but he got the last laugh, for he shit, pissed and bled all over my fairly new living room carpet.

In April, Bandido Cowboy got married to his girlfriend Cheryl in Little Rock. My wife Teresa was the Maid of Honor and Bandido Wiggs was Cowboy's best man. The marriage was a big political event in our world locally, and attracted motorcycle club members, as well as independent bikers from all over Arkansas. I was even quite surprised to see a group of Mongols there from Tulsa. To my relief (and Cowboy's, I think), the marriage was over almost as fast as the ceremony, and by early May Bandido Cowboy was hanging out in Tulsa regularly with a local dancer, Suzanne, who worked at Scarlett's. It wasn't much longer after that, Cowboy and Cheryl got divorced.

Bandido Cowboy & Suzanne
May 1992

Bandido Big John & Girlfriend
February 1992

As soon as I got back from Cowboy's wedding, I replaced Axle with another male Akita pup that I called Thunder. Thunder had a much better disposition than Axle, and since I brought him home as a pup, I planned to learn from my past mistakes and raise Thunder a little differently than Axle had been raised. Thunder would eventually grow up to be a dynamite dog with a great personality; all snow white with black face mask.

In May, for the Memorial Day weekend, I rode down to Mississippi for the annual Gulfport Blowout. There was always a large contingent of Bandidos there, as well as one of the better professional Harley drag races in the country. There were a few members of the Bandidos participating in the drag races, and by sheer coincidence, I got a chance to see the band I managed, Judge Parker, actually play the Crazy Horse Saloon in Biloxi while I was there.

Over the summer of 1992, Bandido Cowboy moved to Tulsa, not far from where I lived. He moved into a little one-bedroom house with Suzanne, and started on the laborious process of convincing his Arkansas federal parole officer that he should be allowed to transfer jurisdictions. Shortly thereafter, to complicate things, another Bandido from Louisiana also moved to Tulsa; his name was Joseph George, and we called him Joe-E. Bandido Joe-E had been convicted in Louisiana of an auto theft charge, and as a condition of his probation, he was told to move out of Louisiana. Tulsa was becoming what we all thought was a great place for Bandidos to serve out their parole or probation. Bandido Cowboy eventually convinced his parole officer to let him transfer to Tulsa, and Joe-E and Cowboy both secured legal employment. Once again, I was starting to think that a Bandidos chapter in Oklahoma was within reach.

In August, on their way to Sturgis, some of the Louisiana Bandidos stopped by Tulsa for a night of rest and some food. Bandido Joe-E, Bandido Cowboy and I were happy to see Bandido Dane, Bandido Osco, Bandido Billy and Bandido Dave, all from the Baton Rouge chapter. Less than two weeks later, on his way home from Sturgis, Bandido Rooster stopped in for a few days, and while here, asked if there was any work around. He was broke from the ride up north to Sturgis and back, so I got him set up with a business associate's construction crew as a laborer.

Bandidos Dane, Joe-E, Billy, Osco,
Cowboy & Dave With Ct Ed August 1992

The first day on the job, before noon, the business associate called to tell me that Bandido Rooster was asleep in a closet in the building that they were working in. Rooster had locked the closet door, figuring that no one would miss him, and no one would be able to find him. My associate, of course, fired him on the spot, but agreed with me to let him continue sleeping. When the construction crew left to go home that night, Bandido Rooster was still sleeping away in the closet. Sometime in the middle of the night Rooster woke up and came back to my house, sniveling that the construction crew had left him sleeping in a closet. He seemed surprised to find out that he had been fired for sleeping on the job before noon, his first day on the job.

In September I made a deal for a brand new bike from a Harley dealer friend in Pennsylvania, to purchase a leftover 1992 FXR convertible. It was blue and had a set of detachable saddlebags, as well as a detachable windshield. I flew into Baltimore from Tulsa; then took a train to Pennsylvania where another old friend, Sam Ceruli, met me at the station. After picking up my bike, I cruised down I-81 to eastern Tennessee, and then headed west on I-40 to the mountains of Arkansas, where I met my wife Teresa and some of the Tulsa crew up in the mountains near Eureka Springs.

In early December, Teresa announced that she was pregnant. Our child would be born in very late July or very early August of 1993. On December 13, 1992, the annual Toys For Tots parade in Tulsa was held, but this year, it was a snowy, rainy type of day; a horrible day for a Toy Run. It was too cold for me to go, the cold now seemed to bother me a lot (maybe I have thin blood?), but Bandido Cowboy and his girlfriend Suzanne decided to try and tough it out. They made the ride safely with no problems, but arrived home covered with ice and snow, freezing.

Once again, I welcomed in the New Year with the Judge Parker band in Fort Smith, Arkansas. Larry and Arthur Pearson put on another dazzling show, and I let my guard down and actually got on stage with them to sing some harmonies on a Judge Parker favorite called "My Missouri". Less than forty-five days later, during a blinding snow thunderstorm, a bolt of lightening apparently hit my house while Teresa, Thunder, Kat and I were in the back shop working.

The lightening had apparently caused a power surge in the house electrical wiring, and somehow started a fire in my back den, either in or near some old stereo equipment or the old console TV. Teresa and I had no idea that a fire had started in the house, since we were in the back shop with the stereo going. We think the fire was burning for about fifteen minutes before it came to our attention. The first sign that something was wrong was when we heard a giant crashing sound of glass breaking, about the same time the dogs started barking.

I initially thought that somebody was breaking into the house, that maybe they had broke the back sliding glass door to gain entry. When I came flying out of the garage, I could not see anything for there was so much smoke. I could see some flames coming out of the space where the sliding glass door had been an hour earlier. The hot tub was even on fire! I got a hose out, hooked it up and desperately tried to put out the fire, but it was way more than I could handle. After only a few minutes, the fire trucks showed up, and fifteen minutes later the fire was out.

The back den/kitchen area and rear of the garage were a total loss; the fire had even burned a little hole through the roof. The rest of the house had sustained massive smoke and water damage, but fortunately the fireman had gathered a bunch of the living room furnishings under a waterproof tarp before they hosed down the room. It took the insurance adjuster and me two days to go through all of the stuff that was no good. The few things that we saved were sent to a special facility where the smoke smell was removed from each item.

The insurance adjuster told me that it would take a construction crew a month to get started repairing the house, but I knew that my friends, business associates and I could fix it much faster. The adjuster allowed me to rebuild the house myself, and within ten days of the fire, I was able to get the demolition started. We cut the house in half and bulldozed the burnt half to the ground. We removed the roof from the other half because of the smoke damage. In early March we poured a new concrete slab on the bulldozed end of the house, and by the end of the month we had it all closed in from the weather. By the middle of May, the outside was painted, the interior of the house was finished and we were able to move back in. All we lacked were some finishing touches to the exterior landscaping.

The whole time we were working on the house, Teresa and I lived in the back shop. I had converted the work area into a bedroom/office. The shop had heat, but no running water. My adopted mom was living in a house just across the street, so we used her place to eat and shower. To complicate our situation, we had to keep the dogs in the shop with us, and Kat chose that time to have another litter of puppies. Between Teresa being pregnant, all of the construction work going on and the whining of the new puppies, it was a wonder I got any sleep at all.

The Burned Hot Tub February 1993

Starting To Rebuild March 1993

Rebuilding March 1993

Just About Done April 1993

I finished the house project just in time to take a motorcycle vacation to Mississippi again. It was Memorial Day weekend, and time for the Gulfport Blowout Rally had rolled around again. This time I was planning on meeting my old tattoo artist buddy from Memphis there, Tattoo Tommy. We had not seen each other in a few years, and I eagerly anticipated our meeting. Tommy and I had spent a lot of time together when I was visiting Memphis on a regular basis back in 1983 and 1984. We had originally met when I was traveling back and forth between Florida and Oklahoma back in 1979. The Gulfport Blowout Rally was a blast, and as always, the Bandidos had a camp there and a racing team participating in the actual drag races.

Bandidos Racing Team May 1993 Tattoo Tommy & Girlfriend May 1993

In June, my buddy Benny Durrett from Checotah was sentenced to federal prison for altering vehicle identification numbers. I had met Benny back in 1987 when I worked for Howard Camron at the Oak Hill auto salvage back in 1988. Benny had a heart of gold, and was an encyclopedia of knowledge when it came to old cars and Chevy pickups. He owned the largest Chevy pickup salvage in the state of Oklahoma, and had sold me Ford parts many times over the years for next to nothing when I was in a jamb. He always told me "that those Ford parts were nothing but junk anyway", which always made us laugh. Benny had no love for Fords; he was and will be a Chevy man until the day he dies.

A prominent local attorney, who also was a state senator, had represented Benny while he was fighting the charges. His "brilliant" attorney had told him right up to the last day that he would never spend a day in prison; while I had told Benny all along that he would probably get between fourteen and eighteen months in prison. In the end, Benny finally knew who was right when he was sentenced to serve sixteen months in a federal prison. (In 2004 his attorney Gene Stipe would be convicted of federal criminal charges and disbarred.) I promised to stay in touch with Benny, because that was what friends were for. To be there when things got tough. And besides, I knew that all his other "friends" would forget all about him after he went off to prison, which is exactly what they did.

In July, I started a quick house-building project for one of my neighbors. My neighbor had watched me rebuild my own house, and had decided that he wanted me to build his new house. I told him that I could build it in about thirty days and it would be about forty days before he could actually move in. We started the house on July 6th, and he moved in the second week of August. I was actually getting the drywall ready for paint when Teresa delivered our daughter, Taylor Leigh Winterhalder, on July 30th, 1993.

At the same time I was finishing up the house project, and trying to get used to having a baby in the house, most all of the Louisiana, Arkansas, Alabama, Mississippi and eastern Texas Bandidos converged on my house while on their way to Sturgis. It was the first week of August, and it just happened to be raining. So instead of getting a break between the small packs as I usually did, a whole bunch of Bandidos wound up piling up at the house while waiting out the rain.

Bandidos Murray & Dane August 1993
While CT Ed Works On A Rebuilder

Part of the Bandidos Stuck At My House Before
Sturgis Waiting Out The Rain August 1993

Bandido Cowboy, Bandido Joe-E and I slept and fed almost forty Bandidos in my new house, while Teresa stayed in our bedroom nursing Taylor. When the pack finally pulled out early one evening, we breathed a sigh of relief. It had been no easy task to handle the new house construction, one of the wrecked trucks I was rebuilding, my wife, my baby and the unusual amount of Bandidos all at once.

Three days after the pack left, I took off for Sturgis like a bat out of hell. I actually left on the day of my 5th wedding anniversary, but at the time Teresa had her hands full taking care of Taylor, so she did not seem to care. I rode up there with a buddy and his wife; we rode first to Denver, then north through southeast Wyoming and northeast to Sturgis. Fortunately I had been able to reserve a cheap room in an old motel in downtown Rapid City, close to the Bandidos clubhouse. I spent a few days there, and got a chance to hang out with some of the Bandidos Racing Team at the drag strip during a severe hailstorm.

Bandidos Crash & Little Red August 1993

At the drag races, I also got to spend some time with an old friend of mine from Florida. His name was Beau and he was a retired Outlaw from Joliet, Illinois. We had known each other since 1980, when Beau had come and stayed with me at my home in Tulsa when I was a member of the Rogues Motorcycle Club. Back then, Outlaw Beau had gifted me a beautiful hand carved club made from cedar. It was really a walking stick, but I kept it strapped to the handlebars of my bike for many years, in case I needed to use it as a weapon.

Retired Outlaw Beau & His Girlfriend August 1993

It would be the last time I ever saw Beau; he was killed in a motorcycle wreck a few months later. A drunk driver had driven the wrong way on a one-way street, and Beau had been following another car until the last second, when it swerved to avoid the drunk. Beau never saw it coming, and was killed instantly. His girlfriend survived the collision, but spent many months in the hospital and eventually lost her leg.

In the fall of '93, I came up with a great idea to start manufacturing Harley rolling chassis kits. I had realized that it was getting difficult to sell some of my rebuilders, and I was beginning to think that the automotive rebuilding industry was dying. I contacted an Ohio frame manufacturer, and contracted with him to provide me with Dyna and Softail style frames. These frames included a seventeen-digit serial number, which was very similar to the serial number used by Harley Davidson. I took the paperwork to the local tag agency (the motor vehicle department here in Oklahoma), where I was able to get titles that said "Harley Davidson" where the manufacturer's name was supposed to go. Where you would normally see the model, it said "Fatboy" or "Heritage" or "Superglide". If you did not note the minor difference in the serial number, you would think you were looking at a real Harley title.

I was ecstatic for I had found a pot of gold, and it didn't take long for me to capitalize on it. I started making rolling chassis kits as fast as I could sell them, and as fast as my finances would allow me to build them. Besides the frame and engine cases, which came from Sputhe, I used nothing but factory Harley parts. I even provided the purchaser with a factory Harley transmission case. I sold about one hundred of those rolling chassis kits before the party was over. In the end, Harley notified the state of Oklahoma that Oklahoma could not issue a title that noted Harley Davidson as the manufacturer, unless the serial number started with 1HD1; my serial number started with 1SD1. In the USA, the first four digits of a serial number always designate the manufacturer of the motor vehicle.

I took off just after Christmas 1993 to deliver some of the frame kits to Michigan and New England, and couldn't have picked a worse time to travel. It had been a snowy winter, and Michigan had gotten its share by the time I got there. From Michigan, I thought I would be smart and cut across Canada to save myself some time. What a mistake that decision was! When I crossed the border, Canadian customs searched my car and found some legal Harley parts and one of my frame kits in the trunk. They made me declare it and post a bond on it to prevent me from selling it while I traveled across Canada to Buffalo. The bond cost me more than $100, and severely cut into the financial resources I had with me for the trip. I saved time crossing Canada ok, but it sure cost me a whole lot of money. In the end, I should have stayed in the United States and taken the long way around the lake.

In Buffalo the snow was worse than Michigan; the piles were the largest I had ever seen. I couldn't figure out how anyone lived up there. I spent two days there visiting the local Outlaws chapter, showing one of them how to research courthouse records. From there I traveled to Boston to attend a swap meet. I had planned on meeting another retired Outlaw from Florida, who was living in Maine, at the swap meet. I also hoped to develop a market for my frame kits in New England. The swap meet was held on the last weekend in January 1994 and while there, I met two guys who were soon to launch a new chapter of the Outlaws Motorcycle Club in Boston. It would be the Outlaws' first chapter in New England, and a point of major contention with the Hells Angels, who had dominated the New England scenery for many decades.

Retired Outlaw Stash, Ct Ed, Future Outlaws Tommy & Rusty Massachusetts January 1994

From Boston, I went north into New Hampshire, where I hung out with Chris Westerman in his new home up in the woods just outside of Laconia. I had originally met Chris at the Grace Recording Studio in Connecticut when I was recording the Crossbar Hotel album back in 1988. Chris had a new wife now, and had built a fantastic recording studio in his home. The home was a spiritual place that sat high up on a snowy hill, very peaceful for me there, and I didn't want to leave. Before heading south, I went west to Vermont and stopped in for a day with another old friend of mine, Stanley Lynde, and his family. New England in the winter was fun to visit, but by now I sure was missing sunny, warm Oklahoma.

From Vermont, I spent a few days in Connecticut visiting my childhood buddy Harry "Skip" Hansen. For years, I had been trying to convince Skip to move to Oklahoma. Skip was a few years older than me, and I had known him since I was eleven. I hung out with Skip's younger brother Pete while Skip was off fighting the war in Vietnam. Skip had been a biker in Connecticut for many years, and was riding with the Vietnam Veterans Motorcycle Club there. It seemed as though my timing was right, for finally Skip broke with tradition and promised me that in the near future, he would at least come to Tulsa for a visit.

From there, it was south into New Jersey to visit another buddy by the name of Frankie "Harmless" Pattica. Harmless had been another Florida Outlaw, but he had been extremely fortunate, for he was not one of the many that were arrested in the RICO roundup by the federal authorities in 1981. Harmless had instead retired and headed back to where he had grown up in central New Jersey. Before he became an Outlaw, he had been a member of the Breed Motorcycle Club; now he was a member of the Breed again. I spent a few days with him, catching up on old times and meeting a bunch of his Breed brothers.

Skip Shoveling Snow   *Breed Harmless & Ct Ed*
Connecticut February 1994   *New Jersey February 1994*

I spent the last few days of my trip visiting Mario Figueroa in New Jersey, who had been a roommate of mine in Oklahoma back in 1984 and played bass on my Crossbar Hotel album. From Mario's house I traveled southwest to visit Fuzz Terreson and his guys at Terreson Harley Davidson in Shillington, PA. Fuzz had sold me my blue 92 FXR that I was still riding. It was one hell of a trip, and I had a blast seeing all my old friends.

But by now, I was homesick for Oklahoma, and couldn't wait to get back to warmer temperatures and no snow. I arrived home just in time for the worst snowfall that Oklahoma had seen in fifty years – eleven inches in one day. The city was completely snowed in, paralyzed for days until the snow melted. I didn't much care though, for it was good to be back home.

19

Waiting On The Bandidos
Spring 1994 To Fall 1995

By early spring, my daughter Taylor was eight months old, and being a dad was starting to sink in. One day while I was filling in some genealogy papers for her, I started wondering how to fill them in, and whether I needed to give her lineage as biological or adopted for my side of the family. I decided that it needed to be biological, but for me to do that I would have to find out who my parents were, for I had been adopted at birth in Hartford, Connecticut, way back in 1955.

I had started thinking about this in the last two years, and had started working on it a little. While on my trip last month, while I was passing through Hartford, I stopped and did some research at the local library and court records office. As a result, I discovered that there are two different types of birth certificates in Connecticut. One is a short form and the other is a long form. On the long form is the name of the doctor that delivered you. While they change a bunch of information when you are adopted, they do not change the name of the doctor nor the time/date when you were born. A few weeks after I got back to Tulsa, my long form birth certificate arrived in the mail. I had ordered it while I was in Hartford at the local vital records office. I had never seen it before, and to my pleasant surprise, there at the bottom of the certificate, was the name of the doctor who had delivered me.

I had already figured out that my parents divorced shortly after I was born, and that the divorce had actually been filed right before I was born. While in Connecticut, I had copied down all of the names involved in about twenty divorce files that I thought might be my parents. When I got the name of the doctor, I was extremely fortunate, for he had an unusual name. I ran his name through the resources I had for locating people, and came up with just a few hits. Within an hour, I had found the doctor. I was shocked to find that he was still alive. He told me that all of his birth logs were in the attic, and if I could give him a day or two, he could locate my birth record. Two days later he called me back, and told me that my biological Mom's name was Jackie.

I cross checked my records and found the divorce file names I had already copied down, and found out my Dad's name, Forrest, as well as both names of my maternal grandparents. Once again, I utilized my resources for locating people, and quickly located my maternal grandmother in Massachusetts. The next day I contacted the daughter of a friend who worked at a phone company in New England, who checked the phone records for my grandmother's phone. There were only a few long distance phone calls on my grandmother's phone bill, and almost all of them were to one number in Austin, Texas. I figured that the Texas phone number was to my biological mom, and I was correct. My biological mom was surprised to hear from me, and told me that I had three half sisters (who lived in Texas) and a half brother (who lived in Boston, Massachusetts).

My biological dad was a little harder to find. In spite of the fact that he also had an unusual name, he normally did not stay in one place for very long. But I finally managed to catch up to him, and he was very happy to hear from me. I was quite surprised to learn that he had been a musician, that he was in the construction business, and that I had another half sister who lived in Michigan. As a result of locating my long lost biological family, I spent the spring and early part of the summer getting acquainted with all of them.

Ct Ed & His Daughter Taylor
March 1994

Ct Ed's Biological Dad Forrest
& His Wife Fall 1993

By now, my Header rebuilders (wrecked cars & trucks) and Paralegal Services (people locating) businesses were almost non-existent, but Connecticut Bike Specialties was booming, mainly due to the sale of my Harley rolling chassis kits. I was producing them in my shop ten at a time. It was almost a fulltime job in itself, but at least I was home to watch Taylor, who sometimes hung out with me in the shop while I built the kits.

Taylor In Ct Ed's Shop May 1994

In April, Dieter Tenter came to visit again from Germany, and bought another load of Harleys. In May, Benny Durrett got out of federal prison and was transferred to a halfway house about a mile from me. To keep Benny from being forced to get a menial labor job while he was at the halfway house, I immediately hired him to work around my place. He basically hung out with me for four months, doing odds and ends to pass the time.

For Memorial Day weekend, my wife Teresa and I went to Austin to meet my biological mom and my half brother and half sisters. It was an interesting weekend, and for the first time ever, we were all together in one place. My mom was an antique book dealer, two of my sisters were homemakers, one sister was working as a production assistant in Austin on movie projects, and my brother was a research laboratory manager. Teresa was all freaked out about leaving our daughter Taylor for the first time back in Tulsa. I should have paid more attention, for it was a sign of what was to come.

Just after the Memorial day weekend, Louisiana Bandido Jack "Jack-E" Tate stopped in Tulsa to stay for a while. He was functioning under an assumed name, traveling with his girlfriend Vicki. Jack-E was on the run from the feds over a minor parole violation, but he wanted to make absolutely sure that it was only a minor parole violation. He had decided to lay low for five years, and let the statute of limitations expire on any other charges the feds might be considering, then turn himself in for the parole violation. He had a large RV trailer that he pulled behind his truck, and was able to travel, to a degree, when he wanted. For about eighteen months while he was on the run, he called Tulsa home.

I had met Bandido Jack-E years before in Pascagoula, Mississippi. A mutual friend of ours, Bandido James "Goldie" Cutrer, had introduced us on one of my many trips to the Gulf coast. Bandido Goldie had called me one day and asked me to stop in and visit him as soon as I could arrange it. Goldie told me that he had a Bandido brother in trouble that needed my assistance. The friend turned out to be Bandido Jack-E, and Jack-E wanted to pick my brain about his legal options. Bandido Jack-E and I spent a day or two together, and from that day on we deliberately sought each other out whenever the opportunity presented itself, whenever we were in the same geographical location.

In the summer of 1994, I started thinking again that maybe the time had come to get the Oklahoma Bandidos chapter kicked off. We had almost enough going in Tulsa to get it started, if I could just get permission from the Bandidos National chapter. Even though Bandido Cowboy and Bandido Joe-E were on parole, and Bandido Jack-E was on the run, they were all living close to me, and were available and willing to supervise us. My best friend Lee McArdle had told me that he was interested, and so was a friend of mine from Michigan, John Fisher. All I really needed was to get my childhood buddy from Connecticut, Harry "Skip" Hansen, to move to Tulsa and I would have my "dream team" ready to go.

Since I had originally seen Bandido El Presidente Ronald "Ronnie" Hodges and asked to put a chapter in Oklahoma back in 1986, I had asked him again a few more times. I was persistent, knowing that it was my destiny to become an Oklahoma Bandido. Every time I inquired about starting a new chapter in Oklahoma, I was told the same story: we will talk about it when the Oklahoma Outlaws get out of prison. By this time, Bandido Ronnie had gone to federal prison for participating in a murder conspiracy, and El Vice Presidente James "Sprocket" Lang had taken his place. Bandido Sprocket also nixed the start of the Oklahoma Bandidos when asked for me by an Arkansas Bandido, while at a party in Lubbock, Texas. Now, Bandido Ronnie was out of prison and poised to take over the club again, or so I hoped. I thought that if Bandido Ronnie did take over again, my chances would be much better, for I had some history with Ronnie.

By now, Bandido Cowboy had broken up with his girlfriend Suzanne. Now he was in love again, and fixing to get married. This one's name was Shawnda, and in July of 1994, they got married at a ranch just outside of Tulsa. The ranch was actually the home of Suzanne's parents, for Shawnda just happened to be a friend of Suzanne's. Shawnda was also a dancer, and once again I didn't think that this marriage would last for long. And I was getting concerned; Bandido Cowboy seemed to be getting out there again. He was using methamphetamine again, and I wondered at the time how long it was going to be before he got busted again. I also wondered about how much time he would do in prison when he got caught.

In mid-August, my next-door neighbor James Perry, who also had a Harley, was at work one evening at a steel distribution plant. Somehow one of his co-workers stuck a forklift in the mud outside the plant, and James offered to help him get it out. James was a young kid at the time, probably about twenty-two. It was his first real job, and in spite of the fact that he worked from 3pm to 11pm, he loved it. When he went to get a chain to pull the forklift out, his foreman told him to get one out of the trashcan. Earlier in the day someone had ruined the chain that was in the trash can by putting too much strain on it, causing it to stretch. James had no experience with this kind of situation, and not knowing any better, James took the chain and went to help his co-worker.

James and his co-worker hooked the stretched, dangerous chain to the forklift, and the other end to a shop pickup. James got in the pickup and started to pull the forklift out of the mud. The chain broke while under tension, and it snapped back through the rear window of the truck, hitting James right in the face. Almost every bone on one side of his face was broken, and he lost his hearing and sense of feeling on that one side as well. It took months before he could talk again, and he never recovered fully from the accident. Years later, he would collect a small workman's comp settlement, but it would pale in relation to the significance of his pain and suffering, as well as his permanent injuries.

waited there at the house with his dad. Just as I heard him shift into second gear, all of a sudden I heard silence. I quickly calculated that he had gotten to a serious bend in the road, and I guessed that he probably missed the curve and crashed into the woods. His dad and I jumped into a truck and drove as fast as we could to the curve in the road, where we found my brother-in-law Steven about ten feet off the road in the woods.

Steven was visibly shaken, and extremely embarrassed. He had multiple abrasions and an injured arm, but fortunately, no broken bones. The bike was surprisingly not hurt too badly; Steven's pride was hurt more than the bike. It took an hour, but I was able to make a few minor repairs to the bike, making it road worthy, and when I got home a few days later, the custom painter was able to touch up the paint job without too much trouble. Now Steven had to go through with the wedding, and it looked like he had been beat up. His arm was in a sling, and his head was covered in road rash. All of the wedding pictures clearly show Steven injured, and some show him obviously in pain. Their honeymoon was spent in Hawaii, and I was told the salt water caused Steven massive pain, so he was forced to watch his new bride go swimming every day without him. In hindsight, I guess I gave my sister and brother-in-law a wedding present that they would never forget!

Steven & April At Their Reception June 1995

On June 30, 1995, Bandido Cowboy's ex-girlfriend, my good friend and roving editor for Supercycle magazine, Marla Garber, was killed while riding her motorcycle in, of all places, Connecticut. The crash occurred along a gradual curve on Route 6 in Andover, when somehow or other, Marla crossed the centerline of the highway and hit a tractor-trailer head on; fortunately she was killed instantly. I was saddened to hear of her death, for she had been a frequent visitor to my home, and had written about my home, my wife and me, both in Easyriders Magazine and Supercycle Magazine.

I packed the bike into the truck and hit the road in late July. I needed some breathing room, for my wife Teresa was driving me nuts. I still had not figured out that she was addicted to methamphetamine, so her behavior, to me, bordered on the insane. We planned for her to join me somewhere on the road, hopefully in about a week, before I got to New England. My first stop on the trip was Dalton, Georgia, and the West Yellow Knife Trading Post, which was a business that handled insurance loss liquidations.

At West Yellow Knife there was a big music equipment loss that had just arrived, and I had been given an opportunity to buy whatever I wanted from it before anyone else. I picked up Larry & Arthur Pearson from the Judge Parker band on my way through Fort Smith, and the three of us got to go music equipment shopping in a ten acre warehouse for the better part of a day. From Dalton, we all went back to Nashville, where I got to see Judge Parker do a live show.

After parting with Larry & Arthur, I drove east through Tennessee and then north through Virginia into Pennsylvania, where I stopped to see Fuzz and Giant at the Harley dealership, and Sam Ceruli in Shillington. From there, I stopped off in New Jersey to see Tommy "Rookie" Sands from the Breed Motorcycle Club and Mario Figueroa, my ex-roommate who had also played bass on my Crossbar album. When I left Mario's house, I went straight up the coast all the way to Maine, where I spent a few days with Randall "Stash" Perkins and his family. Stash was a retired Outlaw from Jacksonville, whom I had not seen since my trip to Buffalo and Boston a few years before.

From Stash's house, I went west through Vermont to New Hampshire, where I stayed with Chris Westerman again at his house up in the mountains. Chris was my musician buddy who had a recording studio in his basement. I always loved that place and the tranquility the surroundings instilled in me. While I was there, I tried desperately to get my wife Teresa to fly there and meet me, to no avail. Every time we made an airplane reservation for her, she missed her flight. She used every excuse imaginable to explain why she could not get to the airport on time. Once she even told me that the driveway had to be washed before she left town, and washing it caused her to run out of time. I should have heard the methamphetamine talking to me, but I didn't. I finally got tired of hearing her excuses, and headed out west to Michigan.

In Michigan, I got to meet my sister Kitty's family for the first time, and got to see how and where they all lived. Kitty was my half-sister from my biological dad's side, and I had actually met her for the first time when she came to Tulsa to visit my dad and me a few months before. Kitty and her husband had three kids, and I enjoyed the visit a lot. While I was there, I tried again to get Teresa to fly to Michigan, but again, I was stonewalled with incomprehensible excuses. I was amazed at her persistence in not getting to the airport on time, in spite of the fact that she repeatedly claimed she wanted to. By now, she and I had made more than ten different plane reservations for her, and she had missed every flight.

From Kitty's, I went west one hundred miles to Grand Rapids, to see another old friend. His name was John Fisher, and he was a master carpenter. John was getting tired of the cold Michigan weather, and was thinking about moving to Oklahoma. I wanted another chance to see him in person, to convince him to come to Oklahoma and be a Bandido in the new Bandidos chapter that I hoped to get permission for in the near future. While at John's, I totally gave up on my wife Teresa ever getting to the airport. To prove the brilliance of methamphetamine-based decisions, Teresa went to the airport at the last minute one day and flew to Detroit, without ever telling me in advance. After all the failed plans we had made over the last week, it turned out that she wanted to be with me for our seventh wedding anniversary.

The only problem was that the Detroit airport was three hours from where I was now, not one hour from where I was a few days ago, when I was at my sisters'. When she called me at 11pm with the surprising news that she was now in Michigan, I was worn smooth out and tired of all her crap. I told her to get a room, and in the morning we would either pick her up or get her to me somehow. The next day, we got her on a bus headed west to Kalamazoo, and John and I rode our bikes down there and met her at the bus station. I was very happy to see her, but it didn't take long for my happiness to wane. Before long, the insanity that hovered around her like a dark cloud was back with a vengeance. If only I had known at the time that she was addicted to methamphetamine, I probably would have handled the situation differently.

By the time we got back to Tulsa a few days later, I knew that I had reached the end of my rope. I instructed my attorney to proceed with the divorce that I had been pondering for many months, and on August 25, 1995, I officially filed for divorce. It was a sad day for me, for I was madly in love with my wife, but still had no idea what had gone wrong. The only thing I knew for sure was that I was no longer willing to put up with the insanity that had become normalcy for Teresa. I had hoped that filing for divorce just might be the catalyst that might propel her to get some help. But to get help, you have to first realize that you need help. And Teresa had no idea that she needed help.

The next night, my best friend Lee McArdle took me out on the town for a while, to talk with me about things and see what he could do to help. Somehow I convinced him that I had everything under control, and we got back on our bikes. When we left the club side by side, as we got out on the main road, we both took off as fast as we could, almost like a drag race side by side. Although our bikes were both quick, I was hoping that mine was faster. In just a few seconds, Lee was nowhere to be found. I pulled over as soon as I could, and looked back to see him coasting down the street. It took him a minute to catch up to me, and then I learned that he had broken a rear drive belt just as he hit second gear. It provided me with a little dose of laughter after such a crappy day.

20

Waiting On The Bandidos
Fall 1995 To Spring 1997

In the summer of 1995, my adopted mom, Dolly, and I decided to go into the construction management business together, so we set up a corporation that we called Blockhead City Construction Company. In August, Blockhead City landed a contract to install the masonry work at a new Office Max in Joplin, Missouri, so by September 1st the project was off and running. I traveled back and forth to Joplin from Tulsa for a little more than a month to manage and facilitate the installation of the concrete block walls for the new store. I had hired a Tulsa masonry crew to install the block, and sold their labor to the general contractor for a little profit per installed block. The only catch was that in commercial construction, it normally takes ninety days to get paid. I borrowed everything I could from every source I had; got the job finished on time and my block crew/masonry materials paid in full. Then I sat back and starved for almost ninety days while I waited patiently for my seventy-five thousand dollar check, which luckily came in just before Christmas.

Unfortunately, filing the divorce paperwork in late August drove Teresa and I further apart, and by mid-September, Teresa and my daughter Taylor had moved back across town, in with her sister Vicki again. Things had gotten worse and worse between us, and there was nothing I could do to alleviate the cloud of craziness that surrounded Teresa. It wasn't long before I soon discovered that Teresa owed more than fifty-five thousand dollars on her numerous credit cards, and that the majority of the debt had been spent on methamphetamine. I was shocked beyond belief, and could have kicked myself in the butt for not having noticed.

I did all I could to make sure that Taylor was doing ok, and tried as best I could to get Teresa some help, while trying all the time to restore our relationship. I was a firm believer that I had married her for better or worse, and just because I had discovered the worse, it was no time to run. At least now I knew that she wasn't completely insane, that the methamphetamine had contributed significantly to the craziness. I even contacted the person that had sold her most all of the methamphetamine, Steve McBride, and told him to never sell Teresa any type of drug again. I had known Steve since I had arrived in Tulsa back in 1975; Steve had been there when Charlie West had bailed me out of jail when I got arrested leaving Arby's. Steve admitted to me at that time, that Teresa had spent more than thirty thousand dollars in the last year purchasing methamphetamine from him.

By October, my biological dad, Forrest, convinced Teresa to move into his house, where there were two extra bedrooms, one for her and a separate bedroom for my daughter Taylor. Throughout most of the week Forrest was away on business; he was home only on the weekends. Since his house was a few blocks from mine, it was easy for me to see Taylor often. Their living arrangement also provided me with an opportunity to frequently try to convince Teresa that we could survive all of this. Unfortunately, Teresa soon turned to alcohol for solace, rather than get help for her substance abuse problems. As she sunk farther and farther into her tiny world of drug and alcohol abuse, our marriage deteriorated more and more.

Christmas was uneventful; although I did get to see Teresa and Taylor for Christmas, the usual Christmas spirit was just not there. I wished for a Christmas like I had known in the years past, but recognized it for what it was: for the kids. I put all my heart and soul into making sure that Taylor thought it was a good Christmas, in spite of what her parents were going through.

In January of 1996, I took off to Nashville with Larry and Arthur Pearson from the band Judge Parker, and went to visit William Lee Golden from the Oak Ridge Boys at his home. It was William's birthday, and we had been invited to attend his birthday party and spend the night at his house just north of Nashville. While we were in Nashville, we took the time to check out some contacts in the music business in an attempt to land Larry a song-writing contract. On the way home, I stopped in Memphis for a day to see Tattoo Tommy and Mouse at Mouse's Tattoo Shop.

Taylor & Ct Ed's Adopted Mom Dolly December 1995

William Lee Golden & Larry Pearson January 1996

A month after I got back from Nashville, my custom bike painter friend Wizard called me up and requested my immediate assistance on a situation he had with a personal bike that he was building. Wizard had contracted with a motorcycle shop across town to assemble his bike for him, and the shop had not performed their obligations in a timely fashion. The shop was giving him the cold shoulder and now ignoring all of his phone calls. Every time he confronted them in the past about the building schedule, they gave him excuse after excuse. By the time I talked to Wizard, he was ready to strangle the shop owner.

At the time, this was going to be one of the most expensive Harleys that had ever been built in the Tulsa area, and would be worth more than $25,000. Wizard wanted his bike done in time to travel to the annual Daytona Bike week in Florida. There were only a few weeks left, and it had dawned on Wizard that there was no way that shop would be able to finish the motorcycle assembly in time for Daytona. It was time for a miracle, and Wizard knew that I would pull a rabbit out a hat for him.

I took a few biker buddies and a truck and trailer, and went straight over to the shop that supposedly was building Wizard's bike, and walked right into the shop area. We immediately started loading all of the pieces of Wizard's bike into the truck and on to the trailer. Although we were prepared for the worst, the shop owner decided the best thing to do was sit back and watch, and in a few minutes, we were on the way to my shop. We did not waste any time, and immediately set to work on the assembly of the bike. Wizard sent over one of his hotshot apprentices, Ian Wilhelm, who helped me a lot with the assembly and running errands over the next two weeks.

I was extremely fortunate that another old friend, Mason Morton, was building the engine. If Wizard had contracted that same shop to build the engine that was supposed to have built the bike, the bike would never had any chance to be completed on time. Mason was like me, he didn't screw around either, and about the time I got as far as I could with the assembly, Mason delivered the engine. From then on, it was a walk in the park for us and in about a week, the bike was complete and running, except for the gas tank, which Wizard was putting the finishing touches on. I actually delivered the bike to Wizard the day before he had originally scheduled the bike to be shipped, and within a few hours, the gas tank was installed and ready for its journey to Florida.

Wizard & His Bike In Ed's Shop February 1996

Wizard's Bike At The Tulsa Bike Show March 1996

In mid-March, as a result of the contacts I made while working on the Office Max project in Joplin late last year, I landed a new contract to do the demolition of a Dillon's Grocery Store in Wichita, Kansas. We only had four weeks to remove everything in the building, leaving the roof and walls intact. It was right up my alley, and I took with me a skeleton crew to supervise the local temporary labor force I would need to complete the job. In the crew was my old childhood buddy from Connecticut, Harry "Skip" Hansen, who by now was living in a new house he bought just south of Muskogee, Oklahoma, with his new Oklahoma girlfriend.

I first hired a bunch of local temporary laborers, and divided them up into four manageable teams, then punched a hole in the front of the building for all of the debris containers. For about three weeks we destroyed everything in the building, saving all of the copper electrical wiring and copper water pipes, as well as anything else of possible value for future resale. At one point, Skip was operating a bobcat loader, pushing around one of the debris dumpsters, when the whole back of the bobcat caught fire. I thought for a minute that he was going to burn up alive, but fortunately, he escaped with no injury, and we were able to put the fire out with no problem.

While I was working in Wichita, Teresa was not working, but had Taylor in daycare so that Teresa could party during the day. All of that came to an end on March 22nd when Teresa showed up drunk at 4pm to pick Taylor up at the daycare. The Manager of the daycare wisely refused to allow Teresa to take custody of Taylor, and called the police. But Teresa was lucky, for the police did not see her driving, so they could not arrest her for DUI. The police even felt a little sorry for her, and did not arrest her for public drunk. Fortunately for Taylor, they did make Teresa call someone to come get her, before the police let her take my daughter Taylor with her.

The next day, my attorney friend Jonathan Sutton went to court and got a Temporary Custody Order for me to take immediate custody of Taylor. Until

Teresa stopped getting high, there was no way I was going to let Taylor be near her. I had no choice but to bring Taylor to Wichita with me, and to simultaneously take care of her while I managed the demolition of the Dillon's grocery store. Between all of us guys, specifically her "Uncle Skip" and her grandfather Forrest, we took care of Taylor surprisingly well. It was the first time I had ever had this much responsibility for taking care of Taylor long term. Although I had taken care of her while she visited me before, I had never experienced anything like this.

All of the guys on the jobsite helped a lot, and we all worked together to keep Taylor in her routines. She played in my jobsite office during the day while I answered the phone and did my paperwork. Taylor loved being there on the job with me, and had lots of fun. We did everything together, and her grandpa Forrest even snuck out occasionally during the day and brought her to the playground at the local park a few times. All of the guys covered for me if I had to change a diaper or put Taylor down for a nap.

By the first week of April, Teresa claimed that she was ready to get some help for her substance abuse addiction, and was willing to do anything to get Taylor back. She also agreed to sign the final divorce decree, which now included a special paragraph that precluded her from "ingesting drugs and/or alcohol" while Taylor was in her care and custody. As part of the divorce decree, I did what I thought was right for Taylor at the time, and agreed to let Teresa have custody of Taylor as long as Teresa agreed to not get high, that Teresa provided Taylor with a suitable living environment, and that Teresa keep Taylor in a daily routine that was suitable for a child. Teresa got a nice apartment on the south side of Tulsa, and the three of us settled into divorced life.

As soon as I finished up the Dillon's demolition job and got back to Tulsa, I purchased an old abandoned house across the street from my biological dad Forrest's house, just a few blocks from my home. As a result of the divorce, I had sold my home; the new owners would take possession in June. It was time for me to find a new home and to make some money. Between April and June, I totally rebuilt the old house. Forrest had also sold his house, but he was going to be out of town on a construction site for six months. Our plans were to move his stuff into two rooms at the new place across the street from him, and we would live there until one of us found another project/place to live.

In May, I took a break and headed off to Fort Smith to relax with Larry and Arthur Pearson from the Judge Parker Band, and to see the Oak Ridge Boys live in concert. They were playing at a new place in Fort Smith called the Red Roper. It was the largest nightclub I had ever seen; supposedly the owners had spent a million dollars building it. The three of us hung out with William Lee Golden all night, and had a blast. It was good to get out of town, and get away from work for a few days.

*Arthur & Larry Pearson, William Lee Golden & Ct Ed
At The Red Roper May 1996*

In late June, I moved out of my home on Madison Avenue, which I had owned since 1981. I felt just a tinge of sadness as I packed up my last load of belongings and moved to the house I had remodeled across the street from my dad's. A few days later, I moved all of my dad's things out of his house and across the street into mine, since he had been conveniently out of town when the moving deadline came. By July 1st, everything that I owned, as well as everything my dad owned, was all safely moved into my new home on North Victor Avenue. I was ready to start my life anew.

*Ct Ed's Dad Forrest & Ed
June 1996*

*Ct Ed's Daughter Taylor
June 1996*

On June 8th, Taylor, my biological dad Forrest, my adopted mom Dolly and I all went together to the marriage ceremony of my old next-door neighbor, James Perry. James had by now recovered substantially from the massive injuries he had sustained as a result of the "snapped chain" accident, and was doing ok considering the circumstances. James had permanent damage to the nerves on one side of his face, could not hear well in one ear, and was having difficulty seeing in one eye, but in spite of it all he seemed to be in good spirits that day. It appeared that he was happy to just be alive.

The first week of August 1996 was extremely interesting. Larry Pearson from the band Judge Parker called and asked me to produce a video of Judge Parker at the last minute. Once again I had to pull a rabbit out of a hat. The video shoot was scheduled in less than a week, but I had absolutely no experience in producing a video. I found the prospect of doing a video a challenge, and took the job, even though it did not pay a dime. I had wanted to take a vacation to southern Louisiana anyway, so I figured that Fort Smith was right on the way, and now would be a good time to take it.

The actual video shoot took place at the Red Roper nightclub in Fort Smith, the million-dollar bar where we saw the Oak Ridge Boys just a few months before. The name of the song that we were going to shoot the video for was called "Guitars and Girls". I suggested that Larry round up as many girls and guitars that he could, and we would just play it as we saw it. I came up with different ideas to shoot around all night long; some of them worked and some didn't. In the end, some of the ideas made it to the actual video, and the rest wound up on the editing room floor.

At one point, I caught an unauthorized guy filming the proceedings with a hand held video camera. When I confronted him, it turned out that he was just a tourist from Germany who was visiting the area, and had heard all about the video shoot on the local radio station. Not knowing any better, he wandered in and just started recording without asking anyone. I made a deal with him: he could continue shooting video as long as he was willing to do one thing, which was send a copy of his video to my biker buddy in Germany, Dieter Tenter.

Dieter had been at a few Judge Parker concerts while here visiting me in the United States, and was by now a big fan of the band. I never expected the German tourist to go through with his part of the bargain, but a few months later, Dieter called me one day ranting and raving about this wonderful videotape he had received in the mail. I had never told Dieter about the German tourist, never expecting the tourist to send Dieter the tape. I then had to explain the whole story to Dieter, who was very appreciative of what had transpired.

From Fort Smith, I headed south to Louisiana to see the Bandidos there in Baton Rouge and Lafayette, and then over to Beaumont, Texas to visit my sister Deedee and her husband Rick. I then went to Galveston to see Bandido Big John, and talk to him again about starting a chapter of Bandidos in Oklahoma. It had now been sixteen years since I had discussed the concept with Bandido Buddy in Mobile, Alabama back in 1980. Bandido John thought that the timing was finally right, and that it would be a good time to bring it up at the drag races in Ennis, Texas, which were scheduled for the first week of October, 1996. Bandido John told me that he would talk to the powers that be, and I already knew that Bandido Jack-E from Louisiana was going to do the same.

While I was in Fort Smith and touring the Gulf coast, my best friend Lee McArdle was on his way to Sturgis, with another good friend of ours, Bill Beaty. Bill had married the widow of ex-Rogue Marvin Brix in May of 1987 (Marvin was my good friend who had died in the spring of 1986). On the way home from Sturgis, Lee got a flat tire coming across Kansas in the heat of the day. They had no jack, and decided that they could pick the bike up, using the kickstand as a fulcrum. When Lee pulled on the bike, to pull it up in the air while Bill picked up on it, the kickstand broke off, pinning Lee to the ground under the weight of the motorcycle. It must have been quite the sight to see for all of the passing cars on I-70 that day.

Bill, being the nice guy he was, and thinking of me, ran for his bike to get his camera, while Lee screamed at Bill, asking Bill to help Lee get the bike off of him. But Bill did the most sensible thing he could do considering the circumstances: he first took some pictures, and then he helped Lee get the bike off. Lee was quite upset, not because Bill took the pictures, but because he knew that Bill would give the pictures to me, and that I would show the pictures to everyone I knew. Fortunately for Lee, in his haste to take the pictures, Bill forgot to remove the lens cover, and the pictures never came out. I was deeply saddened at Bill's thoughtless action, and scolded him for leaving the lens cover on. What I could have done with those pictures.....

In early October, I set off for Austin, to visit both of my sisters there, and on the way home I went to the drag races at Ennis. There I spoke to Bandido El Presidente Craig "Craig" Johnston about getting permission to start the chapter, and before it was all over, got invited to present the concept to a large contingent of National officers up in one of the press boxes above the racetrack. There were Bandidos there from all over the world; who asked me all sorts of questions. I left out of there that evening on top of the world, because I had finally been granted permission to officially start talking to people; to find out exactly who was interested in becoming a member of the Bandidos.

While I was gone to Texas, one of my Tulsa attorneys, William "Bill" Patterson, was successfully sued in a Tulsa court for biting off the nose of another man during a domestic altercation that had occurred in August of 1995. This is the same Bill, whose fingernails I had painted pink while he slept on my couch a few years back. The injured man claimed that Bill got him down on the ground and bit him like an animal. Bill contended that at the time of the incident, it was his belief that he was in danger of serious bodily harm, and that he acted in self-defense. The jury did not agree with my attorney, and awarded the injured man a total of

$850,000 in damages. The initial damages awarded by the jury were eventually reduced to only $75,000. It goes to show you that it is sometimes not a good idea to mess with an attorney, and proves that Bill didn't take any crap out of the courtroom.

November of 1996 was a great month. I was well on track to putting together a crew that would become the first chapter of Bandidos in Oklahoma. I had convinced my friend John Fisher from Michigan to relocate to Tulsa, and he had rented a house not far from me. I had sold the house I was living in, and had bought a wreck of a house about ten miles east of me, in a little town called Owasso. Owasso was a booming town, with one of the best school districts in Oklahoma. The house sat on more than three acres, and had a good-sized shop to work out of. However, the house was infested with wild cats, a bunch of fiddleback spiders, and thousands of wasp nests. In addition to all the construction work that was needed, there was more than $300,000 in liens attached to the property.

By December 1st, my dad and I had moved into the abandoned Owasso house and had started to remodel it. I had taken possession through a federal tax deed, and it superseded all of the liens except the first mortgage. I purchased the first mortgage from the bank for about $30,000, and then got my civil attorneys to do a quiet title, which terminated all of the liens and cleared the title. By Christmas, my dad was living in the living room and I in one of the bedrooms. We had one bathroom working, the laundry functioning, and the rest of the house was a construction zone. There were huge holes in the roof all over the house, and we had garbage pails set under them to catch all of the water when it rained. Teresa and I were starting to see each other again, and Taylor was doing well.

By February of 1997, I had accumulated quite an impressive roster of potential members for the new Bandidos chapter in Oklahoma, which would be based out of Tulsa. Unfortunately, my old friends Bandido Robert "Cowboy" Crain and Bandido Joseph "Joe-E" George were not among them. Bandido Cowboy had gotten so whacked out on methamphetamine, that he had been arrested again. He was destined to do another stretch in prison, this time courtesy of the state of Oklahoma, and then he had to go finish the time that remained on his federal prison sentence, after he got done with his Oklahoma prison time. Bandido Joe-E had also gotten whacked out on methamphetamine, been thrown out of the Bandidos, and was destined to be arrested on drug charges in the near future. Besides myself, to form the new chapter, there were:

Lee "Lee" McArdle	Tulsa
Harry "Skip" Hansen	Muskogee
Lewis "Bill Wolf" Rackley	Broken Arrow
Earl "Buddy" Kirkwood	Sapulpa
Joseph "Little Joe" Kincaid	Muskogee
Mark "Bones " Hathaway	Sapulpa
John "Turtle" Fisher	Tulsa

Joseph "Popeye" Hannah   Muskogee
Keith "Keith" Vandervoort   Tulsa

At the end of February, John "Turtle" Fisher and I took off for Florida and the Daytona Bike Week for the last time as independent bikers. We spent a day together in Daytona, and then went to Orlando, where a good friend of mine, David Gruber, worked at Disney World. David had been a member of the Rogues Motorcycle Club with me back in Tulsa in the early 80's, and we had known each other since the late 70's. David got John and me into Disney World for free, through the gate the employees use, and then into the Indiana Jones show, where David worked, for free as well. David arranged to get me picked out of the audience, to participate in the show. I had to do a bunch of crazy stuff to entertain the crowd, and David and John got a good laugh. After the show, we got an eye-opening back stage tour of the facility and set.

John wanted to spend a few days with some personal friends in Jacksonville and I wanted to head southwest out of Orlando for Tampa, so we split up for the rest of the trip. I tried my best to catch up with my old friend Outlaw Mouse from St. Petersburg, but he was stuck out in the middle of nowhere at an Outlaws Motorcycle Club party site, doing guard duty. Instead, I stopped into see a Florida Outlaw who had just gotten out of prison, and from there I rode to Baton Rouge, Louisiana, where I needed to talk to Bandido Jack-E about getting the Oklahoma chapter off the ground.

While I was there to visit him, Jack-E's Harley broke down, and I was able to okie-doke him by getting a picture of us, with his bike loaded up in a truck behind us. Just as the picture was taken, Bandido Jack-E realized that he had been set up, and as he said something about it, we both laughed.

John "Turtle" Fisher & Ct Ed
Disney World March 1997

Jack-E & CT Ed & His Harley
In The Background March 1997

In April, the Bandidos again sent Bandido Vice Presidente Larry to come see us, to check us out to see if we were Bandidos material. Bandido Big John came up from Galveston at the same time, and most all of us sat down together to work out the details. Bandido Larry and Bandido Big John answered a bunch of questions the guys had about the club. Larry told us that it would be a long time before we would be allowed to become Bandidos, and in the meantime, Bandido Larry told us that he would see what he could do about getting permission for us to wear support shirts. In his opinion, that was all we were worth.

A week later, Bandido El Presidente Craig assigned Bandidos Vice Presidente George "George" Wegers from Washington state to oversee the new Bandidos chapter in Tulsa, effectively saving us from the axe of Bandidos Vice Presidente Larry. I had met Bandido George a few months earlier, when he had come to town with California AIM attorney Richard Lester for an Oklahoma Confederation of Clubs (COC) meeting. Richard Lester and Bandido George had stayed at my house, and we had gone over to the COC meeting together, in spite of the fact that I was not a Bandido yet.

At the confederation meeting, Bandido George had got into a shoving match with Roger Wiley, who was a member of the Rogues Motorcycle Club. I guess Rogue Roger did not realize who Bandido George was, or did not notice the gold Bandidos necklace that Bandido George was wearing. After Bandido George was introduced at the meeting, and gave a little talk about clubs getting along, a humble Rogue Roger ate a large helping of crow pie when he took a long walk with Bandido George and begged for forgiveness.

Bandido George's attitude about us was a whole lot different than that of Bandido Larry. George took us on with the full intention of getting the chapter off the ground. By now, Outlaw John "Little Wolf" Killip from Oklahoma City was out of prison, and had tentatively given the OK from the Outlaws for us to start a Bandidos chapter in Oklahoma. In April, we all went down to Hallsville, Texas, for the annual drag races, as a "chapter" for the first time, proudly showing ourselves off for the Bandidos. For the occasion, we all wore ball caps that we had made that said, "Sooner or Later – Oklahoma" – and the Oklahoma part of the ball cap looked just like a bottom rocker.

While we were all out at the racetrack getting to know everyone, the Bandidos National chapter was in Longview meeting with some of the Outlaws National chapter. During that meeting, the Outlaws National chapter officially gave their OK to our new chapter in Oklahoma. We later heard that some of the Oklahoma Outlaws were totally against it, but the Outlaws National President, Harry "Taco" Bowman told the Bandidos that they could have the new chapter, and that he (Taco) could care less about Oklahoma.

The stage was now set for what was yet to come, but we still had no idea when we would actually get our Bandido patches. In early May, Bandido Vice

Presidente George notified us that we all needed to go to the annual Gulfport Blowout in Biloxi, Mississippi for the upcoming Memorial Day weekend. George told us that he would drive to Tulsa, and then personally make the ride down to Biloxi with us. Everyone else in the chapter wondered if our chapter would be chartered while we were at Gulfport, but for me, it was hard to believe that my dream was going to finally come true, almost eighteen years after I met my first Bandido in Mobile, Alabama.

We were all brimming with excitement when we left for Gulfport on Thursday evening. We all rode over to Little Rock, and spent the night at Bandido Leo "Murray" Murray's house. Six of the potential new Oklahoma Bandidos made the ride down to Biloxi with Bandido George and two other Washington state Bandidos, Bandido Hoot and Bandido Thumper. Four of the guys from Oklahoma did not make it. The next day, Friday, we rode from Little Rock to Biloxi, getting into the Biloxi area early Friday evening. We had not planned on going there, so no one had thought about getting motel rooms in advance. By the time we rolled into town, the only rooms we could find were more than one hundred fifty dollars per night. So we got two rooms, packed three of us into each room, and split the cost of each room between three guys.

To our surprise, at Gulfport all the Bandidos were told that there was going to be a new Probationary chapter of Oklahoma Bandidos, but none of us received our patches. We did meet plenty of Bandidos who were quite excited about our new chapter, but we also met a whole bunch of Bandidos that were not very happy. For us, the ride home was a long one, because we all had expected to get our patches while we were at Gulfport. To complicate the ride home, John "Turtle" Fisher's bike broke down in southern Arkansas. John had apparently forgotten to check his battery water, and it had boiled dry. We were dead in the water, with Little Rock the closest place that had a battery.

It did not take long before Bandido George and I got in an argument. I was used to traveling this stretch of road many times, and knew the only thing to do was to call Little Rock for help. Bandido George did not want to call them for help, and insisted that we figure out some other way to rectify the situation. We tried everything we could, but it was Memorial Day and there was no help available or stores open, in this rural area. I eventually called Bandido Murray for help, in spite of the fact that Bandido George had specifically told me not to.

I had figured out that if I did not call Little Rock, we would be there for the rest of our lives trying to fix something that could not be fixed. Bandido George was mad at me, but soon resigned himself to the fact that help was on the way. We loaded John's bike into the back of Bandido Murray's Ford Ranchero, and finally got into Little Rock just before 10PM. Once again, we spent the night at Bandido Murray's, got John a new battery in the morning, and rode home to Tulsa the next day. Bandido Vice Presidente George told us to all be at my house tomorrow evening for a meeting. He told us that it was an important meeting, and we all had to be there.

21

Bandidos Motorcycle Club Oklahoma
The Beginning Summer 1997

On Wednesday morning, May 27, 1997, an overnight Fedex arrived at my house addressed to Bandido Vice Presidente George "George" Wegers. By the shape, size and feel of the box, I thought that the day I had been waiting for, for almost eighteen years, had finally come. That night, all of us gathered at my house for our first, formal weekly meeting. We had been told that from now on, we had to act like we were a Bandidos chapter, even though we were not Bandidos yet. Acting like a Bandidos chapter meant that we would have to have weekly meetings, which the Bandidos normally referred to as either "church" or "card games".

But on this Wednesday evening, the rumors were flying among us and the anticipation was like a cloud around us. When Bandido George called the meeting to order, he told us that he was in possession of our patches, but first we needed to choose our chapter officers. I became the first Oklahoma Bandidos chapter President, Earl "Buddy" Kirkwood was chosen as the first Vice President, Harry "Skip" Hansen was selected as the first Sergeant-at-Arms, Lee "Lee" McArdle volunteered to be the first chapter Secretary-Treasurer, and last but not least, Bandido Vice Presidente George surprisingly appointed John "Turtle" Fisher to be the first chapter Road Captain.

Bandido Lee May 1997   *Bandido Connecticut Ed May 1997*

Because I was the President, and because I had been around the Bandidos for so many years, I was given an Oklahoma bottom rocker to wear, in spite of the fact that I was a probationary member. All of the other probationary members got

Probationary bottom rockers. The next day we all went out and got our patches sewed on to our vests. We were on top of the world.

Our first trip together as the official Bandidos Oklahoma chapter was to Baton Rouge, Louisiana, for the all Harley motorcycle drag races, a few weeks later in the middle of June. Bandido George flew back to Tulsa, where he had left his bike at the end of the last trip, and once again joined us for the ride down to Baton Rouge from Tulsa. Probationary Bandido Mark "Bones" Hathaway entered his bike in the drag races, but was eliminated in the second round. Later that month, at our initial Oklahoma appearance in public, we set up a booth at the first annual BACA (Bikers Against Child Abuse) fundraiser/party at which we sold t-shirts and ball caps emblazoned with the words "Support Your Local Bandidos". We had two banners made for the event that read "Bandidos MC Oklahoma", which we hung on the fence on either side of our booth.

Bandidos MC Booth At BACA Fundraiser June 1997

Our intent from the beginning was to provide the public with a positive perception of the club. Some of us, who had previously been members of other motorcycle clubs, wanted to make sure we did not repeat mistakes that had been made in the past. We had no intention of beating people up for no reason at all. Quite the contrary, we agreed to do everything we could to avoid a fight; we were adamant that we did not want to alienate the public. Our presence at the BACA party that Sunday afternoon met accolades of approval from everyone, except the Rogues Motorcycle Club. Some of the Rogues found chairs directly across from us, and then proceeded to take pictures of us all afternoon. One of them, a member named Jerry "Jerry" Nelson, got stupidly drunk and made a complete idiot of himself.

Rogue Jerry kept approaching the new Bandidos and making threats concerning what he was going to do about the fact that the Bandidos now had a chapter in Oklahoma. We later learned that the Rogues were upset because we had moved into "their territory" without their permission. But the Bandidos did not need their permission, for the Rogues were not a 1%er club, and the truth of the matter was that the Rogues did not have enough horsepower to even attempt to tell us what to do.

Almost all of the Bandidos there at the BACA fundraiser that day wanted to give Rogue Jerry a serious attitude adjustment. Bandido Keith "Keith" Vandervoort had the worst time keeping his temper in check, for he knew Rogue Jerry well from the days when they were Rogues together, and we ultimately had to physically restrain Bandido Keith from kicking the crap out of Rogue Jerry. The only thing that saved Rogue Jerry that day was the fact that we were all out there in front of everyone, in the middle of a BACA fundraiser, at which we were supposed to be helping abused kids.

Probationary Bandidos Bill Wolf, Turtle, Skip & Buddy
Summer 1997

In late July of 1997, Bandidos Oklahoma hosted a little party at my house in Tulsa for a bunch of Bandidos from all over the United States. It had been a last minute decision by the Bandidos national chapter to come and support us at the Bikers Against Diabetes "BAD" Rally, which was being held that weekend at Mohawk Park in Tulsa. Bandido El Presidente Craig "Craig" Johnston, Bandido Sargento de Armas Terry "Scrufty" Larque, and Bandidos President John "Big John" Lammons from Galveston were a few of the almost sixty Bandidos who made the long journey from other states to Tulsa.

We had planned to show up at the BAD Rally in mass, to make sure everyone and every motorcycle club in Oklahoma knew we were there, and to make a statement. But the BAD Rally was a huge flop, and only three hundred spectators showed up. Our scouts reported back to us that there were almost as many members of law enforcement there, as there were spectators. Instead of going out to the BAD Rally, we decided to take a leisurely motorcycle ride from Owasso, where I lived, down to the heart of Tulsa (that section of town is called Brookside), to a yuppie biker bar/restaurant at 34th Street and Peoria Avenue.

At 6 pm we all saddled up, fired up our Harleys and headed out from my house. We were a sight to see, as a pack of more than seventy-five bikes rode first through Owasso, then through the hills of north Tulsa, then through downtown Tulsa, and then south on Peoria to the parking lot of the nightclub. The rumbling of the bikes sounded like thunder and shook the whole building like there was an earthquake. Our entrance into the bar was electric as we took every chair in the place.

Probationary Bandido Skip, Bandido Tramp, Bandido El Presidente Craig, Probationary Bandidos Connecticut Ed, Turtle, Little Joe And Lee At Ed's House The Day Of The BAD Rally July 1997

The few chairs that were occupied by other customers soon became vacant, and we took all of those as well. The Bandidos completely dominated the night club/restaurant, and spent the entire evening there drinking, eating and relaxing. We were surprised at how little a police presence we found in the Brookside area. We later found out that the contingent of law enforcement gathered at Mohawk Park just to greet us, had spent all day and evening there at the park, anticipating our arrival.

By midnight, we were getting tired of being seen, and hanging around on Brookside, and we slowly dispersed. Some went to their motel rooms, some hit the road to get an early start back home, and the last bunch of us planned to go back to my house for the night. Just as we were walking out to our bikes to leave, the gang squad finally arrived. They had waited for us all day and night at Mohawk Park, and finally heard that we were over at the bar on Brookside. By the time they raced across town to catch a glimpse of us, we were all leaving. In the end, they only got a few pictures of the new Bandidos Oklahoma chapter.

I spent the spring and summer of 1997 remodeling the Owasso ranchette, and between my biological dad Forrest and I, we got a lot of the major problems fixed. We also added a new addition to the house, consisting of a large bedroom, another bathroom, and some more eating space in the kitchen. I took a job late that summer with a local property company, to remodel nineteen residential properties simultaneously. It kept me busy big time, but also provided me with the necessary legal funding to pursue my life as a Bandido. While I was working my ass off, fixing the nineteen properties at the same time, I was working on my house.

Around that time, the Bandidos decided that the new Oklahoma chapter would benefit from the presence of a Bandido Nomad member. Their intention in sending us the Nomad was to make sure we understood the Bandido way, but in the end, caused us much grief and discontent. In spite of the fact the supervising Nomads were friends of mine, they still had no authority to tell me what to do. However, they thought they had the authority. It came to a head within a few weeks, when Bandido Earthquake and I got in a hell of an argument, and I was forced to call on El Presidente Craig to explain to Bandido Earthquake that he was there only to advise me, not to tell me what to do.

In October of 1997, my ex-wife Teresa once again dove off into the world of alcohol and methamphetamine. As a direct result, I petitioned the court and got custody of my daughter Taylor. This time I knew it would not be temporary, and I also knew that I had arrived at a major crossroads in my life. I had to figure out if Taylor was more important to me than being a Bandido, and I needed to make this decision fast.

At the same time, I already doubted my leadership abilities as a Bandido President, and knew that Bandido Lee was not the best choice to be the chapter secretary. During a phone call to Bandidos Vice Presidente George "George" Wegers, after explaining my situation, I resigned my chapter presidency and even attempted to quit the club. Bandido George refused to let me quit, but did appoint Bandido Lee to run the chapter for a few weeks until George was able to come to Tulsa.

When Bandido George once again came to Tulsa, he diplomatically helped us set the stage for a much better Bandidos chapter and simultaneously helped me get a better handle on my life. As a chapter, we hammered out our differences. For the betterment of the club, Bandido Lee unanimously became the new chapter President, and I became the chapter's secretary. This change would require less road time for me, and everyone in the chapter agreed to do what they could, to give me more time at home to take care of my daughter Taylor, who now was almost four and one half years old. I was impressed with the way that George had handled the situation, and proud of the fact that everyone thought enough of me to support this unconventional solution to my problem.

November 1997 was a month of major highs and lows. As I settled into being a single dad, with major child rearing responsibilities, I started attending the local Parent Child Center for much needed guidance in how to be a parent. I also put the finishing touches on a new music CD, which I titled "The Best Of Warren Winters – Forever & Always". Part of the title, "Forever & Always" referred to what I said to my daughter Taylor each night as I tucked her into bed: "I love you, Taylor, forever and always, until the end of time".

Taylor & Ct Ed On the Cover Of Ed's 1997 CD

The music CD was a compilation of the best of my songs, from all three record albums as well as a few studio tracks that had never been published. The songs covered a time span of almost twenty years, from 1979 to 1997, as well as a broad range of musical styles. For the cover, I took pictures of my daughter Taylor and me, walking down the street in front of my home together while I carried my guitar. I used the Bandidos colors, which we called red and gold, as accent colors for the title block. The finished product, although not the best, was to me a significant accomplishment, one that I was extremely proud of. It also marked the closing of an era for me, for I no longer possessed any desire to continue being a musician.

On November 27th, my heart broke. My adopted mom Dolly died peacefully in her sleep. There was no hint of impending doom in those last weeks of her life. I spent my last moments with her just before I left for a trip to Texas with Taylor. I asked her if she wanted to come, and she told me that she was looking forward to being with her friends at church, and she wanted to stay in Tulsa. When Dolly would not answer the door on Thanksgiving Day, her friends from church gained entry to her house, where they found her lying in bed. It appeared that she had gotten into bed for the night, just like always, and had just passed away. Her death was a fitting end for a wonderful lady and great mom, who had spent her entire life in the devotion of others.

I learned of Dolly's passing while I was with my new half sisters in Austin, late in the afternoon on Thanksgiving Day. Ironically, my biological dad Forrest was the one who actually broke the sad news to me. I had a hard time maintaining my composure that evening, and was quite surprised at Taylor's grasp of the situation. Even at the tender age of four and a half, Taylor did all she could to comfort me on the long ride back to Tulsa the next day. As I wrote in her obituary the next day, "Dolly was a generous, kind, loving parent, full of life, laughter and courage". Although she had spent her entire life battling diabetes, and the last ten years of her life blind, never once did she complain.

Christmas of 1997 was a somber event, and the only reason I got through it was Taylor. It was during this time I understood for the first time in my life, that Christmas is truly for kids. For me, it was my first Christmas without my adopted mom Dolly, for she had always been either with me or just a phone call away. This Christmas, though, there was no calling her, and I found that I really missed her. Taylor came through again, and consoled me every time my emotions got the best of me.

By March of 1998, I needed a vacation; being a single parent over the winter had kicked my ass. I made reservations to fly from Dallas to Frankfurt, Germany, and plans for two close citizen friends of mine in Dallas, Greg and Bridgett Johns, to take care of Taylor for the week I would be gone. They had known Taylor since she was born, and also had two daughters her age that Taylor could play with while I was gone. Taylor and I drove down to Dallas, and before I knew what hit me, I was landing in Frankfurt.

22

Bandidos Motorcycle Club Oklahoma
Spring 1998 To Fall 1998

Getting off the plane in Frankfurt, Germany after a ten-hour plane flight from Dallas, I had to force myself to stay awake and find my "land" legs again. I was thankful to find my old friend Dieter Tenter waiting for me there after I cleared customs. As tired as I was, I was able to stay awake and enjoy the four-hour car ride from Frankfurt to Lengerich with Dieter. It was good to be back in Germany again, and good to be away from all the pressures of home.

I spent a few days resting with Dieter and his family, even going to school with his daughter Malisa, who was in the 4th grade. Malisa had told the kids in her school that her "uncle" Ed was visiting from America, and some of them had refused to believe her. When I volunteered to accompany her to school to prove that she was telling the truth, she was elated. The next morning, when Dieter and I walked into the school at her side, Malisa was beaming.

Malisa's schoolteacher and Dieter volunteered to translate, and all the kids in Malisa's class gathered in a circle around me and asked me questions about the United States. I was surprised at the warm welcome I received and the interest all the kids had in me. Before I left, Dieter took a great picture of me with Malisa (she is to my left in the picture), Malisa's class and teacher, as you can see:

CT Ed & Malisa's Class March of 1998

The next day, Dieter and I left by train from Lengerich, Germany for Copenhagen, Denmark. Since July of 1995, when Bandidos Sweden President

Mikael "Joe" Ljunggren had been shot and killed, the Bandidos in Scandinavia (Denmark, Norway, Finland and Sweden) had been embroiled in a terrible war with the Scandinavian Hells Angels. There had been many casualties on both sides from homemade bombs, hand grenades, anti-tank rockets, knives and gunfire. Many on both sides of the war were now in prison or on the run for participating in the carnage.

In addition to Bandido Joe, Bandidos Finland Vice President Jarkko Kokko was shot and killed in January of 1996 at the Bandidos clubhouse in Helsinki. Bandido Uffe Larsen was shot and killed at the Kastrup Airport in Denmark while another Bandido was shot and killed at the Fornebu Airport in Norway – both, on March 10, 1996. Bandido Prospect Jan Krogh Jensen was killed in Drammen, Norway on July 15, 1996, and Bandido Bjorn Gudmandsen was shot and killed in Liseleje, Denmark on June 7, 1997.

In the fall of 1997, after months of negotiations, the Scandinavian Bandidos and Hells Angels had wisely agreed to a truce. Bandidos European Presidente Jim Tindman and Danish Hells Angel Bent "Blondie" Nielsen even got together on TV and shook hands to cement the deal. As part of the deal, the Hells Angels and Bandidos in Copenhagen set up a joint clubhouse for a year, as additional proof that both sides were serious about keeping the peace. I was to be the first American Bandido in Denmark since the war had ended.

I was not exactly sure how we would be received by the Danish police, so I planned to enter Denmark with Dieter disguised as a tourist. I even made sure that all of my Bandidos shirts and jewelry were well hidden in my baggage, and contacted no one until after we arrived. I was also not so sure how the Hells Angels would react to my presence, since most Bandidos in Denmark were still quite nervous about the peace, and at that time were still operating under the impression that war could still possibly exist.

To cross the border from Germany into Denmark, it was necessary to get on a ferry. There is nothing but water between Denmark and Germany. Imagine my surprise when the train stopped and we were told to get off, and I found myself inside the bottom of the ferry. The ferry was so big it carried the entire train, in addition to a whole deck of cars, trucks and motorcycles!

After a short thirty-minute ferry ride, and another two hours back on the train, Dieter and I were greeted at the train station in Copenhagen by a contingent of Bandidos who were surprised to see an American Bandido in Copenhagen. The Danish Bandidos were quite concerned with my safety, and surrounded us with "guards" the entire time we were there. It was at a small café near the train station I met Swedish Bandido Clark for the first time. Clark was an ex-Hells Angel from the Bandidos Helsingborg chapter who had found the Bandidos to be more suited to his way of life.

The first night we were in Copenhagen, Dieter and I attended a reception for a Danish Bandido, who had gotten married that day. There I met too many Danish Bandidos to remember most of their names. I was surprised at how well most of them spoke English; and at the ease of communicating, compared to that of the people in Germany. I was also surprised at how young most of the Danish Bandidos were. Almost all of them were only in their 20's or 30's. I did remember one of the Bandidos I met that night; he was a youngster named Big Jacob, who was out on pass from prison. We agreed to write each other while he finished his prison sentence, and although I held up my end of the bargain, Big Jacob never did write back. I was able to kid him about that for many years.

Bandido Big Jacob & Ct Ed March 1998

After only a few hours at the wedding reception, Dieter and I were prematurely rushed out a back door when the local police raided the party. We spent one more night there in Copenhagen, and the next day we visited the famous Christiana section of Copenhagen. There, Dieter and I were able to temporarily play the part of legal hashish dealers for an impromptu photo session at one of the many open-air hash shops.

One of the Danish guards appointed to keep us safe, Bandido Buller, went out of his way to show Dieter and me all over Denmark, and we got to experience Danish life and food as though we lived there. With Bandido Buller as our guide, we were even able to cross over into Sweden and visit Bandido Clark at the Helsingborg chapter's clubhouse. Like Dieter, Buller made his living buying and selling Harley Davidson motorcycles, so all three of us naturally talked a lot about bike prices, and agreed to try and make some money wholesaling Harleys from country to country.

Buller even offered to drive the two of us back to Germany, and after enduring the day-long train ride from Lienen to Copenhagen, Dieter and I jumped at the chance to relax in a car for the ride back to Germany. While in Germany,

Dieter and Buller planned to check out motorcycles and motorcycle prices and further explore the possibility of doing legal motorcycle business with each other.

Dieter & CT Ed Posing As Hash Dealers At Christiana, Denmark March 1998

Bandido Buller In Germany March 1998

While there, I had talked to Bandido Presidente Jim, the European National President for the Bandidos Motorcycle Club. I had told him that I would be returning to Germany for a few days, and he asked me to contact a motorcycle club there in Germany called the Ghostriders. The European Bandidos were very friendly with the German Ghostriders, and Jim thought that a visit from an American Bandido would promote their friendship. So after a short two-day visit to Denmark, off I went back to Germany for a few more days, to visit the German Ghostriders Motorcycle Club.

I initially made contact with a member of the German Ghostriders, Armin, who had a fairly good grasp of the English language. With Dieter as my guide, we traveled about an hour south to Dortmund, located in the Ruhrpott (coal producing) area of central Germany. There I met up with Armin, Diesel and Les, all full patch members of the Ghostriders. The Ghostriders were the second largest motorcycle club in Germany; only the Bones Motorcycle Club exceeded them in size and strength. At the time Les was their National President; Diesel was their National Sergeant-at-Arms and Armin was their National Secretary.

Ghostrider Diesel owned a tattoo shop in the heart of Dortmund, and we met in a small café nearby. After getting to know each other, Les offered me his motorcycle to ride. Although to me it was very cold out, the German bikers were oblivious to the weather conditions; they informed me that it was a nice day for them. I graciously accepted the use of the bike, and rode next to a German Ghostrider for a few miles across town. At the time, I was unaware that Les was taking pictures of the Ghostrider and me while he followed behind us in a car, as we rode our bikes side by side next to each other. These pictures would eventually become very famous in Germany, as they were apparently the only pictures ever taken of an American Bandido riding side by side with a Ghostrider.

Les ended our afternoon outing by inviting me to a party that was to be held in a few days by one of their new Prospect chapters in Kassel. I promised that I would show up, but first I needed to travel to Luxembourg to visit with a brand new Bandido chapter there. A long-time Luxembourg motorcycle club called Les Copains had recently merged with the Bandidos.

The next morning I set out for Luxembourg via train, and arrived there early that evening. It did not take long to locate a member of the local Bandidos chapter, as this time I had called ahead to warn them of my arrival. When we arrived at their clubhouse, I was quite surprised to find myself in front of a multi-storied building in a nice part of the small town of Esch Alzette. The first floor was a bar, open to the public. The entire second floor was their clubhouse, and the third and fourth floors housed an apartment for the Luxembourg Bandidos President, Angus.

I spent a total of two days with the Bandidos in Luxembourg, and although there was a distinct language barrier, with the help of Bandidos Pirate and Mario (who could both speak a little English), we all got along fine. While there I found the time to visit the local Harley dealer; see some of the local nightlife (where I was first introduced to techno pop – a type of music heard throughout Europe but not popular here in the states); eat some great home cooked food and visit a Luxembourg doctor who helped me sort out a minor medical problem.

Bandidos MC Clubhouse At Esch Alzette, Luxembourg March 1998

Luxembourg Bandidos Angus & Mario March 1998

Early Saturday afternoon, Bandido Pirate and I took off for Kassel, Germany, where we planned to rendezvous with Les, Armin and Diesel of the Ghostriders MC. We did a quick stop at a bar on the way to visit a friend of Pirate's, where we ran into a few members of the Bones MC. Late in the evening, we arrived at the Ghostriders clubhouse in Kassel, where I found the language barrier intense. Although Bandido Pirate was quite fluent in German, English and French, I had a lot of trouble keeping up with the conversation. The Kassel

Ghostriders were all prospects, and weren't quite sure what to make of their two Bandidos visitors. The highlight of the evening for me was watching an obnoxious guest get thrown out of the party.

Bandidos Pirate & CJ Ed, Ghostriders Armin & Les Germany March 1998

The next day Pirate dropped me off at the airport in Frankfurt on his way back to Luxembourg. It had been a great trip, and I was now ready to get back to the United States. Although I had talked to my daughter Taylor nearly every day, I was missing her a lot and knew that she needed her Daddy. I fell asleep on the plane, and before I knew it, we were landing in Dallas. It was about 3pm local time by the time I cleared customs, and unfortunately I had a great case of jetlag. After picking Taylor up, I somehow drove back to Tulsa, getting in late that evening.

I did not spend much time at home before I left to go to Hallsville, an annual drag race event just outside Longview, Texas in early April. While the troops partied at Hallsville, all of the Bandidos Presidents gathered at a house in Longview. After a long day discussing the situation, the bosses decided that Vice Presidente George Wegers would be the new El Presidente when El Presidente Craig Johnston reported to federal prison to begin serving his ten-year sentence. It would be a major turning point for the Bandidos Motorcycle Club in the United States, and a major shift in club policy would soon follow, for George's philosophy was quite different.

The new Bandido El Presidente believed that change was a good thing for the club, and that all motorcycle clubs needed to get along peacefully. He was an active participant in the national Confederation of Clubs, which was a new organization then that was in the process of getting all motorcycle clubs in the United States to peacefully coexist. Bandido George also adamantly believed that in 1998, there had to be a balance in the life of a Bandido. He believed that to be a successful Bandido, a member had to maintain a critical balance between the club, employment and family, or being a Bandido long term would not work. George in fact owned a Harley Davidson dealership in Bellingham, Washington, and knew first hand how important it was to balance the club and your employment.

This reasoning was sound reasoning for if a man lost his family, he would carry that with him while he was a Bandido, and it would be an expensive burden to bear. If a man lost his job, then he would be a Bandido that had no money. Since it takes lots of money to be a Bandido, a Bandido without employment would soon turn to illegal enterprises to provide him with the funds necessary to continue to be a Bandido. Then before long, that Bandido would more than likely be arrested and sent off to prison. Bandido George wanted to break the cycle, and was willing to guide the club through the internal turmoil that was sure to follow when changes were made.

George also wanted the club to grow, but for the club to grow the Bandidos had to change in a big way. For new members to want to join, the old members had to open up and accept new members. There also had to be some type of attraction for new members, and policy change was going to be the only way to assure potential members that the club was worth joining. At the time, there were less than one hundred fifty Bandidos in the United States. Only a third of the members thought like George; another third were dinosaurs that thought the Bandido ways of the sixties should continue forever. The last third was stuck somewhere in the middle. Bandido George possessed the foresight to know that to effect major change, there had to be minor changes in club policy made every day.

For example, the old Bandido tradition of pissing all over a new patch holder and his club colors when he received his Bandidos colors was forbidden as soon as George took over. Other traditions like beating up prospects and/or hangarounds were no longer tolerated. Intimidation and extortion of prospects, hangarounds and independent bikers was strictly forbidden. Bandido El Presidente George also mandated, correctly, that the club needed new members that were men of respect, not pieces of shit. To get them, those potential members had to be first treated with respect; to get respect, you give respect.

Last of all but not least Bandido George was not a fan of methamphetamine at all. He believed, just like Lee and I, that methamphetamine was the biggest enemy that the club had ever faced. All three of us thought that, long term, methamphetamine would eventually cause the total destruction of the club unless something was done to prevent its use by Bandidos members. At a minimum, I secretly hoped that the sale and distribution of methamphetamine by Bandidos members would soon be a patch pulling offense, but that was a tall order of change that the club would not be ready to institute for many more years, if ever.

I was elated when I heard the news that George was going to be the next El Presidente, and I decided to do whatever I could legally to assist him get the job done. I knew that he was going to be a good El Presidente, as long as he kept focused on his plan to change the club and the members that hated him did not kill him. At the same time, I was worried that he too would eventually be corrupted by the absolute power he possessed like so many in the history of mankind that came before him. If that happened, in the end, nothing in the club would have really changed at all.

In late April of 1998, I was in the right place at the right time when I bought a two story, 2600 SF house on five acres of land in Sperry, a small suburb about 10 miles north of Tulsa. The house had been heavily damaged in a fire, but most of the damage was confined to the second floor. I got Harry "Skip" Hanson to help me, and together we rebuilt the entire house, making it like brand new. With no difficulty at all, within a week of its completion, I sold the house to a young couple who had bad credit, by carrying the mortgage myself.

May was a blur to me, between working on the Sperry house and the house I was living in, and the trips I took that month as part of being a Bandido. As Bandidos, we did the Pawhuska Mayfit and the Red River Run in Red River, New Mexico, back to back. At Red River, at the tail end of the Bandidos general meeting that Sunday about 3pm, we celebrated big time when we were handed our Oklahoma bottom rockers. It had been a year since we had started the Oklahoma Bandidos in Tulsa, and the Oklahoma chapter was already down to six of us – Lee, Bill Wolf, Turtle, Buddy, Joe and I had survived. Popeye, Keith, Skip, and Bones had all left the club in good standings, going their separate ways for various reasons.

At the end of a hectic summer, I traveled by car down to Austin and San Antonio for a myriad of reasons. First and foremost, it was going to be my daughter's fifth birthday, and I planned to take her to the Sea World marine water park at San Antonio for a birthday present. I also needed to visit with my newfound sister Julie, who was dying from a rare form of lung cancer called mesophylioma. Last of all, a Bandido I was quite fond of was heading off the prison for quite a while, and I wanted to visit with him a bit before he left.

While in San Antonio, I was quite fortunate when Bandido Bones, whose family had an annual pass to the Sea World water park, decided to accompany us there and act as our tour guide. Taylor got to see the dolphins there, even getting to feed them for a few precious minutes while I watched. That night, Bandido Ramon and his girlfriend threw Taylor an impromptu birthday party, going way beyond the call of duty when they provided her with a birthday cake and a few small birthday presents.

On the way home, we spent two days visiting my sister. It would be the last time I would see her alive. In spite of the horrible disease which had ravaged her body, she was alert and coherent for most of the time I was there. I was thankful for the short time we knew each other, but sad that I had not had more time with her. Shortly after I left Austin, headed for Tulsa in early August 1998, my sister Julie died, leaving this world for a much better place. I knew in my heart then that she would now be one of my guiding angels, watching over me for the rest of my days here on earth.

In October I landed a job for a Dallas based construction company, building a new child care facility for the Muskogee Regional Medical Center in Muskogee, Oklahoma. It would be my first cradle to grave construction project. I felt challenged by the fact that I had been brought in at the last minute, as well as the fact that I was a single dad with custody of a five-year old. I soon got into a routine every day, dropping my daughter off at a Koala Daycare Center near my house at 6:30am, then driving the fifty-five miles to the jobsite in Muskogee, usually getting to work by 7:30am. I would leave every day at 4:30pm, pick Taylor up at 5:30pm, then head to the house and make supper for her and me. It was a hectic pace, to say the least, but I persevered.

I finished off 1998 by attending the annual Bandidos Thanksgiving party, which this year was held in Austin for a change. While there, it was decided that I would be put in charge of publishing a new Bandidos monthly newsletter. The actual conception of a Bandidos newsletter had been originated about ten years prior by a Bandido named Rawhide, but never amounted to much more than a page or two of news. Bandido Super Dave from Baton Rouge had recently attempted to rejuvenate the concept, but had not had much success due to the fact that his computer equipment was antiquated and his knowledge insufficient.

Bandido Rude Richard & El Presidente George At
The Thanksgiving Day Run November 1998

I was to have total control over the content and authority to get the entire Bandido World coordinated, but had no authority to make the USA chapters submit monthly news. Over the next few months, I got the Australia, Europe and USA chapters to all do a monthly newsletter and coordinate the publishing date of each to coincide with each other. It was a monumental task to accomplish, as most of the older USA Bandido members thought that the newsletter was a total breach of internal security; they were all worried about what would happen if law enforcement or our enemies got hold of it. We placated those angry members by reassuring them that no published news would contain any harmful information; all that would be mentioned is general news like: "Baytown Bob broke his leg last Friday and is now at home in Corpus resting".

23

Bandidos Motorcycle Club Oklahoma
Christmas 1998 To December 1999

I had high hopes for Christmas in 1998, and the day before started off the holiday season just right, with the arrival of my sister Kitty, her husband Michael, my nieces Amanda and Kaitlyn, and my nephew Robert. They had traveled from Michigan to Tulsa by plane to spend Christmas with all of us. But my biological Dad Forrest ruined it almost as soon as they had arrived, in a horrific display of anger vented towards Kitty, Michael and me, in the kitchen of the home I shared with Forrest and his new Romanian wife. In front of all of the kids, Forrest screamed, shouted and swore like a deranged, demented man, smashing a book shelf and all that it contained in the process.

We all retreated to my bedroom, where we adults tried our best to calm the kids, who were obviously scared to death. After sorting through our options, we decided to vacate the premises, and drove fifty miles to the peace and tranquility of my construction site in Muskogee. There I proudly showed my sister Kitty and her family the child care facility that I was building. We decided to eat our Christmas dinner right there in the Muskogee Regional Medical Center dining facility. At about $2.50 per person, the meal was probably the least expensive Christmas meal I had ever purchased, but also one of the best. We were all surprised at how good the food was, and very thankful that Forrest was nowhere to be seen.

When we returned to the house, Forrest seemed to be a changed man. It was like nothing had ever happened, in spite of the damaged bookcase that had been reinstalled on the wall. Forrest wanted to have a "family night", where we all opened our presents together. In the spirit of the holiday season, notwithstanding his actions earlier that day, we all gathered around the fireplace in the living room. There, we acted like it was a joyous occasion, when in reality we were all wondering how soon Mr. Hyde would turn back into Mr. Jeckyl again. Thankfully, all went well that night, albeit surreal, and the next day I took my sister and her family to the airport for their return flight home.

But for them, the horrible trip was not over. By the time they got to St. Louis, where they were scheduled to change planes, an unexpected winter blizzard had arrived. The snow caused the whole airport to shut down, and Kitty's family ended up spending two days and nights in an expensive motel, where their only option for food was extremely expensive, hotel room service. Eventually the storm let up and the planes resumed flying, but by then there were thousands of other pissed off passengers all wanting to get to their original destinations as fast as they could. After waiting many more hours, Kitty and her family finally got back home to Flint, Michigan, where they relished the memory of the worst Christmas vacation they could ever imagine.

I spent the first three months of 1999 building the child care facility at the Muskogee Regional Medical Center, attending all required Bandido functions, and trying as hard as I could to be the best dad I could be for my daughter Taylor, who was now 5 and 1/2. In addition to all the demands in my life, I enrolled Taylor in counseling at the local Parent Child Center to help her cope with the absence of her biological mother. I had always been upset that Taylor did not come with an owner's manual, so while Taylor was in her weekly sessions with a child therapist, I spent a quiet hour in the library there at the Parent Child Center, reading and learning everything I could about raising a child, to improve my parenting skills. (Years later I would look back at this as one of the most important things I ever did for my daughter and myself.)

Taylor With Her Very First Cake March 1999

By March of 1999, the entire Oklahoma Bandidos chapter had had more than enough of John "Turtle" Fisher. Unfortunately Bandido Turtle had become addicted to methamphetamine, and was so far out there that no one could reach him. I remember us discussing Turtle's mental condition due to his constant ingestion of methamphetamine. We would joke that Turtle wasn't out in left field, he was beyond the bleachers and the parking lot. After giving him a last chance for the tenth time, Lee finally kicked him out of the club and pulled his patch.

But sadly we were dealing with the methhead and not the man; Turtle decided that he did not want to leave the chapter quietly. His expulsion turned into a fiasco, and instead of paying the chapter the small amount of money that he owed, Turtle told us all to get screwed. That incensed Bandido Joe, our Sergeant-at-Arms. Joe decided that he would teach Turtle a lesson, and that the chapter would take Turtle's bike to even the score and settle the debt. The only problem was that Turtle was nowhere to be found, and when he did turn up, he was so whacked out on the methamphetamine he was unpredictable and extremely volatile. Joe did not want to die for something as trivial as a motorcycle, but on the other hand, it was a matter of respect.

El Presidente George solved the problem for Joe by instructing Bandido Lee to repossess Turtle's bike by filing a civil replevin action in the Tulsa County Courthouse. A replevin lawsuit is how every car, truck and motorcycle dealer repossesses a vehicle when it cannot be located. Although the chapter attorney successfully prosecuted the replevin action, and the Court ordered the return of the motorcycle, Turtle dismantled the bike and sold off all the parts for more dope. The chapter never did collect the money that Turtle owed or locate what was left of his motorcycle.

The Entire Bandidos Oklahoma Chapter Early April 1999
Buddy, CT Ed, Lee, Joe & Bill Wolf

Turtle's methamphetamine addiction finally got the best of him less than a year later, when he was indicted by the feds for drug trafficking and firearms possession offenses. After being found guilty in a jury trial, he was sentenced to twenty-seven (27) years (without parole) in federal prison and will not be released until the year 2024, when he will be more than seventy years old. To this day, I still miss my talented friend John Fisher and think about him regularly, but I do not miss Bandido Turtle at all, for he was living proof that methamphetamine ruins lives.

By April I had pushed myself as far as I could, so when a Bandidos member by the name of Mississippi Charlie in Washington State died, I jumped at the opportunity to travel there for his funeral. On April 23rd, I loaded my daughter Taylor up for her first plane ride, and we arrived in Seattle after a layover in Salt Lake City. While there for only a few days, Taylor and I stayed with Bandido TJ, his wife Cheryl and her two daughters. One of Cheryl's daughters, Ashley, looked so much like Taylor that I was in a state of shock; they could have been blood sisters. I attended the funeral and after-party for Bandido Charlie, and spent a little time hanging out and relaxing with TJ while the girls kept Taylor occupied. (This was the same funeral where I met Alain Brunette, the Rock Machine Motorcycle Club member from Quebec, Canada.)

As soon as I returned to Oklahoma, it was back to the grind and my daily routine. I could see light at the end of the construction tunnel, though, because now the child care facility project was in its final stages. I was determined to see it completed and opened on schedule before July 1, 1999. For once in my life, I was happily employed, and had actually formed a real friendship with two of my bosses, Mike Crowe and Mike Lewis. Both Mikes were decent down to earth regular guys that were easy to relate to and great to work with. Later that summer, utilizing my connections at a Tulsa area Harley dealership, I was able to get both of them fantastic deals on a pair of brand new Twin Cam model Softtails, without them having to endure the mandatory six month waiting period that was common at that time in Texas.

The Muskogee Regional Medical Center Child Care Facility May 2, 1999

In spite of the fact that the Oklahoma Bandidos chapter was not gaining any new members, over the winter of 1998/spring of 1999 we established two chapters of a new motorcycle club here in Oklahoma that we proudly called the OK Riders. Their presence initially helped us look like we were larger than we were and eventually turned into a training operation for future Bandidos, much like a minor league baseball team is to a major league baseball team. Most citizens could not notice the difference in the two clubs; to them the patches were all the same because both had "red & gold" colors. We were also quite surprised when most law enforcement also thought it was the same club. In actuality, the OK Riders patch was the opposite colors as the Bandidos. The Bandidos colors were red on gold; whereas the OK Riders colors were gold on red. The Bandidos center patch was a Fat Mexican; whereas the OK Rider patch was a cow skull w/ snakes set in a diamond. Our top rocker said Bandidos; whereas theirs said OK Riders. Our bottom rockers were Oklahoma; theirs said Chandler or Claremore.

We intended from the outset to make this club a support club for the Bandidos, yet different from all the rest of the Bandido support clubs scattered all across the USA, for we guaranteed that its members would not be treated like shit by members of the Bandidos Motorcycle Club. For years, Bandidos had used the support clubs to do all of their dirty work and had treated support club members as their personal slaves. Our innovative approach to the treatment of Bandido support clubs would send shock waves through the Bandidos Nation and eventually change the way most support club members were treated.

Even though we were a national 1%er motorcycle club and did not need anyone's permission to do what we wanted to do, we did the right thing and approached the three major Oklahoma based outlaw motorcycle clubs (Rogues, Outlaws and Mongols) for their blessing on our new support club. We were surprised at the initial opposition we all received, but with persistence and perseverance, we finally got all three to ok the concept.

The first OK Rider chapter was based in a tiny Oklahoma City suburb called Jones, but we named it the Chandler chapter (Chandler was the name of the town where that chapter's President lived). Another chapter followed shortly thereafter just outside Tulsa in the town of Claremore, which had been the home of the humorist Will Rogers.

Both OK Rider chapters grew like weeds. This was primarily because the chapter members were not being treated like shit, and secondly, that the chapters were being led by seasoned motorcycle club veterans Charles "Snake" Rush and Raymond "Ray" Huffman. OK Rider Snake had been a member of the Rogues Motorcycle Club back in the 70's when Bandido Bill Wolf and I had both been Rogues ourselves. OK Rider Ray had once been a member of the local Mongols chapter in the early 90's.

Bandido Lee and I wanted the OK Riders MC to have a different focus; in essence an extension of what we preached all the time, so OK Rider bylaws dictated that:

1) No methamphetamine addicts are allowed to be a member of the club; and

2) To be a member you must have visible means of support, meaning that you either had to have a job, or a pension, or your

wife/girlfriend needed to be employed in a capacity that obviously provided sufficient income to support your lifestyle; and

3)   Your family and employment came first; the club came third; and

4)   You would not be treated like a slave by a member of the Bandidos Oklahoma chapter.

The Entire Red & Gold World In Oklahoma As It Existed At CT Ed"s House In The Spring Of 1999. From Left To Right In The Back Row: Butch, Donnie, Bandido CT Ed, Bandido Buddy, Bandido Joe, Bandido Lee, Shifter, Ree, George, and Cub. In The Front Row: Mr. Ed, Bandido Bill Wolf, Ray, Snake, Jeff, Doc & Mario

At the time, Bandidos Oklahoma chapter President Lee and I were convinced that the procedures and requirements to be a member in the Bandidos and the OK Riders would prevent the drug dealer/law enforcement problems that all the other outlaw clubs had; in hindsight our perception was a giant miscalculation. Bandido Lee and I would eventually be blindsided when in early 2000, we learned that Bandido Buddy, Bandido Joe, OK Rider Edwin "Sixpack" Collins (Claremore chapter), OK Rider George "George" Schuppan (Chandler chapter) and OK Rider James "Cub" Oleson were all involved in the business of manufacturing methamphetamine.

In the late spring of 1999, I had so much on my plate that I was in a constant state of exhaustion. In addition to my employment with the Dallas based construction firm (for which I was building the new $900,000 child daycare facility for the Muskogee Regional Medical Center), being a single dad with custody, and an Oklahoma Bandido, I had also been instructed by El Presidente George to increase my involvement with the Oklahoma Confederation of Clubs (COC). George asked me to get the Confederation in Oklahoma rolling, but this was no small task, for in Oklahoma, as in the rest of the country, most 1%er outlaw motorcycle clubs could barely tolerate each other. Most hated the others' guts and some were in a state of major war, killing each other on a regular basis. Getting these methamphetamine fueled bikers to sit down in one room and talk about life was a monumental concept, but if anyone could get it done, it was going to have to be me and the Bandidos.

In May of 1998 I had attended the annual meeting of the National Coalition of Motorcyclists (NCOM) at which there was a meeting scheduled for the Confederation of Clubs (COC). In advance, Bandido El Presidente George had asked members of the Pagans, Outlaws, Hells Angels and Sons of Silence Motorcycle Clubs to attend and not fight each other. All of these major 1%er organizations sent representatives to the Dallas, Texas convention, which was held in a large nine story hotel near the Dallas Ft. Worth airport. Bandido George guaranteed the safety of each major club member personally, and to make sure nothing happened, the Bandidos Motorcycle Club were in charge of security for the duration of the convention.

On the first day of the convention, I personally attended initial individual meetings between Bandido El Presidente George and each club. First George and I met with a pair of representatives from the Hells Angles, then the Pagans, then the Sons of Silence, and finally the Outlaws, who arrived with a large contingent of members expecting trouble. Bandido George and I convinced each club to send two members of their respective organizations to a meeting the next day that was to be held in a Bandidos suite. For the first time in history, the five major outlaw motorcycle clubs were all in one room at the same time, which was a major accomplishment. Unfortunately, at the time I was a new Bandido, and was not allowed to attend the actual meeting between the five clubs, but I learned a lot from the experience. I was told afterwards that not much was discussed, but all five clubs did agree to stop fighting and killing each other and to open lines of communication between each other, which everyone hoped would prevent future conflicts from getting blown out of proportion.

Shortly thereafter, there seemed to be some sort of truce among all the major clubs, which passed on to the lesser clubs. So by the spring of 1999, there was some limited participation in the Oklahoma Confederation of Clubs by the Outlaws, Rogues, and Mongols and a lot of participation by the Red & Gold. In the beginning of 1999, I had been voted in as the "Legal Liaison" for the Oklahoma COC, so by late spring I had done a fairly good job at getting all the

Oklahoma motorcycle clubs involved, and trying to keep the ones that were involved from having arguments that would lead to more fighting.

For years, the Sons of Silence MC had been locked in a mortal battle with the Outlaws MC, but over time I had cultivated friendships in both organizations. In early May, I personally invited members from both organizations to be our guests at the annual Pawhuska Rally which was going to be held in the middle of May, 1999. It took a lot to get them to agree, but in the end we got it done. A contingent of Outlaws arrived from Indiana and Ohio to join their Oklahoma chapter, and a larger group of Sons of Silence members arrived from Kansas and Colorado. I put the Outlaws right next to our camp up on the hill, and the Sons of Silence right in front of us. (We later learned that amongst the Sons of Silence were two of their full patch members that were actually undercover ATF agents that had infiltrated their club.)

To get the two motorcycle club members used to being in the presence of each other, I made sure that there was an Outlaw, a Bandido and a Son together for each guard duty shift at the main entrance to the Bandidos camp. It wasn't long before the talk between the three turned to pretty women, the weather, baseball or whatever, and friendships were born. By the end of the weekend, it was not unusual to see an Outlaw visiting with a Sons of Silence member or vice versa. The whole 1%er world everywhere in the United States was rocked by the situation, and how well it turned out. I had taken a huge chance trying this out, but in the end, it was a major turning point in the history of the 1%er clubs in the United States.

All The 1%er Motorcycle Clubs Together At Pawhuska May 1999

The last days of June, I completed the child care facility construction project in Muskogee, Oklahoma. I was very proud of that project, primarily because I had done something for a bunch of kids that would last a lifetime. It felt good to have given something back to the world, after taking so much from it for so many years. I took a week off, and soon got handed new construction projects, both of which I could manage from my office in my home. This was a godsend, because it allowed me much more time to take care of my daughter. It also gave me the income I so desperately needed at the time to keep up the Bandidos lifestyle that I was living. The first construction project was at Fort Huachuca in Sierra Vista, Arizona, which involved the replacement of an existing fire alarm system at the base hospital. The second project was the new installation of a fire sprinkler system at another U.S. Army hospital, at Fort Leonard Wood near Rolla, Missouri. I was going to be the Project Manager for both projects simultaneously, which required a ton of paperwork, with both being federal government construction projects.

As I dived headfirst into both projects in early July, my biological Dad Forrest and his Romanian wife decided to move out of my home and get a place of their own. Forrest and I had been sharing the Owasso farmette while we rebuilt it, but the rebuilding was long over and now it was time for us to part ways. I was quite ecstatic, because now some of my major problems had magically worked themselves out. For quite a while, I had wanted to find a new female partner, since by now I had given up on re-establishing any resemblance of a relationship with my ex-wife Teresa. But I had been unable to, up to this point, for I had been much too busy and had to contend with the piss poor example my dad's Romanian wife would provide to any female that entered my life. She deliberately contributed absolutely nothing to the household, and because she was in her mid-twenties and Forrest was in his mid-sixties, she had him waiting on her like she was some type of princess. There was no way I could be involved with a female that did not contribute to the household financially, emotionally and physically; and no female in my life would willingly contribute to my household while my Dad's wife lived there and did absolutely nothing.

At the end of July, I cashed in some of my Southwest Airlines rapid reward miles, and flew with my daughter Taylor to Michigan for a few days of relaxation. While there, Bandido El Presidente George called and told me that he had to fire me from the National chapter. I had been appointed an El Secretario (a secretary for the National chapter - this would be the first time) at the Red River Rally in New Mexico over the Memorial Day weekend, but still had not sewed on my new El Secretario bottom rocker.

I never had the need to show everyone that I was a National Officer, and really could care less. As a matter of fact, I kind of dreaded the attention that the rocker would bring, both from regular members of the club as well as law enforcement. On the other hand, it was nice to see that I was being recognized and appreciated for all that I was doing for the club. I had been doing National Secretary duties for the National chapter part time off and on for the last year and getting the bottom rocker did not affect or change my job assignments.

Bandido George still wanted me to continue working for the National Chapter; he just wanted me to do it while I was not a member of the National chapter. George told me that Bandido John "Big John" Lammons had cried the blues about me being a part of the National chapter, and to pacify him I had to go transfer back to the Oklahoma chapter. (It would be years before I found out that George had lied to me about what Big John had said, for the truth was that Big John had not said anything about me at all). It really did not affect me that I had been fired before I ever sewed the rocker on, so we all turned it into a little joke. At the time I was just another ex-National officer in a long list of ex-National officers, except my tenure as a National officer had probably been the shortest.

I flew back to Tulsa and left my daughter under the care and supervision of my sister Kitty in Michigan. It felt good to temporarily not have to take care of Taylor, but on the down side, I missed her a lot. I was looking forward to her starting the 1st grade in less than a month. With some extra spare time on my hands, I turned my attention to the fact that I needed female companionship, but in this lifestyle of mine, there was not a very large selection pool of suitable candidates to consider. I had heard of computer dating, so I decided to give it a try. I quickly located a dating website devoted to the biker lifestyle, where I tested the waters over the next few months.

At the end of July, I drove up to St. Louis, stopping on the way to check on my jobsite at Fort Leonard Wood. I caught a Southwest Airlines flight to Detroit, picked Taylor up at my sister's home and then we flew back to St. Louis. It was now Taylor's sixth birthday and you can imagine her surprise when the airplane staff sang Happy Birthday to her over the intercom system, with most of the passengers joining in. After arriving in St Louis, we drove down to Branson, Missouri, where she and I planned to spend a few days celebrating her birthday. We both had a blast at Silver Dollar City, but the highlight of the trip ended up being an outdoor slide and pool at a hotel we accidentally found.

Taylor On The Plane Just After Everyone Sang "Happy Birthday"

Two weeks after we got home, Taylor got on the school bus for the first time and headed off to the first grade. She was now six years old, and I was thinking about how fast time was flying. It was now much easier to take care of her, and I had no more daycare expenses to sustain. My job was going well, and I still had a little time on my hands. I soon got lucky and hooked up with a girl I had met on the biker dating website. She was twenty-one and fresh out of a three year stint in the United States Army. Her name was Caroline Haynor and she lived near Savannah, Georgia, where she was going to college and working at a car dealership. My only problem was the distance between us and the fact that she loved horses more than Harleys.

I invited Caroline to Oklahoma for the September 1999 Pawhuska Rally, and then utilized one of my Southwest Airlines rapid reward tickets to order her plane fare for free. On the day she was supposed to fly out of Jacksonville, Florida, there was a hurricane. Trusting in my decisions that were being made one thousand miles away, Caroline raced southwards on I-95 while thousands of cars headed the opposite way to escape the dangerous storm. Everyone going north that day must have thought that she was crazy. Arriving at the Jacksonville airport with only minutes to spare, she caught the very last plane out before the airport was completely closed. She had dodged a bullet, and we both took it as a sign from the Gods that this was meant to be. After a slight mix up on her plane ticket was resolved in Baltimore, she ended up in Tulsa right on time, the day before Pawhuska started.

We awoke at 5:00am in the morning to the startling sound of Bandido JW Rock (Bandido JW would ultimately be shot to death by a Houston Bandido while sleeping in 2003) from Austin scratching on our window screen, hollering for me to get up and let him in. Caroline just about had a heart attack, but soon calmed down when she found out who he was. After I let JW in and got him settled, I tried to explain to Caroline what it was like, being a Bandido, but that is kind of hard to understand when you have never lived this kind of life before. Over the next few days I knew that she was in for a crash course on being the girlfriend of a Bandido (in the Bandidos, our girlfriends and wives are referred to as PBOL's - Proud Bandido Ol' Lady), and I was not sure how she would react. I knew one thing for sure though: it was going to be interesting in the least, to see how she would act when faced with the stark reality of Bandido life.

Pawhuska went well for Caroline and me, as well as everyone else. For once, all the other Bandidos and a bunch of OK Riders pitched in and took over the operation of our magnificent camp up on the hill overlooking Pawhuska. The only snafu was when I went up there to check on things Thursday afternoon, and found that Bandido Buddy had not arrived to secure the campsite as he was ordered to. (We should have seen it coming, for by now Bandido Buddy was deeply involved in the world of methamphetamine, and doing anything on time was not Buddy's way). I was extremely pissed off, but I made some on the spot decisions and held down the fort until reinforcements arrived. I was looking forward to enjoying myself for the first time, because at every Pawhuska since I had become a Bandido, I had been in charge of our entire camp; the food, security, drinks and all the other responsibilities that come with a campsite for one hundred members of a major 1%er motorcycle club.

Caroline & CT Ed At Pawhuska September 1999

Bandidos JW & Lee At Pawhuska September 1999

Upon my return from Pawhuska, I was quite dismayed because I could not locate my daughter Taylor, who was on a court ordered, unsupervised visit with her biological mother. When I finally made contact with her mom, I found out that Taylor was in the hospital because of her asthma, undergoing periodic breathing treatments. After my initial tendency to blame her biological mother for what happened subsided, I learned that this was the serious side of asthma, and that we all needed to be aware of the different things that would or could set off an asthma attack. Visiting Taylor in the hospital that Sunday night, I realized how much she meant to me, and thanked God that Taylor had survived and was going to be ok.

A few days later, Taylor was released from the hospital and all was well again, until a lady from the Oklahoma Department of Human Services (DHS) showed up at my door. Apparently DHS had received a complaint about my parenting skills, related to my refusal to run out and buy a one thousand dollar breathing machine that some idiot nurse at the hospital told me I needed. For starters, there was no way I could afford that breathing machine, and secondly, there was absolutely no need for it. While Taylor was in the hospital I had done a lot of research on the situation. I had called a brother Bandido by the name of Doc, who happened to be a pediatrician in Texas. I already knew that Taylor was just "slightly" asthmatic, and I had determined that this breathing attack likely was a fluke. Bandido Doc promised to be there for me whenever I needed him or advice.

After letting the DHS lady look all around my home, and explaining to her my situation in detail, including the fact that both Taylor and I were attending the Parent Child Center on a regular basis, she concluded that all was in order. I also had explained to her that if Taylor had any more problems like this in the future, the Indian Hospital was just fifteen minutes away, where Taylor was entitled to free medical care for her entire life because she was a member of the Cherokee Indian tribe. Thankfully the DHS complaint was terminated right then and there, for in Oklahoma, like most other states, DHS has the power to immediately remove the child from the home and place the child into foster care for an indefinite period of time.

Caroline had already returned to Georgia by the time I had my little talk with the lady from DHS, and her trip home, thankfully, was uneventful. The hurricane had not done much damage along the I-95 corridor, and everything at her home was just like she had left it. We remained in close contact throughout October, talking on the phone every few days and exchanging emails daily. I liked her a lot, and was hoping that she felt the same and that things between us would work out.

On October 1, 1999 all members of the Bandidos and OK Riders met at OK Rider Cub's home just outside of Jones for a mandatory meeting. At that meeting, we voted in our first new members in the history of our chapter. Hank "CC" Leasure, David "Doc" Mullikin and Robert "Ree" Thomas had all been OK Riders, and were now Probationary members of the Bandidos Oklahoma chapter. During this meeting, we also took pictures for our annual Xmas card, which came out just great. It was a time of joy for all of us, but if we had opened our eyes, we should have seen the writing on the wall.

By the middle of October, 1999, I somehow convinced my girlfriend Caroline, whom I had met through an online dating service a few months before, to leave Georgia and move to Oklahoma. The week before Halloween, she made the long trip by herself to deliver her old beat up Ford pickup truck, the horse trailer and her horse to her new home in Owasso. She stayed a day, then got in my new pickup and pulled a borrowed enclosed cargo trailer that included my motorcycle all the way back to Georgia.

I admired her tenacity and courage, and thought that our relationship was bound to work out if this was any sign of how it will be in the future. A day after she arrived back in Georgia, I flew down to Jacksonville, Florida and met her at the airport. We then drove the hundred miles to Savannah, loaded up all of her furniture, clothes and Harley Sportster, and took off fully loaded for Daytona, Florida. We wanted to spend a few days there in the sun and warm weather, experiencing the annual Halloween Bike Week, before we returned to winter in Oklahoma.

Bandidos MC Oklahoma Christmas Card December 1999

While there we hooked up with my chapter President and good friend Bandido Lee "Lee" McArdle, who had flown into Orlando, and then paid a visit to the local Outlaws Motorcycle Club clubhouse. We spent the afternoon there with Outlaws Smitty and Fuzzy, both longtime members of the Florida Outlaws, whom I had known for twenty years.

While we were there, two Bandidos from Alabama stopped by to relax, shake off the road and drink a few beers. It turned into quite a party, but not being much of a party person and being very tired from the moving, Caroline and I left about 7 pm and returned to our room. The next day we met up with another old friend who used to be a member of the Rogues Motorcycle Club of Oklahoma with me back in the late 70's, David Gruber, whom I had not seen in quite a while. Our stay in Daytona was way too short, and by the end of the day we left making the long, slow drive back to Oklahoma.

Outlaw Fuzzy & CT Ed Florida October 1999

No sooner than we got back to Oklahoma and got Caroline all settled in, I took off for a week in late November and went to Europe again where I attended the patch over ceremony of the Ghostriders Motorcycle Club in Germany, who had now decided to join the Bandidos. I had been sent down to visit the Ghostriders MC in the spring of 1998, and had a personal interest in this important event in German biker history. The patch party was held in Dinslaken at the new Bandidos MC Germany Dinslaken chapter clubhouse, which had been a Ghostriders MC clubhouse the day before. The party was fantastic, and Bandidos from all over the world were there. I was shocked to see that Bandido John "Big John" Lammons made it all the way from Galveston, Texas with Bandido Knucklehead Dave.

Bandido Big John had me laughing my ass off when he told me about the gift he had brought for the new German Bandidos. As always, he was running late when it came time to take off for the airport in Houston, so at the last minute he grabbed a Bandidos plaque off the wall and threw it in his bag. When he got to Germany, he realized that the plaque had been a gift to him from me, given to him about ten years before. To compound his mistake, he quickly deduced that I was going to be there in Germany with him. The easiest thing for him to do was to tell me the story and hope that it was going to be ok with me. It was so like Big John to do something like this, and what was I going to say anyway, that it wasn't ok? After all, he wasn't known as "Big John" for nothing....he could have done whatever he wanted to. I appreciated the respect and class he showed, and without hesitating, I told him not to worry about it at all. From that day on, it was an inside joke between him and me.

When it came time for the actual ceremony, at which each chapter was handed a ceremonial plaque to mark the occasion, we all went into a huge room at the clubhouse. We were all packed in like sardines; there were more than two hundred Bandidos there. European Presidente Jim gave each chapter a plaque and a big welcome to the Bandido Nation. I was proud to be there, and prouder of the fact that I had helped the Ghostriders decide to become Bandidos. After the ceremony, it was time to bring out the dancing girls, and some of my German brothers had reserved a seat for me right up front. At the time, I thought that the courtesy was an outstanding gesture on their behalf; I should have known that I was the object of a worldwide practical joke conspiracy.

No sooner had the first beautiful stripper got on the stage and started to dance, she came directly to me and led me up on the stage to a chair that she had strategically positioned to entertain my Bandido brothers. As you can imagine, I was like a lamb being led to slaughter, and happier than a pig in shit in spite of the fact that the joke was on me. With everyone cheering her on, and hundreds of cameras taking extortion quality pictures, the stripper performed an exquisite show using me as a center piece. Months later, long after I was home, I was informed that one of these pictures had appeared in the German biker magazine called "Biker News". Like an idiot, I asked Bandido El Secretario Armin to mail a copy to me, and he did. He must have laughed his ass off on the way to the post office, because he added another ten compromising photos of me and the girl to the magazine, as markers for the page where my picture was.

Bandidos Germany Patch Over Ceremony December 1999

Ordinarily, this would not have been a problem at all, but it just so happened that when the magazine arrived, I was out of town for my job, and Caroline asked me over the phone if she could open the package and look at the magazine. I had previously told her that it was coming, never figuring that there was a picture in the magazine of the stripper and me, much less the ten more photos that had been added to it. You can imagine the horror on my girlfriend's face when she opened the magazine and found all the pictures, and as you can imagine, life at home was a little uncomfortable for the next few weeks. Thankfully, Caroline was a great ol' lady, and it did not take her long to realize that it truly had been a great piece of Bandido entertainment.

I did get to spend a night and day at Bandido El Secretario Armin's home, and then left to spend my last day/night with my old citizen friend Dieter Tenter, whom I had known for ten years and had visited about eighteen months before. It was good to see him and his family again, and get some much needed rest before I took the long plane ride home. I was glad to be back in the United States, looking forward to going back to work.

CT Ed Having Too Much Fun In Dinslaken, Germany December 1999

24

Bandidos Motorcycle Club Oklahoma
January 2000 To June 2000

The first day of February arrived with a gunshot. Two Bandidos members and one of their associates were assassinated while eating lunch at a restaurant in Helsinki, Finland. Bandido Bjorn Isaksson, (President of our Helsinki chapter), Bandido Sakke Pirra and Juha Jalonen, a member of the Black Rhino Motorcycle Club, were all killed in a hail of gunshots.

Three Dead In Biker Gang Shootout In Lahti

Three men died and several others were wounded on Tuesday afternoon in a firefight between rival motorcycle gangs in a pizzeria in the centre of Lahti. The dead were all associated with the Bandidos MC club, and the alleged shooters came from the former Lahti chapter of Cannonball MC. First reports indicate that the incident was a revenge attack, after a member of the Lahti club was shot in the leg last October. The Bandidos gang members responsible for this were appearing in court in Lahti yesterday.

Shortly after noon, Lahti police received a report of shooting in the pizzeria-kebab restaurant, which was close to the court-house. Members of the Bandidos gang had gone there for lunch, but there were also some diners who had no connection with the rival gangs. Two cars carrying three men had driven up to the doors of the restaurant, after which numerous shots were heard. Two of the victims died in their seats and four were taken to hospital, where one died later in the day from his wounds. Some of those in the restaurant escaped as best they could, but they later reported to police.

The Lahti police rapidly arrested around a dozen members of the Lahti gang, of whom three are suspected of direct involvement in the shootings. The pizzeria was cordoned off immediately, and police took away a number of weapons. At no point did the police themselves have to resort to firearms, nor were they threatened at any time. The authorities had been on the alert for trouble when the court convened, but everything had gone peacefully.

This is by no means the first such incident in Finland. In the autumn of 1997 the Hells Angels and Bandidos, two of the three biker gangs deemed criminal organizations in Finland, reached a widely-publicized truce. This had been preceded by sporadic outbreaks of violence, including a bazooka attack on the Hells Angels headquarters and the death by shooting of a Bandidos member outside their clubhouse in Helsinki. The truce did nothing to quell the crimes and violence associated with the gangs, but did prevent direct confrontations.

The other party in the Lahti incident were former members of the Lahti chapter of a third (purely Finnish) gang named Cannonball MC. They resigned from Cannonball MC last September over internal differences. Also regarded as a criminal organization by police, Cannonball MC has clubs in Helsinki, Turku and Kouvola. Last spring all of the then ten Lahti members of the gang were serving prison sentences. In the case of the two other international gangs, the work of the authorities is often hampered by the fact that high-profile criminal actions lead to honors from abroad. Finland's Hells Angels chapter received their official membership not long after the Helsinki shooting and incidents at Oslo and Copenhagen airports that left another Bandidos member dead, while the so-called "hangaround club" that became Bandidos mysteriously got its membership shortly after the bazooka-shell flew through the wall of the Hells Angels HQ.

On the 5th of February, 2000, I was in Denver attending the annual bike parts swap meet there, when I received a phone call from Tulsa. OK Riders Edwin "Sixpack" Collins and James "Cub" Olsen had been arrested for "Manufacturing A Controlled Dangerous Substance" and "Trafficking In Illegal Drugs" and were in jail, waiting for someone to post their $50,000 bail bond. I was informed that they had been caught with a significant quantity of methamphetamine, and to complicate matters, their wives were with them and had also been arrested. The wives had $50,000 bail bonds on each of them as well. Since I was in charge of legal matters, it fell on to my shoulders as to how we were going to handle the problem.

I gave OK Rider President Raymond "Ray" Huffman the name of a local bail bond agent I knew very well, who had previously agreed to charge anyone in the red & gold world a 10% bail bond fee, and who was also willing to post their bail immediately, without requiring them to come up with any money. All the other bail bond companies in Tulsa required a 15% fee, and this particular bail bond company was willing to allow the four of them to pay their bail bond fees over the next few weeks. I also advised OK Rider Ray to let all four of them sit in jail for three more days, at which time they would be eligible to have an attorney do a bail bond reduction hearing, at which the bail bond should be reduced to $10,000 or less, for each person.

A bail bond reduction would make a major difference in their respective post-arrest financial lives, for it is a lot easier to come up with $4,000 (10% of the reduced bail bond for all four) vs. $30,000 (15% of the initial bail bond for all four). But before I got back to Tulsa, OK Rider Cub decided that he and his wife had to get out of jail immediately, and that he would rather pay $15,000 in bail bond fees (15% of the initial $50,000 bail bond fees for him and his wife) than wait three more days and only have to pay $2,000 (10% of the reduced bail bond).

To make matters worse, OK Rider Ray located another bail bond firm that we did not have any experience with, which was willing to let OK Rider Cub and his wife make payments to them. By the time I returned to Tulsa, OK Rider Cub and his wife were both long since out of jail, now owing the bail bond company a total of $15,000. OK Rider Ray had even somehow been coerced into co-signing for the bail bond fees, so if OK Rider Cub and his wife failed to make the $15,000 payment, OK Rider Ray could be and would be held responsible. Bandido Lee and I were amazed at their stupidity in handling the bail bond situation, and very upset by the fact that Sixpack and Cub had been arrested on drug charges.

OK Rider Sixpack and his wife waited another week in jail, and their bail bonds were reduced to $10,000 each. But OK Rider Sixpack remained in jail, not willing to postpone the inevitable; instead, he eventually took all the blame for the entire situation, and was sentenced to twelve years in the care and custody of the Oklahoma Department of Corrections, getting credit for all of his jail time. His wife posted her $10,000 bail bond, paid the bail bond agent a $1,000 bail bond fee, and the charges against her were eventually dismissed. OK Rider Cub and his wife ultimately pled guilty and each received two year deferred prison sentences.

Bandido Lee and I were beginning to wonder what was going on, for this was the second time in less than sixty days that OK Rider Sixpack had been arrested. The first time, in early December of 1999, it had been with another OK Rider, Craig "Shifter" Sherman, in Lincoln County, Oklahoma, and we had been told that the charges had just been for knives and guns. We had begun to hear rumors that some of our members (OK Riders & Bandidos) had been manufacturing methamphetamine, and we decided it was time for us to look into it and hopefully put those rumors to rest.

When we eventually learned the truth, Bandido Lee and I were shocked. Apparently OK Riders Sixpack and Shifter had been arrested in Lincoln County for "Possession Of A Precursor Substance" and "Possession Of A Controlled Drug With The Intent to Distribute". To make matters worse, they had both lied to most all of us about the arrest, and lying to any of us was a patch-pulling offense. As soon as we had verifiable proof of what had transpired, which took a few months, both were expelled from the OK Riders organization for drug dealing and then lying about it.

In the Lincoln County case, ex-OK Rider Sixpack once again tried to take the blame for everything, and after pleading guilty to his charges, was sentenced to an additional five years in the care and custody of the Oklahoma Department of Corrections; this now meant that he had a total of seventeen years to serve for his Tulsa County and Lincoln County offenses. Ex-OK Rider Shifter eventually pled guilty and received six years in the care and custody of the Oklahoma Department of Corrections.

By now we were also regularly hearing rumors that Bandido Earl "Buddy" Kirkwood was manufacturing methamphetamine at his home just outside Sapulpa, and then selling the finished product to the Outlaws Motorcycle Club chapter in Oklahoma City, OK. We also learned that Buddy was the driving force behind the arrests of Sixpack, Shifter and Cub, and that all three had been involved in various aspects of his methamphetamine manufacturing business. Obviously, drug dealing was a major problem for our Oklahoma chapter. Doing illegal business with members of another 1%er motorcycle club was now totally against Bandidos National policy and an automatic patch-pulling offense.

We had also ascertained that ex-OK Rider Shifter was buying Red Phosphorus, one of the major ingredients required for the manufacture of methamphetamine, from a Tulsa area informant who was part of a law enforcement sting. Shifter was then selling it to Bandido Buddy and many others, and both ex-OK Rider Sixpack and Shifter had been and/or were still employed by Bandido Buddy in Buddy's significantly large drug distribution conspiracy.

In addition, Bandido Louis "Bill Wolf" Rackley had been busted in Broken Arrow for simple possession of methamphetamine just after Thanksgiving of 1999. Bandido Bill Wolf would eventually, in July of 2000, plead guilty and be sentenced to serve five years in the care and custody of the Oklahoma Department of Corrections. It was starting to look like we had a major methamphetamine epidemic on our hands, and we had no idea how to nip it in the bud. Like the proverbial children's story of an ostrich that hides his head in the sand, Bandido Lee and I looked the other way in the spring of 2000 and hoped that the problem would fix itself.

OK Rider Sixpack January 2000 *Bandido Buddy January 2000*

In spite of all the negativity surrounding some of us, life was pretty good for the rest of the red & gold world here in Oklahoma. Bandido Lee even sold his old Harley and bought himself a brand spanking new 2000 model Twin Cam Softtail Nighttrain. I was quite thankful that I had given up my "Legal Liaison" position in the Oklahoma Confederation of Clubs in January, but in spite of the fact that I still had so much going on in my life, it seemed as though I needed more to do.

So in February, I started lending a helping hand to a Bandido who had been incarcerated for more than twenty-five years in Louisiana, by selling some of the items he was making in a prison hobby craft shop. His name was Jimmie "74 Jim" Graves, and Bandido 74 Jim had been in prison so long that when he was "discovered", it took the club quite a while to actually find a current Bandido member who remembered him and the circumstances surrounding his incarceration. It had been explained to me that the Bandidos Nomad chapter were supposed to be taking care of Bandido 74 Jim, but 74 Jim was not happy with the amount of care that he was receiving. After making initial contact with him via letters and phone calls, I immediately set out marketing his wares worldwide.

Bandido 74 Jim manufactured beautiful Bandido wooden puzzle plaques, belt buckles, wooden clocks, and other fine crafted goods from his small prison hobby shop at the Louisiana State Prison in Angola. He had a regular crew of inmates to assist him in the manufacturing process, so before long we had a pretty good assembly line going. I took orders for his products worldwide, by sending out emails that included pictures of the particular product we were trying to sell. Over the next sixteen months, I sold more than $10,000 worth of goods for him, which was more money than 74 Jim had ever seen in his life. In the process, I pissed off more than a few members of the Bandidos Nomad chapter. It seemed that by selling so much of Bandido 74 Jim's goods (which obviously resulted in a major influx in capital, worldwide attention and care for Bandido 74 Jim), the Nomads thought that I made them look bad for not having done more for 74 Jim in the past themselves.

After repeatedly bitching to El Presidente George and anyone that would listen the Bandidos Nomad chapter finally got their way in the early summer of 2001. In spite of all of my protests, as well as the protests of Bandido 74 Jim, the responsibility for the marketing of his products was returned to the Nomad chapter. It did not take long for the Nomad in charge of selling 74 Jim's goods to screw everything up, and before long, everything in 74 Jim's life was back to the way it had been before I came along.

Probationary Oklahoma Bandido Ree suffered a major heart attack in late February, and by the end of the month we all decided that it was in his best interest to let him leave the club in good standings based on his health problems. Shortly thereafter, we accepted the transfer of a North Houston Bandido by the name of Steven "Steve" Buitron, who had chased his girlfriend to Lawton, Oklahoma, to the Oklahoma Bandidos chapter. At the time, Bandido Steve was a welcome addition to our family, for we now had Oklahoma Bandidos living in

Tulsa, Oklahoma City and Lawton. If we only had had our eyes open, we would have seen him as the lying, two faced coward he really was.

In the middle of March 2000, I set out for Mexico, traveling first to Dallas on Southwest Airlines and then catching an American Airlines flight to my destination, Mexico City. El Presidente George had asked me to attend another Bandidos world meeting with him, and while there, as an added incentive, I had been invited to attend the wedding of Bandido Sargento de Armas Martin "Martine" Gonzalez. Bandido Martine was a new Bandido from Washington State, who had grown up in the Mexico City area and whose family still resided there. He owned and operated a martial arts school in the Bellingham area of Washington State, and because of his extraordinary skills in martial arts and proximity to El Presidente George's home, Bandido Martine had already been appointed a Sargento de Armas in the National chapter.

As soon as I got off the plane, I was met at the airport by a member of the Legionaires Motorcycle Club and Bandido Sargento de Armas John "Big John" Lammons, who delivered me to the downtown hotel where we had all agreed to meet. Already waiting for me there were El Presidente George "George" Wegers, Presidente Jim and Vice Presidente Mike from Europe, Presidente Jason and El Secretario Bullets from Australia, and Bandidos Martine and Jimbo from Washington. All of us talked a lot about world affairs over the next few days, wherever and whenever we could. A couple of times we met officially in one of the hotel rooms to make decisions, and our agenda, as you can see from the notes that I took, was not very illegal:

<u>World Meeting Notes From Mexico – March 17, 2000</u>

1.   New Website Idea:

      a)   check on availability of www.freeharley.com or an equal
      b)   draft a business plan and distribute to all continents
      c)   get contracts between all parties
      d)   Incorporate in the United States
      e)   Look for website designer
      f)   Australia interested – Europe considering – USA interested

2.   5 year patch – anyone can submit a design which will be voted on at a future world meeting.

3.   World meetings themselves are for National officers only.

4.   Support Gear:

      a)   No "Bandidos" or "Bandits"
      b)   Applies to anything you can wear

c) . All designs to be approved by National Presidente in each continent.

d) Remove all unapproved support items from the website.

5. Dizzie – webmaster worldwide.

6. All center patches will be identical – one design on a disc to be supplied by USA to Australia & Europe – all El Secretarios responsible for patches will get together as soon as possible via email or phone.

7. All National Vice Presidente rockers will be changed to "Visa Presidente".

8. ENM patch – see appropriate NSA for approval.

9. TCB patch – ok in Europe - not used in, or to be given to USA & Australia.

10. Probationary rockers will be worn in the USA – for all new Probates.

11. New front patch for hang around clubs in Europe only.

12. USA will check on support patch being worn by USA/Europe club.

13. Asia & Mexico need to be developed.

14. Australia wants visitors from USA & Europe for National Run in October.

15. Australia will send USA club by-laws & bike signing agreement.

16. Australia will send 5 Life Member patches to USA & Europe.

17. Addition to Europe's by-laws only – all motorcycles will be rebuilt in winter months only – in season 30 days downtime rule will apply.

18. Australia & Europe will use the same support items.

On the night before Bandido Martine got married, some of the Legionaires Motorcycle Club members took us out to a local strip joint for Martine's informal, last minute bachelor's party. I still remember vividly, leaving that bar early in the morning, and seeing hundreds of orphaned, disparate children either begging or selling insignificant, trivial items on the sidewalks as we walked by, and being thankful that my daughter Taylor did not have to do that just to survive. Late the next afternoon, we set out for a ride across town to see Bandido Martine and his wife Whitney get married. There in a quaint little Mexican church, along with about fifty of Bandido Martine's family and childhood friends, we were all very surprised to find out that the wedding and reception were going to be done in the tradition of a real Mexican Bandido wedding from the 1800's.

Bandidos Jimbo, CT Ed, Jason, Bullets & Mike Mexico City March 2000

At the reception dinner, all of the Bandidos sat at one table, where we were all served our drinks and food before anyone else. This was as the real Bandidos had been treated many centuries before us. We were told that the original Bandidos were the guardians and the protectors of the town, and in honor of them, as well as to show them respect, the old time Bandidos were always served first at any meal.

Presidente Jim, Sargento De Armas Martine, & El Presidente
George In Mexico City March 2000

Martin & Whitney Gonzalez In Mexico City March 2000

On a personal note, as soon as I returned to Tulsa from my Mexican siesta, my daughter Taylor took her first bicycle ride without the training wheels that she had been using for the last two years. This was for her, as you can imagine, a monumental event; and as for me, I couldn't have been prouder.

With my two construction projects in Sierra Vista, AZ and Rolla, MO now closed out, by early April of 2000 it was time to move on to the next project, which was in McKinney, Texas, completing the Collin County Courthouse. This was a daunting task, because the job was way behind schedule and the two hundred men on the job were primarily Hispanic. Ordinarily this would be no problem, but in this case, the foremen for the various sub contractor crews seemed to be unable to communicate with any of their employees. This was presenting an unusual problem; everywhere you looked there were dozens of Hispanic men standing around doing nothing, in spite of the fact that there was a lot to do.

My first day on the job, I knew that I needed some help, so I got on the phone and called in two of my Bandido brothers from New Mexico. Both Bandido Jessie "Chuy" Wicketts and Bandido "Keiko" were Hispanic, construction experts and bilingual. I made airline reservations for them that afternoon, and by noon the next day, both were in Texas and on the jobsite, working. By the end of the day, we confirmed that the white sub contractor foremen had no love for the Hispanic workers, and that we definitely had a major communication problem. By the next morning, I had made the decision that all work orders to the Hispanic construction workers were to come from either Bandido Chuy or Bandido Keiko, bypassing the respective foremen for each sub contractor work crew.

Collin County Courthouse In McKinney, Texas April 2000

Although unusual, this got all of the Hispanic construction workers working, and kept them working. Within two weeks, we had gained everyone's respect, and turned the job back around to where it was functioning normally. As we finished up the actual jail holding cells part of the project, we found the Collin County Sheriff's deputies there learning to operate the jail. Being the Bandidos that we were, we decided to have some fun with the Sheriff in charge of the training. In the process of constructing the actual jail cells, which were locked electronically, Bandido Chuy had discovered a glitch in the locking mechanism. This glitch allowed him to open the lock with a small piece of metal, from inside the holding cell, *while he was locked inside the cell.*

So I called over the training officer, and had him lock Bandido Chuy in the cell. I then turned the officer around to face me, with his back to the holding cell that he had just locked Bandido Chuy into. Within thirty seconds, Bandido Chuy was tapping the training officer on his shoulder. You can imagine the surprise on the Sheriff's face, when he discovered that his million dollar jail holding facility was not secure. We never told him how we did it, and for the rest of the time we were there no one ever figured it out. We knew one thing for sure: if Bandido Chuy ever got locked up here, there was no way that they were going to keep him in one of those cells!

Before I knew it, May had rolled around and it was Pawhuska time again. By this time I dreaded Pawhuska, because it was always my responsibility to handle all aspects of our campsite. This time, Bandido El Presidente George "George" Wegers and El Secretario William "Bill" Sartelle would be attending, with both their wives. I was hoping that the OK Riders would help me out. To complicate things a bit more, this year the Pawhuska Rally and the Red River Rally were back to back, with only one week between them; normally they were always two weeks apart.

I also had another big problem to rectify. Once again, the Sons of Silence Motorcycle Club and the Outlaws Motorcycle Club were planning on attending, but the Outlaws were having a regional meeting the following weekend in Oklahoma City, and Outlaws were coming from as far away as Ohio. At the time, our (the Bandidos Oklahoma chapter) relationship with the Outlaws chapter in Oklahoma City, who would be camped right next to us, was being strained to its breaking point. Most of the Oklahoma City Outlaws were heavily involved in the manufacture and distribution of methamphetamine, and they were sampling their product on a daily basis. Like trying to talk to a drunk, trying to reason with a methamphetamine addict was next to impossible. We had no idea what was going to transpire.

In the end, all went as well as could be expected. There were no fistfights and no arguments, probably due to the fact that Bandido El Presidente George was there; although there was one local Oklahoma Outlaw who was so obnoxious and arrogant we should have done something about it. That Outlaw, Michael J. Roberts, was a complete asshole that no one liked, but it would take the Outlaws two more years to boot him out of their organization. The funny part about it was that we got along just great with the Outlaws from all the other states. Some of those Outlaws, like Patrick "Pudd" Puttrick (Dayton, Ohio), were old friends of mine from twenty years ago. Others like John "Leadhead" Blackman and Ronald "RT" Taylor (Indianapolis, Indiana Outlaws) I had met the year before at an Outlaws party in Luther, Oklahoma, and personally liked so much that we all kept in touch on a regular basis.

The week after Pawhuska ended, we all headed for the annual Red River Rally, where the Bandidos were holding their annual Memorial Day National run. All Bandidos members in the United States were supposed to be there, or they were in trouble and now had to pay a $500 fine. Bandido El Presidente George and his wife Kelly took off a day early to visit her mom, who was living in Oklahoma City. My girlfriend Caroline and I drove out in a car I had rented for the occasion, because I was carrying the hundred or so t-shirts that the Oklahoma chapter intended to sell while we were in Red River. Most of those t-shirts carried a Red River Rally insignia on the sleeve of the shirts. We had manufactured the t-shirts with that specific design, because we felt that one of the major reasons the t-shirts would be bought was because the t-shirt proved someone had attended the event.

El Presidente George & His Wife Kelly At Ct Ed's In Tulsa May 2000
Sargento De Armas Jack-E From Louisiana Standing In The Background

Unfortunately, no one else in my chapter felt the same as I did about the importance of raising money for the chapter treasury, and my girlfriend Caroline and I spent the whole weekend on the porch of a local bar selling the t-shirts. The Bandidos Oklahoma chapter did stay in style while we were there in Red River, because I had rented two luxury, three-story condominiums for our chapter members just a few blocks off Main Street in Red River. Although expensive, the lodging did make for a nice vacation for all of us, as well as provide a great place for us to entertain our individual guests.

Just a few days after I got back to Tulsa from Red River, we got an emergency call from the Outlaws in Oklahoma City. Apparently two of their brothers, Ronald "RT" Taylor and Mance "Tool" Stephens had been involved in a serious auto accident on interstate highway I-44 just west of Tulsa. Their pickup truck had been hit hard by another truck that had spun out of control in a thunderstorm, causing Outlaw Tool's head to go completely through the windshield. Outlaw RT was in pretty good shape, although shaken up, but Outlaw Tool was a disaster and on his way via ambulance to a local hospital. The Outlaws were still too busy recovering from their own Memorial Day weekend, and asked us to look after RT and Tool.

Bandido Lee and I raced to the hospital, where we found Outlaw Tool's face cut very badly from the windshield he went through: from one ear all the way across his forehead to his opposite eyebrow. The female doctor who was going to do the stitching was terrified that Tool was not going to be very cooperative while she was repairing the damage, so Bandido Lee put on some surgical gloves and helped get Tool cleaned up and ready for surgery, then stayed throughout the actual surgery to calm Tool for the doctor. While Tool was being operated on, I took Outlaw RT to my home for a much needed shower and food, and then I went back to the hospital to pick up Tool, who was being released. The hospital refused to keep him over night because he had no insurance, and the doctor felt that we were competent enough to provide him with the care he needed.

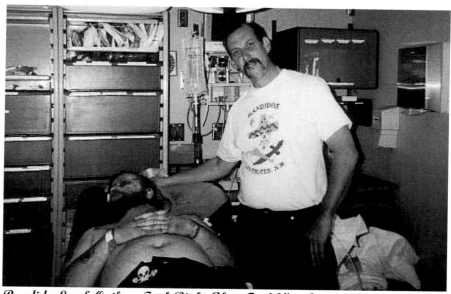

Bandido Lee & Outlaw Tool Right After Tool Was Stitched Up May 2000
Tool Was Unconscious When This Picture Was Taken

When we got Tool home, we immediately tried to get him cleaned up by giving him a bath. His head was a mess, having taken a bunch of stitches across his forehead, and he stank from not having had a bath for the last few days. To complicate the situation, the massive amount of blood he had bled hours earlier was by now coagulated in his hair and ears, turning his head an eerie shade of black. I did the best that I could, and eventually got him cleaned up pretty well, although he did still have some black blood embedded in his hair that I could not remove. I was surprised to see that the bath water he got out of had turned completely black.

After we put Outlaw Tool to sleep for the night, we all realized that he was very lucky to be alive; as a matter of fact it was almost a miracle that he had survived. By now Outlaw RT had called Indianapolis and made flight arrangements for their wives, and by 10 am the next morning both of them were in Tulsa. By early afternoon, Tool's wife had bathed him and he was totally cleaned up. I was even more amazed to find him sitting upright in a chair in my living room, eating a little food. Two more days and Tool was well enough to travel, and they all went home to Indianapolis, where Tool spent months getting back to normal.

In the middle of June, some of my brothers in Washington and Montana were involved in a violent altercation with members of another club, which resulted in the death of a Bandido, Bandido Frederick "Bulldog" Entzel of Missoula, Montana. When I heard the news, I volunteered to represent the Oklahoma chapter at the funeral, for I had known Bandido Bulldog personally.

Talk Turned To Trouble, Then Gunfire At Rally

June 19, 2000

By Wes Nelson

Frederick Entzel and other members of a motorcycle club known as the Bandidos walked away from trouble Friday night at an annual rally near the Yakima River between Toppenish and Zillah.

They had agreed to meet Saturday to talk things out with a small band calling themselves the Iron Horsemen.

But trouble returned to Eagles Park off North Meyers Road where the sixth annual Washington ABATE motorcycle rally to promote motorcyclists' rights was instead pierced by the sound of gunfire that left Entzel, a 48-year-old Benton City resident, dead and two others wounded.

ABATE, short for American Bikers Aimed Toward Education, promotes rider training, safety and educational programs.

Greeted by pandemonium and some drunkenness, up to 40 law enforcement officers from five agencies streamed into the park after the 11:55 a.m. shooting that led to the cancellation of a rally-related parade scheduled to take place in Zillah Saturday afternoon.

Officers found Entzel's friends desperately trying to save his life while another man, an Iron Horseman believed to have exchanged gunfire with Entzel, lay wounded inside a van, Yakima County sheriff's Lt. Dan Garcia said Sunday.

A third man and one of Entzel's fellow Bandido members already had been taken by a private vehicle to a local hospital. He also may have fired shots Saturday, Garcia said.

was made of when he rescued six year old Cheyney Sue from a terrible house fire, by crawling through the flames and smoke, saving her life at the last possible instant.)

After visiting Leadhead, I drove my rental car up to Flint, Michigan, where I spent a night and a day with my sister and her family, before driving back to Indianapolis. From there, my daughter Taylor and I flew back to Tulsa. My thoughts were on Oklahoma; I needed to get back in time for an IRS auction of a downtown mansion house, which was dilapidated and in need of major repair. I also wanted to get back because my friend Dieter Tenter from Germany was coming to visit me for a few days, and I had all sorts of plans for him while he was staying with us here in Oklahoma.

I won the bidding for the old mansion house, and was able to take possession of it the day after my friend Dieter arrived in town for his visit. Being the good host that I was, I immediately put Dieter to work, helping me clean out the three-story home that was going to be my sole construction project for the next three months.

1309 Terrace Drive, Tulsa OK Very Early August 2000

As planned, it was going to be a massive project, for the house had a total of five thousand square feet of living space, with six bedrooms, six bathrooms and two kitchens spread out over its three floors and a basement. I would eventually put almost two hundred thousand dollars of the bank's money into the renovation process, gutting the house to the wooden studs and replacing the electric, plumbing, windows, doors, roof, drywall and HVAC systems along the way.

It was now July 30th, and my daughter Taylor's seventh birthday. Killing two birds with one stone, I took Taylor, her biological mother Teresa, and my friend Dieter on a whirlwind tour of Branson, Missouri. While there, we spent a day and a half visiting Silver Dollar City. My daughter had already been there, so she was quite familiar with the attractions and fun contained there in the park, but for Dieter it was another story. He was like a child in a candy store, and I think that he had more fun on the trip than Taylor. It was also interesting to watch Taylor interact with her mother, for Teresa was now clean, sober and drug free, working at the downtown Home Depot. Teresa and I had been splitting visitation with Taylor for the majority of the last year, and I wanted to see for myself exactly how she was doing with her sobriety. Having Teresa there also gave me time to spend with Dieter, one on one, while Teresa and Taylor also got some time together, one on one. In spite of the fact that I selfishly ignored my girlfriend Caroline's feelings, I knew I had done the right thing for Taylor; and it turned out to be a great birthday present for my daughter.

While I was in Branson, I learned that one of the old-school Bandidos had died, and his funeral was going to be held in Arkansas on August 5th. So as soon we returned to Tulsa, Dieter headed out for Kansas to visit a friend while I took off on my bike and headed east for Little Rock to bury Bandido Donnie "Deadweight" Nichols. It was a beautiful day, not too hot, and the Pinecrest Memorial Park Cemetery was absolutely a great place to be laid to rest; gentle rolling hills covered with giant shade trees. I watched in reserved sadness as other old-school Bandidos Earthquake, Beaudreaux, Sly Willie, DJ, Wiggs, Stubs, Murray and BW carried Deadweight's casket to his grave. After attending the party for Bandido Deadweight that night, I returned to Tulsa on Sunday. The mansion house project was already in full swing, and I was scheduled to do the new wood stud framing myself. If the project was going to progress according to its schedule, I needed to be there to make it happen.

The following weekend, Dieter returned from his visit to Kansas, and we went to Lake Thunderbird, near Norman, for a red & gold family picnic put on by the Chandler chapter of the OK Riders. Having borrowed a motorcycle for Dieter to ride just for the trip, he and I soaked up the gorgeous weather for the two hours that we were on the road. Caroline and Taylor followed us in her pickup truck, and while Taylor played with all the other children there, I was proud to see that Dieter was being treated like he was just another member of the red & gold. When Dieter flew back to Germany the next day, I was convinced that his trip had been memorable, but was sad to see him go.

By mid August of 2000, the situation with Bandido Buddy had come to a head. Everyone knew by now that Buddy had repeatedly lied about almost everything that was going on in his life. We even had Oklahoma Outlaws telling us that Buddy was selling them methamphetamine on a regular basis. So when it came time for our weekly meeting, I was not surprised that Bandido Buddy didn't even show up. Between the Creek County court docket papers and the mountain of the evidence we had all accumulated, it was easy for Bandido Lee to make a decision, and Buddy was expelled from the Oklahoma Bandidos chapter. Bandido Buddy was now no longer a methamphetamine addict riding a motorcycle wearing a Bandido patch; he was now just Earl "Buddy" Kirkwood, the lying sack of shit that methamphetamine had caused him to become. When Bandido Joe and Lee went to collect all of our Bandido property from Buddy, he informed them that he had already burned it all. (We would learn months later, that the DEA had already seized Buddy's Bandido colors and his wife's property patch, while executing the search warrant on his home in June of 2000.)

By the end of August, my attention was on attending the mandatory Four Corners Rally in Durango, Colorado over the Labor Day weekend and simultaneously managing my mansion house construction project. I needed to be at the Rally, or I would have to pay the mandatory $500 fine, but I also needed to maximize the time I spent in Tulsa on the jobsite. So I decided to load my bike into Caroline's truck, and send her out ahead of me on Thursday to make the ten hour drive to Albuquerque, New Mexico, where I planned to meet her the next day. On Friday morning, bright and early, I caught a Southwest Airlines flight to Albuquerque, and met Caroline there before noon. We made the two hundred mile drive up through the mountains in five hours, stopping to visit with the packs of Bandidos we came across along the way and to admire the fantastic scenery.

The Four Corners Rally produced a significant piece of history in the Bandidos world. On Saturday afternoon at our Bandidos USA campsite, we all gathered to take a picture of the entire club, which had not been done since 1970. Many pictures were taken that day, by many different people, and in the end the Nomads chapter settled on one striking photo, and mass produced it in the form of a poster which was sold to anyone in our red & gold world.

Most Of The USA Bandidos Four Corners Rally September 2000

In the photo above that my girlfriend Caroline took, I am second from the left; just to the left of Bandido Marshall who is wearing an unusual tan colored Bandidos vest. This picture is almost identical to the photo that ultimately was used to produce the poster.

On their way to Four Corners, OK Riders Chandler members James "Cub" Oleson and George "George" Schuppan had developed motorcycle trouble, and decided to return to Oklahoma City. In Caddo County, Oklahoma, they had been stopped for a traffic offense by the Oklahoma Highway Patrol. The traffic stop turned into a drug search, and OK Rider George was arrested for "Possession of a Controlled Drug" and "Possession of a Firearm by a Convicted Felon". Just as ex-Bandido Buddy did, OK Rider George lied to my face regarding the circumstances of his arrest, but this time it did not take as long to learn the truth. We had already heard many rumors that OK Rider George had been, and still was dealing with ex-Bandido Earl "Buddy" Kirkwood, but now we were also hearing rumors that OK Rider George was buying and selling methamphetamine with the Oklahoma Outlaws chapter in Oklahoma City.

Within a few days of OK Rider George's arrest, I contacted the Caddo County court clerk's office, and ordered copies of George's court docket to discern the truth. As we had speculated, OK Rider George was charged with being in possession of a small amount of methamphetamine, but when confronted, George denied that it was really methamphetamine. He was adamant that what was found on him that day was not methamphetamine, but something else. Wanting to believe him, and to give him a chance to prove us wrong, we temporarily allowed him to remain an OK Rider. In hindsight, that turned out to be a massive mistake on our part.

At the Four Corners Rally we had invited many Bandidos to the Pawhuska Rally in the middle of September. Some of them, like Bandido Fatcat from El Paso, took us up on our offer, and it turned out that he had family currently living in the Tulsa area. On September 15, 2000, the last night of the party there at Pawhuska, we voted in OK Rider Charles "Snake" Rush as a member of our Oklahoma Bandidos chapter. Probationary Snake became the fifteenth man to wear the Bandidos colors in the state of Oklahoma, and he was proud as can be. He was also quite surprised, because he had not asked to be a Bandido; we had just voted him in without asking him how he felt. We had all decided that if we waited for Snake to ask to be a member, we would all die waiting.

I was very fortunate to get a bunch of help from the OK Riders in handling all aspects of our campsite and Pawhuska passed by peacefully, but by now I was again running on empty. I was well along on my restoration construction project, and the end was in sight. Probationary Bandido Hank "CC" Leasure had volunteered after Four Corners to come up from Oklahoma City and work as a sub contractor on the job, and I was thankful the project was running on time and within budget, just as planned.

On September 21st, the local newspaper carried an article about ex-Bandido John "Turtle" Fisher announcing that he had been convicted by a federal jury after being indicted earlier in the year for a multitude of drug crimes. (John Fisher would ultimately be sentenced to twenty-seven years in federal prison in early February of 2001.) Most of the Oklahoma Bandidos celebrated the news that Turtle had met his Waterloo, but not me. I still remembered my old friend John Fisher from Michigan, the talented construction master craftsman I had known so well.

On October 10th, two members of the Bandidos in Houston, one of whom was a member of the Bandidos National chapter, were arrested and charged with drug crimes. It was alleged that the charges were brought with the assistance of two police officers, who had gained access to those charged by becoming members or associates of a Houston area Bandidos sponsored motorcycle club.

Task Force Reveals Arrests Of Four After Infiltration Of Bandidos Gang

By Peggy O'Hare

October 10, 2000

Swastikas cover the table. A Confederate flag. An array of knives and guns. Christmas cards and photos of leather-clad men with their arms around each other. A T-shirt depicting a gun and reading, "Snitches -- A Dying Breed."

It was a rare peek inside the world of the Bandidos Outlaw Motorcycle Gang, exposed last week when seven homes were raided in Harris County and four key members of the group were arrested on felony drug charges.

The Houston area has long been considered a power base of the group, which has an estimated 400 to 500 members in Texas alone.

Two undercover officers infiltrated the group last year and spent 11 months on the inside, winning members' trust and buying drugs.

That resulted in the Oct. 4 arrests of members from a motorcycle club whose activity has been largely unchecked since police began focusing on juvenile gangs in recent years, the Harris County Organized Crime and Narcotics Task Force announced Tuesday.

David Gregory Smith, 39, of the 500 block of Shawnee, and Kristian Stauffer, 29, of the 3300 block of Ashton Park, were charged with aggravated possession of methampheta-mines. Stauffer also was charged with delivery of methamphetamines.

Carlton Bare, 29, also known as "Bandido Pervert" and described as the group's Web master, was arrested for felony possession of marijuana, as was Angela Clayton, 24. Bare and Clayton live in the 1600 block of Jacquelyn.

Officers said they also seized $250,000 worth of illegal drugs and $175,000 worth of stolen property. They said there may be more arrests.

Police said their investigation offered a glimpse into a tightly knit circle of brotherhood, motorcycles and drugs.

"It takes months and months to develop a rapport with these people," said Houston police Sgt. Frank Miller, a task-force member. "This was done successfully. (The undercover officers) went to the places these people frequent and hung out with them, night after night, day after day. They became known.

"They started to make undercover purchases of narcotics from these people. No one was arrested; nobody went to jail. After a period of time, they were trusted as far as talking other narcotics business with some of the known bikers."

The investigation, begun in November 1999, covered the entire Houston area, originating in east Harris County and expanding to the southwest side of the city.

Officers said they learned that the drugs being purchased belonged to the Bandidos and that their investigation targeted local chapters responsible for the distribution of methamphetamines around the city. Drug buys led investigators to the Bandidos chapters in north, northwest, west and southwest Houston.

For the first time, officers also found evidence linking the Bandidos to neo-Nazi and white-supremacy groups. The swastikas, stamps of Adolf Hitler and even a large colorful image of Hitler making an obscene gesture were among items seized.

But police say they have no doubt that drug deals are the backbone of the Bandidos.

"Our image of Bandidos comes from many years of knowing what they do," Miller said. "We understand there is a secondary image in the public that these people are just misunderstood. ... (Some) will tell you they make donations to certain charities, and they ride for certain causes.

"But the underlying existence of these people, the reason they are here, is to commit crime, sell drugs, to participate in just about everything illegal you can imagine. That's why they are out there; that's how they were formed."

The Bandidos were founded in Houston in 1966, according to law-enforcement officials. The group's base grew to include members in other countries after the

Bandidos began recruiting heavily in competition with such rivals as the Hells Angels.

Police said the Bandidos are about 2,000 strong and have about 110 chapters in nine countries, including Germany, Norway, Denmark and Australia. Several of the group's national officers and its international vice president live in Houston, police said.

The Bandidos expanded worldwide in recent years as police worked to curb the activities of juvenile street gangs, said Capt. Johnny Erikson, the task force's commander.

The two undercover officers who infiltrated the Bandidos did not speak publicly Tuesday but are expected to reveal themselves when they testify in court.

In late October, I finally wrapped up the construction on my 5,000 square foot mansion house near downtown Tulsa, at 1309 Terrace Drive. It had been exhausting, yet I was extremely proud of what I had accomplished. I had even won a zoning dispute in the process, brought on by an overzealous, fanatical, next door neighbor lady, who had taken every opportunity she could get to cause me trouble.

1309 Terrace Drive, Tulsa OK Almost Finished October 2000

The home was now appraised for $350,000, but I had about $225,000 invested in it. I had no idea what I was going to do with the home, but I thought that it would be easy to sell it for $300,000. That ended up being a gross underestimate on my behalf, and over the next six months I did everything I could to sell it, even at one point drastically lowering the price to $260,000.

In early November, Probationary Oklahoma Bandido David "Doc" Mullikin called it quits and left the club. It was a mutual decision, for Doc was having major problems keeping up with all the requirements that were mandated for Probationary members nationwide. Because Doc had done us no harm, we allowed him to leave the club in good standings, which allowed him to still see anyone involved in the red & gold world that he wanted to see. That left us with seven members, and it was beginning to look like Bandido Joseph "Joe" Kincaid would soon be leaving our chapter as well.

In mid November, I took off for Europe again, this time to attend a world meeting in Denmark (explained in detail in Chapter 1) and the one year anniversary of Bandidos Germany, at which time any German member that had been in the club for one year would receive his Germany bottom rocker. As I had been present for the actual patch over ceremony of the Ghostriders Motorcycle club to Bandidos one year ago in Dinslaken, Germany, as well as cultivating the friendship of some of the Ghostriders for the European Bandidos back in the spring of 1998, I personally wanted to be there when the German Bandidos received their bottom rockers in Aachen, Germany. I even brought some of Bandido 74 Jim's wooden puzzle plaques with me to give as gifts to some high ranking German Bandidos that I considered to be my personal friends.

While I was in Denmark I made time to visit the Bandido that had spent so much of his time taking care of me there on my last visit, in the spring of 1998. His name was Buller, and he was serving a short prison sentence for driving a car while his license was under suspension. I contacted Bandido Buller's wife during the day, and fortunately was able to go along with her that evening to visit him. When we arrived at the prison, the guard asked me for my ID, which I gave to him. I was shocked when the guard took a quick look at my Oklahoma driver's license, and let me enter the facility without even searching me.

We ended up in a nice private room that had curtains over the windows and even a curtain over the glass in the door that could be closed for privacy. Buller's wife explained to me that the privacy was needed and ok, because it was legal in Denmark to have conjugal visits. Although this was not going to be a conjugal visit, she reassured me that this was all very normal, and that we would probably be undisturbed for our entire visit. I had wondered what she had carried into the prison in a large bag, and now I found out that she had brought an entire Danish dinner with her, for all of us to eat while we talked. Bandido Buller arrived shortly thereafter, and we settled in for a good two hour visit and wonderful Danish traditional meal. During my visit, I was surprised to find out that Buller even had his laptop computer in his prison cell with him, and could receive and send emails whenever he wanted.

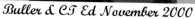

Buller & CT Ed November 2000

Clark, Unknown Bandido & Ct Ed

The next afternoon I took the ferry out of Elsinore, Denmark over to Helsingborg, Sweden, where I met up with Bandido Nomad Clark, who had invited me there while we were both attending the world meeting earlier that week. (Bandido Clark and I had shared a hotel room together when I was in Canada.) I had only a few hours there, which was just enough time to sit down with him and eat a quick meal, before time dictated that I had to leave. I caught the ferry back to Denmark, and then immediately hopped into a car for the long ride back to Germany, where I planned on spending a day with Bandido Nico, who was the President of the Bandidos Cologne chapter. I then would attend the one year anniversary party that night near the Belgium border at Aachen, Germany. Via email, Nico had promised to show me downtown Cologne, where there was a very old church that was supposedly magnificent.

I got into Cologne early in the afternoon, and met Bandido Nico and his crew on the outside of the city. After a short ride into downtown, I was soon standing in the shadow of a church that truly was magnificent. I got a guided tour of that church and was told all of the church's history, and then was treated to a great German meal at a local downtown Cologne restaurant. As soon as dinner was finished, Nico drove me to Aachen, which only took about forty-five minutes.

The Aachen anniversary party was quite interesting; it was like old home week. There were lots of Bandidos there from Europe that I knew, as well as El Presidente George "George" Wegers, El Vice Presidente Jeffrey "Jeff" Pike, and Sargento de Armas Martin "Martine" Gonzalez from the United States. I was pleased to see Bandido Nomad Mick from England there, as he was one of the few that spoke good English. I was also surprised to see some members of the Loners Motorcycle Club from Italy hanging around, who were there as the guests of the

French Bandidos. I tried to talk to them but the language barrier was way too much to overcome.

Geschenke gabs reichlich. Hier ein Präsent aus den USA, genauer von „74 Jim", der seit 28 Jahren im Knast sitzt und dort auch dieses Holzmotiv geschnitzt hat

Biker News January 2001 Issue

At this party, I tried very hard to not fall in the same trap as I had the year before. I knew that there was going to be another stripper show, and I wanted to make sure that I was not going to be part of the entertainment. When the stripper show did happen, I felt very sorry for the poor guy who was "selected" to get up on the stage with the girl. The girl had a squeeze bottle of mayonnaise that she squirted down the front of the guy's pants while he had his eyes closed; don't you know that felt good the rest of the night. The following month, I did end up in the Biker News magazine again, but this time I was just showing off one of Bandido 74 Jim's wooden puzzle plaques.

Seasons Greetings

HAPPY HOLIDAYS
**BANDIDOS MC
OKLAHOMA
2000**

When I got back to Oklahoma, it was time to do the annual Christmas cards for the Oklahoma chapter, as well as assemble the United States Christmas card list and make sure that the overseas Christmas card lists were received by all of the United States chapters. For the Oklahoma Christmas card, I chose a picture that had been taken at Pawhuska earlier in the year, and although dated, was one of the best recent pictures I had access to at the last minute.

I was now working everyday for the El Presidente George and the United States National chapter, but still was officially a member of the Oklahoma chapter. I had been "fired" from the National chapter more than any other Bandido in the history of the club, and was still handling a ton of regular time consuming chores for our National chapter (see Appendix C), such as coordinating the building of a worldwide website, assisting or doing the monthly United States newsletter, arranging airplane flights, and traveling to promote the club. Rarely did I receive any thanks for all that I did for the Bandidos Motorcycle Club worldwide, but when I did it was much appreciated, like the kudos I received from El Secretario William "Bill" Sartelle in a December 2000 newsletter:

Hello Brothers - I want to thank our Brothers in Corpus for another good Thanksgiving Party. Had a good time even if I did not get to visit as much as I would have liked. Welcome to our new Brothers in Canada. Glad to have you in the Bandido Nation, and I hope to visit soon...

Thanks to Connecticut Ed and ALL THE WORK he has done for us. You do a great job Brother, keep it up. I would like to welcome Doc (Laredo) to our Chapter. Doc will be working with me, so help him out....

I would also like to wish ALL MY BROTHERS in the BANDIDO NATION a very MERRY X-MAS and hope everyone has a Happy New Year....
As always, be safe...

All chapters must have an email address by February 1st.

Love, Loyalty, Respect
El Secretario USA
Bandido Bill 1%er
BFFB

In May of 1997, when I became a member of the Bandidos, there were less than thirty chapters in the United States and less than fifty chapters worldwide. On Christmas Day of 2000, there were now forty-nine chapters in the United States and ninety six chapters worldwide. In three and a half years, I had helped to double the size of the club. I was very proud of the fact that I was part of the greatest motorcycle club in the world, and what I had contributed to get it to this point.

After more than three years as a Bandido chapter, Oklahoma only had seven members, with one of those members incarcerated. Lee "Lee" McArdle, Joseph "Joe" Kincaid, Hank "CC" Leasure, Steve "Steve" Buitron, Charles "Snake" Rush, and myself were on the streets; Louis "Bill Wolf" Rackley was in prison. There were about twenty members of the OK Riders scattered across Oklahoma in three chapters; Chandler, Claremore and Comanche.

In Oklahoma, Christmas for my family and me was a wonderful time. Caroline received her property patches, and she gave me one of Bandido 74 Jim's handmade wooden clocks, that stood almost three feet tall. Taylor was content at seven and a half years old, growing like a weed, and half way through the second grade at school. All was well in my world as I made some last minute plans to go to Canada, where, as you already know, my appointment with destiny was waiting.

26

Bandidos Motorcycle Club Oklahoma
January 2001 To Fall 2001

As you are already aware, my trip to Canada turned into a fiasco. When I returned to Tulsa at the end of January, the Bandidos Oklahoma chapter was immediately summoned to a long overdue chapter meeting, which was to be held on January 25th at Harry "Skip" Hansen's home in Muskogee. Skip, who was a lifelong friend of mine, had been an original member of the Bandidos Oklahoma chapter back in May of 1997. He had quit the club in late 1997 because of his dislike for John "Turtle" Fisher and Joseph "Joe" Kincaid; and a minor conflict with Bandido Earthquake. Now that Turtle was long gone, Skip once again desired to become a member of our chapter. Bandido Lee had decided, while I was visiting Canada, that Skip could return to our chapter as a Probationary member at our next weekly meeting.

To complicate matters, we were all now tired of the surreptitious activities of Joseph "Joe" Kincaid, our current Sergeant-at-Arms. We were fairly certain that Bandido Joe had been collaborating against us with the Oklahoma chapter of the Outlaws Motorcycle Club. We had also heard many rumors that Joe had been manufacturing methamphetamine with Earl "Buddy" Kirkwood, and buying/selling methamphetamine with some members of the Outlaws in Oklahoma City. There was no way that we were going to tolerate his activities anymore while he was a member of our chapter.

As soon as the meeting started, before our chapter President Bandido Lee had even said a word about Joe's situation, Bandido Joe quit the Bandidos due to what he cited as his "personal problems". Satisfied that his departure was justified, but not having the paperwork at that time to prove our suspicions concerning his many extracurricular activities, we all voted to let him leave the club in good standings. At that time, Joe turned into us what he claimed were all his Bandido belongings, including his patch, and we all said our goodbyes.

Forty-five minutes later Skip was once again Probationary Bandido Skip. Lee made him our chapter Sergeant-at-Arms, which was Skip's original position when the chapter here in Oklahoma had been started. Our attention then turned to a Chandler OK Rider by the name of George "George" Schuppan. Just before I left for Canada, on January 4th, the Alcohol, Tobacco and Firearms (ATF) branch of the United States Government had served a search warrant on George's home, and discovered a fully functioning machine gun as well as some methamphetamine. So after a short discussion concerning the circumstances surrounding his arrest in Caddo County back in September of 2000 and the January 4th federal search warrant, it was decided that George should be expelled from the OK Riders. His former President, Bandido Charles "Snake" Rush was instructed to immediately locate George, collect his OK Rider patch and tell him to never associate with anyone from the red & gold world again. Unfortunately for us, George would avoid us like the plague for the next thirty-three days, and no one would be able to get their hands on George to collect his OK Rider patch.

A few days later, OK Rider Cub's shop in Jones, Oklahoma, just outside of Oklahoma City, burned to the ground in the middle of the day while no one was home. In the garage shop were about a dozen Harley motorcycles, in various stages of repair. One of the bikes was a one year old Harley Softail, which belonged to ex-OK Rider Sixpack, who was by now residing in the Oklahoma prison system. Most of the bikes and the building were not insured, so the fire was a devastating financial blow to Cub. To complicate matters, Cub was adamant that the fire was arson and that the Outlaws Motorcycle Club was behind it. Cub had been told that Outlaw Michael had been seen at a local gas station filling five gallon gas cans with gasoline, just prior to the fire.

Cub wanted to pay back Michael and the Outlaws in what ever way he could, as soon as possible, but needed our permission to do so. Our relationship with the Oklahoma Outlaws, at this point, was strained to say the least. No one wanted to start a major war with the Outlaws unless we could prove that the Outlaws chapter was behind the fire, and a war with the Outlaws could not be started if Outlaw Michael had burned the garage down for personal reasons. Our investigation ultimately determined that the Outlaws chapter had nothing to do with the fire, but never disproved that Outlaw Michael had set the fire as a result of a personal dispute with Cub.

In February, we all hoped that 2001 was going to be a great year. Now that Joe, OK Rider George and Buddy were out of our red & gold world, we thought that there would be no more problems with the methamphetamine bullshit. Once again, we all grossly underestimated the power of the methamphetamine, for we soon learned that now ex-OK Rider George and his girlfriend Jean had been served with another search warrant, this time by an Oklahoma County drug task force. On February 27th at 5am, George had actually been caught in the act of manufacturing methamphetamine when Oklahoma County law enforcement officers discovered a fully functioning methamphetamine lab in one of the bedrooms of George's home. As you have probably already guessed, George's OK Rider patch vest was there in the house, and seized as evidence that the OK Riders Motorcycle Club was involved in the purchase, sale and manufacturing of methamphetamine. In reality, nothing could be further from the truth.

The funny part about it was that the Oklahoma County Drug Task Force that had served the search warrant on ex-Ok Rider George had called Delbert Knopp, who was an agent with the ATF, instead of taking George directly to jail. Apparently George had told them that he was a confidential informant working for the ATF, and that he was manufacturing methamphetamine as part of a federal criminal investigation. ATF Agent Knopp arrived on the scene at George's house shortly after daylight, took custody of George and later that day had the charges dropped that were pending against George's girlfriend Jean, while she was incarcerated for one whole day in the Oklahoma County jail. It took us months to determine that George Schuppan was a big rat, and to gather the paperwork necessary to prove that George was cooperating with the federal government, which was building a massive criminal case against the Oklahoma City chapter of the Outlaws Motorcycle Club.

When confronted with the mounting evidence that ex-OK Rider George Schuppan was cooperating with law enforcement in the summer of 2001, Outlaws Michael "Michael" Roberts, Thomas "Chameleon" Cain and Virgil "Arlo" Nelson assured me that there was no way that George would ever be a rat. Outlaw Michael was so mad at the mere suggestion that George was cooperating, that he wanted to fight to protect George's honor, for Outlaw Michael was heavily involved in the methamphetamine business with ex-OK Rider George. (Outlaw Chameleon would eventually allow George's ex girlfriend Jean to share his home for many months, while she was also cooperating with federal authorities. Less than two years later, all three Outlaws would be in jail facing federal criminal charges revolving around their association with George Schuppan, along with about one hundred other Outlaws and Outlaw associates from Ohio to Oklahoma.)

In early March, the entire Oklahoma Bandidos chapter took a break and made a fast trip to Mobile, Alabama, where we spent a long weekend at the annual Bandidos Motorcycle Club Birthday Run, celebrating the birth of the Bandidos in March of 1966. There I was fortunate to spend some time with Bandidos Diesel, Les and Armin from the Bandidos National chapter in Germany, who were in the middle of a whirlwind tour of the southern United States Bandidos chapters. Bandido Diesel told me that in a few days, he was going to get to go on a tour of an alligator farm in Louisiana with some of our Cajun Bandido brothers. I patiently explained to him that during the tour, he would get to feed the alligators marshmallows, but to watch out if his fellow Bandidos filled all of his pockets with bags and bags of marshmallows before the excursion. When he asked me why, I whispered to him that if his pockets were filled with bags and bags of marshmallows, then that meant that he was going to be taken into the Louisiana swamps instead of the alligator farm, and that he was going to be thrown out of the boat to the alligators as alligator food. I did my best to keep from laughing while explaining the story, but in spite of my bluff and our language barrier, Bandido Diesel realized that the story was a hoax and we all had a good laugh.

My girlfriend Caroline and I left the Birthday Run party early Sunday morning, and headed over to New Orleans for a day. Caroline had wanted to explore the French Quarter during our trip, but this happened to be Mardi Gras weekend, and it was sheer insanity to go into downtown New Orleans. So instead, we avoided the downtown area and visited Bandido Bradley and his wife at their home just south of New Orleans. Bradley had been in a bad motorcycle accident a few months earlier, and was not yet well enough to travel, so he had stayed home during the Birthday Run. Bandido Bradley owned a tattoo shop in downtown New

Orleans, and I had known him for many years. I felt bad that he was forced to miss the Birthday Run, so I brought a piece of the Birthday Run to him for the few hours we spent together that day.

Three weeks after we had returned home from Mobile, on March 30, 2001, the ATF & DEA served simultaneous search warrants at the homes of Outlaw Arlo, Outlaw Chameleon and OK Rider Cub. Of extreme interest to us was the fact that we now knew for sure that ex-OK Rider George was cooperating with the federal authorities, for the location of a gun that was one of the subjects of the search warrant served at OK Rider Cub's, was known only by George. The search warrant also disclosed that OK Rider Cub was suspected to be in possession of explosives, and although none were found, the mere suggestion got our attention. After all, this was not long after the bombing of the Murrah Federal Building in Oklahoma City, less than twenty miles from Cub's home.

We were also quite concerned that a shotgun and a small amount of methamphetamine were discovered in the master bedroom of Cub's home, and both OK Rider Cub and his wife Glenda were on probation in Tulsa County. Possession of a firearm while under probation was a felony in the state of Oklahoma, and possession of a firearm while using methamphetamine was a federal felony. We all assumed that OK Rider Cub was going to be arrested in the very near future, and sent off to prison for a while. We were also now quite aware that there was a connection between OK Rider Cub, ex-OK Rider George and the Outlaws Motorcycle Club chapter in Oklahoma City, but unsure of exactly how the pieces of the puzzle fit together.

In late Spring, while under a cloud of controversy in Canada, I took off with my girlfriend Caroline on my bike for a weekend trip to Eureka Springs, Arkansas. There I wanted to attend a swap meet/bike show put on by a local area motorcycle club called the 13 Rebels. I had made plans to meet some Tulsa area OK Riders there, and an ex-member of the Outlaws Motorcycle Club from Tennessee by the name of Gary "Andy" McWilliams, who lived in nearby Harrison. Andy and I had met in Pawhuska at the 1999 Pawhuska Bike Rally when Andy was a member of the Outlaws Memphis chapter and over the years had gotten friendly. While Andy and I visited in the parking lot of the swap meet, I met Randy "Randy" Campbell, who lived in Eureka Springs. Randy was wearing a "Support Your Local Bandidos" shirt, and we were immediately attracted to each other for obvious reasons. I was surprised to find out that Randy knew many of my Bandido brothers in Louisiana, for he and his family had lived in the Lafayette, Louisiana area for many years.

Randy, Andy and I spent the entire day and evening together, and then met with the OK Riders from Tulsa for a group breakfast at a local restaurant, Granny's Café, the next morning. The night before I had explained to Randy that I had a lot of interest in setting up a support club in the hills of northwest Arkansas, asking him if he would be interested in helping me do exactly that. I knew that the Arkansas Bandidos chapter based in Little Rock was quite unlikely to ever get any bigger unless I stacked the deck; at the time they only had three active members in the entire state. I thought that I could easily get permission from El Presidente George to get the support club going, and thought that Bandido Arkansas President Leo "Murray" Murray could be persuaded to allow me to start a support club in his area, since the hills of Eureka Springs were closer to Tulsa than Little Rock. But before I did anything or asked permission from anyone, I needed to have some potential members who were interested in being in a Bandido support club.

Randy, CJ Ed & Andy In Eureka Springs April 2001

I had always loved the Eureka Springs-Fayetteville area of northwest Arkansas, and had been vacationing there for more than twenty years. As long as I had been going there, the entire area had been a haven for motorcycle lovers; an independent biker had even been the mayor of Eureka Springs for many years recently. The beautiful, rolling hills were only two hours from Tulsa, and I would not mind a reason to be there on a regular basis. Before I left to ride back to Tulsa, Randy and Andy both told me that they would think about it.

When I returned to Tulsa, I learned that Bandido Hank "CC" Leasure had finally tired of all the crap that Bandido Steve "Steve" Buitron had been giving him in Lawton. Bandido CC had recently been involved in a serious motorcycle accident that left his girlfriend severely injured. He also was facing a DUI charge that had already resulted in the loss of his driver's license. It was hard to function in our world without a driver's license, and to complicate matters, Bandido Steve seemed to hate Bandido CC. Because CC was still a Probationary and Steve was a full patch, Steve ran CC ragged twenty-four hours a day with stupid commands and requests, that Steve spent all his time dreaming up. Steve had a little guy complex and wearing a Bandido patch made him think that he was a man. In reality, Bandido Steve was a piece of shit wearing a Bandido patch.

At the heart of the hatred was the fact that in August of 2000, Bandido CC had bought a 92 Harley Heritage from Bandido Steve, and the bike was one of the biggest pieces of crap I had ever seen. Steve lied to me and CC about the condition of the bike, and Bandido CC suffered for it, costing him hundreds of dollars in repairs that he had no idea were needed. I had actually financed the transaction for Bandido CC and arranged the purchase of Steve's new Road King at a Tulsa Harley dealership. You would have thought that Bandido CC should have hated Bandido Steve, but in Steve's jealous, perverted mind, CC was the offender that needed to be punished.

Knowing full well that Bandido Steve had run CC into the ground, on May 6th we let Bandido CC quit the club to attend to his personal life, and made a deal with him to settle all of his debts simultaneously. To square up with the chapter, he gave me the motorcycle back, and in return I took his equity and used it to pay the chapter all he owed. Some additional equity was used to pay court fines he still owed from the motorcycle accident, and to get him a place to live. Bandido CC was now just CC, and out of the club in good standings. After four years, the Oklahoma chapter was back down to six members; five members on the streets and one member in prison.

Ex-OK Rider George "George" Schuppan was indicted on May 1, 2001, by a federal grand jury for manufacturing methamphetamine, possession of firearms and possession of a machine gun, but we did not find out until a few days before the annual Pawhuska Bike Rally. By now Randy had told me that he had decided to join the support club, if I could get permission to get it together. He indicated that he had a handful of friends that were also interested in becoming members.

I called El Presidente George for permission to start the support club in northwest Arkansas, and he told me that it was ok as long as it was ok with Bandido Murray, President of the Arkansas Bandidos. When I called Murray and explained to him what I had in mind; he blessed it and gave me permission to go ahead and get it going. If it worked, Murray could say that it was his idea and if something went wrong, then he could blame it on me. I decided to call my new creation the Ozark Riders Motorcycle Club.

To launch the club, I settled on the Pawhuska Biker Rally in the middle of May, 2001. Randy and some of his guys rode over from northwest Arkansas to visit with us, and to mark the occasion, I invited the Louisiana Bandidos to see their old friend Randy become the President of a new Bandidos support club. Bandido Sargento de Armas Jack "Jack-E" Tate, Bandido Peck and a few other Louisiana Bandidos made the six hundred mile trip from southern Louisiana to Pawhuska, justifying it as just a rest stop on their way to the Red River Rally for Memorial Day. At Pawhuska, we handed out round red & gold balls that said "I Support Bandidos Worldwide" to six potential members of the first Ozark Rider chapter in Arkansas, which signified to us that they were a part of our world. As you can imagine, I was very proud of my accomplishment.

Randy's Crew May 1999: Spyder, J-Bird, Nasty, Nick, Denny, Randy & Andy

No sooner had we got through Pawhuska, our entire Oklahoma chapter took off in a mad dash for the mountains of New Mexico and the annual Red River Rally in Red River, New Mexico. While there, I was asked by El Presidente George "George" Wegers to officially join the Bandidos National chapter for the third time, and actually sat in on the Bandidos United States National chapter meeting held that weekend. Once again, I rented a pair of magnificent townhouses just off of Main Street for the Oklahoma chapter to stay in. This time Caroline and I fortunately did not have as many t-shirts to sell on the porch of the "Bull of the Woods" bar. And what we did have to sell, sold out fast. It had been a great Memorial Day weekend with the entire Bandido Nation, but on the way home my attitude changed for a minute when I got stopped in Beaver County, Oklahoma for speeding, costing me one hundred dollars that I could not afford.

In very early June, I took one prototype set of rockers with me to Eureka Springs, and Randy "Randy" Campbell became Ozark Rider Probationary Randy. I sold him what was left of ex-Bandido CC's 92 Heritage Softail, and to help him do the deal financed it for him personally by carrying the note. At the time Andy, the ex-Outlaw from Tennessee, had not decided to become an Ozark Rider; he still thought of a support club as a step down from being a one percenter. However, Andy eagerly agreed to hang out with Randy and the other potential Ozark Riders on a regular basis, and teach them all he could about one percenter motorcycle clubs.

I had already decided that the process for becoming an Ozark Rider would be a four step process. First, a potential member would hang around for a while, then become a Prospect when the members of the chapter voted him in. A

Prospect would receive a top rocker and a MC patch. After a minimum of thirty days, a Prospect could become a Probationary, which would get him his bottom rocker. After another minimum of thirty days, a Probationary could become a full patch member, and receive his center patch. I instructed Randy to assemble a crew of potential members, and to make sure that every potential member had visible means of support (jobs or pensions). As always, I mandated that there was no room in the Ozark Riders for methamphetamine addicts.

Andy, Ozark Rider Probationary Randy, & CT ED June 2001

Ozark Rider Randy & Bandido Peck May 2001

which the city of Edmonds, Washington had tried to force a litany of zoning codes upon a local Oxford House to no avail. The Supreme Court ruled that all Oxford Houses were protected by the federal Fair Housing Act and exempt from all local, city and state zoning regulations that might be used to restrict that type of occupancy in a single family dwelling. So armed with the knowledge that the United States Supreme Court decision would protect us, Gregg and I established what would become the showcase of the Oxford House system.

We enlisted the aid of my good friend and attorney, Jonathan Sutton, who donated five thousand dollars, which was utilized to fund the operation. Jonathan's donation was used to purchase thirteen single beds, linen sets and pillows, two sets of living room furnishings, two sets of kitchen utensils, and to pay utility deposits and partial rent for the first three months. Richard Gainer volunteered to be the first resident, and one week later became the first President of the Terrace Drive Oxford House facility. He was happy as a pig in shit to be living in his new elaborate surroundings, I was grateful to be giving something back to the community, and we both were convinced that this was another step up on Richard's ladder of personal recovery.

No sooner had we opened, Maria Barnes led the charge against us, to shut us down for violating numerous zoning codes. The city of Tulsa even filed a frivolous federal lawsuit against us to terminate the operation, but after a month of negotiations with the National office of the Oxford House, that litigation was dismissed based upon the United States Supreme court decision rendered in the Edmonds vs. Oxford House case. Maria Barnes, in spite of all her whining, crying, bitching and moaning, did not have a leg to stand on, and the publicity surrounding the fiasco actually helped us fill the thirteen beds quicker than we had anticipated.

I was thrilled to have a permanent tenant for my problem child, and Gregg was ecstatic to have a three hundred thousand dollar mansion house to launch his chain of Oxford Houses in the Tulsa area. There are now six Oxford Houses in the Tulsa area, and to this day, the Oxford House at 1309 Terrace Drive still stands, and probably will, long after I am dead and gone. I hope that someday it will be seen as a monument to my legacy, but for now you can be assured that it is an accomplishment that I am very proud of. After successfully overseeing the growth of the Oxford Houses in Tulsa, in 2004 Gregg Van Wyck and his wife Wendy established five female-only houses based on the Oxford House (male-only) concept. Gregg and Wendy called their creations the Love 4 Life houses.

On July 30th, Caroline and I took a break for a few days, and headed off to the now very familiar Branson, Missouri area for a short vacation. It was my daughter Taylor's eighth birthday, so with one of her friends Alyssa along for the party, we got a motel room at Taylor's favorite motel. This particular motel had an outdoor swimming pool with a huge slide; and both girls sat on rubber mats and slid down the slide more times than I could count, screaming in glee on every single ride. During the day I took Caroline and the girls to Silver Dollar City, which by now had become another favorite attraction for Taylor and me. We all enjoyed the park and the magic it contained.

At the annual Pawhuska Biker Rally in mid-September of 2001, we had a huge party where we celebrated the splitting of the Ozark Riders Motorcycle Club into two chapters: Rogers and Eureka Springs. Ozark Rider J-Bird had moved from the Eureka Springs area to the western Arkansas town of Rogers, enabling the split. With the addition of the two ex-Flaming Knights, ex-Outlaw Andy, two brilliant entrepreneurs named Steve and Victor, and a few others, the red & gold world now had established a strong presence in the northwest corner of Arkansas. In addition, the Ozark Riders had recruited two members that actually lived in southern Missouri: Steven "Batman" Batson and Mike "Mike" Miller. Both resided in or near Springfield, and for us it would be the first time the Galloping Goose and the El Forastero Motorcycle Clubs became a cause for concern.

Some Ozark Riders (Rogers & Eureka Springs) September 2001

By this time, I had met a young helicopter mechanic from Corpus Christi by the name of Donald "P-Rick" McCaulley. P-Rick was a member of a Corpus Christi Bandidos support club, and had been temporarily transferred to Tulsa for a major United States military helicopter overhaul program. While in Tulsa, P-Rick had been staying with me in my home, helping around the house with chores and contributing some money to my girlfriend Caroline's now-strapped food budget. He was hanging out with us and the OK Riders, and was beginning to think about relocating to the southwestern Missouri area to be closer to his parents, who lived near Carthage.

At the end of September, I broke down and leased a brand new, red 2002 Expedition for my business. I had decided that my old '94 Towncar would just not make it as a work vehicle anymore, and besides, pulling a trailer with a Towncar just looked a little unprofessional. One evening, less than two weeks after I leased the Expedition, there was a weather warning for a thunderstorm with very strong winds. I usually parked my vehicle under the carport by my front door. About ten feet away from my brand new Expedition was a little home renovation construction project. At the time, I had been digging a hole near the foundation, looking for a water leak, and had covered the hole with a piece of sheet metal to keep anyone from falling into it.

Now I was concerned that the sheet metal might blow off in that thunderstorm, and hit my new Expedition, so I moved the Expedition about fifty feet down the driveway, away from the sheet metal, just in case. In hindsight, that was a pretty stupid thing to do, for I inadvertently parked it under an old tree. Sure enough, the strong winds came just like the weather man said they would, and sure enough, a fairly large tree branch broke off and landed on my new truck. When I came out in the morning, there was my truck covered in tree. Miraculously, the only damage I found on the Expedition after I removed the tree limb was a minor dent in the windshield post.

With my daughter Taylor in the third grade, I was surprised when she came home one day after school and announced that she wanted to become a cheerleader. This was a novel concept to me, for I had no idea that kids played organized football in the third grade, much less had cheerleaders cheering for them. Being the dinosaur I am, it never crossed my mind that I would have to take part in Taylor's organized sports activities until about high school time. Soon I found myself going to football games and cheering for Taylor while she cheered for the third grade football team. Although I felt a sense of pride while I watched her, you can imagine how out of place I felt among all of the other parents, secretly hoping that this was just a temporary stop on Taylor's train of life.

Taylor Winterhalder The Cheerleader October 2001

27

Bandidos Motorcycle Club Oklahoma
Fall 2001 To Summer 2002

In late October, the Galloping Goose Motorcycle Club, through the El Forastero Motorcycle Club, contacted the Bandidos National chapter complaining about the red & gold presence within the borders of Missouri. When dealing with the El Forastero or the Galloping Goose, it was for all practical purposes the same organization, even though the clubs wore completely different patches. It was their position that they owned the state of Missouri and no other 1%er motorcycle club was going to wear club colors in Missouri; not even the Bandidos. Apparently the local Goose chapter in Springfield, Missouri, had spotted one of the Ozark Riders riding around, and it had pissed them off. To defuse the situation, El Presidente George sent Sargento de Armas Danny "DJ" Johnson to join us for a sit down with the Galloping Goose and El Forastero in Springfield. Joining DJ for the trip was Bandido Chester from Texas, who was a just-patched new Bandido.

Bandido DJ was chosen because he had known the El Forastero and Galloping Goose in Missouri twenty-five years ago, when the Bandidos had a chapter in Springfield. The only problem was that DJ was one of the oldest Bandidos, now nearly sixty years old. Because of his age, he naturally rode his bike a little slower than all of us, which caused the normal three hour trip (one way) to become a major exercise in patience. After making many stops for Bandido DJ to rest along the way, we finally arrived at the Galloping Goose bar in northwest Springfield at about 2pm. Once there we met with an extremely unfriendly bunch of Galloping Goose and El Forastero members/associates, who outnumbered us three to one. Only Bandido DJ and Bandido Lee "Lee" McArdle were allowed to attend the meeting with about ten El Forastero and Galloping Goose members.

In spite of the horrible atmosphere, the meeting actually produced a truce: the red & gold were allowed to have members living in Missouri, but were never to be allowed to have a Missouri chapter. The Ozark Riders were also allowed to have members living in Missouri, but they also could never have a chapter located in Missouri. In what most Bandidos considered later to be disrespect, the El Forastero and Galloping Goose bosses mandated that any Bandidos support club member wearing his club colors while riding in Missouri must be with a Bandido, or the member would be beat up and their club colors seized. I was shocked to hear that Bandido DJ had readily agreed to this, but it was not my place to argue whatever decision that DJ made.

On the way back to Tulsa, with the autumn cold closing in on us and daylight rapidly fading away, Bandido Lee split the pack up at Joplin for the one hundred mile blast down the Oklahoma turnpike. Everyone was tired of having to stop frequently for Bandido DJ, but no one wanted to admit it, so Bandido Lee used the police helicopter that had been following us from Springfield as an excuse to leave DJ behind. At ten minute staggered intervals in groups of two or three, we all made our way home to Tulsa. I was quite happy to be home by nine that evening and even happier when I heard that Bandidos DJ and Chester had not arrived in Tulsa until six o'clock the next morning.

At the beginning of November, with my troubles in Canada now behind me and the Missouri truce in the back of my mind, I took off for Austin to attend the Bandidos annual Thanksgiving celebration. The Bandidos Oklahoma chapter, in a very unusual move a few nights before, had voted in Ozark Rider Steven "Batman" Batson and Richard "P-Rick" McCaulley in as Probationary members, without either of them knowing it. Their potential membership rested on whether or not Lee and I could convince Bandidos El Presidente George "George" Wegers to allow us to have members in our chapter in spite of the fact that they lived outside of Oklahoma. Bandido Sargento de Armas DJ had offered to speak to El Presidente George in our behalf, and I even took the liberty to ask El Secretario Augie to bring to Austin new colors for both guys.

Although we had only known Batman for a few months since he had become an Ozark Rider, we all liked him a lot. Batman had recently lived in San Antonio, TX for a few years while he was a drill instructor in the United States Air Force. While in San Antonio, before he retired from military service, he regularly associated with a few local Bandidos members. Those members had vouched for his character and integrity when contacted as references. Bandido DJ had vouched for P-Rick, who was well known to DJ when DJ lived in Corpus Christi. Even P-Rick's support club brothers in Corpus had told us that he would make a great Bandido, and had promised to remain quiet about it until they saw him wearing Bandido colors.

Fortunately for all of us, El Presidente George was in a good mood that weekend, and on November 24, 2001, he welcomed Batman and P-Rick into the Bandidos with open arms, full well knowing that they both lived in Missouri. Although this would become a bone of contention in later years, everyone involved at the time was aware of the fact that both men did not live in Oklahoma. So now our Bandidos Oklahoma chapter had eight members and one prospect: one in prison, one in Lawton, one in Oklahoma City, two in southwestern Missouri, one in Muskogee, two in Tulsa, and a prospect in Tulsa.

Overall, our Oklahoma based red & gold world stretched about four hundred miles east to west, and about two hundred miles north to south. It contained only eight Bandidos and one prospect, but those eight Bandidos and one prospect now oversaw about fifteen Ozark Riders and twenty OK Riders. Together with our recognized hangarounds, we were now almost fifty strong and a force to be reckoned with in the state of Oklahoma. We were also now attracting major attention and jealousy within the Bandidos Nation, for the Oklahoma chapter was now well known for getting things done and not sitting on their asses collecting dust on the couch in front of the television.

Bandidos Skip & Lee At The Thanksgiving Run Austin 2001

In early December, some of us broke with tradition and agreed to take part in the annual Tulsa ABATE Christmas Toy Run, which now attracted more than seven thousand motorcycles and ten thousand riders. We had reserved positions up at the front of the pack, where we led the entire pack across town to deliver thousands of toys to needy children just in time for Christmas.

Mongol Lucifer, CT Ed & Mongol Nick December 2001

At the end of the ride, just after I dropped off the toy Caroline had carried, I ran into some Mongols who had with them a member visiting from

California. His name was Lucifer, and I immediately took a liking to this intelligent Hispanic Mongol. He was very outgoing, and in spite of our vast differences, we each vowed to get together as soon as possible. Over the next twenty months we saw each other a few more times, but sad to say, we never found the time we both desired to have for visiting with each other.

For a complete change in pace, the last couple days in December, my girlfriend Caroline, my daughter Taylor and I took off for Las Vegas, where we spent New Year's Day. For all three of us, it was a great time. We stayed at the Excalibur Hotel, where we got to watch the knights jousting while eating food with our hands, in an evening show under the Excalibur. I also took some time away from the girls one night, to visit with some of the local Bandidos, who were in the Las Vegas chapter that I helped start in May of 2001 while on a business trip to Nevada. One was on parole from a Montana prison sentence, and the other was in his first year as a law student. It never ceased to amaze me how diversified the club was, and of the inherent differences I found in its members.

Over the winter, Bandido Lee "Lee" McArdle and I sat down and had several serious conversations about promoting an annual motorcycle drag race at the Tulsa International Raceway. When we both finally committed to the concept, I decided that the name "Living On The Edge" was very appropriate for the venue, and after Bandido Lee talked to Bo Roach, the owner of the race track, Lee set May 12th as the date for the 1st "Living On The Edge" motorcycle drag race. Although we tried to get the chapter behind the idea and turn it into a Bandidos Oklahoma chapter function to raise money for the chapter, no one in the chapter except Skip seemed to be able to see the forest through the trees. On the contrary, feeble minded chapter member Steve "Steve" Buitron thought that the concept was ludicrous and told us to leave the chapter out of it; he thought that the event would involve too much work.

We decided to try an all-Harley drag race, where anyone who owned a Harley Davidson motorcycle could come out and race their bike themselves, with no brackets or prizes. For a ten dollar entry fee, you could either watch the bikes race from the grandstands, or race your own bike as many times as you wanted. If you raced, it was against someone you knew or a bike very similar to yours, and at the end of the race you got a time ticket, showing the speed your bike attained at the end of the 1/4 mile and the exact time it took for you to traverse the 1/4 mile of asphalt racetrack.

As an experiment, I contracted three local bands to simultaneously provide live music at the event, and even hired a stage company to set up and dismantle a professional music sound stage. Lee and I hoped to attract a bunch of kids to the event by having the live music there, thus introducing them to the concept of motorcycle drag racing. In the past, the only type of motorcycle drag racing in the Tulsa area had been where you went out to the track and watched some professional racers do bracket type, elimination racing for prizes. You could go out to the track on Saturday nights from midnight to 6am and race your own bike, but you had to put up with all sorts of drunken kids racing their cars.

So, as Bandido Lee and I spent the spring concentrating on the promotion of the first Tulsa "run what you brung" motorcycle drag race, we found ourselves surprised when on February 23, 2002, more than seventy members of the Pagans Motorcycle Club attacked a crew of Hells Angels at a Harley parts swap meet at Long Island, New York. A Pagan was killed by a Hells Angel, numerous Pagans and Hells Angels were injured and more than fifty members of both clubs were arrested at the scene. After all that had been done by the Bandidos Motorcycle Club in recent years to prevent this type of situation, I was disappointed when I realized that the incident meant that our efforts at nationwide motorcycle club peace had probably failed.

By March 1st, I was involved in another major construction project, this time in Tulsa. I had resolved to not work out of town anymore for more than a few days at a time, for I felt that it took too much of my time away from my family. This job was very unusual; it was a sound mitigation project paid for by the Federal Aviation Administration (FAA). I was the onsite Project Manager and Superintendent for the "quieting" of twenty-six homes that were located in the flight path of the Tulsa International Airport runways. The General Contractor who had hired me was from the Boston area, and was one of the leading forces in the sound mitigation field. My two bosses there, John Millman and Dave Hebert, were great to work with, and gave me full authority to run the project as I wanted.

My main challenge was that the construction on all the homes had to be completed in less than one hundred working days. On each home, we would have to replace all the doors and windows, upgrade the electric systems, install new HVAC systems, install new insulation, install new drywall (double thickness in the bedrooms), and paint most all of the home. All this had to be done while the home was occupied, and the work on each home had to be done in no more than twenty working days. It was a challenge I could not resist, so I got permission from my chapter President, Bandido Lee, to take some time off from the activities of the motorcycle club while I completed this task.

I desperately needed a warehouse manager for this construction project, someone who could handle an inventory of more than three hundred windows and one hundred doors, simultaneously being my second in command. I immediately thought of Bandido Louis "Bill Wolf" Rackley, who was still in the care and custody of the Oklahoma Department of Corrections, but had recently been transferred to a work release program in Tulsa. It was a perfect match: Bandido Bill Wolf needed employment and I needed a right hand man that I could trust.

I found myself a perfect office-warehouse combination only a few miles from the jobsite, near the intersection of Hwy 169 and Pine Street in northeast Tulsa, and took possession of it in the middle of March. Bandido Bill Wolf left his halfway house home early every morning, and actually opened up the facility for me at 7am. He was happier than a pig in shit, and after almost two years in prison, his mind was clear from all the methamphetamine he had ingested before he went to prison; I was thrilled to see my old friend Bill Wolf back in full force.

On March 3rd, OK Rider Rickey "Grizz" Case and his wife Linda renewed their wedding vows in a quiet Sunday ceremony in the backyard of my home in Owasso. All of the members of the Bandidos Oklahoma chapter except Louis "Bill Wolf" Rackley were there, as well as most all of the members of the OK Riders three chapters. After the wedding, we had a Bandidos Oklahoma chapter meeting, where we voted in the first member that had ever prospected for our chapter, Michael "Mick" Barnett. Mick had started prospecting for the chapter just after Labor Day of 2002.

Although none of us knew him when we met him in the summer of 2002, Mick had recently moved to Tulsa from Texas, and his dad was well known to some of the Bandidos in Austin and San Antonio. It was decided at the meeting that Prospect Mick would not receive his Bandidos colors until the annual Bandidos Birthday Run in Houston the following weekend. In hindsight, voting Mick in was not the best decision we could have made; it turned out to be one of those decisions that would haunt us all in the future.

Bandido CT Ed & OK Rider Mario March 2002

The annual Bandidos Birthday Run turned out to be very interesting, although I missed it, staying home to tend to my sound mitigation construction project near the Tulsa Airport. For the first time in history, there were two different party site camps for Bandidos members. One camp was for those members that supported El Presidente George "George" Wegers and the other camp was for the members that were pissed off at Bandido George. The club as a whole was in massive turmoil, for there was a distinct crew of Bandidos (among them was the entire Nomads chapter) that were not very fond of George's new

OUT IN BAD STANDINGS

OUT IN BAD STANDINGS

OUT IN BAD STANDINGS

OUT IN BAD STANDINGS

OUT IN BAD STANDINGS

OUT IN BAD STANDINGS

OUT IN BAD STANDINGS

300# OUT IN BAD STANDINGS

OUT IN BAD STANDINGS

OUT IN BAD STANDINGS

OUT IN BAD STANDINGS

OUT IN BAD STANDINGS

300# OUT IN BAD STANDINGS

300# OUT IN BAD STANDINGS

OUT IN BAD STANDINGS

300# OUT IN BAD STANDINGS

OUT IN BAD STANDINGS

OUT IN BAD STANDINGS

OUT IN BAD STANDINGS

OUT IN BAD STANDINGS

OUT IN BAD STANDINGS
OUT IN BAD STANDINGS

OUT IN BAD STANDINGS

OUT IN BAD STANDINGS
OUT IN BAD STANDINGS

OUT IN BAD STANDINGS

OUT IN BAD STANDINGS

OUT IN BAD STANDINGS

Firearms (ATF) had supposedly wired his home for sound and video, and that Buddy and his wife Karen had agreed to cooperate rather than go to prison for the many crimes that they had both committed.

That fact certainly explained the ten year "suspended" prison sentence that Buddy had received. We had all been shocked when Buddy did not get sentenced to prison, for a prison sentence was mandatory in the state of Oklahoma for a conviction of manufacturing methamphetamine, and on top of that, Buddy had been a Bandido when he was originally arrested. We all thought there was no way he was not cooperating, *if he did not go to prison.*

There was also the fact that his girlfriend Karen Strange had been recently arrested twice for selling methamphetamine, and both times nothing had happened; she was never booked into jail and there were no charges filed. So the first thing I thought when the names of the deceased were disclosed was that somebody had killed Buddy and Karen for being rats. But I was shocked the next day when I learned that law enforcement authorities were looking for a member of the Oklahoma City chapter of the Outlaws Motorcycle Club named Michael J. Roberts.

The local newspaper reported that the slayings were the result of a drug related feud between Buddy and Outlaw Michael. That fact was not surprising, since it was common knowledge that Buddy and Michael regularly did business together and Michael had a violent temper. The local cops were quoted as saying, "that whoever killed Buddy and Karen, there was rage involved". I wondered how long it would be before the authorities located Michael and his two-tone, blue Ford Ranger pickup with a "loud exhaust".

The police said that Karen had been shot in the head with a high-powered weapon, which was found inside the mobile home, and that she was found nude. Buddy's body was discovered outside of the home; he had been beaten to death. I wasn't at all surprised to hear that another methamphetamine lab had been discovered on their property, as well as surveillance cameras and a video monitor.

I was relieved to read that their five-year old son had spent the night with friends and had not been present when his parents were killed. Watching the news on television, I saw federal Drug Enforcement Administration (DEA) agents, Oklahoma State Bureau of Investigation (OSBI) agents and the gang unit of the Tulsa Police Department (TPD) investigating the scene.

I learned that two witnesses had actually seen Outlaw Michael arguing with Buddy about drug business the day before the killing. That was no surprise, since we all had heard that Buddy was selling the methamphetamine he manufactured to the Outlaws in Oklahoma City. Outlaw Michael was well known for his violent tendencies, and he was an obnoxious, arrogant individual who, in my opinion, was quite capable of committing this type of crime.

So when law enforcement authorities announced a few days later that they had eliminated Outlaw Michael as a suspect in the killings, I wondered who had killed Buddy and why. That question was answered a few weeks later, when on April 20, 2002, Mitchell Coleman, Leslie Dobbs and Eddie Simmons were arrested for killing Buddy and his girlfriend Karen, and charged with first degree murder.

It turned out that Buddy and Karen had been killed in a rage of jealousy, for one of the killers' girlfriends had been having sexual relations with Buddy, trading him sex for methamphetamine. Buddy and Karen had both been beaten and bludgeoned in the attack, and Buddy had also been stabbed in the hip and rib cage. The state medical examiner ruled that both of them died from blunt trauma to the head.

All three of the killers, while drinking, had bragged about killing Buddy and Karen to their relatives and friends in the days after the murders. One of the relatives had called the police and reported what he had heard them say, solving the crime for the police in the process. Apparently when the killers arrived at Buddy's house about midnight, Buddy greeted them outside with a shotgun and pointed it at Leslie Dobbs.

Eddie Simmons then reportedly reached around Leslie Dobbs and stuck Buddy with a knife, causing Buddy to drop the shotgun. Leslie Dobbs then picked up the shotgun and struck Buddy on the head several times. Mitchell Coleman then entered the residence and attempted to rape Karen before he was pulled off of her by Leslie Dobbs and Eddie Simmons, who then struck her on the head repeatedly.

Interviewed by Creek County Sheriff's Sgt. Jolen Boyd a few days before the fatal beatings, Mitchell Coleman told Boyd that he had been upset with Buddy because Buddy had been having a sexual relationship with his wife, from whom Coleman was separated. Mitchell begged local law enforcement authorities to arrest Buddy for manufacturing methamphetamine, an endeavor in which Coleman allegedly had assisted in the past.

At the same time, Mitchell had also implicated Buddy in the tattooing of underage children. After learning that local authorities were unable to arrest Buddy because he was being protected by federal law enforcement, Mitchell apparently resolved the situation himself. (Mitchell Coleman, Leslie Dobbs and Eddie Simmons eventually would plead guilty to the killings more than a year later and receive life sentences.)

In very early April, about the same time that we were all patiently waiting to learn who killed Buddy, a Washington state Bandido from Skagit County transferred to the Oklahoma Bandidos chapter. He claimed that everyone in his Skagit County chapter was a piece of shit, and we bought his lies based on the fact that he was a Bandido, and Bandidos did not lie to other Bandidos. His name was James "Smurf" Ragan, and he had lived in the Tahlequah, Oklahoma area for many years when he was younger. There, in Tahlequah, he knew some of the officers of the Mongols Motorcycle Club chapter, for they had all known each other many years ago when Smurf lived in the area.

Bandido Smurf also had ties to southwestern Missouri, which was important for us concerning our future expansion plans, so we welcomed him into our chapter. But just like Bandidos Steve "Steve" Buitron and Michael "Mick" Barnett before him, we had no idea what really made him tick. Bandido Smurf was, like Bandido Steve and Mick, the type of man who needed to wear a motorcycle club patch, for that motorcycle club patch is what made him a man. He was, psychologically, exactly the type of man that we did not want in our chapter: a real piece of shit hiding under a Bandidos patch. We already knew that Steve was that way, and at the time, were already regretting voting Mick in. Smurf became the third bad mistake the Bandidos Oklahoma chapter made, and voting him in to our chapter was like driving another nail into our coffin.

The week before we learned who killed Buddy and Karen, Houston Bandido David "Smitty" Smith received thirty-seven years in prison for selling methamphetamine in Texas. When compared to Buddy's case, it did not take a rocket scientist to determine that Bandido Smitty was not a cooperating witness, and Buddy had been one. It seemed as though Buddy's true colors had shown brightly in the last year of his life.

Biker Gang Member Gets 37 Years
Debate Focuses On Police Use Of Dogs

April 12, 2002

By Dale Lezon

A member of the Bandidos motorcycle gang convicted earlier this week of drug charges was sentenced Friday to 37 years in state prison.

His case was one of several in Harris County at the center of a growing debate over police using drug-sniffing dogs on private property without search warrants, a common law enforcement practice.

David Gregory Smith, 39, of the 500 block of Shawnee, was convicted Wednesday of possession of methamphetamines with intent to distribute.

Smith's attorney, Philip Hilder, will appeal the conviction, saying narcotics officers failed to get a search warrant before taking a drug-sniffing dog to Smith's house Oct. 4, 2000.

Prosecutors claim police officers had a right to be outside the house because the property was not fenced or posted with "No Trespassing" signs.

"If it's allowed to stand, we inch closer to becoming a police state, "Hilder said.

The dog, Rocky, "gave a positive alert" to the odor of drugs at Smith's garage door and officers then obtained a search warrant for the home, according to police.

Smith's case is similar to two others in Houston appealed to the state's Court of Appeals in which officers did not obtain search warrants before allowing drug-sniffing dogs onto private property.

In one of those cases, officers took a drug-sniffing dog through a gate at the Houston home of Hubert Ray Porter Jr. on Aug. 16, 2000, said Matt Hennessy, Porter's attorney.

The dog alerted to the odor of drugs, and officers used that information to obtain a search warrant, according to court documents.

Porter was convicted of felony theft and misdemeanor possession of marijuana, Hennessy said. He is free on bond pending appeal.

     During this time, I was beginning to wonder whether it was all worthwhile; in hindsight, I think it was the beginning of the end for me. I was rapidly getting tired of all the methamphetamine bullshit, and was no longer able to tolerate the drug addicts that seemed to be coming out of the woodwork like ants. I knew that if we did not get it under control, the Bandidos Oklahoma chapter would never be what I intended it to be.

     Just when I thought it couldn't get any worse, it actually got a little better. It was like a breath of fresh air when I read about a Bandido National Officer from Australia who beat a drug case based on the fact that a police officer had planted all of the evidence. A big smile crossed my face when I saw the picture of him plastered all over the Australian newspapers. It was him holding his daughter while he sat on his motorcycle:

Bandido Drug Charges Dropped

By Jeremy Kelly and Jeremy Calvert

April 9, 2002

*Charges dropped: Bandidos
motorcycle club member Kim
Sloan is delighted to have won
his court battle.*

A BANDIDOS motorcycle gang member jailed for drug trafficking plans to sue police, after successfully lobbying for his sentence to be quashed and the charges he faced dropped.

Robert Kim Sloan spent five months of his four-year, four-month jail sentence in prison before the Court of Appeal set aside the verdict and sentence and ordered a retrial.

The court heard the drug squad detective who Mr Sloan accused of helping set him up was charged with drug trafficking.

Yesterday, the office of the Director of Public Prosecutions indicated in the County Court in Geelong it would not be pursuing Mr Sloan's case.

As Mr Sloan, 45, was yesterday being told he was a free man, the former detective, who Mr Sloan has claimed in court had set him up, was appearing in another court to face drugs charges allegedly committed while he was working for the drug squad.

Former Sen-Det Stephen Paton yesterday faced Melbourne Magistrates' Court, where he waived his right to a preliminary hearing and reserved his plea on charges involving at least $1 million worth of illicit drugs he is alleged to have bought from chemical companies.

The court has been told that in 1999 and 2000 Mr Paton was the drug squad's liaison officer for chemical companies, which supplied the squad for legitimate stings.

During his bail application last year, the court heard Mr Paton made at least 12 unauthorised purchases under the pretence they were for drug squad investigations.

The court heard Mr Paton bought more than 500,000 Sudafed tablets, as well as quantities of other chemicals used to make amphetamines and once told the chemical company not to put it on the drug squad's usual account because the drugs were for an investigation into corrupt police officers.

The value of the drugs, none of which have been recovered, was estimated in court to be worth in excess of $1.2 million on the black market.

Mr Paton, 40, who resigned from the force before his arrest last July, was yesterday bailed on a $100,000 surety to appear in the County Court where he will face four charges of trafficking and possessing commercial quantities of amphetamines.

Mr Sloan had maintained in court proceedings that Mr Paton was involved in planting amphetamines in his freezer and a kitchen urn during a search warrant executed on his Geelong house in March 2000.

However, in May last year, a jury found him guilty of possessing and trafficking amphetamines. He was jailed for four years and four months with a non-parole period of three years.

After Mr Paton's arrest, the Court of Appeal took the extraordinary step of releasing Mr Sloan on bail after he had served five months of the sentence.

Yesterday, Mr Sloan told the Herald Sun he was very relieved but also a little disappointed with the DPP's decision.

"I thought they might say sorry," said the father-of-three. "I always said I was set up and now I have been vindicated."

Asked why he thought police would plant drugs on him, he replied: "Probably because I am in a motorcycle gang."

Mr Sloan said he would take civil action against the Victoria Police.

At the end of April, during a large annual Nevada Biker Rally, another salvo was fired in the latest round of biker wars here in the United States. A large group of Hells Angels stormed into a Laughlin, Nevada casino and started fighting with members of the Mongols Motorcycle Club. In the end, three Hells Angels and two Mongols died as a result of the melee, and many members of both clubs were seriously injured. Both sides used hammers, bats, knives and guns during the five minute battle. I was amazed at the arrogance and the fact that this happened in the middle of a very public casino, where there were literally dozens of cameras to record the actions of the combatants.

May 12th was a dreary, cloudy day; not the kind of day you would envision for a motorcycle drag race. I had invested thousands of dollars of my own money in this event, and I got out of bed wondering how much money I would lose as a result of the rain. I prayed that the rain would hold off until after 2 pm, but resigned myself to the fact that I was screwed no matter how good it got. Fortunately, it started raining just before the first band was scheduled to perform, so in the end I did not have to pay the bands because they did not play.

I actually paid all the OK Riders, Ozark Riders and Bandidos that came to help me as staff, and their wives and girlfriends as well, even though I knew I was going to lose money on the event. After all, I had told them that they would be paid, and I am a man of my word. Although no one made a lot of money that day, everyone sure appreciated the money and the fact that they were not working for free.

I was also fortunate that the rain held off long enough for enough participants to come out, so in the end I only lost about five thousand dollars. I was happy with the turnout, and the buzz that the turnout was going to develop, for everyone there was excited about the concept. I had already decided that for the next race, which was going to be held on July 21st, that we were going to open it up to all types of motorcycles.

I figured that the Jap bike riders needed to learn what the Harley riders were all about, and the Harley riders needed to learn what the Jap bike riders were all about. That decision would end up being an important one, for it took a small, specific selection pool of interested motorcycle riders and multiplied it one hundred fold.

At the annual Pawhuska Biker Rally, in the middle of May, OK Rider Ian "Ian" Wilhelm stepped up to the plate and decided that he wanted to become an Oklahoma Bandido. Ian had been around me for a long time, since I built the show bike for the custom painter Wizard back in the early spring of 1997, and I had watched him with pride as he evolved from an independent biker into a well respected member of the OK Riders. At twenty-eight, his youth was exciting, and we hoped that it would propel others his age into hanging around with us.

We were smart enough to realize that clubbing is a dying concept; almost everyone involved around us seemed to be in their forties or fifties. We had to get some younger members, or we would eventually die from attrition. Bandido Ian was one of the keys to our future, and by voting him into our chapter, we started out the summer on top of the world. The Bandidos Oklahoma chapter was now eleven strong, with one member almost out of prison and ten on the street.

Bandido Jan Late May 2002

28

Bandidos Motorcycle Club Oklahoma
Summer 2002 To Christmas 2002

I took off for a lightning trip to Red River, New Mexico, for the annual Bandidos get together at the Red River Biker Rally over the Memorial Day weekend, while Bandido Bill Wolf covered for me at the sound mitigation construction project on Friday. My girlfriend Caroline drove out to Albuquerque the night before and met me at the airport there very early Friday morning, allowing me to maximize my time, getting in a full day at work Thursday and still getting to Red River before noon on Friday. As you already know, I had loaned my bike to my Canadian Bandido friend, Alain Brunette, who was visiting me for two weeks with his girlfriend Dawn. After driving all day Monday to get home in time from Red River, I was able to get back to my office for work early Tuesday morning and have all my faculties still intact.

When I got to work around 7:15am, I was quite surprised to find a crew of sub-contractors waiting for me and the doors still locked. There was no sign of Bill Wolf, and I speculated that the public bus transportation system had possibly failed him. When I had not heard from him by 9am, I got worried and called the halfway house where he was incarcerated, to find out what had happened to him. I was quite dismayed when they told me that he was extremely ill, and laid up in bed unable to move around at will. I asked them to have him call me immediately, but it took more than two hours before he finally did call. When he did call, I knew that something was very wrong, for Bill Wolf did not sound good at all. He told me that he was having massive stomach pain, and that he could barely move.

Over the next few days, I monitored Bill Wolf's health situation the best I could, calling the halfway house twice a day. After a week, I got very concerned, for Bill Wolf was not any better; if anything, he was getting worse by the day. He had seen a Department of Corrections doctor, but she had told him that the pain was a figment of his imagination and that there was nothing to be worried about. The doctor just gave him aspirin for the pain. By this time he had not eaten any food in more than a week, and I was very concerned that he might die. No one there at the halfway house seemed to care if he died or not.

I finally threatened the facility with legal action unless Bill Wolf received immediate health care, and that afternoon he was finally transferred to an area hospital. The doctors there at the hospital immediately diagnosed him as having appendicitis. I was amazed that he had not died, for he apparently had suffered an appendicitis attack over the Memorial Day weekend, and now an infection had appeared in the lining that surrounds the internal organs, due to the fact that he had been misdiagnosed by the prison doctor.

Bill Wolf was immediately rushed into emergency surgery, where his appendix and as much of the infection as they could see was removed. His stomach was not sewn back up, and instead was left open for about a week to allow the infection to be treated properly. When I finally saw him for the first time, I was in a state of shock; he had lost about thirty pounds and looked like death warmed over. I assumed that he would remain in the hospital for quite some time, but when I learned that the Department of Corrections intended to let him "recuperate" in his dormitory bed at the halfway house as soon as his stomach was sewn back up, I blew a gasket.

I instructed my attorney, Jonathan Sutton, to have one of his staff lawyers file an emergency Motion for Post Conviction relief with the Tulsa County Court that had sentenced Bandido Bill Wolf to prison two years before. I assisted the staff attorney in drafting most of the actual Petition myself, and we got it filed at the courthouse the day Bill Wolf was released from the hospital. Bill was terrified that he was going to die while back in the care of the Oklahoma Department of Corrections, and I assured him that I was doing all I could to prevent that.

On the 20th of June, 2002, the Judge that had originally sentenced Bill Wolf to prison heard our Emergency Motion for Post Conviction relief. Judge Gillert, realizing that he had never intended for Bill Wolf to die in prison, ordered Bill Wolf's prison sentence vacated. Judge Gillert immediately sentenced him to time served, and two hours later I was able to pick Bill Wolf up and bring him home to my house.

Bandidos Ct Ed & Bill Wolf July 2002

It took two weeks of care by my girlfriend Caroline, my daughter Taylor and I before Bill Wolf could get up and move around without being in pain. We were all convinced that my actions saved his life, but to me, it was just what friendship was all about: being there when someone needed you. Bill Wolf and I had been friends for almost thirty years; there was no way I was going to do nothing and let the Oklahoma Department of Corrections kill him. As soon as he felt well enough, he returned to work, supervising the warehouse for my sound mitigation construction project. I even hired an extra temporary hand to work only for Bill Wolf, doing all his heavy lifting and physical labor until he was completely well.

In June, my chapter President Bandido Lee accidentally got me involved in an argument with a member of the Bandidos Nomad chapter by the name of Franklin "Stubs" Schmick. Bandido Stubs was pissed off because I had sold a bunch of t-shirts at the Red River Biker Rally that everyone naturally assumed were Bandidos support shirts. The shirts were red with yellow printing, had two crossed swords on the front, and were left over from the May 12th "Living On The Edge" motorcycle drag race event. Bandido Stubs' argument at first was that the t-shirts were illegal only because he did not approve them. According to Bandido Lee, all we had to do was submit the shirt to him and Stubs would then approve the design.

Unfortunately, Bandido Lee's perception of the situation was grossly inaccurate. When Bandido Stubs looked over the design, he immediately rejected it because it contained two crossed swords and the initials SYLB in the handles of the swords. Stubs accurately perceived the initials as meaning "Support Your Local Bandidos", but because internal club rules dictated that there could be no swords used in the design of a Bandidos support shirt, Stubs demanded that all the remaining shirts be destroyed.

The "Living On The Edge" Drag Race T-Shirt From May 2002

My opinion, as you can imagine, was just the opposite, for I was the one who was going to suffer the financial loss. My position was that they were not Bandidos support shirts, that they were "Living On The Edge" motorcycle drag race event shirts that contained a subtle tribute to the Bandidos Motorcycle Club. Bandido Lee and I had included the letters SYLB at the last moment as an afterthought, thinking that all of the other local motorcycle clubs would believe that the person wearing the shirt was a Bandido supporter, when in fact, the person wearing the shirt was wearing it because they found it a neat design or they had been at the actual event.

In the end, in spite of all of Bandido Lee's arguing with Bandido Stubs, my arguing with El Presidente George "George" Wegers, common sense and logic, Bandido Stubs' antiquated line of reasoning won out. Bandido Lee told me that it was starting to look like if an idea was mine, the club would be against it no matter how much good it was going to do for the club. Jealousy seemed to be alive and well in our club and regularly raising its ugly head. So Lee and I changed the initials on the printing for the next round of drag race event t-shirts, and instead of SYLB on them, it now said SYLMC; which stood for Support Your Local Motor Cyclist or Support Your Local Motorcycle Club. It was crazy to think that the club did not want to be a part of this, but to make sure the argument was settled once and for all, I applied for a federal trademark over the t-shirt design in July of 2002. (It took almost a year, but I was eventually granted a federal trademark on the design and the slogan it contained: "If You're Not Living On The Edge, You're Taking Up Too Much Room".)

At the end of June, the Bandidos in Australia announced that they had agreed to act as expert consultants on a new movie which was based on the Milperra Massacre in 1984. The Milperra Massacre movie was based on the day-long shootout that occurred between the Comancheros Motorcycle Club and the Bandidos Motorcycle Club in which seven people had been killed. The Australian Bandidos even blessed the project by agreeing to allow the Bandidos colors to be used in the movie in return for future royalties. I was amazed at how smart the Australian Bandidos were, and how stupid some of the United States Bandidos seemed to be.

At the other end of the spectrum here in the United States, I was pleased to see that there were other Bandidos chapters that thought just like the Oklahoma chapter, when I saw the following newspaper article from the Pueblo, Colorado newspaper:

The Club's All Here - Bikers Reject 'Gang' Stereotype

By Kirsten Orsini-Meinhard

July 7, 2002

Bandido Billy, pictured with his son Little Billy, 5, of Pueblo, is a member of the Bandidos Motorcycle Club.

Everyone calls him Magic.

They say it's because of the coin tricks he pulls off flawlessly, or maybe he's just good at making some details about his life seem less important.

He won't tell you his real name, but that's normal for members of the Bandidos Club.

He'll talk about his motorcycle, but not how long he's been part of the group or how he gained his membership.

Bandidos members don't often give away any information about their exclusive motorcycle club - referred to as a gang by everyone except members - because it paints them in a bad light.

"We don't do a lot with the media," said Magic, wearing a leather biker vest with a bright yellow Bandido patch sewn on it.

"They don't find out if we're really the way we are."

Bikers tend to be crippled by raging stereotypes that paint them as fighters and drunks, but Bandidos members claim they don't live up to this generalization.

Their group is actually a brotherhood, they say.

Sure, you have to initiate - they call this "prospecting" - before you're accepted, but then you become part of the family.

"We're the ones that get up and fight Congress for safety regulations," Magic said at the Rocky Mountain Motorcycle Rally Saturday.

"We spend a lot of time fighting against laws."

Still, the Pueblo County Sheriff's Department felt the need to staff the four-day rally with a slew of county and out-of-county officials: the Colorado Springs tactical unit and K-9 unit, the La Junta Police and the Fremont County tactical unit, just to name a few.

On Saturday, there seemed to be as many camouflaged officials talking on walkie-talkies at the Fairgrounds as there were bikers.

"We have a number of groups out here who have a reputation for not abiding by the laws," said Pueblo County Sheriff Dan Corsentino. "We wanted to have more officers because we knew there would be more gangs out here."

The Bandidos weren't the only group the Sheriff's Department was watching out for - anyone who was breaking rules would be ousted, not just club members, he said.

In the world of motorcycles, riders are either "independents" or they join a club.

"There's a lot of clubs around, but there's a lot of people who just like to bike," said Lenny Schmidt of Canon City. Tattooed and wearing a bandana, Schmidt looked similar to many members of the Bandidos. The only difference was the lack of patch.

Bikers who aren't members of a club are called "independents" because, as Schmidt explained, they can ride with anyone they want. If they're part of a club, they must follow the rules of that group.

It's not always easy joining a club, either, Schmidt said. Hopeful members go through a "prospecting period," where the club will determine if they are eligible to join.

Although Bandidos were vague when asked how they choose new members, Magic said they look for "quality-type people who don't show-up and show off."

As part of most motorcycle clubs, Schmidt said members sign over the rights of their bikes to that club. That way, if a group member is arrested and brought to jail, they can use the bike as collateral.

Magic wouldn't talk about how the club reprimands members who disobey rules, but said disciplinary action depends on the situation and the group member.

In the Bandidos, there is a hierarchy among the members, but they won't say how their president received that title.

"This is a big family," said the president of the Bandidos, who calls himself Tooter.

"We take care of our own."

The Bandidos is actually a national club with chapters in different states. At the motorcycle rally Saturday, Bandidos members were from all over the country.

Although he understands why motorcyclists might have a bad name, Stig Jantz of Pueblo said they're not all trouble.

"There is a concern because of some problems with local bike gangs," he said. "But in reality, they're almost all people like dentists."

Christian Bell, who was visiting from Denver, agreed.

"You have a few bad apples and it makes them all look bad."

So far, officials have had minimal problems at the motorcycle rally. There's been three minor fights and a few bikers carrying knives or guns were asked to leave the rally, Corsentino said. With so many law enforcement officials around, he said these problems were taken care of quickly.

But Bandidos members were offended that security had increased so much at this year's rally. They say it's taking away their independence. To them, it's just perpetuating the stereotype.

"If anyone wearing leather goes into a bar," Tooter said, "they look at him like 'uh-oh.'

On July 21st, Bandido Lee and I held the 2nd "Living On The Edge" motorcycle drag race, but this time it was for all types of motorcycles. As a matter of fact, as long as it was not an automobile or a truck, we let it run. We had motorcycles of every kind and make there, even four wheel ATV's. All types of people were there, and the Jap bike riders seemed to tolerate the Harley riders, and the Harley riders seemed to tolerate the Jap bike riders. This time we held a bikini contest and broke up the races with some typical Harley bike games, like a slow race, which surprisingly amused the Jap bike riders because they had never seen bike games before. Once again, I used many OK Riders, Ozark Riders and local Bandidos, as well as their wives and girlfriends as my event staff, and paid them all as I had done the first time. There was no trouble at all, and besides the hot weather, the event was a success. Financially, I only lost about two thousand five hundred dollars this time, and I was thrilled.

The approach of the Labor Day weekend brought a certain amount of trepidation in the entire Bandido Nation, as there had been three recent, violent incidents between members and/or supporters of the Bandidos and Hells Angels in the Albuquerque area. Although I chose to not travel in that direction that weekend, I was wondering if the Hells Angels would be foolish to fight a war on three fronts. They were already fighting with the Pagans on the east coast and the Mongols on the west coast, and it looked like they were flirting with disaster by encouraging a conflict with the Bandidos. An article in the Durango, Colorado newspaper summed it all up:

Officials Report Sightings Of Hells Angels, Bandidos As Bikers Arrive

August 31, 2002

By Jennifer Kostka

The smell of leather and the roar of motorcycles hung in the air Friday, amid sightings of arriving Hells Angels and Bandidos members and talk of an unscheduled motorcycle parade.

More bikers streamed into town for Labor Day weekend, when the Four Corners Iron Horse Motorcycle Rally usually takes place.

Law-enforcement officials in the area began to prepare for the busy weekend. The La Plata County Sheriff's Office heard that Hells Angels members had rented a house east of Bayfield, and Durango police officers learned about an unexpected parade down Main Avenue in Durango Sunday afternoon.

Some sheriff's deputies spotted Hells Angels and Bandidos motorcycle gang members in town, and Sheriff Duke Schirard said he had heard that Hells Angels members had rented a house near Sauls Creek, east of Bayfield, for the weekend.

Sheriff's Lt. Dan Bender said it wouldn't be unusual for the gang to rent houses and hotel rooms or stay at friends' homes in the area during Labor Day weekend.

"They've been here every weekend for several years," Bender said. "We don't anticipate this year to be any different, because the rally isn't being held."

The sightings of Hells Angels and Bandidos members could become a big concern for law-enforcement officials in the area, after the two gangs were involved in a gun fight Aug. 21 in Albuquerque.

The president of the Santa Fe chapter of the Bandidos, Teodoro "T-Bone" Garza, was grazed in the head by a bullet and struck with shotgun pellets at the home of two men with ties to the Hells Angels, according to an Aug. 24 story in the Albuquerque Journal. Garza was not critically injured in the fight.

The Bandidos are the second-largest biker gang in the world behind the Hells Angels, and they control New Mexico, according to Conrad Chavira, a gang specialist with the New Mexico Department of Public Safety who is quoted in the Albuquerque Journal article.

The fight in Albuquerque does not mean the Sheriff's Office will change any of its enforcement plans for the weekend, Bender said.

"Because of the competition between different patch clubs, any time you have a large number of people gathered together and there's hard feelings between them you have that potential (for conflict)," Bender said. "We've been very fortunate thus far, and we hope their peaceful existence, at least while they're in La Plata County, continues."

A manager at Iron Horse Inn said about six Hells Angels members stayed at the hotel in the beginning of August, but she didn't believe they would be back this weekend, because they didn't feel welcome in Durango.

The gang had reserved about 10 rooms at the hotel, but it canceled them all, the manager said. About 90 of the inn's 143 rooms were filled for the weekend with other bikers.

The Durango Police Department began to gear up for the big bike weekend as well, after learning about an unscheduled biker parade Sunday.

Bright orange fliers with the words, "The Rebel Rally's 10th Annual 'Stealth ' Iron Horse Parade," began to appear around town Friday afternoon, and the fliers were a surprise for the Durango Police Department.

"We have no plans for a parade Sunday," said Capt. Dale Smith with the Durango Police Department. "We'll notify the officers to make them aware."

The flier instructs motorcyclists to "just show up and ride" at noon Sunday on Main Avenue in Durango. It also says the parade is sponsored by "The Party Poopers of La Plata County and the Southern Ute Indian Tribe."

*"Hell, if this was an organized event we would have to have 42 public hearings
and pay big bucks - so express your freedom by showin' up, lookin' good and
making some noise," the flier says.*

*Smith said the police department has 10 officers scheduled for Sunday, but it will
have to add more officers and examine what it will do if hundreds of motorcyclists
take to Main Avenue and run red traffic lights to follow the parade.*

*"We're hoping that the intention is that they plan to stop at the traffic-control
lights," Smith said. "Each and every one that runs a traffic light can get a ticket."*

*Motorcyclists continued to roar through Durango Friday. Lynn and Dixie Ruffell,
of Idaho Falls, Idaho, pulled into the parking lot at Adobe Inn after a day and a
half on the road. The Ruffells decided to come to Durango for the first time
despite the cancellation of the official rally.*

*"Just because they canceled their plans doesn't mean we have to cancel ours," Mr.
Ruffell said.*

*M.C. Wellesley, of Amarillo, Texas, was getting his black leather boots shined in
the parking lot at Albertsons on West College Drive. Wellesley decided not to
cancel reservations he made nine months ago.*

*"We had a great time last year," Wellesley said. "It's pretty country. We really just
want to do a little riding."*

By the Labor Day weekend, my sound mitigation construction project
near the Tulsa International Airport was over. Bandido Bill Wolf accepted a job
offer with the Boston area General Contractor we had been working for, to go to
work at another sound mitigation project in Baton Rouge, Louisiana. Although I
too, had been offered a job there, I had no desire to be out of town for the four or
five months it would take to get the job done. Bill Wolf was single, had no family
and had just got out of prison; the job situation was perfect for him because it gave
him an opportunity to make some money, traveling in the process. Besides, there
just happened to be a chapter of Bandidos in the Baton Rouge area, and Bill Wolf
was friendly with many of its members.

While Bill Wolf headed to Louisiana, and some of our other Oklahoma
chapter members headed to Durango for the annual Four Corners Biker Rally, I
took off for Perry Lake in Kansas to meet up with a crew of guys we had recently
met from the Atkinson, Kansas and St. Joseph, Missouri areas. There I spent the
weekend with them, and rode into the annual Perry Lake Biker Rally side by side
with the Sons of Silence Motorcycle Club, in a show of solidarity against the El
Forastero and Galloping Goose Motorcycle Clubs. By now things were starting to
heat up in Missouri for the Kansas Sons of Silence members that lived just outside

Caroline had a great time, too. Visiting Mickey Mouse and his crew was like a breath of fresh air; after all I had been through in 2002. I hoped that things would get better, but I was at this time losing faith in Bandido El Presidente George and his administration. I could not put my finger on the problem, but some of what the older Bandidos thought about our El Presidente was making more sense to me now. The saying "being hung out to dry" had crossed my mind more than once in the last year, and I had a bad feeling that I had been used over and over again by El Presidente George in more ways than one. I also was hearing lots of rumors that El Presidente George would regularly tell one person one thing, and then tell another just the opposite. There were even rumors that he was telling us Bandidos one thing and telling other 1%er motorcycle clubs just the opposite. By Christmas of 2002, I was wondering now if all those rumors were true, and starting to believe that where there was smoke, there had to be fire.

Fueling my thoughts were two specific incidents that occurred in 2002. First, thinking back to November of 2001, when Bandido Skip and I had traveled to Kansas to attend a Sons of Silence party at their Hutchison clubhouse, we had met up with Bandido El Presidente George. He was temporarily stuck in Wichita because the van he had been traveling in had broken down. At that Sons of Silence regional party, El Presidente George gave me permission to open a Bandidos support club chapter of Hermanos based out of the Atkinson, Kansas and St. Joseph, Missouri area. Three of the prospective Hermanos members traveled to Hutchison to meet me and the Kansas members of the Sons of Silence. At the time, I had a lengthy conversation with the Sons of Silence National President, Terry, about setting up the Hermanos chapter, and during that conversation, Terry also granted me permission to open that Hermanos chapter as well.

The first Hermanos Motorcycle Club chapter in that area was started in March of 2002, and by Christmas of 2002 was flourishing. By the end of the year they had two chapters, one in Atkinson, Kansas, known as the Jamesland chapter and the other based out of St. Joe, Missouri, known as the Blacksnake Hills chapter. Already there were multiple rumors floating around the Bandido Nation that El Presidente George had never given me permission to open any of the Hermanos chapters, and that I was a "loose cannon", operating on my own. In reality, nothing could be further from the truth.

Secondly, during the summer of 2002, Bandido El Presidente George called me from Oklahoma City where he was visiting his wife's mother, and asked me to come down and bring him back to Tulsa for a night, so he could visit with Lee and me. On the way from Oklahoma City to Tulsa, George had told me a tall tale about Bandido Jack "Jack-E" Tate that I knew was a lie. I said nothing about it to Lee, until after Bandido Lee took El Presidente George back to Oklahoma City the next day. When I told Lee about what George had told me concerning Bandido Jack-E, and the fact that I knew it was a lie, Lee told me that El Presidente George had told him the same thing, and when George told the story to Lee, Lee knew it was a lie also. Bandido Lee and I just looked at each other; because now we both knew for sure that El Presidente George had lied to us at least once. Lying to a Bandido was a patch-pulling offense, and now there seemed to be a set of double standards in the club's hierarchy.

So as the year ended among all of my disparaging thoughts, I tried to end it for our chapter on a positive note. As a Bandidos chapter, for a change, we sent out two different Christmas cards that year that I had made. One was totally for fun, kind of a joke to be played on the minds of those lucky enough to receive it, and the other, a sincere Christmas yuletide greeting. The joke Christmas card made it look like we had a huge mansion for our chapter clubhouse; when in reality there was no way any motorcycle club could ever afford a clubhouse like that here in the United States.

Bandidos Oklahoma Chapter Joke Christmas Card December 2002

29

Bandidos Motorcycle Club Oklahoma
January 2003 To Summer 2003

It was now the beginning of 2003, and no sooner had I returned from my family vacation in Florida, than I dove off right back into the shit pile as soon as I got home. It was painfully obvious to me, now that I had gotten away from the Bandidos world for a while, that I had some serious internal problems to contend with. I had always been unpopular with a minority of Bandidos, but I had always dispelled that to the "you can't please everybody all the time" line of reasoning. Now, I seemed to have most of the entire Bandidos United States National chapter pissed off at me on a regular basis. In reality, I was facing a battle that I could never possibly win; a battle that would ultimately cause me to quit the club I loved. On January 1, 2003, I was beginning the last nine months of being a member of the Bandidos Motorcycle Club.

On January 3rd, I rented a car at a Tulsa area car rental company, and took off for the annual Sons of Silence/ Iron Horsemen Motorcycle Club New Year's Party in St. Louis, Missouri. Bandidos Skip, Mick and I first stopped in Springfield, Missouri, where we picked up our Bandido brother Batman, then stopped near Rolla to meet Probationary Bandido Gary "Andy" McWilliams from the Arkansas chapter. Andy had originally been a member of the Memphis chapter of the Outlaws Motorcycle Club, then helped me start the Ozark Riders Bandidos support club in Arkansas, eventually becoming a member of the Ozark Riders himself. Recently, against the wishes of the Outlaws, the Arkansas Bandidos had voted Andy in as a member of their chapter.

The Sons of Silence Motorcycle Club party was being held this year at the Crowne Plaza Hotel complex, and as soon as we arrived, everywhere we looked we saw Iron Horsemen and Sons of Silence members. It was a great place for a National Run, and for those two motorcycle clubs; its geographic location was perfect, right in the center of the country. While I was there, I ran into Terry, the National President of the Sons of Silence. We sat down and talked about the situation with the El Forastero and Galloping Goose Motorcycle Clubs in Missouri, and Terry asked me if I would join the Sons and the Iron Horsemen who were going to a swap meet in Belleville, Illinois on Sunday.

I had already heard about the swap meet there and thought about going, but now I made up my mind and assured him that I would be there. Terry expected that there was going to be some El Forastero and Galloping Goose there, and he wanted to make a good showing of the unity between the Sons of Silence, the Iron Horsemen, and the Bandidos for the benefit of the El Forastero and Galloping Goose. It was Terry's subtle way of telling the El Forastero and

Galloping Goose that they were not the only show in town, and definitely not in charge of the state of Missouri.

Terry and I also talked about the two Hermanos chapters I had set up near Kansas City, and he told me that Bandidos El Presidente George had no recollection of granting me permission to set them up, and had told the El Forastero and Galloping Goose that all Bandidos and their support club members would move out of Missouri in the near future. I was surprised to hear this in some ways, and in other ways it did not surprise me at all; it seemed that I was learning more about El Presidente George every day.

Sons of Silence National President Terry complained to me that El Presidente George had not advised him that the Bandidos were going to open another chapter in Colorado, and was talking to me like I was a member of the Bandidos National Chapter. I volunteered to call Bandido George and find out where the breakdown in communication went wrong. It turned out that Vice Presidente Chris (Chris had recently been promoted from El Secretario to Vice Presidente) from South Dakota had forgotten to call Terry, to notify him about the new chapter in Colorado. It dawned on me then that even the Sons of Silence looked to me to get things done, because they knew that I always got things done and that I always did exactly what I said I would do.

On Sunday, Bandido Andy took off early and headed for Arkansas, and Bandido Skip, Mick, Batman and I drove over the Illinois state line into Belleville, where we rendezvoused with a large contingent of both Sons of Silence and Iron Horse members. As we flooded into the swap meet hall, I was immediately struck by the look of horror on many of the faces of the public there. For every one of us club members that entered the hall, it seemed as though ten citizens or independent bikers left. We soon located a booth of about ten members of the El Forastero and Galloping Goose members, selling their Harley parts. They seemed overwhelmed by the hundred or more Sons of Silence and Iron Horsemen that surrounded them, and even more surprised to see the Bandidos there with them.

I only spent a few minutes there close to the El Forastero and Galloping Goose before I decided that we should walk around the rest of the building and let the whole world know that the Bandidos were there. Ten minutes into my tour of the swap meet hall, I ran into some Hells Angels, one of whom I knew. His name was Monster, and he had been in another motorcycle club for many years, and recently had decided to jump ship and join the Hells Angels. Monster was only a Hells Angels prospect at the time, but his reputation and huge build dictated that he was a force to be reckoned with. He wasn't named Monster for nothing!

When I saw Monster, and he saw me, he came running over to me, picking me up off the ground when he hugged me. Bandido Skip jumped to attention, but by the expression on my face he soon figured out that it was a reunion, and not the beginning of a fight for our lives. Monster and I chatted for a few minutes, and he told me that one of the Hells Angels wanted to talk to me.

Monster asked me if I would mind, and I told him I would be willing to meet with him and discuss whatever was on his mind. We agreed that I would meet his Hells Angel boss over by the food area in ten minutes, and parted ways. (Six months later I heard that Monster became a full patched Hells Angel.)

Bandido Skip was ready, Bandido Batman a little concerned, and Bandido Mick scared shitless. But this is what I did best, so I did it on my own, with Skip, Batman and Mick watching from about thirty feet away. A small contingent of Hells Angels soon came into view, and one broke off from the pack and left the others not far from Skip, Batman and Mick. As the Hells Angel walked into the food area to greet me, you could cut the tension in the air with a knife. Independent bikers, citizens and even the food court staff abandoned the area for fear of a gang war, leaving the Hells Angel and me completely by ourselves.

The Hells Angel boss introduced himself as "Pulley"; I later learned that his real name was David Ohlendorf and that he was a member of the Illinois Nomads chapter. I was pleased to find out that he was also a single dad with custody, and a regular working guy who told me that he hated methamphetamine as much as I did. I was amazed to find a Hells Angel who was so much like me; it was almost as if I was looking in a mirror. To my surprise, which I tried not to show, the topic of discussion was Arkansas and the Bandidos National chapter. Apparently Hells Angel Pulley thought that I had been sent there to see him by the Bandidos National chapter because he had called Bandido El Vice Presidente Jeffrey "Jeff" Pike. Pulley wrongly assumed that I had the authority to talk to him about the Hells Angels intention to expand into Arkansas.

Pulley told me that he had recently emailed Bandido Gary "Wiggs" Wiggs, a former Bandidos President for the state of Arkansas, and Bandido Wiggs had responded in a manner that Pulley failed to understand. Pulley had then called El Vice Presidente Jeff twice in the last week, and Bandido Jeff had failed to return his calls. After listening to Pulley explain the situation, knowing that Bandido Wiggs hated Hells Angels and that Bandido Jeff was ignoring him, I volunteered to contact both Bandidos and see what I could do. All Pulley wanted to do was talk about the situation in Arkansas, before one of the players there resorted to violence to prove a point, which I considered to be the right thing to do. Before I walked away, I made sure to tell Pulley that I was no longer a National officer, but that I would see what I could do.

When I called Bandido Wiggs, and told him where I was and what had just occurred, Wiggs told me to tell Hells Angel Pulley that there would never be a Hells Angel chapter in the state of Arkansas. I then called Bandido Jeff, and when I told him what had transpired, he told me that he had no reason to talk to Pulley, and that was to be the end of it. I was amazed, for everything that I had been taught by El Presidente George was now just the opposite of what was happening. Once again, I was left out on the end of the limb, and the club had cut off the branch I was hanging from.

I met up with Pulley again about a half hour later, and told him that I had no luck talking to Bandido Wiggs and Bandido Jeff, and that he would need to talk to Bandido El Presidente George himself to resolve the issue. I volunteered to contact Bandido George as soon as I got back to Oklahoma; we exchanged contact information, and parted ways. As soon as I got home, I called El Presidente George and told him everything that had happened. He told me that he would personally contact Hells Angel Pulley, but as I expected, he never did. I called Pulley later that day and told him that I had contacted El Presidente George, explaining the situation at length, and told him that El Presidente George had told me that he was going to call Pulley. I told Pulley that I had done everything that I could and that there was nothing more I could do.

On the 19th of January, another ex-member of the Miami, Oklahoma based Loners Motorcycle Club, Mike "Stymie" Loring, decided that he wanted to be a Bandido, and our chapter voted him in. Unfortunately he did not last very long, for his girlfriend was not very happy and made him quit February 2nd. It turned out that Stymie was a little too pussy whipped to be a Bandido anyway, and quitting as soon as he did was the best for all parties concerned.

In very early February I purchased a wrecked 2002 Harley Davidson FLHT from a broker in San Antonio, Texas. It was smashed up really bad, requiring a new frame, front fork assembly, engine cases and transmission case before it was road ready. It was the first dresser I had owned since the late 70's, and I was very proud of it. I even scored a killer deal on a brand new factory CD player for it from the local Harley dealer, and a premier Tulsa graphic artist painted a Bandidos mural on the front fairing depicting a crazy Bandido holding a stick of dynamite. The mural very accurately depicted what was on my mind at the time; I just did not know who I needed to blow up.

The Bandidos Mural On Ct Ed's 2002 FLHT March 2003

In February I also helped Probationary Bandido Ian with his own wrecked bike project, a 2001 FXDXT. Up until now, Ian had been riding a Sportster and now he would have a big Harley to ride, which would make his life a lot easier. I even went way out of my way, and financed the purchase and rebuild of the motorcycle, the same as I had done for Bandido Mick and the others before him. Both Mick and Ian, our younger members, were hotrods, and both now had relatively new Twin Cam Harleys to show off on that I had helped them to attain. Both Ian and Mick failed to acknowledge the fact that neither one of them would have had new bikes unless I had done the financing, and that should have clued me in for what was to come from both of them in the near future.

On March 7th, just before the annual Bandidos Birthday Run to Jasper, Texas, Probationary Bandido Red Dog quit the club and turned in his club colors. He was having a tough time keeping up with his club financial obligations, and we let him leave the chapter in good standings. Although he owed us about two hundred fifty dollars at the time, he made statements promising us that he would settle his debts in the very near future. The very next day, at Jasper, the Oklahoma chapter took on the third prospect in the history of the chapter; his name was Walter "Levi" Willis. But to make it happen, I was talked into buying another wrecked motorcycle, which Levi, Bandido Ian and I built in about ten days. And just like Ian and Mick before him, Levi offered no thanks for what I had done for him. You would have thought that by now I would be a wee bit wiser, but somehow I thought that I was doing a good thing, helping these guys realize their dreams, and I was blinded; I failed to see them for what they really were.

After the party at Jasper, we did have a good laugh when the local newspapers reported that there were three thousand Bandidos present for the Birthday Run. In fact, there were less than two hundred fifty there.

Bandidos Meet In Newton

March 8, 2002

Texas troopers are letting their presence known in Newton County this weekend. That's because the Bandidos are in town.

The notorious biker group is holding it's 37th annual reunion at the Sawmill which is on Highway 190 in Newton.

Authorities tell us the 3000 Bandidos can't come outside the compound during the meeting.

20 troopers are patrolling the area making sure nothing goes wrong, normally there are just two troopers making rounds in Newton County.

All was quiet in Oklahoma for almost a month after the Birthday Run. Then on April 8, 2003, federal authorities finally arrested almost the entire chapter of the Oklahoma City Outlaws, as well as a bunch of their associates, for a variety of drug and firearms charges. Only two actual Outlaws members were not arrested, probably because both were new members. The arrests were the culmination of a two year investigation, and it was officially disclosed that one of the main informants was ex-OK Rider George "George" Schuppan. By the time the summer of 2003 was over, fifty-nine people eventually were arrested, all facing charges that resulted from illegal activities they committed while members of, or associated with, the Outlaws Oklahoma City chapter. What had started with the co-operation of ex-OK Rider George had become the largest investigation of a motorcycle club in the history of Oklahoma.

Two Day Sting Puts Brakes On Biker Gang

April 10, 2003

By Nick Trougakos

OKLAHOMA CITY -- Twenty-seven Oklahomans with ties to a national motorcycle gang were arrested and charged with a score of gun and drug offenses after a two- day sweep by local and state law enforcement officials. U.S. Attorney Robert McCampbell announ-ced Wednesday the arrests netted six members of the Outlaws Motorcycle Club, including the group's chapter president and vice president.

The president, Thomas Burl Cain, 58, one of 16 people arrested Tuesday, could face up to 20 years in prison on federal charges of possession of firearms by an unlawful drug user and possession of an unregistered sawed-off rifle. The vice president, Virgil Earl Nelson, 48, could go to prison for 30 years on three federal charges of being a felon in possession of a firearm.

The sweep was the culmination of a two-year joint investigation involving more than 160 officials from the U.S. Attorney's Office; Oklahoma County District Attorneys' Office; the Bureau of Alcohol, Tobacco, Firearms and Explosives; the Oklahoma City Police Department; the U.S. Marshal's Service and the Drug Enforcement Administration. The investigation was aided by confidential informants, who provided investigators with information about alleged illegal drug activity, a court affidavit shows.

McCampbell said 16 search warrants were executed Tuesday and Wednesday. Fourteen were in Oklahoma County and the others were in Tulsa and Grady counties. McCampbell would not confirm whether there will be more arrests, but said officials are examining evidence obtained through the search warrants and the investigation is ongoing. He also declined to disclose the amount of drugs, primarily methamphetamine that turned up in the investigation.

While not all of the 27 arrested were members of the Outlaws Motorcycle Club, McCampbell said they were all affiliated with the club in some way. The club has chapters in 16 states and several countries, according to the court affidavit. Group members are normally identified by a vest with a patch on the back featuring a skull with crossed pistons colored black and white, and the word Outlaws above the skull.

The Oklahoma chapter of the club was founded in the early 1980s, court records show. Founding members of the club include Nelson; John Scott Killip, who faces 10 years in prison on a federal charge of being a felon in possession of a firearm; and Darcy Earl Swearingen, 62, charged with possession of a controlled substance with intent to distribute.

Other gang members arrested include Michael Roberts, 45, charged with three counts of being a felon in possession of firearms and ammunition; Gary Gene Hatfield, 42, charged with two counts of being a felon in possession of firearms and ammunition; and Richard Deeter, who faces state methamphetamine charges.

McCampbell also announced two outstanding warrants in the case. The first seeks the wife of Nelson, Dawn Marie Nelson, who is charged with possession of methamphetamine with intent to distribute. The second names Charles Shannon North Jr., who is charged with distribution of methamphetamine.

All fifty-nine people charged in federal court as a result of the Outlaws Motorcycle Club investigation eventually either plead guilty or were found guilty after trial. All the members of the Outlaws Oklahoma chapter plead guilty except one, John "Little Wolf" Killip, who was one of the very few that actually went to trial. Outlaws Virgil "Arlo" Nelson received a twenty year sentence, Michael "Michael" Roberts (who had been originally sought in connection with the murder of ex-Bandido Earl "Buddy" Kirkwood) received a fourteen year sentence, Thomas "Chameleon" Cain received a ten year sentence, John "Little Wolf" Killip received a four year three month sentence, Richard "Sir Rick" Deeter received a two year ten month sentence, and Gary "Hateful" Hatfield received a two year six month sentence. Ex-Outlaw Darcy "Darcy" Swearingen received a ten year seven month sentence, while ex-OK Riders James "Victor" Wall received a nine year sentence. The man who started it all, ex-OK Rider George "George" Schuppan plead guilty and ultimately received a six year sentence in return for all the informing he did.

What surprised us the most was the April 9th search warrant that had been served on ex-Bandido Joseph "Joe" Kincaid in connection with the federal investigation of the Oklahoma City chapter of the Outlaws Motorcycle Club. I legally obtained a copy of the search warrant application and affidavit for the residence of Joseph Kincaid, when federal authorities in Muskogee forgot to have it sealed. It was an amazing tale of illegal activities that led up to the search warrant, all chronicled in minute detail. (In all federal criminal search warrants, this affidavit was a required predicate that had to be submitted to a Judge before obtaining a search warrant.)

In spite of being involved with the sale of a Sten 9mm machine gun, the sale of a pound of "ice" (a pure form of methamphetamine), numerous drug manufacturing allegations, numerous liaisons and/or meetings with members of the Outlaws, and a history of working for the informant ex-OK Rider George "George" Schuppan, ex-Bandido Joseph "Joe" Kincaid somehow miraculously escaped arrest. To this day, we have no idea why he was never charged for the myriad of illegal activities that were detailed in that search warrant application.

In the late afternoon of April 21, 2003, I received an urgent call from one of our two hangarounds, John "LJ" Engelbrecht in Wichita, Kansas. The call was not a surprise, for over the last few weeks, LJ and our other hangaround, Devin "Devin" Quattlebaum, had both been subjected to repeated threats from members of the local chapter of the El Forastero motorcycle club. Over the last few days, Devin had received a very specific threat: either stop wearing a baseball cap that said "Support Your Local Bandidos", which Devin had bought at a recent Bandido function, or die. The threat was an arrogant attempt to dictate what clothes people could wear in Wichita, and Devin had been advised to defend his life if he was attacked by anyone associated with the El Forasteros.

But the nature of the call did surprise me, for apparently two full patch members of the El Forasteros had attacked Devin after work, in the parking lot of the Big Dog motorcycle manufacturing plant where Devin worked, as he walked to his truck, which was parked in the company parking lot. Devin had defended his life, and in the process had shot both of the attackers, killing one and seriously injuring the other. In everyone's opinion, both El Forasteros got exactly what they deserved, like the saying goes: "If you mess with the bull you should not be surprised when you get gored". Needless to say, the El Forasteros did not feel the same, in spite of the fact that the one El Forastero who survived readily admitted that the two members had stalked, threatened and attacked Devin intending to do him bodily harm

As soon as LJ briefed me as to what had transpired, I instructed him to drive out of town with Devin and get a motel room for the night. I told him that I did not want to know what town or where they were, but to call me back in a few hours from a pay phone collect, when they were safe and secured. I then called the Sons of Silence motorcycle club President in Kansas, Jerry, who lived near Wichita and knew me well. When Jerry immediately recognized my voice, he told me that he knew why I was calling, because the news of the shooting was all over the television. Jerry advised me that according to the television, the police were already looking for Devin. I had Jerry chase down the names and contact information for two prominent criminal defense attorneys, which he provided to me within the hour.

When LJ and Devin called me back, I told them that I was going to arrange Devin's surrender through one of the two Wichita criminal defense attorneys, and to try and get a good nights' sleep. I asked them to call me again in the morning, and then I would give them the contact information for the attorney I had chosen to turn them in. Sons of Silence Jerry called me frequently to keep me updated on the television reports concerning the police search for Devin, and when he told me that the police had Devin surrounded at a house in Wichita, I knew that Devin's and LJ's actual location was still a secret. Throughout that evening, I had multiple discussions with the two criminal defense attorneys, and in the end I settled on one, Les Hulnick. The next morning, accompanied by Mr. Hulnick, Devin turned himself into the authorities.

Suspect In Downtown Wichita Shootings Turns Himself In

By Sarah Bahari

April 25, 2003

The suspect in Friday's double shooting in downtown Wichita turned himself in Saturday morning as police were searching for him.

Devin Quattlebaum, 32, of Wichita, is being held in the Sedgwick County Jail on charges of first-degree murder and attempted murder, police Lt. John Speer said.

John Dill, 45, of Wichita died Friday after being taken to Via Christi Regional Medical Center-St. Francis Campus. Injured was Bret Douglas, 43, also of Wichita. He was upgraded from critical to serious condition Saturday, a hospital official said.

Police think the shooting involved rival motorcycle gangs.

Dill and Douglas confronted Quattlebaum when he got off work Friday at Big Dog Motorcycles manufacturing plant on East Douglas. Speer said the shooting stemmed from an earlier argument, but would not elaborate.

Quattlebaum's father, Fred Quattlebaum, said he thinks his son acted in self defense. He said the men confronted his son at an earlier time and threatened bodily harm.

"He feared for his life and had to protect himself," he said.

Douglas' family declined to comment, and Dill's family could not be reached.

Speer said Quattlebaum should be formally charged early this week.

Saturday afternoon, police searched the ground along the canal under I-135 between 13th and 21st streets for the gun used in the shooting.

Police are now processing for evidence a blue pickup the suspect left the scene in. Detectives found the truck late Friday night at a house near 13th Street and Maize Road, that belongs to an acquaintance of the suspect, Speer said.

Officers surrounded the house Friday night, evacuated two nearby homes and blocked off Maize from 13th to 21st, but eventually found the house empty.

Police also contacted friends and family of the suspect and searched bars and nightclubs but were unable to locate him, Speer said.

"We do consider him armed and dangerous," Speer said Friday night.

Homicides involving rival motorcycle gangs are very rare in Wichita, Speer said.

"The whole thing is interesting," he said.

A few days later, after determining that Devin did not have enough money to pay for his own defense, Mr. Hulnick withdrew as counsel and a Kansas Public Defender, Sarah McKinnon, was appointed to represent him. Because of the nature of the charges, Devin remained in jail without bond pending trial, which was anticipated to occur in late summer or early fall. Over the next few months, Sarah and her lead investigator Jenny Blaine would determine that both members of the El Forastero motorcycle club were high on drugs at the time they attacked Devin. This, of course, was no surprise to anyone. We were surprised that Devin was being charged with first degree murder, since he had obviously been defending himself during the attack. A newspaper article from the Wichita newspaper dated May 31st, tells a fairly accurate depiction of the events that occurred in the parking lot of Big Dog Motorcycle manufacturing plant that day in March:

Jury To Hear Cycle Slaying Case

Devin Quattlebaum is charged in the death of one man and the shooting of another at Big Dog Motorcycles.

BY Ron Sylvester

which the Bandidos Motorcycle Club had been founded, way back in March of 1966.

Hanging out with the Danish Bandidos was like a breath of fresh air, and I already missed them by the time Buller and I rolled off the ferry onto German soil. I hoped to return to Denmark soon and see them all another day, but I knew in my heart that it was highly unlikely I would ever do so again, at least not as a Bandido. I knew that the clock was ticking, and there was not much time left for me as a member of the Bandidos.

Bandidos Ct Ed & Nomad Clark May 2003

30

Bandidos Motorcycle Club Oklahoma
Summer 2003 To Fall 2003

Bandido Buller dropped Caroline, Taylor and me off at an autobahn rest stop, where we met my German buddy Dieter Tenter. Dieter was not a member of the Bandidos, but had many friends who were. He was an independent biker from Lengerich whom I had known for many years. I made it a point to always visit him when I was in Europe, and he did the same when he was in the United States. In Germany, his home and family were my home and family. Seeing him standing there in the autobahn parking lot, I felt like I had arrived home again.

After a short ride in his delivery van we arrived at his home. After getting settled in, we sat down on his porch and caught each other up on what had happened in our lives since we had seen each other last. I was surprised to see that his two kids had grown up a lot, and especially surprised at the young lady his daughter Malisa had become. It seemed just like yesterday I had accompanied her to her elementary school class, now more than five years ago, and spent time talking to her entire class.

Bandidos Fossey (far left), Wolfgang (2nd from right) & Crew With CT Ed At The Bandidos Clubhouse Muenster, Germany June 2003

Late that afternoon, we drove over to the Bandidos Muenster clubhouse, which was not far from Dieter's home. There, some of the Muenster and

much time left to spend with her. I also wanted to spend more time with Caroline, and devote more time to my business. And I started thinking that if I stayed in the Bandidos, none of that could happen. There was no way I could do it all. Something had to give, or maybe I could change the way the Bandidos were heading.

I felt like the club was a train out of control, coming down a mountainside. There was no engineer in the locomotive, and if left alone, the train was going to crash. No ifs, ands or buts; the question was *when the train would crash, not if it would crash.* I wondered if I could somehow get control of the train, but I knew I could not do it myself. I also knew that I wanted no part of running the club, in spite of what many were thinking. On the flight across the ocean, I resolved to do what I could to help the members of the Bandidos who wanted our El Presidente to be replaced as the man who ran the entire club. Among those Bandidos who hated El Presidente George and everything he stood for, was Bandido Joe "Little Joe" Benavides. He was a legend in the Bandidos red & gold world, and had been around for more than twenty years. Bandido Little Joe had a crew of about fifty Bandidos who thought the same about El Presidente George as he did, and I decided to help them get organized. I figured that once they were organized, El Presidente George could be replaced easily without any of them resorting to violence.

For once in my life, the overseas flight went by very fast, and by the time we landed in Detroit, I was again dragging ass from a case of jetlag. Once again, I had not slept in almost twenty hours and it was only late afternoon, and I knew I had to remain awake for a few more hours to get past the jetlag. We settled into a local hotel, ate some dinner, and were all sound asleep by eight. The next morning we caught an early flight to Tulsa, and after tending to all of my important email and phone messages, I eased right back into my normal daily life. The only exception was that during a late evening conversation with Bandido El Secretario William "Bill" Sartelle, in the heat of the moment, I let it slip that I was finished helping El Presidente George, and as a matter of fact, I was now on the side of all the dissenters, whom I called "the other guys". Thinking that El Secretario Bill was a good friend, and knowing that he and I had many "heart to heart" talks over the years, I thought that my statement to him would be taken as me just "venting" a little. I had no way of knowing that he would immediately tell George, and that conversation would end up being a nail in my own coffin in the near future.

As soon as I could, I explained everything that happened on my trip to Europe to my chapter President Lee "Lee" McArdle, and I also told him how I felt and the decision I had made. Then I sat Bandido Lee down, and had him watch the video I had shot at the Biker Rally in Sweden. You should have seen his face when he watched that gorgeous Swedish Playboy Playmate tell him, "If you would have been here this weekend, I would have been your girlfriend for the whole weekend." It was priceless, giving me a good laugh at a time when I needed some humor in my life.

A few days later, Bandido Lee announced that I had to accompany him on a trip to town. He wanted to take me out to dinner for my forty-eighth birthday, and then surprised me with tickets for the ZZ Top concert, which was to be held that night. Bandido Ian, Bandido Lee and I went to the ZZ Top concert, having a blast. Afterwards we rode over to the other side of downtown Tulsa to a new nightclub called "Bad Girls". "Bad Girls" was a takeoff on the "Coyote Ugly" theme, where the waitresses danced on the top of the bar for entertainment. Although I had seen the movie "Coyote Ugly", seeing this in person was way better. I was having a great night, albeit a bit too smoky, until the local gang task force descended on us when they saw us step outside for a breath of fresh air.

I had nothing to fear because I did not drink, but Bandido Lee was a little drunk and Bandido Ian had no driver's license. When the task force ran the tag numbers on the three bikes, fortunately two came back registered to me. Bandido Ian's bike had been originally purchased by me when it was a wreck, and apparently my name still showed on the ownership records. That was a stroke of luck, for the cops knew that Bandido Ian had no license. The cops asked me who was riding the third bike, which was the one that Ian had parked out in front of the bar, and I told them that there was another Bandido down there in the downtown bar district, hanging out with a female friend. After enduring a shakedown that lasted more than ten minutes, the gang task force cops decided to leave us alone. Leaving the local police in a patrol car to watch us, I rode off by myself to Bandido Ian's house, where I borrowed the keys to his wife's car. I then drove back downtown and picked Bandido Ian up, giving him a ride to his house. I was pleased that none of us had gone to jail, but pissed that the night had ended on a sour note.

In the middle of June, a Houston Bandido showed up in Tulsa, explaining that he had been hired temporarily by a Tulsa drafting company. His name was Scott "Scooter" Musslewhite, and Bandido Scooter thought that he would be in our area for about three months. If all went well, he might move here and left the door open to join our chapter, since he had just gotten divorced. Relocating at this time of his life seemed to be a way to start anew, but for the time being, Bandido Scooter just wanted to hang out with us. We should have had the brains to realize that he had been sent here as a spy for Bandido El Vice Presidente Jeffrey "Jeff" Pike, and that his showing up was not a mere coincidence.

Bandido Scooter immediately started hanging out with Bandido Mick, Bandido Smurf, our Prospect Levi, and Bandido Steve, who by now was almost dead from pancreatic cancer. We should have seen the writing on the wall, but at the time were blinded by the façade Bandido Scooter put on. If we had seen it, we would have noticed the first signs of what would soon become a major internal Oklahoma chapter uprising. There was going to be a mutiny, but we were going to have to walk the plank. We just did not see it coming. There were too many things to do, and as always, not enough time to do them.

To add some gasoline to our little internal, mini mutiny fire, we added another Prospect to our chapter on July 25th. His name was Glenn "Glenn" Vermillion, and Glenn seemed to be harmless at first glance. But Prospect Glenn soon started running with the other chapter dissenters, and by the time we went to Sturgis the first full week of August, the minority problem children were now a force to be reckoned with. Like a festering pimple, the events of the last few months would soon come to a head and pop. With the addition of Prospect Glenn, we were now a Bandidos chapter that was sixteen strong, and Bandido Lee and I thought that it was all downhill from here on in.

I left for Sturgis, South Dakota a few days early, planning on taking the long way around. I first traveled west to Amarillo, where I sat down with Bandido James "Tucker" Atkins for a few hours. I wanted to talk to him about the way I felt, give him a chance to tell me how he felt and get some advice from him. I knew that he had no love for El Presidente George, but needed to know if he was one of the ones that really wanted a new El Presidente. While I was there he told me to be extremely careful, because now some of my own Bandido "brothers" intended to kill me if they had the chance. The rumor was that El Presidente George wanted me out of the club as soon as possible, in any way possible; if I was dead or alive, it did not matter. This did not surprise me, for I had been told this by a few other Bandidos in recent weeks, but one more thing did surprise me: El Presidente George wanted me gone so badly, he was willing to destroy the entire Oklahoma chapter in the process.

As I rode west from Amarillo into New Mexico, I had a few hours to think about the reception I likely could expect when I rode into the Bandidos clubhouse campsite in Rapid City, South Dakota. I knew that there were only a few Bandidos I could really trust, and all it would take would be one to set me up. Even a Bandido that was loyal to me could easily be convinced to betray me without knowing it. If I was going to survive Sturgis, then I had to be at the top of my game. For starters, I decided to sleep at a local motel, and not in the camp ground. I also made up my mind that there was no way that I would be in our camp unless it was during daylight hours.

I arrived in Albuquerque just before the heat of the day cooked me like a fish in a frying pan, hooking up with my old friend Bandido Jessie "Chuy" Wicketts at a local tattoo shop. Bandido Chuy had worked with me at the Collin County Courthouse project in Texas a few years back, and we had become close over the years. While I watched him get a tattoo on the back of his shaved head, we reminisced about the good times we had had over the years.

The next morning Chuy and I stopped at a local restaurant for breakfast, before riding the hundred miles from Albuquerque to Sante Fe. There we planned to stop and spend the night visiting the new Sante Fe chapter of Bandidos. After awaking to a chilly sunrise, Bandido Chuy and I set out for Denver, Colorado early in the morning. We planned to make the entire ride that day, hoping to stop during the heat of the day at Pueblo, where we would visit a Pueblo chapter

Bandido. The entire day's ride was outstanding, with the New Mexico and Colorado weather cooperating to the fullest. After waiting out some late afternoon thunderstorms in Pueblo, we finally arrived at the home of Bandido Victor "Victor" Marquez shortly after dark.

Bandido Chuy In Albuquerque August 2003

Bandido Victor had been the President of the Denver chapter for as long as I could remember, and one of El Presidente George's biggest vocal critics. Bandido Little Joe also lived with Bandido Victor, and I hoped like hell that Bandido Little Joe was there. To my dismay, I soon found out that Bandido Little Joe was nowhere to be found. I did get to spend a few hours with Bandido Victor, and the same discussion that I had with Bandido Tucker a few days ago, I had again with Bandido Victor. Once again, I told him how I felt, and he gave me basically the same advice that Bandido Tucker had told me: I had better watch out for El Presidente George was definitely out to get me.

Bandido Victor added that he thought I was a huge liability to El Presidente George, because I knew a lot about the El Presidente, his inner circle and the decisions that he had made over the years. El Presidente George also thought that I was out to take his job from him, and was worried that I might have enough stroke to do so. Victor and I resolved to get together at Sturgis if possible, all of us in one room: Bandidos Jack-E, Tucker, Victor, Lee, Little Joe and me.

Bandido Chuy and I spent a short night at the home of a Denver chapter member, leaving at five the next morning to beat the heat we anticipated running into later that day. We traveled north up through Cheyenne, Wyoming, then northeast into the Black Hills region of South Dakota. At one of our last rest stops before we entered into Sturgis, Chuy and I talked for quite a while about my situation and whether I would leave Sturgis as a Bandido. I made him promise me that he would not get involved in my situation, and that he would keep his eyes wide open to all that he thought were his "brothers". Bandido Chuy was well educated after spending three days with me, riding side by side more than a thousand miles.

Our first stop in Sturgis was to visit with the Sons of Silence Motorcycle Club, at their private clubhouse and campsite just north of downtown Sturgis. Bandido Chuy and I were welcomed there with open arms, and after a few hours of visiting, we set out for Rapid City and the Bandidos clubhouse. Riding in through the gate at our clubhouse, I had a distinct sense of imminent danger. Like riding in through the gates of hell, I knew I only possessed the power to alter my destiny a little. By and far there was not much I could do to make a major change in what was going to happen, in spite of all my advance warning. It is said that stupidity is just one notch past bravery; but being stupid is not a part of the game that I intended to play.

The first thing I did was to locate myself a safe haven, which in this case became a local Rapid City motel room. I spent about a half hour at the Bandidos camp, before I took off to the motel room for a shower and a meal. If I was going to survive the next few days, I needed plenty of sleep and regular meals. About four in the afternoon, I headed back over to the clubhouse party site. As soon as I rode through the gate and got off my bike, I saw Bandidos El Presidente George "George" Wegers. Bandido George was madder than I had ever seen him, and the first words he screamed were at me. The El Presidente ordered me into his personal travel trailer camper, and with him came three of his Sargento de Armas, and El Secretario William "Bill" Sartelle. I was obviously up shit creek without a paddle, with no way out. So when the El Presidente started questioning me about a conversation that I had over the phone with El Secretario Bill back in June of 2003, I was quite surprised, for it was not what I expected at all.

It was easy to admit the truth, and the truth is what I told Bandido George. I admitted that I had told El Secretario Bill in that phone call that I was no longer interested in assisting the National chapter or the El Presidente, and in fact was going to do all I could to help out the other side; the Bandidos that wanted a new El Presidente. I also explained that at the time of the phone call, I was venting my frustrations to what I considered a friend, and I had not anticipated that he would exploit the confidence I had in him by "ratting on me". The El Presidente then asked me if I was after his job as El Presidente, and when he did, I realized that was what this interrogation was really all about. Bandido Victor, in our conversation a few days ago, had been dead on the money in his assumptions.

I patiently and quietly explained to Bandido George that there was no way I wanted his job at all, and that I was no longer as upset as I had been back in June when I made the call to El Secretario Bill. I also explained that it was true; there was no way I was going to do any more for him or his national chapter, that as far as I was concerned, I had already done enough in the last five years to last a lifetime. After Bandido George explained to me that he should have me beat up right there on the spot, I told him I understood why he felt that way.

But for some strange reason, instead of ordering his three Sargento de Armas enforcers to kick my ass or kill me, the El Presidente let me walk out of that trailer. As I hopped out of the back of the tiny travel trailer, I thought maybe I had just cashed in my one time free "get out of trouble" card. It had always been a running joke between the El Presidente and me that because I had done so much for him and the club that I always had one "get out of trouble" free pass that I could use whenever I needed it. In reality I had completed every task he had ever asked me to do, and I felt that I had been entitled to use my free pass.

For the next twenty-four hours, El Presidente George and El Vice Presidente Jeff both kept trying to come up with a valid reason to expel me from the club. It seemed like their whole focus was to come up with some type of stupid excuse to expel me from the club; an excuse that could be passed off as a valid reason to the entire club worldwide. Time after time, a Sargento de Armas was sent to interrogate me about something mundane that had happened since I had become a Bandido. Most of the accusations were so petty they amused me; some were once the truth, but in their present form so far removed from the truth that the accusations were now total lies.

Every one of the accusations had already been settled, back when they had occurred. Some of the accusations had been settled multiple times, over and over again, because a Bandido did not remember or understand that a decision had been rendered. In every situation I had been vindicated, and here at the Bandidos clubhouse in Rapid City, South Dakota in August of 2003, I was vindicated for those same accusations again. I was amazed at how many times they could figure out a new way to "beat a dead horse", and at the lengths they would go to find an excuse to kick me out of the club.

Bandido Skip, who I had now known for more than twenty-four years, convinced me to take off for awhile to escape the tension early Saturday afternoon. Leaving the Bandidos clubhouse campsite, which had by now become a pressure cooker, Skip and I went exploring the exhibits and entertainment that were scattered all over the Rapid City and Sturgis area. We deliberately stopped in at a carnival-type set up of tents, just off the interstate, that surrounded the new Harley Davidson dealership halfway in between the two cities. There we were surprised to find the Orange County Choppers booth, and more surprised to see Paul Tuetul Jr. finishing an autograph session.

Bandido Skip asked me to follow him, and try to get a picture of him with Paul Jr. if I could. Knowing that this was going to be impossible, I followed, holding the camera ready for action just to see how much fun it would be watching Skip make the attempt. To my utter surprise, we both easily got through the security that surrounded Paul Jr., and when Skip shouted to Paul Jr., Paul Jr.

turned around and shook Bandido Skip's hand as if they were old buddies. It all happened in a split second, and as fast as it happened, it was over. I knew I had got a picture of something, but doubted that the picture would turn out. On the contrary, I thought that the picture might be of half of Skip and the other half sky, or maybe of Paul Jr.'s hand and Skip's chest. I advised Bandido Skip to not hold his breath, and to count on seeing a crappy picture. To my surprise, the picture turned out great as you can see:

Bandido Skip & Paul Tuetul Jr. At Sturgis August 2003

When Skip and I returned to the Bandidos campground at Rapid City, I found a few minutes to visit with my good friend and Bandido brother Jack "Jack-E" Tate, and Bandido Jack-E told me the same thing as Bandidos Victor and Tucker had in the last week. El Presidente George and El Vice Presidente Jeff were out to get me, and it did not matter to them what they had to do to achieve their goal. Their words echoed through my mind when the entire Oklahoma chapter was summoned into the clubhouse for an interrogation by the El Presidente George, El Vice Presidente Jeff, and their entire National chapter.

The subject of the meeting was to find out who was really running the Oklahoma chapter, and how everyone in the chapter felt. Bandido Lee and I, as well as most all of the chapter, were in state of shock when three of our own chapter members sold us down the river. First, Bandido Steven "Steve" Buitron, who was everything but dead from his pancreatic cancer, devastated us with his version of what our chapter was all about. Bandido Steve, in a babbling monologue that almost was almost comical, equated the Oklahoma Bandidos chapter to a support club. Speaking directly to Bandido Lee and me, Bandido Steve told everyone that I really ran the chapter, and that Bandido Lee was just my puppet. All this stupidity came from a jerk who did not even own a motorcycle at the time, and had only me to thank for providing the financing on all three of his last three motorcycles. All three of those motorcycles had been repossessed because Steve had not paid the monthly loan payments as he agreed to. Not owning a motorcycle was a valid reason for immediate expulsion, and was a major violation of the Bandidos By-laws.

I knew we were in trouble as I saw the look of joy come over El Presidente George's face while Bandido Steve was lamenting at what an awful chapter of Bandidos he belonged to. I was thinking that I wanted to wring his neck on the spot, and what an ungrateful piece of shit he was. If it was not for the Oklahoma chapter helping him over the last three years, he would have been expelled a long time ago, either for not owning a bike or for not paying his chapter monthly donations.

About the time I had realized the damage that Bandido Steve had done, next up at bat was Bandido James "Smurf" Ragan, who also concurred in what Bandido Steve had said. The third one up at bat was our newest member, Bandido Michael "Mick" Barnett, who had not a clue what was going on. But Bandido Mick also agreed with what Bandidos Steve and Smurf had said, and the same bullshit story that came out of three of our members' mouths was more than anyone could fathom.

After listening to all of their sad stories about our incompetence, El Presidente George decided that the Oklahoma chapter needed to be split in two chapters at the next Pawhuska Biker Rally in mid-September. Bandidos Oklahoma would then have a new Oklahoma City/Lawton chapter and for the time being, a Tulsa/Joplin/Springfield chapter run by Bandido Lee. That was not so much a problem, as we had all planned on doing that anyway in the next six months. What surprised us is that El Presidente George suggested that Bandido Steve would be perfect to run the new Oklahoma City/Lawton chapter, when we all expected Bandido Charles "Snake" Rush to be the President of the new chapter. Fortunately for us, the decision of who was going to be President of the new Oklahoma City/Lawton chapter was not going to be made until Pawhuska.

Before we even got over the shock of that, Bandido Smurf announced that he wanted to be President of his own chapter, and El Presidente George announced that Smurf would make a great President. And so it was also ordered that the new "Tulsa" chapter would be split again before the end of the year, and that Bandido Smurf would be the President of that new chapter. Bandido Smurf's new chapter would be headquartered out of the Joplin, Missouri area and would contain all the Oklahoma members that lived in Missouri and northeastern Oklahoma. The notion was ludicrous, for Bandido Smurf was incapable of taking care of himself, much less controlling a Bandidos chapter.

Of all the members in our chapter most incapable of leading a Bandidos chapter, all three of the complaining whiners, Bandidos Steve, Smurf and Mick, were at the top of the list. As the rest of us came out of the meeting in the clubhouse, we knew that we were all screwed, and that Bandidos Steve, Smurf and Mick were two-faced, lying traitors. Bandido Lee and I realized that it was just a matter of time before Bandido George got what he wanted, which was for me to be forced out of the club. We now knew for certain, to get what he wanted, that he most certainly was willing to destroy the Oklahoma chapter in the process.

As I rode home alone from Sturgis that Saturday evening, I thought about my situation even more than I had thought about it on the plane coming home from Europe three months ago. I knew that I had dodged a bullet. I was amazed that I had survived the ordeal, and could not believe that I had somehow just barely avoided being beat up. I realized for the first time, that I was much more likely to suffer bodily harm from my own organization, than another motorcycle club. I also realized that there were few Bandidos that I could really trust and that the Bandidos I had helped the most, were the ones that whined, complained and bitched the most. It also seemed that the ones I had helped the most were the ones most likely to stab me in the back. Riding into North Platte, Nebraska just before eleven that night, as lightning lit up the skies all around me and the cool rain soaked through my clothes, I wondered what the future would bring and thought that the storm was a fitting end to a most horrible Sturgis.

The next day, I stopped in Wichita, Kansas, at the home of our hangaround LJ's home for a few hours, arriving just before the heat of the day. I was so mentally drained that I immediately fell asleep for four hours, waking up to the sound of the voice of Bandido Skip, drenched in sweat. I was glad to figure out that he had caught up to me, and as soon as it started to cool off, we rode back to Tulsa side by side. When we stopped for awhile to gas up and get a quick drink, Bandido Skip let his composure fly to the winds. On the long ride home, he had stewed over what had happened at Sturgis, and wanted to beat up Bandidos Steve, Smurf and Mick as soon as he saw them. I did my best to calm him down, but in my heart I was thinking the same. No matter what happened after we got back to Tulsa, I knew that nothing would ever be the same again, and that the motorcycle dynasty known as Bandidos Oklahoma was dead and stinking.

On August 22, 2003, Bandido Steve was officially accused by Bandido Skip in a written statement with lying to a National officer (Bandido El Presidente George at the meeting in Sturgis), failure to own a motorcycle, failure to be loyal to your chapter and President, and faking medically inactive status when really active. Each of the accusations in themselves were patch-pulling offenses, and in a normal situation, would result in that person being expelled from the organization and losing his club colors. But Bandido Steve was no ordinary Bandido because his nose was buried in El Presidente Jeff's ass; everyone now knew that Bandido Steve was the El Vice Presidente's boy.

At the next Bandidos Oklahoma chapter meeting, which occurred at my house in Owasso, Bandido Steve was conveniently too sick to attend. But we did have Bandido regional boss Jack "Jack-E" Tate and Mississippi Bandidos President James "Sluggo" Gilland join us, since Bandidos Jack-E and Sluggo were in Tulsa for a few days, still on the road traveling home from Sturgis to Louisiana. Bandido Smurf was also conveniently absent, crying the blues about one of his many convenient medical problems. Only Bandido Mick had the balls to show up at the meeting, making a feeble plea that he did not understand what was going on when he spoke up at the meeting, and did not mean to say what he did. No one believed him for a moment, but fortunately for him, Bandido Steve was the main focus of the meeting.

Bandido Lee, as the Oklahoma Chapter president, decided in an open meeting with all of us present, that Steve should be immediately kicked out of the club and his club colors returned to the club. Every chapter member present agreed that Steve was a traitor, a liar and that he did not own a motorcycle. Even Bandido Jack-E and Bandido Sluggo agreed that Steve should be kicked out of the club posthaste. So Bandido Lee sent our Sergeant-at-Arms, Bandido Skip, down to Lawton the next day to repossess all of Steve's Bandidos property. Bandido Skip was all too happy to comply, for he hated Bandido Steve's guts with a passion. No sooner had Skip returned to Tulsa with all of Steve's club colors, than the shit hit the fan.

Subj:	Steve
Date:	8/23/2003 6:08:49 PM Central Standard Time
From:	bandidobill@hotmail.com
To:	okbandidoboss@aol.com
CC:	
	bandido_george@hotmail.com, bandidojeff@hotmail.com, OKbandido@aol.com

Sent from the Internet (Details)

MAKE SURE LEE GETS THIS MESSAGE RIGHT AWAY!!!

AS PER JEFF, STEVE IS TO GET HIS PATCH BACK IMEDIATELY! STEVE IS TO CALL JEFF BY TOMORROW (SUNDAY, 8/24/03) AND LET HIM KNOW HE HAS RECEIVED IT!!!!!!!

IF THIS IS NOT DONE, LEE WILL BE THE ONE LOSING HIS PATCH!!!!

SEE IF THIS TIME Y'ALL CAN FOLLOW INSTRUCTIONS, JUST DO IT!!!!!!!

Love, Loyalty, Respect

El Secretario, USA
Bandido "Big Deal" 1%er
B.F.F.B

Apparently now ex-Bandido Steve had immediately called El Vice Presidente Jeffrey "Jeff" Pike, and whined to Bandido Jeff about what had happened. El Vice Presidente Jeff was livid, and through an email from El Secretario William "Bill" Sartelle, ordered Bandido Lee to immediately return to Steve the Bandidos club colors that had been taken from him, or suffer the consequences. We were all in a state of shock when El Vice Presidente Jeff stuck his nose in the middle of our chapter business, for it was standard policy that no one in the National chapter except El Presidente George had any authority to get involved with any chapter's business.

For us, this was just another situation where a member of the National chapter was making up new rules as he went, but this was a serious intrusion into the sovereignty of our chapter. Before responding to El Vice Presidente Jeff, Bandido Lee called a half dozen Bandido National officers and a dozen individual Bandidos chapter Presidents, and all of them agreed that El Vice Presidente Jeff was way out of line. In a carefully worded response to Bandido Jeff, with Regional President Bandido Jack-E advising him, Oklahoma chapter President Lee responded as follows:

Subj: **Regarding Steve**
Date: 8/24/2003 3:59:25 PM Central Standard Time
From: Okbandidoboss
To: bandidobill@hotmail.com
CC:

        bandido_george@hotmail.com, bandidojeff@hotmail.com,
        OKBandido

To set the record straight, Friday night (8/22/03), after discussing Steve's situation, the entire Oklahoma chapter agreed with my decision to pull Steve's patch for the following reasons:

1) <u>Failure To Own A Motorcycle - In Violation Of The BMC National By-Laws</u>
Steve does not own a motorcycle; and has not owned a motorcycle in more than a year.

2) <u>Lying To Brothers - In Violation Of The BMC National By-Laws</u>
Steve lied to the National chapter when he told Bill Sartelle that he was building a motorcycle.

3) <u>Lying To Brothers - In Violation Of The BMC National By-Laws</u>

Steve lied to the National chapter & the Oklahoma chapter at the Oklahoma/National meeting inside the Sturgis CH @ Sturgis when he told them that some members of the Satans Bros MC were ready to become Bandidos.

4) <u>Lying To Brothers - In Violation Of The BMC National By-Laws</u>
Steve lied to the entire Oklahoma chapter at a chapter meeting 8/15/03 when he told them that he was told by the National chapter to move to Lawton, Oklahoma to start a support club; and that was why he moved to Oklahoma.

5) <u>Failure To Be Loyal To The Chapter & His President</u>
Steve went behind the chapter and Lee's back and discussed chapter business with the National chapter at Sturgis

6) <u>Failure To Be Loyal To The Chapter & His President</u>
Steve told the National chapter & the Oklahoma chapter at the Oklahoma/National meeting inside the Sturgis CH @ Sturgis when he told them that the Oklahoma BMC chapter was run like a support club.

7) <u>Being Active While On Medical Inactive Status</u>
Steve has been on medical inactive status for almost a year - he has no vote, no right to talk to anyone about any chapter business until Lee puts him back active.

As we are all aware of the fact that only George can give orders to a chapter President, thank Jeff for his input as I value his opinion. However, after consulting with many Chapter Presidents and other National officers, my entire chapter and I feel that this is internal Oklahoma chapter business, and therefore we do not require National assistance concerning this matter at this time.

We will hold off with the new Oklahoma City chapter until Pawhuska, as directed in my recent phone conversation with George. Also be advised that regular meetings (with all Oklahoma members) have been held every week as directed upon in Sturgis until the new Oklahoma City chapter is formed.

Bandido OK-Lee 1%er
Bandidos MC Oklahoma

Instead of terminating the problem, this compounded it. Bandidos El Presidente George, anticipating repercussions, had already given El Vice Presidente Jeff permission to do whatever he wanted when it came to the Oklahoma chapter. This time Bandido Lee received a personal phone call from the El Vice Presidente, in which Bandido Lee was ordered to immediately return the patch taken from Steve. If the patch was not returned to Steve immediately, then

Bandido Jeff threatened to expel Lee from the club himself. Bandido Jack-E advised Lee to comply now, and to try and fix the problem at the next big President's meeting. Bandido Lee did not want to wait that long and asked Bandido Jack-E to bring a crew of Louisiana Bandidos with him to the next Pawhuska Biker Rally, which would occur in about three weeks. Bandido Jack-E agreed to, and it was decided that Bandido Victor in Colorado would also be asked to come to the Pawhuska Biker Rally with his crew. We all felt that it was time to settle this once and for all.

When Bandido Victor was contacted, he immediately volunteered to bring all of his crew, and to bring Bandido Little Joe as well. We expected to have more than one hundred fifty Bandidos there, all on our side. And we expected to leave there with Bandido Snake in charge of the new chapter in Oklahoma City/Lawton, and Bandido Steve kicked out of the club. Bandido Lee also planned on demoting Bandidos Smurf and Mick back to Prospect, so that they could learn again what our club was all about. We also expected to make such a strong showing that the National chapter would stay out of our chapter business and leave us alone forever. If only things had worked out that way......

On Tuesday, the 10th of September, our Hangaround Devin Quattlebaum in Wichita, Kansas, went on trial for first degree murder for the death of the El Forasteros member "Big John" in the fight for his life in the parking lot of the Big Dog factory last March.

Trial Begins In Shooting At Big Dog Motorcycles

September 10, 2003

By Hurst Laviana

A turf dispute between rival motorcycle clubs led to the fatal shooting outside Big Dog Motorcycles, jurors were told Tuesday.

Devin Quattlebaum, 32, who is standing trial in Sedgwick County Court for first-degree murder, was associating with the Bandidos, a club with roots in Oklahoma and Texas, lawyers on both sides said.

The victim, John Dill, 45, was described as a key member of the El Forasteros, a club that claims turf rights across Kansas.

Defense lawyer Jeffrey Wicks said Dill, who was called "Big John," was known as an "enforcer" for the El Forasteros.

"When they wanted something done, they'd send Big John," Dill told the jury in his opening statement. "When they wanted to get a message across, they'd send Big John."

Wicks said his client had repeatedly been threatened and warned about associating with Bandidos and wearing their clothing. On the day of the shooting, he said, Quattlebaum "was advised he is now going to pay the price for not doing what he was told."

Wichita police said Quattlebaum was wearing a Bandidos cap on March 21 when he killed Dill and wounded Bret Douglas, 43, during a confrontation outside the motorcycle plant where Quattlebaum worked.

Assistant District Attorney Jim Puntch said in his opening statement that the victims had no firearms when they were shot. He said witnesses would suggest that Quattlebaum acted with premeditation.

"The evidence will show you that on March 21, the defendant shot John Dill -- shot him in the chest, shot him in the back, shot him at close range," Punch said. "He got out of his truck, shook out the empty cartridges and began to fire again."

Wicks, meanwhile, said his client emptied his gun in self-defense. When Quattlebaum reloaded, Wicks said, he had just one bullet that he fired into the ground in an effort to scare the men who were attacking him.

The trial resumes today in the courtroom of District Judge Karen Langston.

The weekend before the Pawhuska Biker Rally, at the last Bandidos Oklahoma chapter meeting I attended, it was decided that Bandido Charles "Snake" Rush would be the President of the new Oklahoma City/Lawton chapter. As part of that new chapter, at the Pawhuska Biker Rally, two OK Riders from the Shawnee chapter were going to be voted in as Probationary members of the new Bandidos Oklahoma City/Lawton chapter (to be called the Oklahoma City chapter), and Prospect Walter "Levi" Willis was going to be made a full patch member of the Tulsa chapter.

As we looked forward to the confrontation with our Bandidos National chapter at the Pawhuska Biker Rally in less than a week, our eyes and ears were riveted on Devin's ongoing trial in Wichita, Kansas. We all waited, holding our breath; if he lost, we all knew that Devin would be in prison for many years. Knowing the facts, it was hard to see how he could lose, but trials were funny. One could never tell for sure in advance how they would turn out. Even knowing that both members of the El Forasteros had been high on methamphetamine when they went down to the Big Dog factory to confront Devin, and knowing that they intended to do him serious bodily harm, there still was no way for sure to predict how the jury would react. We also had no idea that the El Forasteros would be willing to assist in Devin's defense, by having one of their own attempt to intimidate the jury.

Jurors Feel Uneasy After Seeing Victims' Associates Watch Them Leave Courthouse

Devin Quattlebaum looks at the cap that led to a shooting last spring at the Big Dog Motorcycle factory in Wichita that left one man dead and another wounded.

By Hurst Laviana and Brian Corn

September 16, 2003

Devin Quattlebaum took the witness stand Monday at his murder trial to explain why he felt he had to shoot two men to protect himself -- the same day some jurors voiced concern over their own safety.

Quattlebaum's trial, entering its second week, centers on the somewhat volatile relationship between the local chapter of El Forastero motorcycle club and another club, the Bandidos.

Quattlebaum, who supported the Bandidos, said he feared two of Wichita's El Forastero members would kill him in the parking lot of the Big Dog cycle factory last spring. Instead, he shot at them, killing one.

Monday's trial began with some jurors saying they felt uneasy that some of the associates of the victims had watched them leave the courthouse near the end of last week. Sedgwick County District Judge Karen Langston cleared the courtroom to question the jurors, saying she didn't want them to feel further intimidated by having to answer her questions in public.

Langston, however, honored a request by The Eagle to inspect the court record of the closed session.

Two jurors told Langston they recognized some of the people they had seen in the courtroom, sitting with family and friends of the victims, hanging out across from the courthouse parking garage after the trial Thursday and Friday. One juror expressed concern the panel could be followed.

But all said they would not let the incident interfere with their decision. They should get the case this week.

Quattlebaum then followed with nearly a full day's testimony and cross-examination about his frame of mind the afternoon of March 21, when he opened fire on John Dill and Bret Douglas. Dill died. Dill and Douglas were members of El Forastero and didn't like Quattlebaum's cap, which read: "Support Your Local Bandidos Worldwide."

Quattlebaum, 32, said he had focused on a lifelong interest on motorcycles to fill a void left after he quit drinking in 1991.

Seven years later, he found camaraderie with other Wichita motorcycle enthusiasts who also were on the wagon. These enthusiasts introduced Quattlebaum to biker clubs and to his friend "Little" John Engelbrecht. Quattlebaum called him "L.J."

It was through trips to Tulsa and Texas with L.J. that Quattlebaum said he met members of the Bandidos, a large motorcycle club that boasts national and international membership. Quattlebaum picked up T-shirts and caps at various outings with the Bandidos. Quattlebaum claimed he even wore a shirt he had gotten from a Wichita El Forastero member in support of their club to a Bandidos function. No one said a word.

But back in Wichita, Quattlebaum said some members of El Forastero and the Newcomers -- another motorcycle club -- began taking exception to his Bandidos hat in December at the Riverside Perk coffeehouse.

"Why didn't you quit wearing the hat?" public defender Sarah McKinnon asked.

"It's not just the hat," Quattlebaum said. "I was supposed to quit hanging around my best friend. I was supposed to quit riding with the same people."

On March 20, Quattlebaum said Dill and another man visited him at the Big Dog plant. The El Forastero members didn't want Quattlebaum wearing the Bandidos hat anymore.

"Next time I see you on the street wearing that... it's not going to be pleasant," Quattlebaum remembered Dill saying. "I'm going to take it all the way."

The next day, March 21, Quattlebaum still had the hat -- and after his shift ended, he found Dill and Douglas waiting. There was a struggle at Quattlebaum's pickup.

"I thought they were going to kill me," Quattlebaum said. "I thought I was never going to see Regina again." Regina is Quattlebaum's wife.

Prosecutor Jim Puntch asked on cross-examination why Quattlebaum resorted to deadly force.

"You knew you couldn't miss at that range, didn't you?" Puntch asked.

"I wasn't thinking about that," Quattlebaum said. "I just wanted them to get away from me and not kill me."

The trial continues today.

On Thursday September 18th, the jury was deliberating on Devin's first degree murder trial, and I was getting prepared for a much bigger showdown at Pawhuska than Bandido Lee and I had anticipated. Complicating things, Bandido Cain of the Lafayette, Louisiana chapter had died the night before. Now Bandido Jack-E and his entire crew needed to stay in Louisiana and prepare for the funeral, so no Louisiana Bandidos would be here to help us. We also now knew that Bandido El Vice Presidente Jeff was coming to Oklahoma with seven Sargento de Armas and two Bandidos Nomads members.

The rumor going around the entire Bandidos Nation was that the "Oklahoma problem" was going to be fixed once and for all, no matter what it took. If Bandido Victor did not show up with his crew, we knew that we would have no chance against the unprecedented show of force by the Bandidos National chapter. I bought up canisters of police grade pepper spray and miniature aluminum baseball bats to be used to defend ourselves at Pawhuska, in the event that Oklahoma chapter members were attacked by any of the Sargentos de Armas or Nomads.

On Thursday evening, I got a call from Devin to let me know that he had been acquitted on all charges. We both knew that his great defense attorney Sarah McKinnon and her lead investigator, Jenny Blaine, were responsible for the acquittal. Without their extraordinary efforts, Devin would have probably spent the rest of his life in a Kansas prison. I was ecstatic, but only for a brief moment, and then my mind was back on the current confrontation brewing at our Pawhuska Biker Rally camp site. I had been told that the normal festive atmosphere was nowhere to be found, and instead you could cut the air with a knife, it was so heavy. It was like we were preparing for a major battle in a world war, and no matter what I did, there was going to be no happy ending. When I read the Friday morning Wichita newspaper online, it gave me another ten minute break from the thoughts going through my over-stressed mind, as you can see:

Verdict In Biker Slaying: Not Guilty

Jurors Agree With Devin Quattlebaum's Argument That He Was Defending Himself When He Shot Two Members Of A Rival Motorcycle Club, One Fatally.

September 19, 2003

BY Hurst Laviana

A Wichita man was justified when he shot two members of a motorcycle club who had confronted him for wearing a ball cap that promoted a rival club, a Sedgwick County jury ruled Thursday.

Devon Quattlebaum, 32, wept and hugged his lawyers after a court official read the initial verdict: not guilty of first-degree murder.

His tears turned to sobs that were heard throughout a packed courtroom when the second and final verdict -- not guilty of attempted murder -- was read at 3:20 p.m.

Most of those seated in the courtroom had ties to the defendant, and they exchanged hugs and shed tears with the realization that Quattlebaum was about to be freed after spending nearly six months in jail.

During the nine-day trial, all witnesses agreed that Quattlebaum shot and killed John Dill, 45, and wounded Bret Douglas, 43, in the parking lot of the Big Dog Motorcycles plant where Quattlebaum worked.

Witnesses said both victims were members of Wichita's El Forastero motorcycle club. They said Dill had warned Quattlebaum the day before about wearing clothing that promoted the Bandidos, a rival group.

Dill and Douglas were shot in the chest after confronting Quattlebaum in his pickup on the afternoon of March 21. Dill was also shot in the back.

When he testified Wednesday on his own behalf, Quattlebaum said he fired at the men in self-defense.

"I thought they were going to kill me," he told the jury. "I just wanted them to get away from me and not kill me."

Prosecutors had argued that Quattlebaum acted with premeditation because he shot Dill in the back and because he reloaded his revolver during the confrontation and continued to fire.

After the verdict, Quattlebaum's lawyers said he did not want to talk to reporters. Members of the Sedgwick County Public Defender's office said Quattlebaum later left the jail quietly through a side door for security reasons and to avoid publicity.

District Judge Karen Langston said the jurors in the case did not want to talk to lawyers or reporters.

Sarah McKinnon, one of Quattlebaum's lawyers, said she thought the not-guilty verdicts were justified.

"We had confidence this jury was going to do the right thing, and I think they did," she said.

"We are extremely happy, to say the least," said Jeffrey Wicks, who also represented Quattlebaum.

Outside the Sedgwick County Courthouse, several of Quattlebaum's relatives said they were relieved.

"It's been a roller-coaster ride for the last six months," said Fred Quattlebaum, the defendant's father.

"I'm not surprised that it was not guilty. I know my son. I raised him."

Friends and relatives of the victims -- at least one of them wearing an El Forastero vest -- left the courthouse without talking to reporters.

District Attorney Nola Foulston said she was disappointed with the verdict, but she said it was important that the facts of the case were presented to a jury.

"A jury has made a determination in this case, and we'll live with their verdict," she said. "I think the facts and circumstances warranted that the case be prosecuted. That's what we have juries for. They make the decisions.

"I think that is an example of how the justice system works in the United States."

Friday was uneventful, as I pondered the pending confrontation between the Bandidos National chapter and the Bandidos Oklahoma chapter. Bandido Lee and I both made a decision to not go to Pawhuska at all on Friday. Both of us needed to get all of our work related business done first, and I had no intention of being up there after dark in case there was an attempt on my life. Early Saturday morning the 20th of September, Bandido Lee stopped by my house, before we both rode to Pawhuska together. Just before we left, I called Denver to find out what was going on with Bandido Victor and his crew. Lee and I hoped that they were already en route to Pawhuska, and at best more than halfway there. Instead I was surprised when Bandido Victor answered the phone, and even more surprised that he did not sound too good. When I asked him what was wrong, he sadly informed me that Bandido Joe "Little Joe" Benavides had died unexpectedly during the night. Because Little Joe had died, there was no way that any of the Colorado Bandidos were coming to Pawhuska. We were screwed.

Bandido Lee and I felt like we had been blindsided, and for me it was the straw that broke the camel's back. I made my decision right then and there to quit the club, turning in my club colors to my chapter President Bandido Lee. Accepting my resignation with regret, Bandido Lee told me that I would be out of the club in good standings, and if I ever wanted to come back, I was more than welcome. I made arrangements for him to pick up all the rest of my Bandido possessions Monday, as soon as he returned from the Pawhuska Biker Rally.

As I watched him ride off to Pawhuska without me, I hoped that he would be ok, and that no one would get hurt during the confrontation that would soon occur between the Bandidos National chapter and the Oklahoma chapter. I hoped that my quitting would defuse the situation enough to ensure that there was no violence. And for the first time in as long as I could remember, I felt good. It seemed as though there was a hundred pound gorilla off my back, and I knew in my heart that I had made the right decision.

31

After The Bandidos
Fall 2003 To Summer 2005

I spent the next four hours with my girlfriend Caroline and my daughter Taylor packing up all of my Bandidos clothes, pictures and mementos. Then I moved my Harley to the home of my attorney, Jonathan Sutton, for safekeeping in the event that the National chapter attempted to steal it. There was an unwritten rule when you quit the club that if you were weak enough, then it was ok for a Bandido to take your motorcycle. In Oklahoma we had never exercised that option, thinking that there was no reason to treat an ex-brother that way. If the ex-brother owed the chapter ten thousand dollars, then it would be another story, but to take a man's Harley just because you wanted to was not reasoning we subscribed to here in Oklahoma. But the National chapter was here in Oklahoma, and taking my bike could easily be an option that they might elect to pursue.

Just before noon, my cell phone rang. It was El Secretario William "Bill" Sartelle, calling to tell me that it was mandatory that I show up for the meeting, and to find out where I was. I was surprised that he did not know I was no longer in the club, and told him so. He responded by telling me that I needed to give the club my bike, and I told him that was never going to happen. As I hung up the phone on him, I thought what a two-faced piece of shit he had become. There was a time when he and I were real close, but in the last six months he had lost most all of his integrity, and was now trading his soul just to get closer to El Presidente George and El Vice Presidente Jeff.

All afternoon my phone rang over and over again, as people heard the news. Many of my close Oklahoma chapter brothers called to inform me of what was going on at Pawhuska. Apparently El Vice Presidente Jeff had already decided to replace Bandido Lee as President of the Tulsa chapter as soon as he arrived, when he ordered all members to "talk to him one at a time before he made a decision" about what was going to happen. The funny part was that Bandido Smurf was telling anyone who would listen, that he was going to be the new President of the Tulsa chapter after the Oklahoma chapter was split in two. Two Bandidos actually overheard the conversation between Bandido Smurf and El Presidente Jeff during which Bandido Jeff told Smurf that he would be the new Tulsa chapter President. That conversation actually occurred *before* the El Vice Presidente announced to everyone that they had to "talk to him one on one, before he made a decision". Apparently the El Vice Presidente was becoming as much a liar as El Presidente George, even though lying to a Bandido was a patch-pulling offense. Maybe the El Vice Presidente had Alzheimer's disease as well?

After six hours of "one on one" meetings, and supposedly listening to every Oklahoma chapter member's side of things, Bandido Jeff announced that he had made a decision. Apparently about half the chapter was very unhappy with the way Bandido Lee had been running things, so it was time for a change. The Oklahoma chapter was then split in half, with Bandido Charles "Snake" Rush to be the new Oklahoma City chapter President. OK Riders Curtis "Mario" Eppihimer and Robert "Robert" Taylor traded in their OK Riders club colors for that of Probationary members in the brand new Bandidos chapter, which was to be called the Oklahoma City chapter.

The new Oklahoma City chapter would consist of the following members:

Charles "Snake" Rush	President	Full Patch
Walter "Walt" Lopez	Vice-President	Probationary
James "Cub" Oleson	Sergeant-at-Arms	Probationary
Curtis "Mario" Eppihimer	Secretary	Probationary
Steven "Steve" Buitron		Full Patch
Garland "Little Horse" Kirkes		Probationary
Robert "Robert" Taylor		Probationary

The new Tulsa chapter would consist of the following members:

James "Smurf" Ragan	President	Full Patch
Scott "Scooter" Musslewhite	Vice-President	Full Patch
Harry "Skip" Hansen	Sergeant-at-Arms	Full Patch
Steven "Batman" Batson	Secretary	Full Patch
Lee "Lee" McArdle		Full Patch
Louis "Bill Wolf" Rackley		Full Patch
Ian "Ian" Wilhelm		Full Patch
Michael "Mick" Barnett		Full Patch
Walter "Levi" Willis		Full Patch
Glenn "Glenn" Vermillion		Prospect

The El Vice Presidente then informed everyone that effective immediately, Bandido Smurf was in charge of the new Tulsa chapter. What a surprise. When I heard that, I laughed out loud. Bandido Smurf was not smart enough to lead a group of kindergarten kids to the bathroom. The only Bandidos stupid enough to follow Smurf were Mick, Levi (who had just patched out that weekend) and Scooter (who finally got off the fence and transferred from his old Houston chapter to the new Tulsa chapter that weekend).

Even if I had not quit the club earlier that day, I would have quit that night as soon as I heard that Smurf was in charge. There was no way I was going to be told what to do or where to go by that moron. As I drifted off to sleep, I wondered who else was feeling like I did, and who would quit the club just because Smurf was now in charge. I also thought about El Presidente George, and how happy he must have been that day. Two of his worst nightmares were now over and done; Bandido Little Joe was now dead and I had quit the club. My last thoughts were about how long it would take Bandido Smurf to destroy everything that Bandido Lee and I had built over the last six and one half years. I was betting on ninety days, as I slept with one eye open just in case I had any unwelcome visitors in the middle of the night.

Arising very early the next morning, I spent all of Sunday morning preparing for a pack of National chapter Bandidos to arrive at my door after Pawhuska, even moving my daughter Taylor across town. It did not take me long to find a few volunteers to hang out nearby, in case they were needed. All of them were licensed to carry firearms, and some even had automatic weapons permits. They had all been friends of mine for many years, and most would do whatever it took to help me defend myself, if my family or I were attacked. If there was going to be a battle at my home, I was going to stack the deck and make sure that there was no way I was going to lose.

By the middle of the afternoon, it was apparent that there was no resemblance of organization left in the Oklahoma Bandidos. When asked to make the simplest of decisions, Bandido Tulsa chapter President Smurf was dumbfounded. As members of the OK Riders stopped by my house to say goodbye, it dawned on me that maybe the El Vice Presidente had been ordered to put Smurf in charge by El Presidente George, just because he knew there was no way I could follow Smurf; he knew the decision would make me quit. I remembered what other Bandidos had recently told me: Bandido George was willing to destroy the Oklahoma chapter to get rid of me.

I stayed up almost that entire night, waiting for the National chapter attack that never came. It was a long night, but I did not regret the decision I had made to quit. On the contrary, I felt better and better about it as time passed. By the time the sun arose, I figured that there was a good chance that most all of the out of town Bandidos had returned to their hometowns. I figured there was now a good chance I could get out of the club without the club resorting to violence.

Later that week, on the twenty-fifth of September, 2003, my childhood buddy Bandido Skip, as well as Bandido Steven "Batman" Batson, quit the club, following my footsteps. Neither of them had any love for Bandido Smurf, nor any desire to follow an idiot around. Bandido Smurf had told Bandido Skip that he could no longer associate with me, and Skip had asked Smurf, "What are you, an idiot? I grew up with Ed. I'm not going to stop associating with him because you tell me to."

Wisely, new Tulsa Bandidos chapter President Smurf did let both leave the club in good standings, with Batman actually leaving for "medical reasons" due to a bad back. By the end of that first week, the Bandidos National chapter overruled the decision of Bandido ex-President Lee and Bandido President Smurf, mandating that Skip and I were now out of the club "in bad standings". Being out of the club in bad standings meant that no member of the Bandidos worldwide was supposed to associate or talk to us, and we were not allowed at any function if there were Bandidos there, even if it was a public event like the Pawhuska Biker Rally.

For Skip it was a blessing in disguise, although initially he did not see it that way. I considered my new status an honor, for it told me that I was a serious threat to the National chapter in my own little way. I knew why that decision had been made, since the Bandidos had an agreement with the other five main 1%er motorcycle clubs nationwide, that if a man was put out of a 1%er club "in bad standings", then no other club could take him in as a member. With the knowledge I had of the internal workings of the Bandidos Motorcycle Club nationwide, it was imperative that I not be allowed to join another 1%er motorcycle club.

It would be like leaving a major business and taking all their trade secrets with you, and the business you just left exercising their right to protect their intellectual property. Besides, if you are going to quit, then it is better to quit cold turkey, rather than seeing and talking to Bandidos members every day. I also knew in my heart that the Bandidos who considered me their friend would disregard that mandate anyway, and still stay in touch with me no matter what anyone in the National chapter told them.

By the time the annual "Living On The Edge" all motorcycle drag races came around on September 28, 2003, Bandido Lee and I wondered what Bandidos Smurf, Mick, Scooter and Levi would do to sabotage the event. It was a serious proposition, because in the few days since I had quit the club and the fiasco at Pawhuska was over, the Tulsa chapter was now decisively split in half.

On one side were Bandidos Lee, Bill Wolf and Ian; on the other side were Bandidos Smurf, Scooter, Mick and Levi. Prospect Glenn was stuck in the middle because he was a prospect. Members of each side hated the members on the other. Bandido Ian even kicked the bushings out of Bandido Mick at the first meeting of the new Tulsa chapter. Due to all of the hostility and threats, Bandido Lee and I wondered if the races would go off without an act of violence marring the event. Fortunately for us, the event went off without a hitch and the weather was absolutely beautiful for racing motorcycles.

Over the weekend, while Bandido Lee and I were concentrating on a successful motorcycle drag race, Bandidos Mick and Levi decided that because I was now out of the club in bad standings, there was no reason for them to continue paying their motorcycle loan payments to me, notwithstanding the fact that I had a valid lien on both bikes and possessed legal promissory notes signed by both. Apparently El Vice Presidente Jeff had told them that they did not have to pay me anymore, because I was no longer a Bandido. They were so stupid or high on methamphetamine, that they believed what they were told. When I found out that they would not pay me what was owed, I immediately sold my entire motorcycle loan portfolio to my attorney, which obviously included both Bandido Mick and Levi's loans, as well as Bandido Ian's and Prospect Glenn's. Selling the loan portfolio to the attorney, even at the loss I did, was well worth the while, for now I no longer had to make contact with them for any reason.

(Both Mick and Levi continued to not pay their monthly motorcycle loan payments, in spite of the fact that an attorney now owned the notes. It only took a few months for my attorney to get tired of their attitude and file repossession court cases in Tulsa County court system. Both Bandido Mick and Levi bragged that they were going to beat the attorney in court, and that he would never get their motorcycles, but by the early spring of 2004, both of those two "smart" guys lost in a big way. Bandido Mick paid the attorney five thousand dollars to settle a two thousand, two hundred dollar loan balance, but got to keep his bike. Bandido Levi gave his bike back to the attorney, but like the idiot he was, beat the crap out of the bike before doing so. That was an extremely stupid thing to do, for when the attorney sold the bike at auction, the bike only brought about three thousand dollars. The balance owed on his loan account now totaled about fifteen thousand dollars, and the attorney got a judgment for the same amount against him, liening his home in the process, all over a four thousand dollar loan balance.)

In early October, just a few days after the drag races, Bandidos Smurf, Mick and Levi went to ex-Bandido Batman's home and in only what can be considered an act of extortion, took Batman's motorcycle. Batman was laid up in bed unable to move due to back pain when they showed up. Unable to defend himself, higher than a Georgia pine on his medication, and the only one home at the time, Batman reluctantly let them have his 2001 Harley Road King. Almost every Bandido in Oklahoma was pissed at what the three stooges did, and I was livid. It was one thing to take a man's bike when he was out of the club in bad standings, but this was the first time a member out for medical reasons had been the victim of a motorcycle hijacking. (It would take six months of political wrangling by Bandidos Lee and Snake to get the motorcycle returned to Batman. The National chapter initially said that it was ok, because I owed them a bike, but later changed their minds and ordered it returned.)

In November of 2003, Bill "Bill" Reynolds and Edwin "Kahuna" Rita became the thirty-first and thirty-second men to wear the colors of the Oklahoma Bandidos, when they became Probationary members of the Oklahoma City chapter. Bandido Bill had been an OK Rider and Bandido Kahuna an independent biker in Oklahoma City for many, many years. When Thanksgiving rolled around, there were nine members in the Oklahoma City chapter and eight members in the Tulsa chapter.

By the late fall of 2003, I was concentrating on spending more time with my family and devoting more attention to my business. When I heard about a bank that had foreclosed on five new, unfinished homes located in Owasso, I made the bank an offer they could not refuse. It took me about a month to get them all finished, and another month to sell them, utilizing an "Owner Carry, No Qualifying" loan program I had developed just as an experiment. I had used this program many times on older homes that I had renovated, but never on a new home. I was happy to learn that the loan program worked with new homes as well as it did with the older ones. I was also reaping the benefits that came with putting my time and energy into my own business, rather than into the Bandidos Motorcycle Club, which never appreciated what I did or ever made me any money.

One Of The Homes Ct Ed Bought December 2003

A few days before Christmas, I held an informal Christmas party at my home. It was an all day event, starting at noon and ending at eight that night. People came and went all day long, coming from all over the state of Oklahoma to visit. In the crowd were Oklahoma Bandidos, OK Riders, independent bikers, ex-Bandidos, ex-OK Riders and other citizen friends of mine. Over the course of the day, Caroline and I had about fifty visitors and their wives/girlfriends. It was a great day, and we all had a fantastic time.

You can imagine my surprise when I heard just before the end of the year that Bandidos Smurf, Mick, Levi and Scooter were pissed off at me. The reason was that I had held a recruiting party at my home for a chapter of the Outlaws Motorcycle Club that I intended to start in the immediate future. When I heard that I laughed so hard I nearly fell out of my chair, and I wondered exactly how much battery acid had been in the methamphetamine they had been snorting. I was still laughing about it when Bandido James "Tucker" Atkins from Amarillo showed up to visit me at my home on New Year's Day, 2004. I was glad to see him again, for he and I were very close; our relationship went back more than twenty years. As soon as he arrived, I contacted Bandido Lee, who immediately came over to join us.

As Bandidos Tucker and Lee sat in my office discussing all of the recent events, there was a knock on the front door. Caroline answered the door, and there was Bandido Smurf asking for me. Caroline told him that she would get me, and closed the door in his face. When she announced to all of us who was at the door, Bandido Tucker immediately responded that if Smurf caused any trouble, Tucker personally would kick the crap out of him. We all wondered if Bandido Smurf had noticed all of the "Support Your Local Bandidos" stickers or the Texas license plate on Tucker's truck which was parked in the driveway out in front of my house.

When I stepped on the porch, Bandido Smurf immediately started the conversation off with a big lie. He told me that the Bandidos National chapter had asked him to stop by my house and wish me a Merry Christmas and a Happy New Year. I could barely contain my amusement, and I wondered if he really thought I was that stupid. Smurf then launched into the real reason he was here. He had heard that I was starting an Outlaws chapter, and as far as he was concerned, that was not going to happen. At that point, I could not restrain my amusement any longer, and I laughed out loud at him. What an idiot, I thought, as I reassured him that there was no way I was going to be a member of any 1%er motorcycle club ever again. Pacified, Bandido Smurf left about five minutes after he arrived. When I returned to my office, I explained to everybody what had transpired with Bandido Smurf. As you can imagine, we all had a good laugh.

In the middle of January, 2004, Prospect Glenn was voted into the Tulsa chapter as a full patch member, having successfully completed his six months of prospecting duties. A few days later, Bandido Gary "Andy" McWilliams of the Bandidos Arkansas chapter was arrested for what he thought was going to be a sexual liaison with a thirteen year old girl. Bandido Andy had at one time been a Tennessee member of the Outlaws Motorcycle club and had helped me start the Ozark Riders in Eureka Springs, Arkansas a few years ago. Andy had become a member of the Ozark Riders a few months thereafter, and after a year in the Ozark Riders, he had recently become a Little Rock Bandido. We were all shocked to learn that there was a child sexual predator in the Bandidos.

Charges Filed Against Man In Internet Sex Sting

January 24, 2004

By Jessica Graves

Charges were formally filed Friday morning in Yell County Circuit Court against a 50-year-old man arrested Monday in Dardanelle, accusing him of attempted rape and computer child pornography.

According to John Riedel, Yell County chief deputy prosecutor, Gary Anderson McWilliams of Compton was arrested Monday in the Wal-Mart parking lot in Dardanelle after allegedly arranging to meet with an underage girl over the Internet with the alleged intent of having sex with her. The person he had met over the Internet and thought was a 13-year-old girl was actually an undercover operative.

One count of attempted rape is a Class A felony punishable by 6-30 years in the Arkansas Department of Correction. The charge of one count of computer child pornography is a Class B felony, punishable by 5-20 years in prison.

McWilliams remains detained at the Yell County Detention Center in Danville on a $75,000 bond set by David H. McCormick, 15th Judicial District circuit judge, on Tuesday. He is scheduled to appear before Circuit Judge Paul Danielson on Feb. 17 for a formal arraignment and trial setting, according to Riedel.

The Yell County Sheriff's Department Criminal Investigation Division and the 15th Judicial District Prosecuting Attorney's Office began an investigation earlier this month into Internet communications designed to lure underage females for sexual activity with older men. An investigator created an online profile on the Yahoo member directory indicating that they were a 13-year-old white female, according to information filed in Yell County Circuit Court on Friday.

The investigator went online using a profile and went to a Yahoo chat room under the sub-category of "Teens" named "very young girls wanting sex/relationship w/older guy." She received a message from the name "toms_hard_candy." The person using that name communicated to the investigator that he was 40 years old, according to court documents. He continued asking her sexually-oriented questions, asked the investigator which direction she was from Russellville and if she was still 13 years old, to which the investigator responded, "Yes, I am still 13," according to court documents. He arranged to meet the "girl" on Jan. 19 at 11 a.m. at the Dardanelle Wal-Mart. McWilliams earlier indicated that he drove a white Chevy 4x4.

Court documents indicated that McWilliams pulled into the Wal-Mart parking lot at approximately 11 a.m. on Jan. 19, driving a white Chevrolet four-wheel-drive pickup. He pulled next to the undercover operative, posing as the 13-year-old girl, in front of the store on a bench. The operative was wearing a transmitting device for the meeting that was being recorded by Det. John Foster Jr. of the Yell County Sheriff's Department, who led the investigation.

After McWilliams was identified by the undercover operative, he was transported to the Dardanelle jail where he declined an interview and asked for an attorney after being advised of the nature of his charges.

A search warrant was obtained and executed on McWilliams' vehicle in Dardanelle. Investigators recovered a vase of a dozen artificial pink roses, a pair

By Kim Morava

A Shawnee man died early Sunday morning when his motorcycle collided with a car at 45th and Kickapoo Streets. Police have arrested the car's driver on a negligent homicide complaint.

The motorcyclist, Robert Dale Wright, 55, was pronounced dead at the scene from head and trunk injuries, a Shawnee police report shows.

The accident occurred just after 1 a.m. as Wright drove his 1994 Harley Davidson southbound on Kickapoo Street. He collided with a northbound 2000 Pontiac Grand Am driven by Travis Earl Baker, 27, Tecumseh.

Sgt. Tom Cartwright's investigation report shows the accident occurred when Baker, trying to turn onto westbound 45th Street, turned his Grand Am into the path of Wright's southbound motorcycle. At impact, Wright vaulted into the passenger side door frame of the Grand Am, the report shows, then was thrown 10 feet.

Wright had no pulse when emergency personnel arrived.

A police narrative shows Cpl. Khris Steadman arrived and found Baker "staggering" in front of the Grand Am. Officer Steadman reported a strong odor of alcohol on Baker's breath and Baker was unsteady on his feet with slurred speech. Baker admitted he had been drinking, the report shows, and failed field sobriety tests. A cold, quart-sized bottle of beer was found broken at the scene.

Baker had no signs of injury and refused a breath test at the scene. Police transported him to Unity Health Center, North Campus, for a blood test after REACT medics checked him at the scene.

While waiting at the hospital, Baker told officers the accident "wasn't his fault," according to Steadman's report. He also told police his traffic light was red, then green, the report reads. After refusing medical treatment, Baker was arrested and booked into the Pottawatomie County Public Safety Center on a complaint of negligent homicide. He has since posted a $10,000 bond.

Sgt. Cartwright's report shows Baker was driving about 10 mph and Wright was traveling about 25 mph at impact. That area is a 40 mph zone. There was no improper action on Wright's part, but the report shows Baker failed to yield to oncoming traffic.

Wright reportedly was not wearing a safety helmet.

Shawnee Patrol Officer Becky Oblien assisted at the scene and officers responding included Pottawatomie County sheriff's deputies and a state medical examiner. REACT EMS and Shawnee firefighters worked the scene.

Wright is survived by several family members, including his mother, wife, children, siblings and grandchildren. Swearingen Funeral Home of Seminole is in charge of arrangements.

The accident report will be turned over to the District Attorney's office for consideration of formal charges.

As I headed into the start of summer, my daughter Taylor graduated from the fifth grade, getting ready to turn eleven. In just a few months she would start her sixth grade year, and I was amazed at how fast she was growing, and what a social butterfly she was becoming. I had started her counseling with the therapist from the Parent Child center again, mainly as a preemptive strike at any possible trouble she might have dealing with the differences that she experienced between the rules at her biological mother's home and mine. I also figured that it would help her, in general, getting through the often turbulent pre-teen years.

Just before the Memorial Day weekend, on May 14th, Bandido Lee patched out Michael "Pinhead" Simecek, Rick "Grizz" Case and Ronald "Hun" Warren as the newest members of the Tulsa chapter of Bandidos. The following week, at the annual Red River Rally in Red River, New Mexico, the Tulsa chapter was officially split into two different, distinct chapters. Bandido Lee was now President of the Tulsa chapter, and Bandido Scooter President of the North Tulsa chapter. Bandido Levi, now part of the North Tulsa chapter, did not even go to the mandatory Bandidos National party, because he no longer owned a motorcycle and was too ashamed to admit it. I was amazed that he was still a member of the Bandidos, since the Bandido by-laws clearing stated that to be a member you had to own a motorcycle, and he had not owned one in months.

By the first of June, 2004, the child I had originally conceived had now evolved into three chapters, consisting of twenty members:

The Oklahoma City chapter consisted of the following members:

Charles "Snake" Rush	President	Full Patch
Walter "Walt" Lopez	Vice-President	Full Patch
James "Cub" Oleson	Sergeant-at-Arms	Full Patch
Curtis "Mario" Eppihimer	Secretary	Probationary
Garland "Little Horse" Kirkes		Full Patch
Bill "Bill" Reynolds		Probationary
Edwin "Kahuna" Rita		Probationary

The Tulsa chapter consisted of the following members:

Lee "Lee" McArdle	President	Full Patch
Louis "Bill Wolf" Rackley	Vice-President	Full Patch
Rick "Grizz" Case	Sergeant-at-Arms	Probationary
Ronald "Hun" Warren	Secretary	Probationary
Ian "Ian" Wilhelm		Full Patch
Michael "Pinhead" Simecek		Probationary

The North Tulsa chapter consisted of the following members:

Scott "Scooter" Musslewhite	President	Full Patch
Michael "Mick" Barnett	Vice-President	Full Patch
John "John" Burzio	Sergeant-at-Arms	Probationary
Glenn "Glenn" Vermillion	Secretary	Full Patch
James "Smurf" Ragan		Full Patch
Walter "Levi" Willis		Full Patch

Three things came to a head in July of 2004 that were of significance. First, Bandido President Scott "Scooter" Musslewhite of the North Tulsa Bandidos chapter finally rectified the failure of Bandido Walter "Levi" Willis to show up at the mandatory Memorial Day Bandidos National Run by allowing Bandido Levi to quit the club "in good standings", after being without a bike for more than six months, and in spite of the fact that he owed the chapter hundreds of dollars. Secondly, Oklahoma City Bandido James "Cub" Oleson was allowed to continue being a Bandido, even though he had not repaid Tulsa OK Rider President Raymond "Ray" Huffman a multi thousand dollar debt owed over the posting of Bandido Cub's bail bond back in early February of 2001.

Once again I was amazed that the situation with Cub was not rectified by Oklahoma City President Charles "Snake" Rush. OK Rider Ray had originally co-signed for the bail bond that secured the release from jail of then OK Rider Cub. OK Rider Cub had bankrupted the bail bond agent less than a year later, without paying the bail bond agent the thousands of dollars that he owed. After the bankruptcy had been finalized, and the bail bond agent screwed out of her money, she naturally exercised her option to pursue the co-signor for the full amount plus interest owed. The case went all the way to the Oklahoma Court of Appeals, and when OK Rider Ray finally lost, everyone expected that now Bandido Cub would immediately pay the debt. When that did not happen, no Bandido boss rectified the situation and OK Rider Ray's pleas for help fell on a sea of deaf ears. As a result, OK Rider Ray immediately quit the OK Riders. I could not blame him, for he had been treated with absolute disrespect.

Last of all, Arkansas Bandido Gary "Andy" McWilliams plead guilty and was sentenced to fifteen years in the Arkansas prison system for the attempted child molestation charges in Arkansas. Bandido Tulsa President Lee "Lee" McArdle was actually the one that broke the news about Bandido Andy's situation to the Little Rock Bandidos, by delivering to them a copy of the following

Arkansas newspaper clipping. Bandido Lee and I were in a state of shock, for the Arkansas Bandidos were completely in the dark and had no idea that Andy had plead guilty and was now a convicted child sexual predator. Apparently the Arkansas Bandidos did not read the newspapers, nor had enough interest in one of their own members to attend one of their own members' court appearances.

Compton Man Pleads Guilty, Sentenced To 15 Years In Prison

July 29, 2004

By Sean Ingram

A 51-year-old man arrested by Yell County authorities in January — charged with attempted rape and computer child pornography — pleaded guilty last week and was sentenced to serve 15 years in prison.

Gary Anderson McWilliams of Compton (Newton County) appeared in Yell County Circuit Court on July 19, pleaded guilty to computer exploitation of a child and was sentenced to 20 years in the Arkansas Department of Correction with five years suspended. McWilliams was also ordered by pay a fine of $1,000, court costs and Act 1262 fee totaling $155, and a DNA sample fee of $250.

Charges of attempted rape and computer child pornography were filed against McWilliams by the 15th Judicial District Prosecuting Attorney's Office on Jan. 23 following his Jan. 19 arrest in the Wal-Mart parking lot in Dardanelle. He pled innocent to the charges Feb. 17 in Yell County Circuit Court after posting a $75,000 commercial bond Feb. 4 to gain release from the Yell County Jail.

One count of attempted rape is a Class A felony punishable by 6-30 years in the Arkansas Department of Correction. The charge of one count of computer child pornography is a Class B felony, punishable by 5-20 years in prison.

Previous reports indicate McWilliams was arrested at Dardanelle after allegedly arranging to meet with an underage girl over the Internet with the alleged intent of having sex with her. The person he had met over the Internet and thought was a 13-year-old girl was actually an undercover operative.

The Yell County Sheriff's Department's Criminal Investigation Division and prosecuting attorney's office began an investigation into Internet communications designed to lure underage females for sexual activity with older men. An investigator created an online profile on a Yahoo! member directory indicating that they were a 13-year-old white female, according to information previously filed in Yell County Circuit Court.

The investigator went online the morning of Jan. 15 using a profile and went to a Yahoo! chat room under the sub-category of "Teens" named "very young girls wanting sex/relationship w/older guy." She received a message from the name "toms_hard_candy." The person using that name communicated to the investigator that he was 40 years old, according to court documents.

He continued asking her sexually-oriented questions, asked the investigator which direction she was from Russellville and if she was still 13 years old, to which the investigator responded, "Yes, I am still 13," according to court documents. He arranged to meet the "girl" at 11 a.m. Jan. 19 at the Dardanelle Wal-Mart. McWilliams earlier indicated that he drove a white Chevy 4x4.

Court documents indicated that McWilliams pulled into the Wal-Mart parking lot driving a 1992 Chevrolet white four-wheel-drive pickup. He pulled next to the undercover operative, posing as the 13-year-old girl, in front of the store on a bench. The operative was wearing a transmitting device for the meeting that was being recorded by lead investigator Det. John Foster Jr. of the Sheriff's Department.

After McWilliams was identified by the undercover operative, he was transported to the Dardanelle jail where he declined an interview and asked for an attorney after being advised of the nature of his charges.

"We are committed to stopping Internet predators who attempt to lure teenagers in unlawful sexual activity," Prosecutor Tom Tatum II stated after McWilliams' arrest. "Our office and the Yell County Sheriff's Office, as well as other counties in the district (Conway, Logan and Scott) will set a high priority to intercept Internet predators."

A search warrant was obtained and executed on McWilliams' vehicle in Dardanelle. Investigators recovered a vase of a dozen artificial pink roses, a pair of binoculars, seven live rounds of .45-caliber ammunition, 40 live rounds of .22-caliber ammunition, a cell phone, a .22-caliber revolver fully loaded with six live hollow-point rounds recovered from a jacket pocket lying in the front seat, and a softball bat recovered from under the driver's seat.

Another search warrant was obtained for the McWilliams residence outside of Compton, executed by Foster and Newton County Sheriff's deputies. Authorities there recovered a computer and peripherals, discs, correspondence, notes, magazines depicting nude females, McWilliams' U.S. passport, videotapes, film, biker pins and a telephone answering system.

In the middle of August, a few days before the start of school for my daughter Taylor, she was hit by a car while riding her bicycle. The car actually came to a stop with one of the rear tires resting on top of her foot, causing serious burns to her foot in three different places. Her collar bone was also broken as a result of the bicycle handlebar hitting her a perfect shot, but we were all elated that she did not get hurt more seriously. As I sat in the hall at the Claremore

OUT IN BAD STANDINGS

Indian hospital, listening to her screaming in agony as the hospital staff worked on her, I thanked God again for saving her life.

Slowly recovering from her injuries, Taylor hobbled around from class to class as she entered the sixth grade. The Owasso school system jumped right into help by letting Taylor help out in the office while she healed up, instead of doing the mandatory physical education classes. (Taylor would eventually heal from her broken collar bone in six weeks, but the burns on her foot took more than six months to completely heal.)

While I worked on my new home all summer long, the Bandidos nationwide were experiencing increasing internal conflict, which resulted in many time honored traditions being shit canned. A good example of this occurred in the second half of August when active San Antonio Bandido Richard "Scarface" Merla killed a popular Mexican boxer named Robert Quiroga, who was a world title holder. The killing happened while the two were socializing together at the home of another San Antonio Bandido, Rick Casas.

Instead of standing behind the Bandido who had committed the murder, Bandidos El Presidente George "George" Wegers and El Vice Presidente Jeffrey "Jeff" Pike came up with a brand new strategy to deal with all of the negative publicity. This time, contrary to almost forty years of Bandidos club policy to never cooperate with law enforcement, they ordered Bandido Rick Casas to assist the police in prosecuting Bandido Scarface.

Sargento de Armas John "John" Portillo was also ordered to hold a press conference at which he told the world that Bandido Scarface was no longer a member of the Bandidos Motorcycle Club, and in fact was now out of the club "in bad standings". So much for the time honored traditions of standing behind your brothers when the going got tough and never cooperating with the police. It looked like things were changing after all, just not the way anyone ever expected. I figured that El Presidente Ronald "Ronnie" Hodge must be rolling over in his grave.

Witness Says Argument Led To Boxer's Slaying

August 20, 2004

By Jaime Castillo

It started out as a friendly night of drinking among motorcycle buddies. But it ended with a bitter fight that took the life of ex-prizefighter Robert Quiroga.

Rick Casas, the man who says he witnessed the stabbing death of the former world title holder, broke his silence Thursday.

He said an argument erupted between Quiroga and Richard Steven Merla, a convicted felon known by some as "Scarface," moments before the two grappled on the driveway of Casas' Northwest Side home.

"It took only two seconds," Casas said. "I went to close the garage door and then (Merla) was on him."

Casas said he went to break up what he thought was a fistfight after 3 a.m. Monday, but then noticed Quiroga was bleeding.

"I told Scarface, 'What the hell is wrong with you?'" Casas said. "And he ran off while I got Robert to his feet."

The details are the first public account of the events that left San Antonio's first world boxing champion lying mortally wounded in Casas' driveway on the Interstate 10 West access road.

Police have issued an arrest warrant for Merla, 38, who remained at large Thursday.

Members of the Bandidos motorcycle club have distanced themselves from Merla. They say he's no longer a member.

Casas said he decided to speak because he wanted to deliver a message to the Quiroga family.

"The family is thinking I didn't call 911. They're saying I ran inside and locked the door (after Quiroga was stabbed). It's just not true," said Casas, a member of the Bandidos who rents the home where Quiroga was killed.

Casas and other group members said Quiroga was a friend who shared their enthusiasm for motorcycles, but who never joined the Bandidos.

Casas, 31, said widespread media reports that a passer-by alerted authorities to Quiroga's nearly lifeless body aren't correct.

"My first reaction was to call 911 and get my gun," he said. "I needed to protect my wife and children who were sleeping upstairs."

Police confirmed Thursday that two emergency calls directed authorities to or near Casas' residence on Fallen Leaf Lane. One call came from Casas' home and the other from a passer-by within seconds of each other at 3:22 a.m.

Casas said he, Merla and Quiroga, contrary to previous reports, were not playing cards in the hours before dawn Monday, but drinking beer in his back yard.

Casas said there was an argument between the 34-year-old retired boxer and Merla, which escalated to the point that Casas intervened. Casas said he didn't know exactly what the argument was over, but remembers Quiroga saying he was tired of Merla "picking on me."

"I said, 'Hey, hey, hey, the party's over. Everybody go home,'" Casas said.

Merla got up to leave while Quiroga hugged Casas and apologized for causing a ruckus at his home, Casas said.

Moments later, Merla, whom Casas described as a "big old monster of a guy," was on top of Quiroga, a much smaller man, who won his world title in 1990 in the 115-pound class.

After breaking up the fight and realizing Quiroga had been stabbed several times, Casas said he ran inside to call 911 and to get his handgun.

When he returned, Casas said a disoriented Quiroga had stumbled onto the access road, prompting Casas to run out and grab him and bring him back to the driveway, where they remained until an ambulance arrived.

"People say, 'If I was there, I would have done this and done that.' How do you know what you would have done?" Casas said, gazing blankly.

"There's nothing I could say to (Quiroga's family) that will change their minds. And I understand that," Casas said. "But hopefully one day I'll get to talk to them and tell them that it wasn't that way."

On October 19, 2004, my daughter Taylor and I stopped into visit some friends of mine from Dallas who worked for the promoter in charge of the annual Edgefest event, the largest rock concert of the year in Tulsa. One of those friends, Paula McElheney, I had known for more than twenty-five years. The other, Billy Morgan, was the actual Production Manager for this huge event. The rock band Velvet Revolver was scheduled to be the headlining band, and I had a keen interest in seeing them play live, for the band was made up of some of the original members of the band Guns N' Roses. Slash, the famous lead guitar player from Guns N' Roses was now the lead guitar player for Velvet Revolver.

When we arrived at three in the afternoon, all we had intended to do was hang out and watch the bands for a while, since we both had back stage passes courtesy of Paula and Billy. Unfortunately my friend Paula was overloaded with remaining tasks that had to be completed to facilitate the concert, so Taylor and I volunteered to help her. We set about doing a myriad of assignments given to us by Paula, running the gambit from setting up all of the band hospitality suites to stocking the personal dressing room of Velvet Revolver. After we finished helping Paula, Taylor and I got up on the stage for a few hours to watch the bands perform and look out on the crowd.

Taylor On The Edgefest Stage October 2004

Slash (On The Speaker) & Velvet Revolver At The Edgefest October 2004

I had my girlfriend Caroline pick up Taylor at dark thirty, and hung around to watch Slash and Velvet Revolver sing all their songs, from a private area at the rear corner of the stage. My friend Billy had made sure that I got a special pass that allowed me to be on the stage when Velvet Revolver played, and I sure appreciated his gesture of friendship. For the entire concert, I stood only a few feet from all of Slash's guitars, and there were many times I was only about ten feet from Slash as he played his guitar. I am sure that there were thousands of Velvet Revolver fans out there in the audience watching me up on the stage, who would have given anything to be where I was.

On September 26, 2004, Bandido Lee put on the sixth "Living On The Edge" all motorcycle drag race event. To keep his association with me distinct, since he was not supposed to be socializing with me because I was out of the Bandidos "in bad standings", I turned over to him all aspects of the promotion for the drag race. I even drafted contracts between him and me, giving him temporary use of my federal and state trademarks that were associated with the name "Living On The Edge". Since the last event in September of 2003, the ownership of the Tulsa International Raceway had changed, and the track had undergone about a million dollars in renovations. This time the event was a huge success, with more than a thousand paid admissions and dozens of financial sponsors. It appeared now that the "Living On The Edge" all motorcycle drag races was going to be a Tulsa tradition. Everyone all over the Tulsa area now knew the name and what it meant. Bandido Lee and I agreed to hold this annual event the last Sunday of every September, every year from now on as long as we were alive.

On October 31st, Caroline and I celebrated our "living together" anniversary of five years. Although she had her sight on getting married to me, I still was extremely gun shy. Like the old saying goes, "Once bitten, twice shy". I definitely had no intention of going through another divorce again, but by now, my emotional wall was slowly but surely being demolished by Caroline, one brick at a time.

I closed out the year 2004 by purchasing five more homes in Owasso, this time in the Country Estates addition just northwest of town. Once again, they all sold in a matter of weeks, and now I knew that I was onto something. I sat down with my Keller Williams real estate agent, Joe John Edwards, and my attorney, Jonathan Sutton, and decided that I needed to seriously pursue this as a nationwide business. I spent the January of 2005 perfecting a federal patent application that would protect my business method forever. After filing the application for the patent in February, I spent the next two months doing the necessary paperwork to franchise the concept and secure investors. By the summer I had successfully expanded my operations into Texas, and had plans to expand into other areas of the United States in the near future.

On Memorial Day weekend, in May of 2005, as Bandido Lee and all the Bandidos nationwide headed off to the various mandatory National Runs, I was busy running all of my businesses. I had now been out of the club for more than a year and a half, and had never looked back. I was amazed at how much I had accomplished and how far I had come since leaving the club, and wondered how far I could go in life. I was thankful for all the time I had spent with Caroline and Taylor, and the effort I had put into my businesses.

I knew that there was no way that I could have done all of this if I had still been a member of the Bandidos Motorcycle Club, but in a strange way, felt like I had a spiritual connection to the club that could never be broken. I wondered most of all, when Bandidos El Presidente George "George" Wegers and the house of cards he had built would come crashing down, and who would be left standing free on the streets after the feds finished indicting what I perceived to be a large percentage of the club. There was a price to be paid for all the stupidity that by now was rampant in the organization, and a heavier price to be paid for allowing methamphetamine to be used and sold by so many Bandidos members. I knew that someday it would be acknowledged that methamphetamine was the biggest and strongest enemy the Bandidos Motorcycle Club had ever faced since the club had been founded in the spring of 1966. I just did not know how long it would be before the majority of the Bandidos would wake up and smell the roses, and how many lives would be destroyed before the club recognized that the situation had to be rectified.

In Oklahoma, by the summer of 2005, most all of the members of the North Tulsa chapter of the Bandidos were running wild, fueled by an endless supply of methamphetamine distributed by themselves and their associates. Even my old friend Ian "Ian" Wilhelm, who had helped me put together Wizard's show bike back in 1996 and went on to become an OK Rider and then a member of the Oklahoma Bandidos, was not immune to the destruction brought about by the influence of the methamphetamine. Caught up in a world where self medicating with alcohol and/or drugs is an accepted practice, Ian first got in trouble for riding his motorcycle while drunk back in the spring of 2003.

Bandido Ian was luckily admitted to a two year drug court program, where if he did everything that the Court requested him to do, he would not end up as a convicted felon. But hanging out with the Bandidos North chapter during the fall of 2004, in spite of his chapter President Bandido Lee's orders for him not to do so, had its own drastic set of consequences. In drug court in February of 2005, Ian got his drug court supervision violated after failing a series of dirty urine tests, and as a result was sent off for six months to pluck chicken feathers in a chicken processing plant in eastern Oklahoma.

As another direct result of his methamphetamine use, Ian also had decided that paying his motorcycle loan payments was not a priority. (If you remember, my attorney had bought Ian's loan from me back in October of 2003) By May of 2005 Ian had, just like Walter "Levi" Willis before him, his motorcycle repossessed. With no motorcycle to ride, and being caught by his chapter President Bandido Lee more than once lying about his use of methamphetamine and supposedly paying his motorcycle loan payments, Bandido Ian unfortunately got kicked out of the Bandidos in May of 2005.

32

The Bandidos Motorcycle Club
The Big USA Bust Summer 2005

It did not take long for me to find out what was going to happen to Bandido El Presidente George "George" Wegers, for on the ninth of June, 2005, he was arrested by federal authorities in Washington, charged with a myriad of crimes. Indicted along with twenty-one other members of the Bandidos Motorcycle Club in Washington, Montana and South Dakota, Bandido George was arrested for ordering the kidnapping of a rival motorcycle club member in Montana back in May of 2003, when I was visiting Bandido Vice Presidente Mike in Denmark while I was still a Bandido.

Caught up in the two year long, federal investigation along with Bandido George had been three other members of the Bandidos National chapter, and two Bandido chapter Presidents. One of those indicted was Vice Presidente Christopher "Chris" Horlock, who had been an El Secretario for a few years at the same time I was working for the National chapter. Numerous sources were reporting that this was just the beginning salvo in a nationwide war against the Bandidos, and to expect many more arrests before it was all over. I, for one, was not surprised when I heard of the indictment; I had anticipated it for many years.

Biker Gang Leaders Plead Not Guilty To Federal Charges

June 10, 2005

By Gene Johnson

Two leaders of the Bandidos biker gang pleaded not guilty to federal charges Friday as more than a dozen people arrested in a three-state bust of the club's alleged crime ring made their first appearances in U.S. District Court.

Among the 15 defendants in court Friday were the group's international president, George Wegers, 52, and Hugh Gale Henschel, its national sergeant-of-arms. Both men pleaded not guilty to charges against them, including racketeering and witness tampering.

Federal agents and police launched an offensive against the gang Thursday, serving arrest and search warrants in Washington, Montana and South Dakota. Nineteen people were arrested.

U.S. Attorney John McKay in Seattle said the crackdown against the Bandidos has likely been the nation's most significant bust of a motorcycle gang in 20 years. The sweep was centered on Bellingham, a city near the Canadian border where authorities say the Bandidos based their international criminal network.

"On the backs of Harleys, they brought violence and drugs to Whatcom County and across the Northwest," McKay said at a news conference Friday.

All the defendants appearing Friday either pleaded not guilty or declined to immediately enter a plea.

After the court proceeding Friday, Wegers turned to two of his supporters and said "I'm not guilty, you know, so it's not going to be a problem."

His attorney, Jeffrey Lustick of Bellingham, said the charges were a case of guilt by association.

"What's interesting is that some of the charges are a complete surprise to him," Lustick said of Wegers. "He doesn't remember being in the places he was alleged to have been or making the statements he was alleged to have made."

Wegers' former brother-in-law, Tracy Latham of Bellingham, said Friday that Wegers gave him a place to stay and helped him find work when he was a troubled teenager. "He helps people out. He's not this guy who he's alleged to be," Latham said.

Agents were still pursuing 10 others wanted in the investigation. The fugitives — including Bandidos secretary Christopher Horlock, 44, of Bellingham, and Missoula, Mont., chapter president Bernard Russell Ortman — were among 26 people named in two federal indictments.

The Bandidos have about 170 chapters in 14 countries, including 90 in the U.S. and 14 in Washington state, the indictment says. Membership is estimated at 2,400 bikers, all of whom must ride Harley-Davidson bikes.

The 300 agents working the case also served 19 search warrants, including one at a Harley-Davidson dealership in Bellingham. They seized weapons, drugs, stolen motorcycles and more than $25,000 in cash.

The Bandidos have operated for more than two decades in Bellingham, said Police Chief Randy Carroll, and they held picnics and performed other civic activities to mask their criminal enterprise.

"There is a public face that they put forward to give the community and the public a perception that they're helpful, and they can be, in the light of day," Carroll said. "They'll stop and help you change a tire. They'll help you if you run out of gas. But that is the surface; that's the face of the organization."

"We got the international president. We got the sergeant-at-arms," said U.S. Marshal Eric Robertson. "I would assume we've got the picnic coordinator, but we haven't confirmed that yet."

The first federal indictment named 22 gang members and said they engaged in a pattern of threatening behavior to protect their turf and criminal enterprises. Several bikers from the Bandidos' Missoula chapter were charged with kidnapping an individual identified as SS in May 2003.

The other indictment charges four men with weapons violations. The investigation began in 2002, said officials with the federal Bureau of Alcohol, Tobacco, Firearms and Explosives.

I did laugh my ass off when I read the part about the El Presidente's attorney stating that Bandido George had no memory of what he was accused of saying, concerning the fact that the El Presidente's own words had been the basis for some of the charges in the indictment. All I could think of was the European Bandidos telling me back in May of 2003 that Bandido George had Alzheimer's, and I wondered if having Alzheimer's was eventually going to be his defense. I did feel a little sorry for Bandido Sargento de Armas Jimmie "Jimbo" Garman, who had returned to the Bandidos three years ago, after being retired for more than ten years, only because El Presidente George had talked him into it.

Biker Sweep Continues
Law Officers Pleased With Raid On Outlaw Gang

By Kira Millage

June 10, 2005

One day after a three-state, multi-agency raid on the Bandidos motorcycle gang, local and federal law-enforcement agents were breathing a little easier, but still working hard.

"We're entering the fourth quarter of the game and looking to our quarterback to throw the touchdown pass," said Kelvin Crenshaw, a Bureau of Alcohol, Tobacco, Firearms and Explosives agent in charge, during a news conference Friday morning.

Of the 26 people indicted by a federal grand jury, 16 have been arrested, including the international and national president, George Wegers, according to the U.S. Department of Justice. Federal agents are still looking for at least eight fugitives.

"We are very pleased with the outcome of yesterday's operations," said John McKay, U.S. attorney for the Western District of Washington.

"We do think it's very important that the individuals that were arrested are now, for the time being anyway, removed from the community," he said. "It's obvious on the backs of Harleys they brought violence and guns into Whatcom County and across the Northwest."

The raid is the result of a 2-year investigation into the motorcycle gang. Charges include: violent crimes with racketeering, kidnapping, assault, witness tampering, distribution of marijuana and methamphetamine, trafficking motor vehicles and parts, sale of firearms and illegal possession of firearms.

"The indictment in this case is not as thick as one might expect for an international organization," said Jeffrey Lustick, attorney for Wegers. "It doesn't have the kind of pow for this organization as the government has described. ... I don't see how this is a crackdown."

STILL SOUGHT

Federal agents are actively looking for these Bandidos biker gang members:

Bernard Russell Ortman: President of the Missoula, Mont., chapter.

• Wanted for crime in aid of racketeering and conspiracy to tamper with a witness.

• White, age 46, 5-foot-10, 185 pounds.

Christopher Horlock: National regional secretary and president of the Rapid City, S.D., chapter.

• Wanted for conspiracy to tamper with a witness.

• White, age 45, 5-foot-10, 225 pounds.

According to the indictment, Wegers is charged with violent crime in aid of racketeering, conspiracy to traffic motor vehicles and parts, conspiracy to tamper with a witness and trafficking of motor vehicle parts.

"My client is looking forward to his day in court because he believes he will be vindicated and acquitted on these charges," Lustick said.

If convicted, all the defendants will face sentences ranging from five years up to life imprisonment, according to the U.S. Attorney's Office in Seattle.

Nineteen search warrants were executed in Washington, Montana and South Dakota on Thursday, including one at the Harley-Davidson of Bellingham dealership downtown.

"Harley-Davidson of Bellingham fully cooperated with these authorities and has not been accused of any illegal activity," said Barbie Jackson, the general manager of the store. "We were shocked and stressed to see some of our customers accused of serious crimes."

ATF agents and local law enforcement closed the store Thursday morning and seized items, including the store computers, Jackson said. The computers were returned later that night, and the store is open for business again.

"It is our full intention to continue to serve these valued customers and we will post any additional information about our responses to this situation on our Web site," Jackson said. The site is: http://www.harleyofbellingham.com.

Some people in Whatcom County have come to the defense of the indicted gang members, saying they were nice people and always willing to help.

"There is a public face they put forward to give the community and the public a perception they're very helpful," said Randall Carroll, Bellingham police chief. "We see them in a different light than the public - what we see is under the surface."

People arrested in Whatcom County on Thursday were transported to Seattle on Friday morning to make their initial appearances before a federal judge. The indictments are allegations, but they are yet to be proven, McKay said.

People have been starting to call authorities, Carroll said. They've been giving their names, telephone numbers, addresses and information about the Bandidos and their actions, something they were unwilling to do before, he added.

Bellingham police are asking anyone with information about the Bandidos to call 676-6913.

The ATF issued a press release announcing further details of the investigation and arrests on June 10, 2005:

TWENTY-SIX INDICTED FOLLOWING 2 YEAR INVESTIGATION OF "BANDIDOS" MOTORCYCLE GANG

A Federal Grand Jury in Seattle has indicted twenty-six members and associates of the Bandidos Motorcycle Organization for serious violent offenses.

The two indictments charge various defendants with: Violent Crime in Aid of Racketeering: Kidnapping (VICAR); Violent Crime in Aid of Racketeering - Assault; Conspiracy to Tamper with a Witness; Tampering with a Witness; Conspiracy to Distribute Marijuana and Methamphetamine; Distribution of Marijuana; Distribution of Methamphetamine; Carrying a Firearm During and in Relation to a Drug Trafficking Crime; Conspiracy to Traffic in Certain Motor Vehicles and Motor Vehicle Parts; Trafficking in Certain Motor Vehicle; Sale of a Firearm to Prohibited Person; and Felon in Possession of Firearm. During the course of the investigation 14 firearms were sold to or by individuals with several felony convictions.

Nineteen search warrants were executed in four judicial districts including the States of Washington, Montana, and South Dakota. Several weapons, including firearms and knives; methamphetamine and marijuana; stolen motorcycles and motor vehicle parts; and over $25,000 in cash have been seized. 19 individuals have been arrested, 16 of whom are indicted defendants, and three of whom were arrested on probable cause for drug charges. Ten fugitives are outstanding.

The defendants were arrested in raids yesterday in Whatcom County, Kitsap County, and Okanogan County, Washington, and in Montana. The arrests follow a two year investigation into a variety of criminal activity by the Bandidos Motorcycle gang. Among those facing federal charges are the national president, Bellingham chapter president, and other chapter presidents of the Bandidos.

These individuals were indicted by the grand jury:

GEORGE WEGERS, 52, National President, Bandidos, Bellingham
CHRISTOPHER HORLOCK, 44, National Regional Secretary, Bandidos
JIMMIE GARMAN, National Sergeant-at-Arms, Bandidos
HUGH GALE HENSCHEL, National Sergeant-at-Arms, Bandidos
GLENN W. MERRITT, 64, Bellingham Chapter President, Bandidos
WILLIAM E. JAMES, 53, Secretary/Treasurer, Bellingham Chapter, Bandidos
BERNARD RUSSELL ORTMAN, 46, Missoula Chapter President, Bandidos
DALE ROBERT GRANMO, 49, Member Missoula Chapter, Bandidos
AARON KENNETH WISE, 34, Member Missoula Chapter, Bandidos
ROBIN WADE HUNDAHL, 40, Member Missoula Chapter, Bandidos
WILLIAM BLAINE BEACH, 54, Member Missoula Chapter, Bandidos
STEPHEN DALE KOESTER, 47, Member Missoula Chapter Hermanos
ROBERT RANDALL ALEXANDER, 44, Member Missoula Chapter, Hermanos
RICKY THOMAS LOOKEBILL, 47, Member Missoula Chapter, Hermanos
MICHAEL TRENT McELRAVEY, 56, Member Missoula Chapter, Bandidos
FRANK OFFLEY, 49, Member Whatcom County Chapter, Bandidos

VINCENT STACY REEVES, 50, Associate Bellingham Chapter, Bandidos
JAMES AUSTIN PENNELL, 44, Associate Bellingham Chapter, Bandidos
BRITT AUGUSTUS ANDERSON, 34, Whatcom County Chapter, Bandidos
WALTER BAIL, 48, of Blaine, Washington
JULIE ANDERSON, 35, of Custer, Washington
RICHARD MacMILLAN, 49, of Bellingham, Washington
DARRELL MORRIS, 42, of Everson, Washington
MICHAEL BARTOLO, 39, of Canada
STEVEN GLENN, 34, of Everson, Washington
JASON R. GORDEN, 34, of Seattle, Washington

"The Bandidos are an organized criminal enterprise that virtually held communities hostage," stated United States Attorney John McKay. "This investigation by federal and local law enforcement has loosened the stranglehold of fear and intimidation that the Bandidos had on communities throughout the northwest."

"This operation illustrates ATF's commitment to lead the fight against gangs and violent crime. The culture of violence and those who deal in illegal guns, drugs and death will be exiled from our community. This investigation does not end here," stated ATF Special Agent in Charge Kelvin Crenshaw. To that end, during enforcement activities, agents and officer's recovered narcotics, firearms, U.S. currency, evidence of trafficking in stolen motorcycles and 70 marijuana plants.

"Yesterday, the Bandidos Motorcycle Gang's drug trafficking, violent tactics, and firearms violations were answered with decisive enforcement operations by numerous Federal and State law enforcement agencies around the region. This criminal organization, which operated under its own terms and outside the law, will now face justice," stated Drug Enforcement Administration Special Agent in Charge Rodney G. Benson.

"The international leadership of the Bandido organization has been operating in Whatcom County with perceived impunity for many years. Hopefully this case will serve to dismantle the Bandido Motorcycle Organization in our area and will have a significant impact upon methamphetamine distribution, thefts, burglaries, crimes of violence and other nefarious activities that plague our community," added Whatcom County Sheriff Bill Elfo.

Bellingham Police Chief Randall Carroll spoke of the gang's long history of violence and intimidation saying, "For over 20 years the Bandidos have been tied to armed narcotics trafficking and related violence and the crime narcotics bring to our community. This operation is about Bellingham's Homeland Security."

If convicted of the charges, defendants face sentences ranging from five years up to life imprisonment.

An indictment contains allegations that have not yet been proven in court beyond a reasonable doubt.

The case was investigated by the Bureau of Alcohol, Tobacco, Firearms & Explosives (ATF), the Whatcom County Sheriff's Office, and the Bellingham Police Department. The Drug Enforcement Administration, the U.S. Marshal's Service and numerous state and local law enforcement officers assisted with Thursday's arrests. The defendants will make their first appearances at approximately 2:30 today in the Magistrate's courtroom, 12th floor of the U.S. Courthouse at 700 Stewart Street. Because of the number of defendants, the Court may change the scheduled time.

For additional information please contact Doug Whalley, Assistant United States Attorney, at (206) 553-4882.

But what interested me the most in the days that followed all of the arrests, was the Motion filed by the United States Attorney's office to deny bond to Bandido El Presidente George. It appeared that Bandido George had not seen the worst of it yet, and I was shocked when I learned that he was found to be in the possession of a Hells Angel patch and four handguns; the Hells Angels patch for obvious reasons and the guns because he was a convicted felon. It also appeared that everyone was in way more trouble than had been initially calculated, for it indicated that the club was likely to face Racketeering (RICO) charges in the very near future. The Motion that appears as follows is in relation to Bandido George only:

WESTERN DISTRICT OF WASHINGTON
AT SEATTLE

UNITED STATES OF AMERICA,
Plaintiff,

NO. CR05-231C

SUPPLEMENTAL
MEMORANDUM
IN SUPPORT OF
DETENTION MOTIONS

v.

GEORGE WEGERS,
GLENN WILLIAM MERRITT,
HUGH GALE HENSCHEL,
JIMMIE GARMAN,
WILLIAM EDWIN JAMES,
ROBIN HUNDAHL,
FRANK OFFLEY,
BRITT AUGUSTUS ANDERSON,
RICHARD MacMILLAN,

JAMES AUSTIN PENNELL,
JULIE ANDERSON,
WALTER BAIL,
Defendants.

The United States of America, by and through John McKay, United States Attorney for the Western District of Washington, and Ye-Ting Woo and Bruce Miyake, Assistant United States Attorneys, submit this supplemental memorandum to the Court in support of the United States' motion for detention as to George Wegers, Glenn Merritt, Hugh Henschel, Jimmie Garman, William James, Robin Hundahl, Frank Offley, Britt Anderson, Richard MacMillan, James Pennell, Julie Anderson, and Walter Bail. The purpose of this memorandum is to acquaint the Court with additional information that should be considered in support of the government's request for the Court to detain the defendants through the course of these criminal proceedings.

A. Indictment

On June 8, 2005, a federal Grand Jury in this District returned a twenty-count indictment as follows:

Count	Offense	Penalties
1	*Violent Crime in Aid of Racketeering: Kidnapping*	*Life imprisonment* *$250,000 fine* *3 years supervised release* *$100 special assessment*

Bernard Ortman
Dale Granmo
Aaron Wise
Robin Hundahl
William Beach, Jr.
Ricky Lookebill
Michael McElvary
Frank Offley
Stephen Koester
Robert Alexander

2	*Violent Crime in Aid of Racketeering Assault*	*25 years imprisonment* *$250,000 fine* *3 years SR* *$100 SA*

Britt Anderson

3	*Conspiracy to Tamper with Witnesses*	*10 years imprisonment* *$250,000 fine* *3 years SR* *$100 SA*

George Wegers
Jimmie Garman
Christopher Horlock
Hugh Henschel
Bernard Ortman
William Beach
Britt Anderson

| 4 | Tampering with a Witness | 10 years imprisonment
$250,000 fine
3 years SR
$100 SA |

Britt Anderson
Hugh Henschel

| 5 | Conspiracy to Distribute
Methamphetamine/Marijuana | Life imprisonment
10 year mandatory minimum
$4 million dollar fine
5 years SR
$100 SA |

Glenn Merritt
Walter Bail
Julie Anderson

| 6 | Distribution of Marijuana | 5 years imprisonment
$250,000 fine
2 years SR |

Glenn Merritt

| 7 | Distribution of Methamphetamine | 40 years imprisonment
5 year mandatory minimum
$2 million dollar fine
4 years SR |

Glenn Merritt

| 8 | Distribution of Marijuana | 5 years imprisonment
$250,000 fine
2 years SR |

Glenn Merritt

| 9 | Distribution of Marijuana | 5 years imprisonment
$250,000 fine
2 years SR |

Glenn Merritt

| 10 | Distribution of Methamphetamine | 40 years imprisonment
5 year mandatory minimum |

$2 million dollar fine
4 years SR

Glenn Merritt
Walter Bail

11   Carrying a Firearm During and in   20 years imprisonment
        Relation to a Drug Trafficking Crime   5 year mandatory minimum
                                                  $250,000 fine
                                                  3 years SR

Glenn Merritt

12   Distribution of Methamphetamine   40 years imprisonment
                                                  5 year mandatory minimum
                                                  $2 million dollar fine
                                                  4 years SR

Glenn Merritt
Walter Bail

13   Distribution of Methamphetamine   40 years imprisonment
                                                  5 year mandatory minimum
                                                  $2 million dollar fine
                                                  4 years SR

Glenn Merritt
Walter Bail

14   Distribution of Methamphetamine   40 years imprisonment
                                                  5 year mandatory minimum
                                                  $2 million dollar fine
                                                  4 years SR

Glenn Merritt

15   Conspiracy to Traffic in Certain   5 years imprisonment
        Motor Vehicles and Motor Vehicle Parts $250,000 fine
                                                  3 years SR

George Wegers
Glenn Merritt
William James
Vincent Reeves
James Pennell
Richard MacMillan

16   Trafficking in Certain Motor Vehicle   10 years imprisonment
                                                  $250,000 fine
                                                  3 years SR

Glenn Merritt
Vincent Reeves
Richard MacMillan

| 17 | Trafficking in Certain Motor Vehicle | 10 years imprisonment $250,000 fine 3 years SR |

Glenn Merritt
James Pennell
Richard MacMillan

| 18 | Trafficking in Certain Motor Vehicle | 10 years imprisonment $250,000 fine 3 years SR |

Glenn Merritt

| 19 | Trafficking in Certain Motor Vehicle | 10 years imprisonment $250,000 fine 3 years SR |

George Wegers
Glenn Merritt
James Pennell
William James

| 20 | Sale of a Firearm to a Prohibited Person | 10 years imprisonment $250,000 fine 3 years SR |

Glenn Merritt

The indictment also alleges two bases for criminal forfeiture, Title 18, United States Code, Sections 512 and 982, Title 28, United States Code, Section 2461(c), relating to the trafficking in stolen motor vehicles and motor vehicle parts, and Title 21, United States Code, Section 853, relating to drug offenses. The government has seized numerous motor vehicles and motor vehicle parts during the course of this investigation and the execution of search warrants, and will file a bill of particulars and/or seek a superseding indictment to provide notice of its intent to seek the criminal forfeiture of seized assets, including motor vehicles and motor vehicle parts.

B. Search Warrants

On June 9, 2005, law enforcement agents and officers executed search warrants at nine-teen locations in Western Washington, Eastern Washington, Montana, and South Dakota. A total of 100 firearms were located and seized from these various locations. Many of the firearms were loaded and ready for use. Additionally, over 30 knives ranging from several inches in length to two feet in length were seized. Most of the knives were seized from the residence of the National President, George Wegers. Voluminous documents of important evidentiary value were also seized at most of the search locations.

The following chart provides a summary description of seized weapons, drugs, currency and stolen vehicles from residences and businesses of the defendants arrested in the Western District of Washington.

Location	Defendant	Items Seized
6395 Portal Way, Ferndale, WA	Glenn Merritt	18 firearms, ammunition, two ounces methamphetamine, 22grams cocaine, 10 grams marijuana, 1999 Chevrolet truck
7462 Sunset Blaine, WA	William James	$10,000 cash
7628 Portal Way Custer, WA	William James	$3,500 cash
5870 Portal Way Ferndale, WA	James Pennell	FX Harley Davidson, 100 plant marijuana grow, ½ lb. hash
3535 McAlpine Street, Bellingham, WA	George Wegers Richard MacMillan	4 handguns w/ammunition, 33 knives, 1 machete, VIN plates for stolen vehicles, bullet proof vest
6046 Portal Way Ferndale, WA	Hugh Henschel	6 firearms, small quantities of methamphetamine and marijuana, $400 cash
5568 Doren Road Acme, WA	Glenn Merritt	34 firearms, ammunition
5192 Hannegan Road, Bellingham, WA	Jimmie Garman	30 firearms, ammunition
2955 Iverson Lane Custer, WA	Julie Anderson	small quantity of methamphetamine
545 Peace Portal Drive Blaine, WA	Walter Bail	small quantity of methamphetamine
280 West Pole Road Lynden, WA	Frank Offley	1 handgun, ammunition

C. Summary of Facts in Support of Detention

Section 3142(g) of Title 18, United States Code, sets forth the factors that are to be con-sidered by the Court in determining whether conditions of release will reasonably assure the appearance of the defendant, and the safety of any other person and the community. The United States believes that these factors, as applied to each defendant, strongly militate in favor of detention. Furthermore, pursuant to Section 3142(e), a rebuttable presumption arises that no condition or combination of conditions will reasonably assure the safety of any other person and the community if the applicable offense involves a felony drug crime that carries a term of imprisonment of 10 years or more.

Specifically, the factors under 3142(g) are:
. The nature and circumstances of the offense charged;
. The weight of the evidence against the person;
. The history and characteristics of the person, including physical and mental condition, family ties, employment, financial resources, length of residence, community ties, past conduct, history relating to drug/alcohol abuse, criminal history, court appearance record, and whether the person was on pre-trial release or on probation at the time of the offense or arrest; The nature and seriousness of the danger to any person or community posed by the defendant's release.

1. GEORGE WEGERS

George Wegers, as the National and International President of the Bandidos Outlaw Motorcycle Organization (OMO), oversees the activities of over 2,400 members in 168 chapters or more in fourteen countries around the world. As alleged in the indictment, George Wegers is a member of the racketeering enterprise, referred to as the Bandidos OMO. This racketeering enterprise is known to be engaged in violent crimes, trafficking of motor vehicles and motor vehicle parts, including the transportation, sale, and altering of stolen motor vehicles, drug trafficking, and witness tampering. Bandidos OMO members are required to wear "colors," which are clothing with patches that symbolize the club, including a "1% patch" denoting that they belong to a club that prides itself on being non-law abiding.

Numerous patches, including "El Presidente" Bandidos OMO patches and memorabilia were found at, and seized from, Wegers's residence. Possession of "colors" of rival gangs, such as the H ell's Angels Outlaw Motorcycle Club, a long-standing competitor of the Bandidos OMO, is highly prized and considered to be noteworthy of confrontations between the gangs. A Hells Angels patch was also located at Wegers's residence which leads investigators to believe that he was involved in, or has knowledge, that the patch was stolen or forcibly removed from a Hells Angel member.

George Wegers is charged with conspiracy to tamper with witnesses, conspiracy to traffic in certain motor vehicles and motor vehicle parts, and trafficking in certain motor vehicle. The government is seeking authorization from the Organized Crime Racketeering Section of the United States Department of Justice approval to present a superseding indictment to the Grand Jury to charge Wegers with the offenses of Racketeer Influence and Corrupt Organizations (RICO) and Conspiracy to Commit RICO.

We also continue to investigate Wegers for his involvement and participation in, including the directing, sanctioning, and approval of, the kidnapping incident charged in Count 1 of the indictment, the assault incident charged in Count 2 of the indictment, and other law enforcement reports of assaults and threats to assault made by private citizens. The government anticipates that additional charges against Wegers will be forthcoming, and that it is particularly essential to ensure the safety of the community by continued detention of Wegers to encourage private citizens to come forward and cooperate with law enforcement agents and officers in the ongoing investigations.

As stated in the Indictment at Pages 3 and 4, "Witnesses to their criminal acts are typically the victims of acts of intimidation or harassment and are too afraid to approach law enforcement or testify in court proceedings." Law enforcement agencies have already reported to the United States Attorney's Office that victims and witnesses are coming forward to report information they have about acts of violence and intimidation believed to involve Bandidos members. Release of the National President, George Wegers, would seriously thwart and jeopardize the United States's continuing investigative efforts.

As stated in Overt Acts (e) through (h) of Count 3 of the Indictment, George Wegers was immediately notified by co-defendants and National Sergeant-at-Arms Jimmie Garman, Hugh Henschel, and Christopher Horlock that federal agents had contacted William Beach and were attempting to contact Frank Offley. Both Beach and Offley were arrested by the Great Falls Police Department on May 27, 2003, for their participation in the arrest of S.S. The telephone conversations between George Wegers and Garman, Henschel, and Horlock, as well as a conversation between Wegers and Beach, were recorded by law enforcement. As reflected in the Indictment, upon being advised that federal agents were contacting Bandidos OMO members about the kidnapping incident, Wegers promptly directed Henschel and Horlock to enforce a gag order. These facts establish the significant authority and control of Wegers over his national officers and other members.

Most recently, since the arrest of Wegers, Garman, Henschel, Horlock, and others, law enforcement has received an anonymous tip, and a separate witness report that there is a "hit" ordered on Kinsmen members in Montana. Law enforcement has also received a report that Bandidos OMO members have also been ordered to destroy and remove evidence, such as firearms, documents, and other valuable items. Agents are conducting follow-up investigation of these reports. We will not reveal the identity of the witnesses who have provided this information to law enforcement in an effort to protect their safety. The witnesses have expressed a fear of retaliation if their information and identities are revealed at this time.

Specifically, as to Wegers, agents located four firearms with loaded magazines stored in a bedroom of the residence. When Wegers was arrested, there were three other men found at the residence. One of them was Richard MacMillan, who was living at Wegers's residence. The other two men stated that they had traveled from Texas to Washington recently and were staying with Wegers. One of the men claimed that the four firearms belonged to him. The second man declined to indicate whether he knew about the firearms, but agents confirmed that the second man had felony conviction and is prohibited from possessing firearms.

Also found in the residence were numerous knives and swords. Thirty-three of the knives were seized from the residence and retained as evidence. The knives range from several inches in length to two feet in length. Agents also seized a machete from the residence. Agents have learned that knives are frequently used by Bandidos OMO members to intimidate individuals, particularly prospective witnesses in criminal cases. Moreover, Bandidos members in the Montana kidnapping incident also carried knives during the confrontation.

As to flight risk, Wegers resides within 30 minutes of the United States/Canada border. We have learned from witnesses and confirmed from intercepted calls on the wiretap that he travels to Europe and Hawaii on at least a yearly basis. Due to loyalty to the Bandidos OMO and to George Wegers, he has access to worldwide support to assist him in fleeing from this jurisdiction and concealing him from the Court. For all of these reasons, the United States requests that this Court find that defendant George Wegers poses a danger to the safety of persons and the community, and that he poses a serious risk of flight, and to enter an order of detention.

By the middle of the next week after the indictment was unsealed, Bandido Bernard "Bernie" Ortman had been located and arrested by federal authorities in Lubbock, Texas. When arrested, Bernie was found to be in possession of guns and methamphetamine. A few days later, Bandido Vice Presidente Christopher "Chris" Horlock turned himself into federal authorities in Houston, Texas. As of July 2005, all are awaiting a January 2006 trial, most held without bond, and El Vice Presidente Jeff is running the club worldwide. El Presidente George is being held in solitary confinement, allowed only two fifteen minute phone calls each week.

Epilogue

These days I consider myself a retired biker and a simple family man, spending most all of my time running my businesses and taking care of my family. I treasure the time that I have left with my now 12 year old daughter Taylor before she becomes a teenager, discovers boys, and has a life of her own that more than likely will not include much of dear old Dad. At this age one tends to reflect on one's life, and I am quite surprised that I am alive, and much more surprised that I have not spent more of my life in prison. I am extremely proud of the fact that I have gone through my life never sacrificing my integrity or principles, and that I have always been a "man of my word".

In spite of the fact that I am just now starting to show my age, I can easily look myself in the mirror every day. There are a few things that I regret doing in my life, but nothing I regret not doing. The majority of what I do regret having done involves people that I hurt, when I was young, as a result of my behavior then. I am pleasantly surprised that I do not miss the life of a Bandido; in fact, am quite relieved that I no longer am required to do things that I now have no desire to do. I realize that I have been blessed to have lived the life I have led, and quite fortunate to have traveled all over the world doing so.

There have been some major milestones in my life; some of which you have read about in this book and some others that you may read about in the future. I am honored to have had the privilege of knowing most the men that I have written about in this book, and consider many of them to be friends of mine for the rest of my life. Many of them also have been my mentors, and some have taught me a lot about life. I only hope that I have had half the impact on them that they have had on me. Some, like my close friends Jonathan "The Shark" Sutton, Robert "Cowboy" Crain, Harry "Skip" Hansen and Lee "The Boss" McArdle, are truly the greatest friends a man could hope to have.

Robert "Cowboy" Crain and I have spent a lot of time together through the years, and done a lot of stupid things, which obviously we now regret. It never ceases to amaze me at how time changes the way you think, as well as your priorities. Robert is a case in point; he has been a devoted Christian since 1996, now living with his wife in Denver, Colorado. More than twenty years have now passed since he and I forged a truly remarkable relationship that continues to this day. Our friendship has survived multiple prison terms, drastic changes in lifestyles for both of us, marriages, and the fact that both of us are no longer part of the Bandidos Motorcycle Club. In hindsight, it seems ironic that a friendship as strong as ours could be born in such a time of so much confusion and turmoil.

Harry "Skip" Hansen is currently living in Muskogee, Oklahoma with his wife; spending his days wishing that he was sailing around the world in a sailboat, but still riding his Harley nearly every day. We still communicate almost daily, and I hope that this will continue until the day I die. Skip, who has no plans on ever returning to the Bandidos, is also enjoying his retirement from the 1%er world.

Lee "The Boss" McArdle is still a Bandido and probably will be until the day he dies. He still lives just a few miles from me, and I talk to him almost every day. I know that our relationship will continue until one of us dies, in spite of what Lee has been told to think about me. I could not imagine my life without Lee, since both of us have been through so much for so long.

Alain Brunette is now serving an eight year prison sentence, and will be released from prison in June of 2006. When released, Alain plans on living in the country on a farm somewhere in Ontario with his girlfriend, who has faithfully remained at his side throughout his ordeal. I also communicate with him on a regular basis, and plan to see him once a year in Mexico or the Bahamas, since Alain cannot come to the United States and I cannot travel to Canada. Alain, like Skip and me, also has no desire to be a member of the Bandidos ever again.

I suspect that the Bandidos Motorcycle Club will undergo major changes in the near future, as it is more likely than not, that wave after wave of federal indictments will incarcerate many of its six hundred United States members. Many more members will probably quit, rather than endure the stigma of being involved with what is perceived to be a criminal organization. I am sure that the club will survive in some shape, fashion or form, but I am willing to bet that someday soon methamphetamine use and sales by its members will be prohibited and no longer tolerated. If not, then I think the club will ultimately perish, for it is hard to attract and retain quality members, if those members have to deal with methamphetamine addicts on a daily basis.

The Bandidos, just like all of the outlaw motorcycle clubs in the United States, will have to figure out what it takes to beat old age attrition if they hope to survive for the long haul. The average Bandidos member is now in his late forties and many members are now in their fifties and sixties; very few are in their thirties and almost none are in their twenties. If nothing is done soon to alter these trends, then in twenty years the average Bandido will be in his late sixties with many members in their seventies and eighties, and their youngest members in their fifties. If they avoid change, the only territory that they will "control" in twenty years will be nursing homes.

I think that at some point in time it will become impossible to attract younger members purely due to the fact that no twenty year old potential member will want to hang out with a fifty or sixty year old member. The interests of that potential twenty year old will not be the same as that fifty or sixty year old, and the priorities of that fifty or sixty year old member will have nothing in common with the priorities of that potential twenty year old member. When this happens, the inevitable is that the club will eventually fade away, for every year it will lose more members than it gains.

The only way to change this is to change the entire focus of the Bandidos over time. To change the focus of the club will require a major change in leadership, as well as forced retirement for some of the older members that espouse the continuation of antiquated concepts and ideas. The by-laws of the club will have to be amended, and the Bandidos will have to learn to treat all of its members equally. Last of all, but not least, all Bandidos members will have to accept these changes to survive, for fighting progress is an exercise in futility; nothing remains the same forever.

If nothing is done to alter the track of the train as it makes its way through time, then the course the train is on will never change. If the train track is moved just a little every year, then over a period of time the train eventually follows a completely different course than it would have if the track was not changed. If the Bandidos, as well as all the other outlaw motorcycle clubs, do not change their ways, just like every other thing in history that did not change, they will eventually fade away and die out, never to be heard from again.

I did what I could while I was a member to effectuate change and organize the Bandidos, but I was just one man, and one man cannot do much by himself. I did succeed in helping to bring the Bandidos into the 21st century, teaching them along the way to open lines of communication, both internally and externally. I introduced the club as a whole to the concept of the worldwide web, and did what I could to get them to look at themselves as a worldwide business. I desperately tried to get them to incorporate, and argued for years that the club needed to apply for a federal trademark that would protect their club colors.

In 2004, El Presidente George finally took my advice and applied for a federal trademark, but did so in his own name, which I think will come back in the end and bite him in the ass. The club still needs to incorporate, and be run as a business to survive long term. The corporation needs to control the trademark, so that it will never be controlled by one man. Drugs like methamphetamine need to be banned from club life, and drug/alcohol treatment for its members will have to become an acceptable way to help Bandido members that need the same.

Unfortunately, I think that I was a little ahead of my time, and in some ways I am sad that my attempts at change were rejected by a few. The real catastrophe was that those few made all the decisions for the masses, and most of the decisions that the few actually made, were in no way made to benefit the masses. On the contrary, most of the decisions made by the few in charge were made for the benefit of themselves.

History will remember that the Bandidos recently missed a divine opportunity to effect change, under the leadership of El Presidente George "George" Wegers. For whatever reason, Bandido George somehow forgot his values and ideals, and lost his integrity along the way, rather than guiding the club non-traditionally as he initially set out to. Someone famous once said that absolute power always corrupts, absolutely; and I think that in this case, more truthful words have never been spoken.

As I sat and contemplated the recent arrest of El Presidente George, I couldn't help but think that the stage was now set and ready to go. What will happen next is anyone's guess. But one thing I know for sure though, is like a Phoenix arising from its' ashes, the Bandidos Motorcycle Club will learn from this experience and probably live on forever.

Glossary

El Presidente

The United States National President and International President of the Bandidos Motorcycle Club. The El Presidente is the boss of all members of the Bandidos worldwide; his corporate equivalent would be the Chairman of the Board. The El Presidente is the only Bandido that wears an El Presidente bottom rocker on the back of his club colors.

El Secretario

The secretary in charge of all other Secretarios in a particular area or country for the Bandidos Motorcycle Club. The area or country that the El Secretario is in charge of is signified by the country or area rocker he wears on his side under his arm or a small ribbon he would wear on his chest. The El Secretario assigns all Secretarios their job assignments, is usually the keeper of the club treasury. His corporate equivalent would be the CFO.

El Vice Presidente

The United States National Vice-President of the Bandidos Motorcycle Club; the El Vice Presidente is the underboss to all the Bandidos in the United States; his corporate equivalent would be the CEO.

Hangaround

In the normal process for an individual to become a member, he will hangaround" for a year or many years, then "prospect" or "Probate" (Probationary), and then "full patch".

Hangaround Club

A hangaround club is normally an existing motorcycle club that wants to join a larger motorcycle club. The first stage of the process is for that smaller club to "hang around" with the larger club; hence the name, "hangaround". The actual term puts everyone on notice, from both clubs as well as the rest of the biker world that the smaller club wants to join the larger, and the larger is considering the change. Usually a hangaround club will hangaround for a year or more, then the larger club will take a vote as to whether the members of the smaller club are worthy of the larger club's patch. If so, then there is a patchover, where the old club's patches are swapped for the new ones. In the Bandidos world, usually the members from the old club retain the old patches, and sometimes they have been burned.

Patch

The club colors of any motorcycle club. A Patch can be the entire vest with the club colors sewed on it, or could refer to just the actual club colors by themselves.

Patchover

A patchover is when the members of a smaller club change their patches, and then start wearing the patches of a larger club; the actual assimilation of a smaller motorcycle club into a larger motorcycle club.

Presidente

The European or Australian President of the Bandidos Motorcycle Club; the Presidente is the boss to all members of the Bandidos in that particular country or area; his corporate equivalent would be the President. The area or country that the Presidente is in charge of is signified by the country or area rocker he wears on his side under his arm or a small ribbon he would wear on his chest.

Probationary

In the Bandidos motorcycle Club, if a potential member has previous motorcycle club experience, then that potential member is eligible to become a "Probationary" member, which will last for a minimum of one year. While he is a Probationary, he is retrained in the ways of the Bandidos Motorcycle Club. A probationary wears the Bandidos Fat Mexican center patch and Bandidos top rocker, but wears a bottom rocker that says "Probationary".

Prospect

Prospecting is like trying to join a fraternity when the prospect has no experience with the motorcycle club lifestyle. So he undergoes an intensive 6-month minimum period of "learning", before becoming a full patch member. While he is prospecting, the prospect only wears one rocker at the top of his back that says Prospect".

Sargento de Armas

An enforcer for the Bandidos Motorcycle Club; in charge of enforcing the clubs rules and decisions both internally and externally. The area or country that the Sargento de Armas is in charge of is signified by the country or area rocker he wears on his side under his arm or a small ribbon he would wear on his chest.

Secretario

A secretary or treasurer for the Bandidos Motorcycle Club. The area or country that the Secretario is in charge of is signified by the country or area rocker he wears on his side under his arm or a small ribbon he would wear on his chest. His corporate equivalent would be the Secretary or Treasurer.

Vice Presidente

A Vice President for the Bandidos Motorcycle Club. The area or country that the Vice President is in charge of is signified by the country or area rocker he wears on his side under his arm or a small ribbon he would wear on his chest.

Appendix A

BY – LAWS OF THE BANDIDOS MOTORCYCLE CLUB

June 2002

1: Requirements for a Chapter:

Five (5) member minimum – One (1) "Charter Member".
Charter Member = 10 years.
Keep pictures and information on all members.
Hold weekly meetings.
$25.00 per month, per member to National Treasury (by the 1st of each month).
Probationary Chapters (new) will pay a one-time donation of $1000.00 to National Treasury.
Probationary Chapter members' bikes and titles will be pledged to National Chapter for the first year.

2: Patches:

Only a Top and Bottom rocker, Fat Mexican, 1% diamond and MC patch should be on the back of your cut-off. It should be visible from 150 feet.
A 1%er diamond will be worn over the heart.
Anything else is up to the individual.
Year patches & buckles are not to be given early.
National can grant a "Lifer" patch or membership on a person to person basis.
One Property Patch per member. If she rides her own bike it is NOT to be worn while riding with or around Patcholders or Prospects. It should not be worn in public without her old man in view.
There is no limit on Property Belts.

3: Do's:

Labor Day and Memorial Day are MANDATORY RUNS.
A Chapter may leave one (1) member behind from a mandatory run. A member on medical leave or a Life Member is that member. This is for security reasons; that person should have access to a phone as much as possible.
When you are traveling, you should attend your host chapter's meetings.
You must abide by those chapters' By - Laws and policies.

4: Don'ts:

Things that will cost you your patch:

You don't lie.
You don't steal.
This includes OL' Ladies as well.
Needle use will not be tolerated
Neither will smoking of any chemicals – coke, speed, mandrax…if it didn't grow, don't smoke it!

5: Motorcycles:

Each member will OWN at least one (1) Harley Davidson or facsimile of at least 750cc.
No more than 30 days a year down time.
After 30 days that members Chapter will pay National $500.00.
Have a good reason? Ask for more time.
Road Captains should inspect all bikes regularly.
*** If you are visiting another area, chapter, state or country and you borrow another brother's property (bike, tools, money, etc.), you are responsible for the return of that property. It will be returned in as good or better condition than when you borrowed it.

6: Membership:

*Hangaround period to be determined by chapter President.
*Harley Davidson Motorcycle or facsimile capable of meeting the demands of Pledge period.
*Members must be at least 21 years of age
*Sponsor – May be individual (preferably charter member) or may be Sponsored by chapter as a hole.
*Sponsor,
Do not turn your Pledge loose without help. If you think enough of him to sponsor him into this club, it's up to you to teach him the right way, the BANDIDO WAY. If you're not ready to sacrifice your time and share your knowledge, don't do it. The simple things – Who's the neatest M.F. in the world? Or don't wear your Patch in a vehicle. Trivial things that will get a Prospective BROTHER run off.
* Pay $275.00 to National Treasury.
* Pledge bike and title.
* Be voted in as Pledge by Chapter (100% vote).
* Receive your Patch or Rocker.
*DO YOUR TIME.
Prospect: 6 months MINMUM.
Probationary: 1 year MINIMUM.
This man is pledged to the whole BANDIDO NATION, not just one Chapter or area, City or State. He will attend every meeting, party, bike event or gathering of any kind in his area where Bandido Patcholders will be present.

He will not miss any National or Regional runs, especially Funerals.
This club is about sacrifice. Get used to it! His motorcycle should be in up and running condition his whole Pledge period, ready to go anywhere. In other words, NO DOWN TIME.

* Pledge is not eligible for vote if there are any outstanding debts, Chapter, National or Private, (inside club). He should start into this club on a level playing field.

* After the mandatory time period has passed, and the Sponsor feels the Pledge is ready, a meeting should be called. All surrounding Chapter Secretaries should also be notified, (in advance).

* The Pledge should be voted in by a 100% Chapter vote. Club members outside the   chapter should have a chance to voice their opinions. The Pledge's Sponsor should base his decision on these things, for he is the one who will have to fade it if things go foul.

It is a life long commitment: DON'T RUSH IT.

*Charter Member is 10 years of unbroken service.

* National may grant Leave of absence – this is not automatic.

Two (2) year members are eligible for transfer, only if both Presidents involved have agreed and a $50.00 fee is paid to National Treasury.

***** Suicides: Any Brother who commits suicide, WILL NOT be allowed to have a BANDIDO funeral.....

* Other national Fees:

New Patch Fee	$ 275.00
Transfers	$ 50.00
New Charter	$1000.00
30 Day Downtime rule	$ 500.00

Appendix B

PROJECTS & JOB ASSIGNMENTS FOR EL SECRETARIOS

March 2001

1) Money
2) Commissary program & inmate affairs
3) USA website
4) USA website – graveyard
5) USA website – history of the club
6) T shirts
7) All other merchandise (except t shirts)
8) Life insurance
9) Support clubs – members list & email list & phone list & club list/cities
10) Patches & stickers
11) Newsletter
12) Travel arrangements for the National chapter
13) World email list
14) USA secretary list
15) USA phone list
16) Time in club – members & chapters – actual date of entry into club
17) Legal issues & oversight of all criminal cases
18) Public relations issues
19) Club tattoos – uniform rules & regulations worldwide
20) Dress shirts - uniform rules & regulations worldwide
21) PBOL guidelines – merchandise & patch
22) List of deceased Brothers – each chapter – grave sites for same
23) Business – incorporation & trademark administration
24) Funeral guidelines – one guy from every chapter (however you can get him there) for any funeral; two guys from each chapter within 500 miles (on bikes); every chapter sends flowers or money for each funeral.

Appendix C

CT ED'S PROJECTS & JOB ASSIGNMENTS FOR NATIONAL CHAPTER

March 2003

1)   Keeper of the USA Phone List & USA email list & USA 15 year member list & USA support club chapter/member list

2)   Keep tabs on the Fat Mexican trademark

3)   Monitor most internal federal criminal cases (Bandidos members) & some state criminal cases

4)   Provide occasional internal travel arrangements worldwide

5)   Provide occasional national public relations services

6)   Provide suggestions for forms of communication between the national chapter and the national chapter members

7)   Provide suggestions for forms of communication between national chapter & all United States chapters

8)   Provide suggestions for design changes to the USA website

9)   Provide suggestions for legally structuring the club's financial affairs

10) Provide emergency backup for publishing the USA newsletter

Appendix D

BANDIDOS SUPPORT CLUB CHAPTERS

August 2003

Name of Club/State	City	Members
ALABAMA		
Pistoleros	Auburn	5
Pistoleros	Birmingham	6
CMA	Birmingham	2
Soldiers of the Cross	Birmingham	3
Wayward Wind	Birmingham	5
Pistoleros	Dothan	2
Pistoleros	Huntsville	
Pistoleros	Jasper	5
Iron Hawgs	Jasper	5
Pistoleros	Mobile	4
Soldiers of the Cross	Mobile	12
CMA	Mobile	2
Alabama Riders	Montgomery	5
Pistoleros	Montgomery	5
ARKANSAS		
Ozark Riders	Eureka Springs	7
Ozark Riders	Rogers	6
COLORADO		
Peligrosos	Denver	16
No Names	Grand Junction	5
Los Bravos	Denver	11
John's Guys	Pueblo	12
LOUISIANA		
West Bank	Baton Rouge West	5
Louisiana Riders	Baton Rouge	6
Louisiana Riders	Bogalusa	4
West Bank	Point Coupee	7
Hole in the Wall	Lafayette	5
Road Shakers	Acadiana	7
Rat Pack	Lake Charles	12

Grey Ghosts	Minden	3
Grey Ghosts	Nacadoches	4
Louisiana Riders	New Orleans	6
Grey Ghosts	Shreveport	14

MISSISSIPPI

Asgards	Biloxi	6
Asgards	Gulfport	6
Pistoleros	Hattiesburg	5
CMA	Jackson	10
Pistoleros	Jackson	2
Asgards	Kiln	6
Asgards	Pascagoula	6
Mississippi Riders	Tupelo	5

MISSOURI

Hermanos	Jamesland	11

MONTANA

Hermanos	Kallispell	5
Hermanos	Missoula	4
Amigos	Ronan	1

NEW MEXICO

Native Thunder	Acoma	3
German MC	Alamogordo	9
Black Berets	Albuquerque	9
Native Thunder	Albuquerque	4
Bandoleros	Albuquerque	4
Pacoteros	Artesia	4
Native Thunder	Dine Nation	2
US Vets	Hobbs	10
Regulaters	Roswell	7
Bandoleros	Sante Fe	6
Bandoleros	Truth/Consequences	3
US Vets	Tucamcari	7
Native Thunder	Zuni	3

OKLAHOMA

OK Riders	Tulsa	9
OK Riders	Shawnee	8
OK Riders	Comanche	9

CMA	OKC	2

SOUTH DAKOTA
Hermanos	Sioux River	5
Ghost Dance	Pine Ridge	6

TEXAS
Iron Riders	Amarillo	28
Companeros	Austin	10
Iron Riders	Borger	29
Southern Pride	Beaumont	3
Border Brothers	Brownsville	20
Rebeldes	Corpus Christi	10
Macheteros	El Paso	4
Del Fuego	El Paso	5
Coyoteros	El Paso	6
Amigos	Estralla Sola	3
Rebel Riders	Fort Worth	14
Aces & Eights	Fredericksburg	12
Amigos	Galveston County	8
Macheteros	Hill Country	5
Los Dorados	Hill Country	5
Soldiers of Jesus	Houston	10
Amigos	Houston State	5
Amigos	Houston East	5
Amigos	Houston North	8
Amigos	Houston West	4
Southern Raiders	Houston West	5
Los Malos	Jefferson County	
Renegades	Laredo	4
Aces & Eights	Levelland	37
Desperados	Longview	8
Los Cabboleros	Killeen	5
Amigos	Montgomery County	13
Los Riders	Plainview	39
Macheteros	San Antonio NW	14
Southsiders	San Antonio SW	12
Westsiders	San Antonio	9
Campesinos	San Antonio	9
Malditos (Bad Lance)	San Antonio SW	9
Texas Wheels	Waco	80
Equestrians	Waco	12

<u>WASHINGTON</u>

Warriors	Everett	7
Destralos	King County	5
Amigos	King County	8
Hermanos	King County	4
Hombres	La Costa	4
Hombres	Olympia	4
Amigos	Pierce County	10
Hombres	Seattle	6
Amigos	Snohomish County	9
Hombres	Snow Valley	4
Hombres	Tacoma	6
Hermanos	Tacoma	5
Destralos	Thurston County	5
Hombres	Wenatchee	4
Canyon Riders	Whatcom County	11
Unforgiven	Yakima	6

<u>WYOMING</u>

Hermanos	Gillette	5

47 Support Clubs   **Total Members**   929

Appendix E

Credits For Newspaper Articles